REAL ESTATE PRINCIPLES & PRACTICES

A CONTEMPORARY APPROACH

Second Edition

REAL ESTATE PRINCIPLES & PRACTICES

A CONTEMPORARY APPROACH

Second Edition

Arlyne Geschwender

Randall School of Real Estate

Gorsuch Scarisbrick, Publishers

Scottsdale, Arizona

To all who are interested in learning more about real estate, with special thanks to the many students who have encouraged me along the way.

The publisher makes every reasonable best effort to ensure the accuracy and completeness of the information and answers contained in this book. Due to the ever changing nature of applicable laws and practices, the reader is cautioned and advised to always consult with the instructor when questions arise. Test questions have been checked for correct correlation with the question answered. If the reader encounters a questionable answer, the reader should always consult the text or the instructor for a more complete answer and analysis of the answer. Should the reader believe that an alternative interpretation of the information contained in this book is possible, s/he is encouraged to consult with the instructor.

Cover photo by Kristine Daines

Gorsuch Scarisbrick, Publishers
8233 Via Paseo del Norte, Suite F-400
Scottsdale, Arizona 85258

10 9 8 7 6 5 4 3

ISBN 0-89787-911-2

Printed in the United States of America.

Contents

Preface

At some point in life every person is involved with real estate. Since the time when early humans sought refuge in caves, the need for shelter has been a fact of life. Furthermore, with the great housing boom of the late 1970s and early 1980s, people began to realize that real property ownership was a hedge against rising inflation. A look forward may well reveal even greater emphasis on the value of real estate as an investment.

After many years of teaching real estate classes, I felt strongly that there was a need for a principles and practice textbook written in a clear and concise manner—one that would be easy for the novice entering the world of real estate to understand. Furthermore, it seemed only logical to follow the natural sequence of events in a real estate transaction. Consequently, this text is divided into five sections: an introduction to real estate, the process of a sale, other aspects of ownership, fair housing and license laws, and basic tools for the salesperson, broker, or investor.

Part One begins by giving the reader a brief overview of the impact that real estate has on our country's wealth as well as on fulfilling our personal housing needs. The contribution real estate makes to the employment rolls is reviewed in this introductory chapter. Chapter 2 explains property rights and ownership interests and introduces the reader to a basic knowledge of real estate ownership. Chapter 3 covers land descriptions and survey systems to acquaint the reader with legal descriptions. Chapter 4 explains estates, deeds, and the various methods by which title to real property can be taken.

Part Two follows the orderly process of a real estate transaction. Beginning with Chapter 5, the reader is introduced to the important role that contracts play in the process of listing, selling, leasing, and optioning real property. Using the sale of a single property as an example, Chapters 6 through 10 illustrate the natural sequence of the process, beginning with the listing contract and concluding with the final closing of the sale. Chapter 6 covers the function and purpose of the brokerage firm and explains the listing contract. The offer to purchase the property follows in Chapter 7. Lending sources (Chapter 8) and financing the purchase (Chapter 9) are the next steps in the process. Chapter 10 covers the closing procedures from both the lender's and the real estate company's viewpoint, showing settlement statements for the seller and buyer.

Part Three deals with other aspects of ownership. Other forms of residence such as condominiums, cooperatives, and time-sharing units are covered in Chapter 11; leases are explained in Chapter 12, followed by a discussion of management in Chapter 13. Investments and tax aspects of real estate ownership are investigated in

Chapter 14. A discussion of appraisals (Chapter 15) is followed by material on land use controls and regulations (Chapter 16).

Part Four covers the federal fair housing laws as they apply to sales and rentals of real property (Chapter 17). A brief overview of the license laws act, which mandates the licensing of persons engaging in the real estate business, is offered in Chapter 18.

Finally, Part Five considers the various math problems encountered in real estate transactions (Chapter 19). Problems on computing interest, profit and loss, taxes and commission, ratio and proportion, and loan amortization are provided as examples of basic real estate arithmetic.

The text concludes with an appendix containing various forms and documents not previously introduced, a supplementary glossary, and an answer key to the chapter review questions.

A note about writing style: Because both women and men are active in real estate, I made a conscious choice in this new edition to avoid the use of generic "he". Unfortunately, the English language offers no suitable concise substitute; I have used instead "s/he" and "his or her". If this makes the presentation a little more wordy at times, I hope readers will understand the intent behind my choice.

Never before has real estate been so complex or challenging. It is my hope that this textbook will provide you with the foundation of knowledge you need to enter the fascinating field of real estate.

Arlyne Geschwender

To The Student

This text has been written especially for the person who is taking his or her first course in real estate. It provides an easily understood introduction into this complicated and many-faceted subject. Whether the reader plans to pursue a career in real estate or is interested in learning for the purpose of buying, selling, leasing, or managing personal real estate investments, the text covers the fundamentals of real estate principles and practice.

To assist you in using this text, I recommend the following:

1. Read the chapters in sequence. It may help you to better understand the strange new language of real estate if you reread portions of some of the chapters. The wide margins are for your use in making notes and jotting down any questions you have. By placing your questions in these margins, you will have them readily available to ask in class.
2. Review the key terms and concepts that are at the conclusion of each chapter.
3. Answer the review questions at the end of each chapter and check your answers with the answer key at the end of the book. If you have missed a question, reread the pages on which the material appears.

While text headings outline the contents of the book, the special terms placed in the margins bring out important topics and ideas. As you review the material, these marginal notes will help you identify and locate the main concepts in each chapter.

Since Part Two of the text follows the natural sequence of events in a real estate transaction, it will help you put the process in perspective. Legal documents are introduced as they are used in the listing and sale of real property and each instrument is explained in detail. Understanding these documents and the part they play in a real estate transaction will enhance your ability to become a true professional in the field.

There will always be more people,
but there will never be more land.

Real Property

PART

ONE

Real Estate and the Economy

Each of us at some time in our lives becomes involved with real estate. Since we all need shelter, we either rent or purchase a place in which to live. Moreover, as one of the largest industries in America, real estate has a direct influence on our economy, community, and society. Thus, it seems appropriate to begin this text by exploring the role and contribution of real estate.

As the concept of home ownership being available to the common man and woman at affordable prices developed, it became a vehicle through which people could prosper and through which this nation grew. The largest portion of the estate the average person acquires in a lifetime is the equity built up through home ownership. It serves as a forced way of saving.

More immediately, real estate provides us with a sense of belonging in a very mobile society. Better housed than people in any other nation, Americans in all age groups and economic levels take pride in their homes. Home ownership in the United States is the underpinning of the ideal of the American way of life and assists in promoting pride in citizenship.

HOUSING NEEDS

The United States Census Bureau in their 1980 report predicted that our population would swell to 245 million people by 1990. This anticipated growth in population will accentuate the importance of land and housing as a merchantable commodity. The population increase can in part be attributed to the "graying" of America, as our citizens are living longer and more productive lives. Housing provisions for this segment of the population have been springing up in all parts of the country, with special emphasis in the Sun Belt areas of Arizona, Texas, Florida, and California.

Changes in population distribution patterns are continually monitored by real estate analysts. Any rapid growth in a particular area of the country will require additional housing units. Conversely, if statistics reveal a decline in population, housing needs will be lessened. Tracking these changes includes determining the population characteristics since that will affect not only the number but the type of housing units needed. For example, provisions for the single student in college cities is evidenced by dormitories and apartments surrounding the campuses. A trend throughout the country, the number of single households is on the increase, with many unmarried young people opting for ownership rather than renting. Condominiums are popular since they provide ownership without the care and maintenance required in a single family home. (See Chapter 11 on condominiums.) At an early age the young adult can begin to accumulate an equity in home ownership.

An increase in "mingles" (unrelated singles) purchasing real estate together is also prevalent; young adults join together to purchase living quarters. Another market is that first time buyer who later decides to upgrade his or her investment, moving up to a larger home. These young adults are discovering that the size and location of one's home is an important aspect of social mobility.

The rights and benefits inherent in real property ownership contribute to the economy of our country. Through taxation, real estate provides the monetary base upon which schools, parks, recreation areas, public transportation, utility services, and roads are built and maintained. Large corporations establish factories and businesses in areas where employees can live "the good life". The community that can offer a favorable and attractive economic environment will prosper and grow. In some communities, blighted areas are reclaimed and restored or redeveloped by concerned community members, ultimately adding to the tax roles of the area. Buildings with historic significance are renovated and become prized landmarks.

REAL ESTATE CREATES EMPLOYMENT

At a national level, real estate accounts for a substantial share of the Gross National Product (GNP). The Gross National Product is the sum (value) of all goods and services produced and used in the country. When the GNP is divided by the population it gives us a means of measuring the flow of income for that particular year, indicating our standard of living, although inflation changes the impact of these figures to a degree.

Consider the tremendous number of people who are either directly or indirectly involved with housing. Begin with the plotting of a subdivision, which requires the services of engineers and surveyors. Operators of heavy equipment construct the roads and workers install public utilities in preparation for the homes. The construction of the house itself requires a general contractor, subcontractors, and suppliers and builders of all the materials that compose the structure—from the foundation, siding, drywall, windows and doors and cabinetry to the plumbing, electrical, and gas connections. Appliances and furnishings that ultimately go into the house must be supplied and installed.

The services performed include the savings and loan institutions financing the sale, the title companies insuring the title, the insurance companies insuring the premises, and the appraisers placing a value on the property. Attorneys oversee the closing, city offices record the documents, and nurseries provide the lawn and plantings. Local, state, and federal government have departments devoted entirely to real estate issues.

Local government interests include land use planning and zoning laws. The U.S. Department of Housing and Urban Development (HUD) was established solely to monitor and administrate housing needs. Lastly, real estate agents—750,000 agents belong to the National Association of Realtors®—service the public in the listing and selling of real property.

As one can see, the numbers of people added to the employment rolls through transactions in real estate are indeed large, adding to the prosperity of the community. Clearly, real estate is big business.

PURCHASING THE HOME

At an individual level, the decision to purchase a home is one of the most important decisions made by the average person. That first home is a most meaningful step and is looked upon by the owner as much more than mere shelter. It represents pride, accomplishment, and security. In making a selection, the considerations faced by the purchaser include deciding upon the location, the style, the condition, and the size of the home, and its proximity to public transportation, schools, shopping, and employment. Buyers' needs vary; what is perfect for the young family with school age children may not meet the needs of a childless couple.

The new home owner becomes involved in the "happenings" of his or her new neighborhood and contributes to the socio-economic existence of the community, participating in the school system, churches, and neighborhood associations. Some become involved in the local political arena, taking an active part not only with their votes, but also by campaigning for their choice of candidate. They make purchases at the nearby shopping centers, contributing to the success of the business community.

THE OWNERSHIP CYCLE

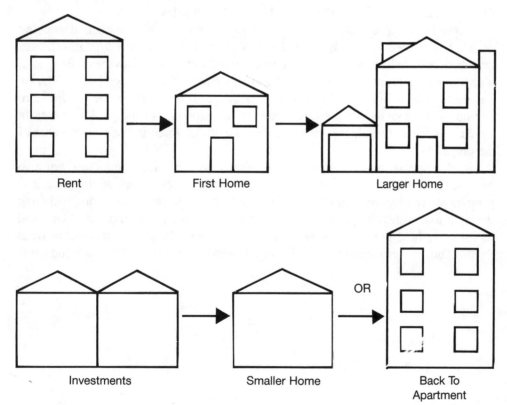

Rent   First Home   Larger Home

Investments   Smaller Home   OR   Back To Apartment

FIGURE 1.1
The ownership cycle.

The cycle of an average person's experience in real estate usually begins with renting, creating a need for apartment units. The first move into a home allows the individual to begin building an equity that will supply the basis for the next move into a larger home. Often moves are necessitated by employment transfers to other parts of the country. As an owner's equity builds and salary increases, he or she seeks a place to put savings to work. For many, investment takes the form of the purchase of additional real estate. Whether the purchase is residential income property or an office building or commercial structure, the investor adds to the prosperity of the area since each individual property affects the community. After the family is raised and people grow older and retire, their needs change and they choose smaller homes with less maintenance. Some of this senior citizen group may return to renting.

HOW ECONOMIC CONDITIONS AFFECT REAL ESTATE

Our free enterprise system is based on the premise that the more you produce, the more you receive. The open market system allows the consumer to decide what he or she wants and the producers compete to supply those needs. Extremely successful in encouraging economic progress, the open market system forces suppliers to be competitive in offering goods for consumption, giving both buyers and sellers choices.

Business cycles create problems, however, especially for the real estate industry. The economic conditions of the country play a great part in the real estate cycle. One can track the fluctuations of real estate values to the conditions in the market place. When interest rates rose to an all time high of 17% in most areas of the country, sales slowed dramatically. As interest rates fell, buyers once again began the home search and the market place hummed with sales.

However, each region experiences "buyer's" and "seller's" markets depending on what is happening locally. In 1985-86 a sluggish land market was in effect in the farm belt. When farmers with overextended credit failed to meet their loan obligations, the farms were foreclosed and auctioned off to the high bidder. During this same time, astronomical prices were being paid for homes in the northeastern section of the country. Real estate relates to the economy of the particular area in which it is located, with supply and demand a strong force in the market value of the property.

Real estate is exciting—not only because it is a needed commodity but also because "owning a piece of the earth" has long been the dream of the American people. Many early immigrants came to our land for personal freedoms, including the right to own real property. Today, the desire to own one's own piece of land and the promise held out that it is possible to do so are a large part of our American dream. Thus real estate has implications far beyond the exchange of money and land.

Land: Its Characteristics and Acquisition

2

It all begins with the land. Historically, land acquisition has been the crux of major battles throughout the world. Land ownership has played a part in everything from the rise of great political powers to the development of individual self-worth. We have learned a great deal from the past; many of today's fundamental ideas concerning ownership and transfer of real property have been handed down relatively unchanged from medieval times.

The evolution of land ownership began when wandering tribes of nomads stopped roaming to settle and form communities. Staying in one area, they began to cultivate crops and build shelters. Tribal chiefs controlled the village, allocating areas of land to individual families to use. The tribe often found it necessary to fight off aggressors who sought to infringe on their possessionary rights. As time passed, the feudal concept developed.

The evolution of land ownership

The *feudal system* prevalent in Europe during the Middle Ages gave the king control of all the land. Feudalism formed the political, economic, and social organization of medieval Europe. Under the feudal system, social position was determined by the amount of land held. The king maintained control of the land, distributing it among lords and nobles who in return pledged to support the king with taxes and their allegiance. The lords supervised serfs who worked the land. In the early Middle Ages the lords did not own property as we do today; they merely had the right to use or administer the land.

Our system of land ownership is the **allodial** system, which gives individuals the right to own land. We can acquire real property without government interference and buy, sell, exchange, option, lease, or will the real estate we own.

Perhaps the most exciting chapter in the history of land acquisition occurred during America's westward expansion. Pioneers explored and settled a wilderness, carving out homesites for their families and for generations to come. Promises of individual land ownership through grants by the United States government prompted thousands of early Americans to forsake the comforts of established cities for the spartan life of the western frontier. To encourage the settlement of public lands, Congress gave land to all settlers who complied with the homestead laws. There was little exchange of properties in those early days, but as the territories and states became more settled, the need for land to supply food and shelter for new arrivals became apparent and people began to sell off portions of their holdings.

Land remains the most prized possession of the average individual in the United States. The pioneers of a century ago would view with amazement the concrete empires that have replaced their sod houses. In fact, with an evergrowing population, land development has been so rapid that scientists are now exploring the possibilities of communities under the sea or in space, orbiting the earth. Creativity is a key characteristic of today's developer. Each parcel of land is unique; no two are alike.

CHARACTERISTICS OF LAND

The distinct characteristics of land can be classified into two general categories: physical and economic. These characteristics determine its utility and value.

Physical Characteristics

The physical characteristics of land are its immobility, its indestructibility, and its nonhomogeneity.

Immobility

Land consists of various types of soil, rocks, and minerals. It contains valleys and plains, lakes and rivers, mountains and canyons. Whatever the makeup of the land, it is fixed; that is, it is not movable. It remains permanently in a fixed geographical location. This *immobility* of land determines its value. That a parcel of land will always be exactly where it lies does not, however, guarantee that its value will remain constant. Economic conditions in an area dictate if its worth will rise or fall. Demand and scarcity are the greatest influences on its value.

Indestructibility

Since land remains in a permanent location, except for erosion and depletion, it never wears out. Hills have been leveled in the construction of highways and building sites, rivers have changed channels, minerals have been taken from the soil, but the land is still there; it is literally *indestructible*. We are living on the same land as our ancestors and the natives before them. When improvements (buildings, utilities, etc.) are added to the land, they too are of a permanent nature, though unlike the land they will depreciate and need to be replaced over a period of time. Land's durability makes it an ideal commodity for investors, though the economic climate of an area can have an impact on its value.

Nonhomogeneity

Since there are no two identical parcels of land, land is *nonhomogeneous*. Unlike manufactured goods, that are duplicated many times, any two parcels of land will vary. The fact that the location of each parcel is different creates a variance in itself.

Recognizing that land is nonhomogeneous has resulted in its being legally referred to as *nonfungible* (not substitutable). One property cannot be substituted for another. While the same house plan may be followed on several sites, differences in material and craftsmanship will occur in the construction. The parcels of land, though similar to the eye, will also vary.

Because of the differences in the physical characteristics of land, it is divided into agricultural, residential, commercial, industrial, and recreational uses. The use to which land is designated is determined to a great degree by that to which it is best suited.

Agriculture began with the early settlers who farmed the valleys and plains and cleared forest lands that lent themselves to cultivation. Some agricultural land is best suited for raising wheat, as in the central plains states. In warmer climates, the temperature and soil are ideal for orange groves. Irrigation can supplement the lack of rainfall, but northern temperatures would freeze many fruit crops.

Residential

As cities developed and their populations grew, and as they are growing still, they encroached onto neighboring farmland. While the land was physically suited to raising crops, it was put to a new use. The desire for workers to live near employment creates a demand for housing in close proximity to the job centers. Home sites must be adaptable to construction. Extremely steep hills are a detriment, particularly in areas of the country where snow and rain could create travel problems. Known flood zones and areas with the possibility of mud slides are also to be avoided as home sites.

Commercial property is located where business will be generated for the mer-   *Commercial*
chants. The busy streets along which traffic flows beckon to the builders of the restaurants and shopping centers. Their properties should be easily accessible for the shopper.

Industrial land is generally located near transportation facilities, such as rail-   *Industrial*
ways, trucking, airlines, and waterways. Industrial tracts are developed around these services.

Land unsuitable for other uses may be perfect for recreational purposes. The   *Recreational*
mountains of Colorado abound with ski lodges and nature trails. Rivers and lakes are used for boating, fishing, and water sports. Resort areas are developed near ocean beaches, especially in warmer climates. Stated briefly, the physical charac-teristics of land determine to a great extent its use.

Economic Characteristics

While its physical and economic characteristics overlap to some degree, land has some distinct economic characteristics, including *scarcity, situs* (location), and *durability* (permanence).

Land acquires value when it is desired. Since we cannot develop or manufacture   *Scarcity*
more land, the supply is fixed. If there is a *scarcity* of usable land for homesites in a given area, the value of the land tends to rise. Creativity has resulted in more high-rise construction in congested areas where the supply of open land is limited. The air about us is absolutely essential to us, but because of its abundance, we do not have to purchase it; it is free. Likewise, when too many homes in a similar price range are placed on the market in a given area, the abundance may cause a decrease in value and a *buyers market* will occur. That is, a large selection may lead the prospective buyer to offer less than the asking price. If, on the other hand, few homes are available and the buyer needs one, he or she may be willing to pay more. Demand for a commodity is created in part by it scarcity. The law of supply and demand dictates that scarcity influences supply and desire influences demand.

The *situs* or location of the land also determines its value. Travel twenty miles   *Situs*
out of the city and the land is not as costly because it is further from the center of employment. We are not in short supply of land across the United States but the available sites near heavily populated areas are limited. Near large metropolitan cities such as Chicago and New York, many workers spend hours commuting daily to and from their employment. Homes by the sea will command a higher price than similar homes situated two blocks from the shore. Lots with views or with trees are considered more valuable than those without these amenities.

Value is further determined by what the soil contains. Land rich in oil and gold will be far more valuable than arid desert void of minerals. Fertile agricultural land will be more productive and hence more valuable than dry, rocky, grazing land.

To the economist, land is the supreme substance from which all our nation's goods are produced. The farmers use land to produce crops, the lumber mills cut trees to supply wood for houses and furniture and to provide the pulp for the paper upon which this book is printed, and so on. To have an economically sound base, each community must produce commodities (goods or services) that they can sell and in turn use the funds they earn to purchase what the community does not produce. Cities like to maintain a broad economic base rather than relying on one industry because if that industry should collapse and the city's residents were without jobs it could mean the decline of property values and tax bases. The ghost towns near the abandoned mines that ran out of ore are examples of communities that died out because they were dependent solely upon one commodity. In modern times, similar problems arose in Detroit when the automobile industry encountered financial difficulties.

Durability

While land is considered indestructible, the *durability* of the improvements that have been made to it must be considered. Although, unlike land, such improvements are vulnerable to natural disasters such as earthquakes, tornadoes, or fire, with proper maintenance they can have an indefinite economic life. However, the use for which a structure may have originally been intended may change. For example, obsolete warehouses in downtown areas of large cities are being renovated and converted into residential apartments, condominiums, and specialty shops. Houses over one hundred years old have been updated and modernized and continue to be used as residences. Many cities have historic preservation committees that bestow landmark designations on old, architecturally aesthetic buildings to preserve our heritage. A move back to urban city areas, especially by young professionals, has been due in part to the aesthetic value of these older homes.

Land is indeed where it all begins; it produces food for animals and humans; it provides water and minerals; it provides for recreation.

REAL PROPERTY RIGHTS

Private ownership of real property gives the owner the right to possess and use the land to the exclusion of all others. All legal rights attached to the property are the owner's, including the right to possess, exclude, sell, lease, mortgage, give away, exchange, and will (figure 2.1). This combination of privileges is often referred to as a **bundle of rights.** It gives the owner the surface rights, the subsurface rights, and the air rights above the land as well. However, one owner could have the surface

Bundle of rights

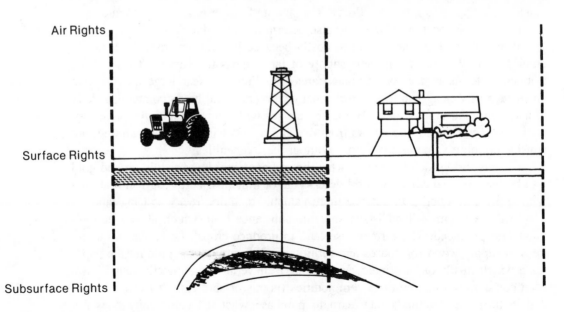

FIGURE 2.1 Rights in land.

rights, another the subsurface rights, and even a third the air rights. A landowner may lease or sell the surface rights to farm the land to one party and the subsurface rights to explore for oil to another. A purchaser receives whatever rights the seller holds.

The surface rights are the rights to use the surface of the real property, for example, in building a residence or farming the land.

Surface and subsurface rights

The subsurface rights give the holder the right to drill for oil or gas, to dig for gravel and sand, and to extract other minerals. While the owner may own either specific or unlimited minerals, the right of exploration and/or removal of these minerals may be severely restricted due to deed restriction or environmental laws.

The owner of land also possesses the air rights over the property (figure 2.2). **Air rights** may be leased or sold and allow the holder to occupy the open space above the designated space of another. This can be in the form of a walkway over a busy street or between buildings. A restaurant may be built over a freeway or a building may be erected over railroad tracks. The original concept of land ownership was that not only did one own the surface rights but also from the core of the earth and to the heavens above. With the emergence of air travel the courts decreed that it is reasonable that air flights over one's property are not considered trespassing.

Air rights

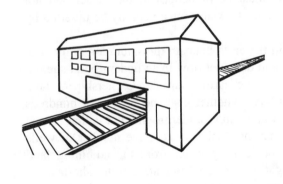

FIGURE 2.2
Air rights.

Water is one of our most valuable natural resources, essential to our very existence. Since rainfall is distributed unevenly across the United States, most areas have a water problem of some kind. Considering this, the appropriation of water rights is of prime importance in some states. Water rights are established by either the *doctrine of riparian and littoral rights* or the **doctrine of prior appropriation.** The lakes and flowing streams are *surface waters* available for use under these doctrines. (See figure 2.3.)

Water rights

If an owner's land borders a moving body of water such as a stream or waterway, under *riparian rights* the landowner is entitled to share in the use of the water. These rights do not extend to damming the water and depriving a neighbor downstream of the use of the water, nor do they extend to actual ownership of the water, but merely to its use. If the water is nonnavigable, the landowner has rights out to the middle of the stream. Under riparian rights, if a shortage of water develops, first priority is given to necessary household use. When that need is filled, agricultural use will be served followed by commercial and industrial uses.

Riparian rights

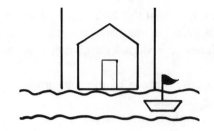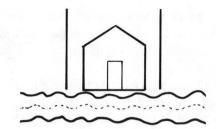

FIGURE 2.3
Water rights.

Doctrine of prior appropriation

If the property borders water that is not flowing, such as a lake or ocean, the landowner abutting the water has *littoral* rights. The owner may use and enjoy the water bordering his land but cannot divert the water. In some states, however, this right has been reduced by the **doctrine of prior appropriation.** Adopted in the arid western states, this principle was originally based upon custom and necessity and finally established in law. Colorado adheres strictly to this doctrine. Simply said, the first owner is privileged with the first claim on the water. This law allows the first user to channel the water for his or her use, depriving other landowners along the watercourse of their equal share. This right established by the appropriator stays with the landowner. However, this use must be of benefit to the owner and not diverted by the owner for another's use and the water must actually be diverted by an artificial structure.

Ground water refers to that water in the earth beneath the saturation point. The water passes beneath the land's surface and does not flow in an underground stream, nor is it supplied by streams flowing on the earth's surface. Ownership of land includes the right to drill below the surface, whether near the surface or hundreds of feet below. *Percolating* water is the water found underground and is that tapped by the farmer for a well. The farmer may not drill an excessive number of wells and sell the water, thus draining this percolating water from the adjoining land owner. In agricultural areas, heavy irrigation uses could create a water shortage.

Gaining and losing land

An owner whose land borders a body of water may actually gain land due to the slow build-up of soil caused by natural forces such as wind and waves. This process is referred to as **accretion,** and the land gained by accretion is *alluvion*.

The rapid washing away of land is known as *avulsion*. Boundary lines remain the same regardless of how much land is swept downstream. *Reliction* (or *dereliction*) occurs when the body of water recedes, exposing dry land.

Erosion

The opposite of accretion, *erosion* results in the loss of land. The erosion of soil is a gradual process created by the action of the natural elements. Rain, wind, water, and extreme weather changes erode the earth's surface. Terracing cultivated land and planting trees helps to absorb water and preserve fertile top soil from being washed or blown away. Some types of erosion can also be controlled by building dams. The Grand Canyon of Arizona is an example of thousands of years of erosion by the Colorado River.

RIGHTS OF GOVERNMENT

Taxation

Ever since feudal times when land was controlled by the king, it has been necessary for governments to protect their citizens in time of war. In the Middle Ages, taxes were collected and allegiance was pledged to the king in return for this protection.

So it is today. The Constitution of the United States provides for the collection of taxes for the general welfare and common defense of the nation. Consequently, taxes are collected on all real property according to its value. On new property, the cost of construction determines to a great extent the real value of the property. In many cities buyers are required by law to disclose the purchase price on a tax assessment form that must accompany the deed when it is recorded. The property is then placed on the tax roles at the new sale price. To unify tax on property in the area, the assessor's office may periodically call for a reappraisal of all property values. This enables the assessor to keep the values that have risen due to inflation current with the market place.

Property taxes will vary greatly between cities because of the different needs and services a community may offer. If a city offers schools, libraries, public transportation, parks and community centers, public utilities, trash hauling, and well maintained streets and parks, the cost of these services must be borne in part by property taxes. On the other hand, the property's value is indirectly enhanced by these services. The more properties on the tax roll, the greater number of people there are to contribute to the cost of the services.

Location will also determine the cost of property taxes. The costs of road maintenance will be higher in areas of the country where snow removal and subsequent additional street repairs are necessary. If a community is basically a retirement city, services such as schools and playgrounds may not be in the tax budget.

Other revenue generated by the city from sources such as taxes placed on gambling casinos and lotteries, or oil royalties received from property owned by the city will assist in offsetting high property taxes. An equal charge of taxes is made on all real property according to value and is known as an **ad valorem tax.** The assessor appraises the property for taxation purposes and the assessed value is provided by the law of the municipality. The city, county, or state then sets the **mill levy** (or the tax expressed in dollars) according to the amount of money needed to meet the budget and expenses of the government. One mill equals one tenth of one cent. *Tax by mill levy*

To determine the amount of taxes on a property, the assessed value is multiplied by the mill levy:

	$80,000	*appraised value*
×	35%	*percentage of taxation*
	$28,000	*assessed value*
×	.080	*mill levy*
	$ 2,240	*taxes*

Taxes are sometimes expressed in dollars, for example, $2.75 per $100.00 of appraised value: *Tax by dollars*

	$80,000	*appraised value*
×	.0275	*per $100 of value*
	$ 2,200	*taxes*

Special Assessments

To pay for the cost of improvements such as pavement, sidewalks, curbs, street lights, and public utilities, an assessment is levied against adjacent property. For example, if a street is paved each of the abutting home owners will pay their proportionate share, which is based on the front footage of each property. If a sewer line is being extended into a specific neighborhood, each of the property owners in that area will be equally assessed since it will benefit the entire area.

Eminent Domain

The right of eminent domain permits the government to take private property for public use with just compensation to the owners. The act of taking the property is accomplished through condemnation proceedings. The United States Constitution prohibits the confiscation of private property without just compensation.

A series of events takes place when a unit of government finds it necessary to take private property. The condemnor (the county, city or state) negotiates with the condemnee (the owner) as to the purchase price. If an agreement can be reached, the condemnor purchases the property for the agreed upon price and no condemnation action is necessary. However, if an agreement cannot be reached, legal proceedings are in order. A petition is filed in the county court to condemn the property. Appraisers (usually three) are appointed by the judge of the county court to appraise the property. Market value is established by these fee appraisers who may be called upon as witnesses to validate their appraisal. After a hearing is held, where evidence from both the condemnee and the condemnor is given, a determination of price is made. If either of the parties feels the award is not just, an appeal may be made to the district court and a trial by jury will be held.

Many times only a partial segment of a property is taken and the appraisers must determine what the value of the portion taken was and what the remaining value is. This is referred to as the *before and after value*.

Examples of eminent domain proceedings can include the need for public recreation areas, the widening of streets, or the expansion needs of a university.

FIGURE 2.4
Eminent domain.

Escheat

The state acquires the property of an **intestate** (a person who dies without leaving a will) who has no heirs. Each state's statutes will set out the perimeters and the judicial process for establishing the right to acquire the property. Many states cannot claim the property until the court so orders, while others acquire title immediately upon the death of an intestate. In the latter situation, the state must go to probate court to establish ownership. If no heirs come forth, the sovereign state succeeds to the property according to statute.

The right of **escheat** also extends to abandoned property. The doctrine of escheat dates back to feudal days when all land was ultimately owned by the king. While we are now under the allodial system of ownership with absolute rights to property, the state succeeding to ownership of abandoned property or the intestate owners property is for the benefit of the people. The majority of decedents have either made wills or have heirs so escheat is not an ordinary means for the state to acquire property.

Police Power

The governmental powers within a local municipality may impose additional restrictions and controls upon land. These imposed limitations over the private use of land are necessary for an orderly growth pattern within the community. This power of the government to regulate land use is referred to as police power and must be in the interest of the public welfare. Zoning laws, building codes, and planning laws are all examples of police power.

PERSONAL PROPERTY VS. REAL PROPERTY

Fixture as real property

Ownership of land gives us the right to use and possess it to the exclusion of all others. Real property refers to the land and anything that is permanently affixed to the land, such as a house. Personal property is referred to as **chattel** or *personalty* and is any kind of property that is movable in nature, such as a chair or table, and is therefore not *real*. A tree is real property until you fell it and then it becomes personal in nature. Build a bookcase from this wood and it would be considered personal, but attach it to the wall in the library of the house and it becomes real property once again. When selling farm land, the crops are normally considered personal since they are replanted annually. If there is a question as to whether a particular piece of property is real or personal, *intention* is considered. If the owners intended to take the object in question with them when they conveyed the property, then it is considered personal property.

A memory device for whether an object should be considered real or personal is MARIA:

Manner of attachment

Appropriateness to use intended

Relationship of parties

Intent of parties

Agreement to the contrary

Manner of attachment

The manner in which the item was attached to the real property determines if it should remain real property. The drapery rods are nailed to the wall and are considered real, but the draperies that hang on the rods are easily slipped off and are therefore personal. A mail box is permanently affixed to the house or to a post beside the driveway and thus becomes real property. The gas line that is run to the pole on which the gas grill sits is for the sole purpose of supplying gas to the grill. While the grill could be easily removed, the "appropriateness to use intended" dictates that the grill is real property. The hot water heater, a necessary item in any dwelling, is installed with piping in a very permanent manner. While it could be removed, it is essential to the property and therefore considered a part of the real property. If there is a question as to whether an item is real or personal, the intention is considered. Clearly the intention of the parties who had the water heater installed was that it remain with the property.

Appropriateness to use intended

Relationship and intent of parties

To be positive that no unpleasant circumstances arise from a misunderstanding on the part of either party upon the transfer of real property, it is prudent to list articles that are to be included with the sale in the purchase contract. Certain questionable items that are to be considered real property should be clearly stated as being transferred in the sale. Built-in bookcases, television antennas, gas grills, and built-in appliances are a few examples of articles that could trigger misunderstanding. If the seller states that s/he is taking the gas grill or the mail box this should be so stated in the contract.

Common examples of real property:
land
buildings
carpeting, tacked down
trees and shrubs
furnace
built-in appliances

Common examples of personal property:
furniture
annual crops
farm machinery
trade fixtures (store display cases, dentist's equipment, printing press)

Fixtures are items of personal property that become real once they are affixed to real property, for example, light fixtures, cabinets, book cases, plumbing fixtures, carpeting, and shrubbery. Once attached they are considered a part of the real property.

Trade fixtures   Items that have been affixed to real property by a tenant to be used in the tenant's business or trade are *trade fixtures*. The tenant clearly needs the items to conduct his business but when the lease expires will expect to remove the fixtures. Examples of trade fixtures include

- coolers, stoves and ovens in a restaurant
- shelving and display cases in a retail store
- printing presses in a print shop
- a dentist chair and equipment

If a fixture is purchased on a payment plan, the supplier can secure his interest by fixture filing before the goods become fixtures or within ten days after the item is affixed. If the business should fail, the supplier would have a right to remove the fixture. Many times fixtures are used as collateral for a loan and if recorded prior to the fixture filing, the loan would take precedence.

ACQUIRING OWNERSHIP

While the government can acquire property through its right of eminent domain and by escheat, there are many avenues by which an individual may assume title to real property. Real property can be obtained by *purchase*. The owner sells it voluntarily

By purchase

(voluntary alienation) to the purchaser.

Ownership of real property can be obtained through a *will*, a formal written document that permits the distribution of an owner's property after death. To be legal a will must be in writing, signed, witnessed, and attested. The maker of the will has died **testate** and is said to have left his last will and testament. The person who made the will is the *testator* (masculine) or *testatrix* (feminine). The will states who is to inherit the property. Willed real property is known as a *devise* and the receiver is the *devisee*. An *executor* (masculine) or *executrix* (feminine) should be named in the will to carry out the terms of the deceased. If no executor is named, an *administrator* (personal representative) is court appointed. If personal property is being willed, it is referred to as a *legacy* or *bequest* and the receiver is the *legatee*.

By will

The parties named in the will have no rights until the death of the owner. Most state laws mandate that the will be filed for probate with the court prior to distribution to the devisee. The validity of the will is determined at a hearing held by the court and the terms of the will are carried out by the executor or the administrator.

The laws of each state must be adhered to for the will to be legal. In community property states, the surviving spouse is entitled to one half of all property jointly acquired during the marriage. If the will provides for less than this statutory right, the surviving spouse can renounce the will and request the minimum rights as stated under the law.

The person who dies without leaving a will has died **intestate** and his or her property passes to heirs by *descent*. The laws of inheritance are statutory and vary from state to state. The premise of these laws is that the intestate descendent would undoubtedly desire his property to succeed to his or her heirs. In the majority of the states, the surviving spouse receives one half or one third of the estate. In some community property states, the surviving spouse will succeed to all the property jointly acquired since the marriage. The children receive the estate if there is no surviving spouse. Any claims and debts against the estate will be satisfied first.

Twenty-seven states* recognize the *holographic* will, which is a handwritten will, dated, written, and signed entirely in the maker's handwriting. It is important not to have any printed words in or on the holographic will or it becomes invalid.

A written amendment to an existing will is a *codicil*. The codicil changes some conditions of the will without the need for rewriting the entire document. Just as with the original will, the codicil must be signed, dated and witnessed. The amendment by a codicil to a will is the only way to change the terms of the will since to alter the will by penciling in notations or deletions is not acceptable under the law.

LOSING OWNERSHIP

Under certain conditions property may be taken from the rightful owner. A true owner may lose ownership if another person occupies the property for a prescribed statutory period in a hostile, continuous, distinct, visible, and actual way. This is known as **adverse possession.** Do not confuse adverse possession with squatters' rights. The latter pertains to the right to occupy land by undisturbed and lengthy use but not with legal title. In acquiring land by adverse possession, the adverse claimant must make an actual claim of ownership to the occupied property. This claimant brings a **quiet title action** suit in a local court against anyone who may have any claim to the property. If the claim is valid, the court will award title

Adverse possession

*The following states recognize holographic wills: Alaska, Arizona, Arkansas, California, Colorado, Idaho, Kentucky, Louisiana, Maryland, Mississippi, Montana, Nebraska, Nevada, New Jersey, New York, North Carolina, North Dakota, Oklahoma, Pennsylvania, Rhode Island, South Dakota, Tennessee, Texas, Utah, Virginia, W. Virginia, and Wyoming.

Adverse possession by tacking

to the claimant. If the adverse claimant has been paying taxes on the land, it reveals some appearance of ownership and is referred to as **color of title.** Many states will permit one adverse claimant to tack his or her possession onto a previous adverse occupant if the first occupant is a relative or if the tacking is done by contract. For example, a mother may occupy a property for three years, after which her son takes possession of the premises and tacks on to the previous possession of his mother.

Adverse possession by contract

An example of taking property by contract would be "A" sells his "rights" to "B" and "B" could take possession, continue to occupy the property, and file claim to the property when the statutory term has been met. The adverse claimant must follow the procedure in filing claim as outlined in the state's statutes. States vary in the occupancy requirements of an adverse claimant from five years to twenty-five years. The adverse possession law encourages true owners not to abandon their property.

The statute of limitations determines the adverse claimant's rights. His possession must be open and notorious, exclusive and uninterrupted. The fee title owner must commence legal action from the wrongful occupant within the period of time stated in the state's statutes or is subject to losing the property.

Real property rights acquired through use

Prescription is an easement one acquires in the land of another through continuous use for a statutory period. It is sometimes referred to as an *easement by prescription*. An example would be a privately owned road used continuously by the public. The owner should permanently post a sign stating that the road is private property or barricade the road once a year, indicating it is indeed privately owned, to avoid losing rights of ownership through prescription.

PUBLIC ACQUISTION OF PROPERTY

Title to property may be obtained by private grant, such as a gift by dedication in which real property is transferred by an individual to the public and accepted by someone on behalf of the public. An example of a gift by dedication would be a street dedicated to the city when a new subdivision is formed. The developer must lay the streets in the subdivision, but by dedicating them to the city, any maintenance responsibility would be transferred to the city.

SUMMARY

This chapter began with a short comparison of land rights under the feudal system in contrast to the allodial system of today.

The physical characteristics of land have a great effect on its value. The use to which the land can be put largely determines that value. Therefore, a farmer would value a valley not a mountain, since to cultivate a mountainside would not be sensible when the valley below lends itself far better to agricultural pursuits. Similarly, the mountain would have more value to a ski resort owner.

The economic characteristics of land involve the location, the scarcity, and the demand for land. Value depends on where the property is and how much is available. The last lots in a subdivision usually are more expensive since the supply is scarce. The obvious fixity of land makes it permanent and unmovable in nature.

Ownership of real property gives the owner a bundle of rights (possession, quiet enjoyment, use, disposition) that are determined by the ownership rights of the past owner. These rights may include surface, subsurface, and/or air rights. While owning real property allows for exclusive doctrine over the property, the government does exercise certain controls. If the property is needed for public use, the government can condemn it under the right of eminent domain. Property taxes must be paid on all real estate to support some of the costs of the local government.

The methods of acquiring ownership in land include purchase, will and descent. Ownership can be lost through adverse possession and certain rights can be acquired by another under an easement prescription. Finally, the public can obtain land through dedication, such as a gift of land for a park or school.

KEY WORDS AND CONCEPTS

Accretion: The gradual gain of land through the build-up of soil.

Ad valorem tax: All real property is taxed or assessed according to market value.

Adverse possession: Rightful owner loses land to occupant who has taken possession in a hostile, distinct, continuous, visible, and actual way for the statutory period.

Air rights: Right to occupy and use the airspace above the surface of another's land.

Allodial: Individuals have right to own land in fee simple title.

Avulsion: The loss of land through the actions of water.

Bundle of rights: The legal rights an owner of real estate acquires, such as the right of possession, use, enjoyment, the right to sell, will, mortgage, and so on.

Chattel: Personal property, movable in nature.

Codicil: A written amendment to a will.

Color of title: Indicates person has some rights of ownership.

Descent: Property of intestate passes to heirs.

Devise: A gift of real estate by will.

Doctrine of prior appropriation: The first owner or user has right to divert water for his use.

Eminent domain: Right of the government to take private property for public use upon just payment to the owner.

Escheat: Right of the sovereign state to succeed to the property of an intestate without heirs.

Fixture: Personal property that becomes real when attached to real property.

Intestate: Person who dies without leaving a will.

Mill levy: A tax rate expressed in tenth of a cent per one dollar of assessed valuation.

Police power: Right of the government to pass legislation governing the use of land to protect the safety and welfare of the public.

Quiet title action: Court action brought to acquire the land of another through continuous use.

Riparian rights: Right of a landowner to use waters of an adjacent stream or lake.

Testate: Person who dies leaving a will that designates the distribution of his estate.

REVIEW QUESTIONS

1. Possession of property through the removal of the true owner's rights is called
   a. adverse possession
   b. codicil
   c. dedication
   d. reliction

2. Title to real property may be obtained by means of
   a. adverse possession
   b. inheritance
   c. devise
   d. all of the above

3. When a person dies intestate and no heirs can be located for intestate succession, the real property of the deceased will revert to the state through a process known as
   a. reconveyance
   b. escheat
   c. reversion
   d. condemnation

4. Land can be taken by adverse possession
   a. if adverse claimant cultivates crops
   b. if it is possessed in a manner hostile to owner
   c. if possessed with owner's knowledge and consent
   d. if owner receives rent

5. When property is transferred by adverse possession
   a. it is involuntary
   b. it is governed by statute
   c. both of the above
   d. neither of the above

6. Abandoned private property redeemed by local government is an example of
   a. police power
   b. eminent domain
   c. taxation
   d. escheat

7. If a person dies testate, his or her property will
   a. come under the laws of escheat
   b. go into a life estate
   c. pass to the heirs
   d. be titled to the devisee

8. The act of the state exercising its right of eminent domain is
   a. escheat
   b. police power
   c. both of the above
   d. neither of the above

9. All of the following are governmental rights, except
   a. taxation
   b. police power
   c. eminent domain
   d. adverse possession

10. The physical characteristics of land include all of the following, except
    a. scarcity
    b. fixity
    c. permanence
    d. nonhomogeneity

11. The legal rights attached to real property are referred to as the
    a. situs
    b. bundle of rights
    c. severance rights
    d. reliction rights

12. Rights in real property can include all of the following, except
    a. surface rights
    b. subsurface rights
    c. water rights
    d. avulsion rights

13. All the following are real property, except
    a. garage
    b. television antennna
    c. tractor
    d. fixture

14. The doctrine of prior appropriation of water rights provides for
    a. the first owner has first claim on water
    b. the water rights are held by the state
    c. water rights are leased from the local government
    d. prevention of erosion

15. A tax levied against a property because it will benefit from the improvement is
    a. escheat
    b. special assessment
    c. ad valorem tax
    d. percentage tax

16. The most prominent economic characteristics of land include
    a. scarcity, durability, nonhomogeneity
    b. scarcity, situs, durability
    c. situs, permanence, immobility
    d. permanence, immobility, indestructibility

17. Because no two parcels of land are identical, land is referred to as
    a. permanent
    b. durable
    c. quaint
    d. nonhomogeneous

18. Common examples of personal property include all of the following except
    a. farm machinery
    b. trade fixtures
    c. furnace
    d. annual crops

19. A right acquired in another's real property through continuous use is
    a. eminent domain
    b. adverse possession
    c. easement by prescription
    d. easement by Color of Title

20. Taxation of real property provides in part for all of the following services, except
    a. schools
    b. street maintenance
    c. libraries
    d. airline transportation

Land Descriptions

The surveying of land dates back to early times. As all legal descriptions are founded upon surveys, some of the historical background in the development of land surveying will be of interest to the novice in real estate. Surveying is important because it is necessary to have a sufficient description of the property to correctly identify and locate it. Every parcel of land that is sold or mortgaged must have a legal description. While a street address is the commonly used means of identifying the location of a property, legal documents require the legal description. Street addresses may be changed. For example, when a city annexes a nearby subdivision or village it is not unusual to extend the streets of that city into the newly annexed area. This occurred when the city of Omaha, Nebraska annexed the city of Millard and changed the names of many of the streets that aligned with Omaha streets.

To arrive at an accurate description of a particular parcel of land, several methods are followed.

METES AND BOUNDS

The metes and bounds method of measuring land is the oldest known method used in the United States. The original thirteen colonies were surveyed by this method but precise directions and measurements were not used. A selected **monument** *Monuments* served as the reference point or point of beginning, and the particular piece of land was described in terms of other natural and artificial monuments. Natural boundaries are created by nature, such as trees, rivers, and lakes. Artificial monuments are highways, section corners, and roads. Because of the vagueness involved, descriptions using monuments usually are concluded by referring to the area as being "xx acres, more or less". A typical description would read as in figure 3.1.

Because of the possible destruction of natural boundaries, the description lacks the permanence needed to correctly identify the property in later years. Today metes and bounds descriptions usually make reference to government survey lines as the place of beginning. If an owner sells off a portion of his land that is irregular in shape or if it cannot be identified except by using courses and distances, the surveyor will elect to use the metes and bounds in combination with the rectangular system.

Metes refers to the measurement of length or distance from one point to another. **Bounds** pertains to the direction of the course. In the **metes and bounds** description in figure 3.2, the metes (distance) are shown in feet and the bounds (direction) are in degrees, minutes, and seconds.

Beginning at a point at the southeast corner of Fish Lake; thence south to the burr oak tree; thence west along the northern boundary of the Blake farm to the fence at the corner of the Masterson farm and the Blake farm; thence north to Fish Lake Road and east to a large boulder; thence north to Fish Lake.

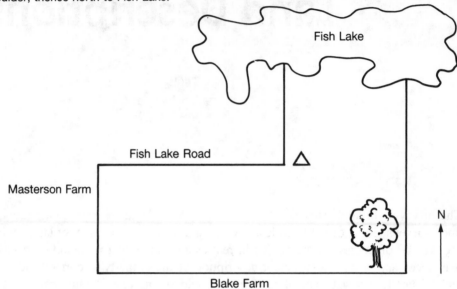

FIGURE 3.1

A metes-and-bounds description of this area: Beginning at a point 80' south and 40' west of the NE corner of the NE ¼ of Section 1, thence south 250', thence SW 30°17'10" for a distance of 500', thence North 330', thence 45° northeast for 320', thence east 220' to the point of beginning.

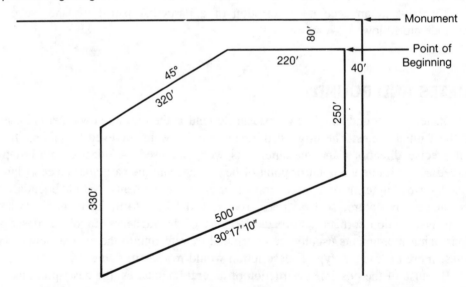

FIGURE 3.2

In Figure 3.2 note that the description began with a permanent marker called a **monument.** This monument is used as the reference point and the surveyor will go to the nearest corner of the property being surveyed. In Figure 3.2 the surveyor traveled 80 feet south and 40 feet west to the point of beginning. Reading through the legal description and traveling clockwise, we come back to the true point of beginning. The surveyors place iron pins or stakes into the land at the corners of the boundaries.

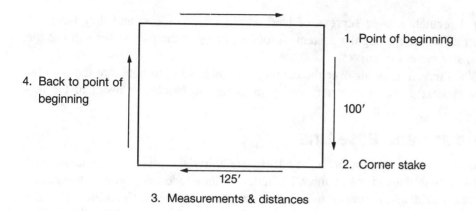

1. Point of beginning

4. Back to point of beginning

100'

2. Corner stake

125'

3. Measurements & distances

FIGURE 3.3

All land descriptions (see figure 3.3) contain

1. a point of beginning
2. corners defined by iron pins
3. definite measurements and distances
4. back to the point of beginning

In the metes and bounds description, the course will usually not run due east and west or due north and south, but will be angular, such as south 40 degrees east. In this instance, it is necessary to measure the angles by the units of degrees, minutes, and seconds. A degree is 1/360 of a circle and is divided into 60 minutes; each minute has 60 seconds (see figure 3.4). Measuring angles in a plat is done by using an instrument called a protractor.

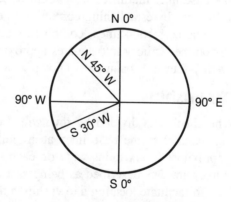

FIGURE 3.4
There are 360 degrees in a circle; each quarter contains 90 degrees.

Bench marks are permanent reference marks placed by United States government surveyors to designate locations and elevations. Surveyors use them as references when locating boundaries of a particular parcel of land. Bench marks may also be the brass markers surveyors place into a concrete drive or sidewalk.

Bench marks

THE GOVERNMENT RECTANGULAR SYSTEM

The rectangular system of land description was adopted by the federal government in 1785. It was used by most of the United States except for the original thirteen colonies and the Atlantic Coast states, with the exception of Florida. Upon admission to the Union, the states of West Virginia, Tennessee, Texas, Kentucky, and Hawaii retained regulation over surveys of land within their borders, and they have not conformed to the rectangular system. A total of thirty of the fifty states still use the rectangular system of survey.

When traveling by air over the country it is interesting to note that the land far below appears as an orderly series of squares and rectangles, a result of the rectangular survey system.

Meridians and Base Lines

Surveying land by latitude and longitude

In the rectangular system of survey there are thirty-six principal meridians and thirty-two base lines in the country. Latitude and longitude lines provide these base lines and meridians. A **meridian** is a line that runs directly north and south, and a **base line** is a line that runs east and west. These imaginary lines grid the surface of the earth. Starting from some tangible landmark, the surveyors ran a line due north through the area to be surveyed. This line running north and south was designated as the meridian for that particular state or area. In some states, these lines were called the first or second meridian. In others, they were actually given names, such as the Indian Meridian in Oklahoma. A base line was fixed at right angles to the meridian, to run due east and west, and this line was designated as the base line for that area. The surveyors would use the point where the meridian and base line intersected as their point of beginning (see figure 3.5).

Correction Lines

Because of the curvature of the earth, it was necessary to place **correction lines** at twenty-four mile intervals along the meridians to the north and south of the base lines. While the eye cannot see this curvature, it is very real. The north line of a township is 50 feet shorter than its south line. At every fourth township north of the base line, the difference would be 200 feet. The surveyors compensate for the difference by establishing correction lines at 24 mile intervals.

The correction lines, combined with guide meridians, enable the surveyors to divide the territory into squares approximately twenty-four miles on each side. The

Checks

twenty-four miles square is known as a *check*.

Townships

Townships contain 36 sections

The check was divided by **township** lines into smaller tracts of land. These lines run parallel to the base lines at six-mile intervals, resulting in a grid of squares approximately six miles wide on each side of the township lines. These grids and ranges are thus described as being east and west of the principal meridians.

Base lines

To facilitate locating a township in the grid, the townships have both a township number and a range number. The first township adjacent to and parallel to the base line was numbered one, the next two, proceeding on until reaching the next base line.

Likewise, a range number was given to each township running parallel to the principal meridian, commencing with number one east if it was directly east of the meridian or range one west if it was west (see figure 3.6).

Sections

The townships were further subdivided into thirty-six **sections** each, with a section containing 640 acres. These sections were numbered 1 to 36, beginning with 1 in the northeast corner of the township and proceeding west and east alternately, ending in the southeast corner with section 36 (see figure 3.7).

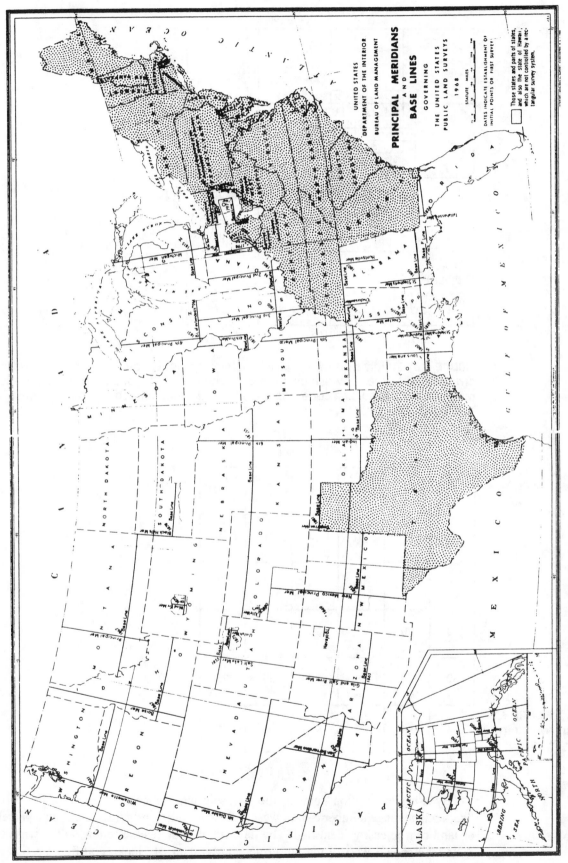

FIGURE 3.5 The meridian and base line system of surveying.

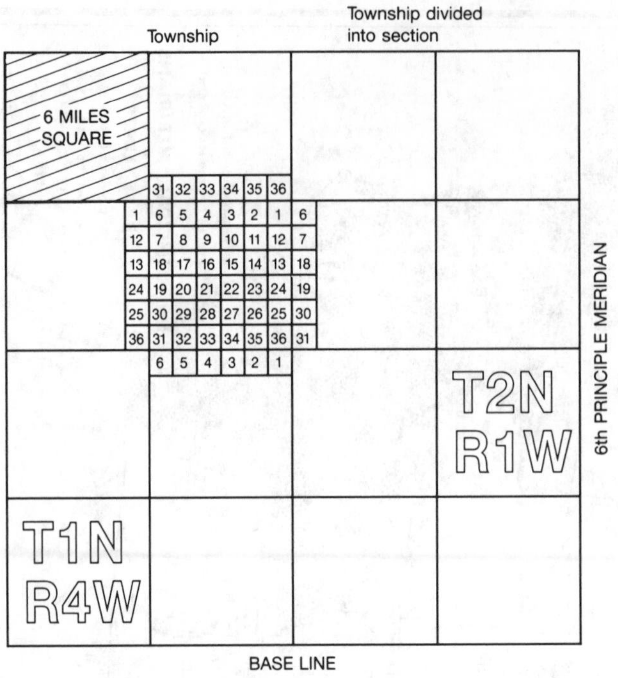

FIGURE 3.6 Subdivision of a check. A check is twenty-four miles square and is divided into sixteen townships, each of which is six miles square. Townships and ranges are signified by a code; for example, township 1 north and range 4 west is T1N, R4W.

6	5	4	3	2	1
7	8	9	10	11	12
18	17	16	15	14	13
19	20	21	22	23	24
30	29	28	27	26	25
31	32	33	34	35	36

FIGURE 3.7 A township containing 36 sections.

By using the section number, the township number north or south of the base line, and the range number east or west of the controlling principal meridian a parcel of land can be easily identified. The description may read: Section 8 of Township 3 North, Range 3 West of the 6th Principal Meridian. By looking at figure 3.6, we can locate the section.

Let us take it a step further. A legal description reads: The NE¼ of the SE¼ of Section 5 in T5N, R11W of the 6th PM. Legal descriptions are always read starting backwards, thus we would locate the range and township and then the section. The SE¼ would be identified and then proceed on to locate the NE¼ of said SE¼ (see figure 3.8).

Not all sections form an exact square because of the convergence of the meridians or due to bordering areas of water. To make allowances for this, the government added or deducted from one row of sections—from sections 1 through 6 (the northeast row) of the township if the difference occurred when measuring from south to north, and from the west row (sections 6, 7, 18, 19, 30 and 31) if the excess or deficiency occurred in the east or west measurements. These sections bordering on the north and west sides of a township are referred to as *fractional* sections (see figure 3.9).

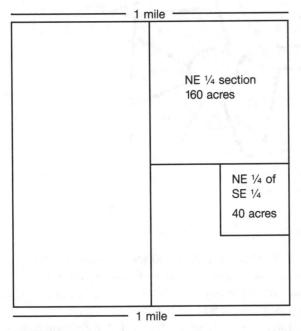

FIGURE 3.8

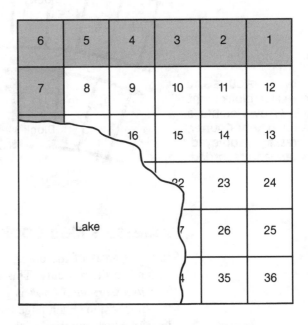

FIGURE 3.9 The shaded lots and the lots bordering the lake are fractional sections. The lots bordering the lake are called *government* lots.

The law further provided for any portions of land that could not be divided into equal fractional portions to be termed *government lots*. Fractional parcels were also created by bodies of water converging into a particular area (see figure 3.9).

Existing Indian reservations were excluded by law from the rectangular system, as were military reservations and land privately owned. As time passed and reserves were abandoned the surveyors were unable to establish exact lines with the original survey, thus fractional sections resulted.

THE LOT AND BLOCK SYSTEM

The **lot and block number** system of land description is used by developers in the platting of subdivisions of land. This can usually be considered the final platting of an area. The tract of land is divided into blocks, which are separated by streets. The blocks are platted into lots for single family dwellings and the lots numbered in sequence for easy identification. Usually the subdivision is given a name to further identify the area. Once the developer decides the manner in which the area is to be laid out, a surveyor prepares a survey sketch establishing the boundaries and legal descriptions of the area. The plat (detailed plan) will be certified by the surveyor and signed by the developer. Upon approval by the planning board of the local municipality, the plat is recorded and placed in a map book, which contains plats of all the subdivisions in the county. The book is indexed and may be inspected by anyone (see figure 3.10).

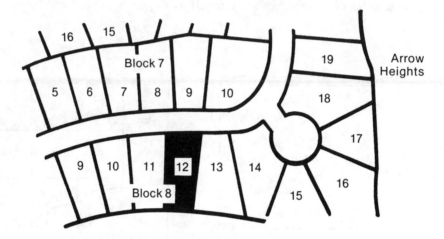

FIGURE 3.10
Lot twelve (12), block eight (8) in Arrow Heights, a subdivision in Kent County, Nebraska, as surveyed, platted, and recorded.

Assessors Map Book

In many areas of the country assessors attach a number to every registered parcel of land in their county. This method assists the assessor in preparing the tax roll. The *assessors map book* is prepared from the plats submitted by the developer of the subdivision. Each page has the assigned parcel number, book and page, and the lot and block number of the parcel. The book is generally available for purchase and many real estate offices find it convenient to have a copy for reference.

VERTICAL LAND DESCRIPTIONS

Chapter 11 relates how the condominium and townhouse type of ownership divides the single lot even further. In a highrise, the owner owns an *air lot* plus an interest in the common elements of the property. The master deed permits individual fee

Air lots   simple ownership within a larger estate. This horizontal property law has permitted owners of apartment houses to sell individual units and give fee simple ownership to the purchasers.

In preparing a survey of an air lot, a surveyor describes each unit by reference to the elevation above the lot and the land beneath it. The point from which the lot is measured is referred to as a *datum*. The datum is a level surface from which heights are measured. It may be mean sea level (zero feet) or the city may have established its own datum. The surveyor will start from this datum when measuring air lots.

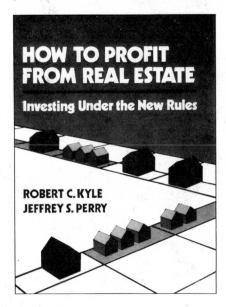
at
in
by

a
p-
ty
ly

s,
s-
re
ge
of
re

a

onspicuous object that helps estab-
es.

ers: A system of dividing an area
dividual lots, used in platting a

nning north and south to aid in
der the rectangular survey system.
A method of measuring land by
rections.

Monument: A marker set by surveyors to establish land boundaries.

Plat: A map of an area that delineates the boundaries of the parcel as they were surveyed.

Section: An area of one mile square, containing 640 acres.

Survey: The measurement and establishment of the boundaries of a particular property, usually identified by metal stakes imbedded in the ground on the corners of the lot lines.

Rectangular survey system: A means of dividing up the land by using meridians and base lines.

Township: An area of land as described in the rectangular survey system that contains thirty-six sections and is six miles square.

REVIEW QUESTIONS

1. To simplify and improve the system of determining individual parcels of land, the federal government adopted this type of land description
   a. metes and bounds
   b. lot and block number
   c. monuments
   d. rectangular survey

2. Section 36 of a township can be found at the
   a. northeast corner of the township
   b. northwest corner of the township
   c. southeast corner of the township
   d. southwest corner of the township

3. An acre contains
   a. 3,840 square feet
   b. 6,490 square feet
   c. 4,356 square feet
   d. none of these are correct

4. Which of the following are true of a section of land?
   a. it contains 640 acres
   b. a half section is a quarter-mile square
   c. both a and b
   d. neither a nor b

5. The NW¼ of the SE¼ of the SW¼ of section 9 contains
   a. 160 acres
   b. 80 acres
   c. 40 acres
   d. 10 acres

6. Section 9 of a township is directly below
   a. section 5
   b. section 3
   c. section 4
   d. section 16

7. The length of the north side of the NE¼ of the SE¼ of a section is how many feet?
   a. 660 feet
   b. 2,640 feet
   c. 1,320 feet
   d. 5,280 feet

8. Because of the curvature of the earth, it is necessary to compensate for shortages in the rectangular survey system through
   a. correction lines
   b. fractional lots
   c. bench marks
   d. principal meridians

9. The legal description of the shaded area in the diagram is

   a. NW¼ of the SW¼
   b. SW¼ of the NE¼
   c. SW¼ of the NW¼
   d. SW¼ of the SW¼ of the NW¼

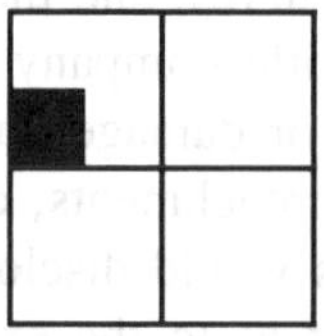

10. Give the township and ranges for the four areas surrounding township 9 north and range 1 west of the 6th principal meridian.

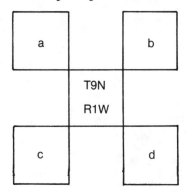

a.

b.

c.

d.

11. Establish the number of acres in the following description of a section of land: Beginning at the NE corner of the N½, thence in a diagonal line to the SW corner of the NE¼, thence in a diagonal line to the SE corner of the SE¼, thence north to the point of beginning.
    a. 80 acres
    b. 160 acres
    c. 320 acres
    d. 40 acres

12. Special provisions in the rectangular survey system were made for all of the following except
    a. Indian reservations
    b. fractional lots
    c. schools
    d. churches

13. Below is a diagram of a section of land. Establish the following parcels and the number of acres in each.

    a. SE¼ of the SW¼
    b. SE¼ of the SE¼ of the NW¼
    c. S½ of the SW¼ of the NE¼
    d. W½ of the SE¼

14. A land developer is going to subdivide the N½ of the SW¼ of the NW¼ of a section of land into residential lots 70 feet × 110 feet. He is allowing 420,450 square feet for streets. How many lots will be realized?
    a. 5
    b. 58
    c. 59
    d. 100

15. Identification objects used by surveyors to establish description points are referred to as
    a. metes and bounds
    b. correction lines
    c. monuments
    d. meridians

16. This surveying method uses boundaries and measurements of length in distances from one point to the other.
    a. monuments
    b. metes and bounds
    c. rectangular survey
    d. lot and block

17. Fractional sections that contain more or less than 640 acres are referred to as
    a. government lots
    b. irregular plots
    c. lots and blocks
    d. school sections

18. Which of the following would not be included as part of the legal description of a parcel of land?
    a. metes and bounds
    b. street address
    c. lot and block
    d. rectangular survey

Estates, Interests, Deeds, and Title | 4

ESTATES

An *estate* in land determines the legally recognized interest the person has in the real property. There are two main types of estates in real estate—freehold and less than freehold.

Freehold Estates

A **freehold estate** is ownership for an indefinite duration. The length of time a freehold estate will exist cannot be predetermined. Freehold estates include fee simple, fee simple determinable, and life estates. These freehold estates may be an *estate of inheritance* giving the holder the right to pass the real property on to his or her heirs. A *not of inheritance* freehold estate does not carry the right to will property but is only for the duration of the owner's life.

Fee simple absolute is the most complete type of estate, giving the estate holder complete rights to the land with absolute ownership. The owner of an estate in fee simple title can sell it, will it, give it away, or retain possession for as long as he or she desires. While the estate is subject to governmental and land use restrictions, the owner has the most power over the land that may be acquired in real estate.

Fee simple absolute

The *fee simple determinable* limits the estate holder to the terms set forth by the grantor. A parent may deed property to a child with the stipulation that it can never be sold, but must be passed down to the next generation. Land may be given to the city for a park on the condition that it never be used for any other purpose. The deed will specifically make reference to the fact that the estate is conditional "as long as" the land is used for the purpose stated. If the city vacates the property as a park deciding instead to use it for a parking lot, the land will revert back to the original grantor, his or her heirs, or a remainderman named by the grantor. That person holds a future or contingent interest in the property.

Fee simple determinable

The *fee simple* to a *conditional subsequent* gives the same possession and use rights as the fee simple determinable. However, when the fee simple is subject to a conditional subsequent, the original grantor must take action to reenter the property and gain possession if the condition has been broken— as in the city abandoning the property as a park. If the grantor does not take action to regain the property, the fee simple subject to a conditional subsequent will continue even though the terms have been broken. To summarize, the basic variance of the conditional subsequent is that the violation of the conveyance must have occurred and the original owners must go to court and demand return of the property.

Life estate

A **life estate** is granted to a person by will or by deed for the holder's lifetime. The estate holder, referred to as a *life tenant*, loses all rights to the estate upon death. During his or her life, while the estate is in effect, the life tenant has all the rights of ownership, including the rights of use, possession, enjoyment and income. The life tenant is responsible to maintain the property in reasonable repair and to pay property taxes. The life tenant can do nothing to diminish the value of the real estate, which is referred to as laying *waste* to the property. Nor can the life tenant change the use of the property; a farm could not be subdivided into housing lots or dug up for a gravel pit.

While the life tenant may lease the property, all leases will automatically be cancelled upon the death of the life tenant. Similarly, while the property may be mortgaged, the mortgage would terminate upon the life tenant's death. The mortgagee would thus want the protection of being named beneficiary of a term life insurance policy on the property or the cosignature of the remainderman on the mortgage note. The life tenant may sell the property, the grantee receiving only the rights of the holder. The remainderman could also sell his interest, which would be subject to the life tenant's interest. The purchaser would not come into possession until the life tenant's death. If the remainderman and the life tenant both convey their interests, the grantee would receive fee simple title. Since the life estate ceases to exist upon the death of the holder, it cannot be bequeathed.

Remainderman

The grantor of the life estate makes provisions for the property upon the life tenant's death by either naming a *remainderman* or creating a *reversionary interest*. The remainderman is the person named in the establishment of the life estate to succeed to the property. For example, Jones gave a life estate to his mother and upon her demise his daughter will become the remainderman. The daughter will

Reversionary interest

have a future interest (nonpossessory estate) in the real estate. If Jones does not name his daughter (or anyone else) as remainderman, upon the death of his mother the estate will revert back to Jones. If Jones is not living, it will pass to his devisee as stated in his will or to his heirs. This is known as a *reversionary interest*.

FIGURE 4.1

Less Than Freehold Estates

A **less than freehold estate** gives a possessory interest in real property for a definite period of time. These estates, often referred to as *leasehold interests,* encompass the rights a tenant has in the property of an owner. Generally conveyed by contract, they include an estate for years, periodic estate, estate at will, and a tenancy at sufferance. Less than freehold estates will be covered in detail in the chapter on leases.

THE DEED

After becoming aware of the estate that is granted in real property, it is important to understand the document that transfers title to that estate.

Title (evidence of ownership) is acquired by transferring the property to the new owner with a written instrument known as a **deed**. The deed conveys the grantor's interest in the real property to the grantee. This means of conveying ownership of land has been in existence for many years. Prior to this, it was customary to merely go out on the land, break a twig, and shake hands. By this basic ritualistic action the land was transferred. This act was referred to as **livery of seizin,** which simply means "transfer of possession." The **grantor,** the seller of real property, conveys title to the **grantee,** the purchaser.

Conveying title

A deed must be properly executed, delivered, and accepted for title to pass. According to statutes in most states, the deed must be in writing. The deed is executed (signed) only by the grantor(s).

Acknowledgment

Most states require that the grantor's signature be *acknowledged* (sworn to under oath) for it to be recorded. The grantor signs the deed in the presence of a notary public and agrees that this is a voluntary act and deed. The deed is witnessed and the notary public attests to the fact that the signatures are genuine by placing his or her seal and signature on the deed.

Delivery and Acceptance

It is necessary to establish that the deed has been delivered and accepted for title to pass. This delivery must be made by the grantor. For an owner to place a deed in a safety deposit box with the intention that title pass after his or her death is not allowable; the deed must be delivered within the grantor's lifetime. A third party, such as a real estate agent, an escrow agent, or an attorney who represents the grantee may accept the deed and delivery is presumed. In most states, delivery to a third party must be acceptable to the grantee.

Recordation

The purpose of **recording** any instrument is to give notice to the world of the transaction. State laws require mandatory recordation of liens against a property, and assessments against real property for public improvements, divorce decrees, and unpaid taxes. However, recording a deed or any document that affects ownership in land is not compulsory in most states, but is a right of the holder. If such documents are recorded, the "chain of title" continues on record. The recorder will endorse in the instrument the correct filing number and the exact time at which the document was filed, including the year, month, day, hour, and minute that it was received. The contents of the document are then transferred in writing to the appropriate book of records and the instrument is returned to the person who left it to be recorded. Thus, anyone desiring to look up information regarding a particular piece of property may do so by visiting the county courthouse where the document was recorded.

Documenting title

Contents

A deed must contain certain elements, including:

1. competent parties
2. consideration
3. words of conveyance (granting clause)
4. description of the real property
5. restrictions
6. the quantities or quality of the interest being conveyed (habendum clause)
7. signatures of the grantors

Competent parties

As in any legal contract, the parties involved must be *competent;* that is, capable of entering into a contract. Minors and persons adjudged insane are considered to be not legally competent. The deed would be voidable by the incompetent. For example, if a grantee is determined to be mentally incapable of decision making, the deed may be revoked by the grantee.

Consideration

The *consideration,* or the price paid for the property, must be recited on all deeds (see figure 4.2, number 2). Even a token amount may be stated, such as; "One dollar ($1.00) and other valuable consideration." If the property is being conveyed as a gift, the simple phrase, "for love and affection" may be used. The full consideration must be stated if the transfer is by order of the court or if the deed is from a trustee or a corporation.

Words of conveyance

The *words of conveyance* are the words that expressly grant the title to the grantee. Various kinds of deeds will state the granting clause differently, but all must express the grantor's intention to convey the property. The grantee(s) names will follow the granting clause and will spell out their relationship. In the warranty deed (figure 4.2) Kurt and Susan Kindly, husband and wife, are taking title. If Kurt Kindly was taking title by himself the deed would state: Kurt Kindly, a married man.

Following the grantees' names their specific rights are recited. In the example shown, the Kindlys are taking title as joint tenants, vesting their entire rights in the survivor. This is a very important phrase in any deed since it determines the rights of the survivor should one of the parties die.

Description

The *description* of the property must be sufficient to identify the real estate. In most states the legal description, citing the lot, block, and subdivision is preferred (see figure 4.2 number 5).

Restrictions

Restrictions may be written into the deed such as, "subject to real estate taxes and subsequent assessments." If the grantee is assuming an existing mortgage, it would also be recited in the "subject to" section of the deed. Generally, the phrase "subject to easements and restrictions of record" does not recite what these easements and restrictions may be. The subdivider filed the covenants and restrictions that relate to the subdivision and so the deed merely refers to this fact. The grantor may place further restrictions in the deed limiting the use of the property.

Quality and quantity of interest

The *qualities and quantity of the interest* being conveyed by the grantor will be shown in the deed. In the warranty deed, the grantor warrants the title through him- or herself, his or her heirs, and even his or her predecessors. However, when a grantor conveys title with a quitclaim deed s/he gives no warranties.

Signatures

The *signatures of the grantors* (figure 4.2 number 10) must also appear on all deeds. All the owners of the property must execute the instrument. In most states if a married person holds title alone, the spouse must still sign the deed to extinguish any rights to the property. If a grantor cannot write his or her name, s/he must place

NO. 342—WARRANTY DEED, VESTING ENTIRE TITLE IN SURVIVOR.   OMAHA PRINTING COMPANY

KNOW ALL MEN BY THESE PRESENTS, That

         Harvey J. Wender and Della J. Wender, husband and wife, **1**

in consideration of Eighty Four Thousand and no/100 ($84,000.00)----- **2** ---------- DOLLARS
in hand paid, do hereby grant, bargain, sell, convey and confirm unto **3**

         Kurt K. Kindly and Susan A. Kindly, husband and wife   **4**

as **JOINT TENANTS,** and not as tenants in common; the following described real estate, situate in the County of
     Kent   and State of Nebraska, to-wit:

         Lot Eight (8), Block One (1), in Confusion Hill
         subdivision, an Addition to the City of Big Red, **5**
         Kent County, Nebraska, as surveyed, platted
         and recorded.

      STATE
DOCUMENTARY **6**
    STAMPS
    $126.00

together with all the tenements, hereditaments, and appurtenances to the same belonging, and all the estate, title, dower,
right of homestead, claim or demand whatsoever of the said grantors   , of, in or to the same, or any part thereof,
subject to covenants, restrictions and easements of record, all regular taxes and
subsequent taxes and assessments. **7**

    **IT BEING THE INTENTION OF ALL PARTIES HERETO, THAT IN THE EVENT OF THE DEATH OF
EITHER OF SAID GRANTEES, THE ENTIRE FEE SIMPLE TITLE TO THE REAL ESTATE DESCRIBED
HEREIN SHALL VEST IN THE SURVIVING GRANTEE. 8**

    TO HAVE AND TO HOLD the above described premises, with the appurtenances, unto the said grantees as
JOINT TENANTS, and not as tenants in common, and to their assigns, or to the heirs and assigns of the survivor of
them, forever, and we the grantors named herein for ourselves **9** and our heirs, executors, and
administrators, do covenant with the grantees named herein and with their assigns and with the heirs and assigns of
the survivor of them, that we are lawfully seized of said premises; that they are free from incumbrance except
as stated herein, and that we the said grantors have good right and lawful authority to sell the same, and
that we will and our heirs, executors and administrators shall warrant and defend the same
unto the grantees named herein and unto their assigns and unto the heirs and assigns of the survivor of them, forever,
against the lawful claims of all persons whomsoever, excluding the exceptions named herein.

    IN WITNESS WHEREOF we have hereunto set our hands this 14th day of

     May   A. D., 1987   *Harvey J. Wender*
                             (Harvey J. Wender)
      In presence of   *Della J. Wender*   **10**
Judy M. Selling   **11**   (Della J. Wender)

STATE OF NEBRASKA,   } ss.
County of Kent   }   On this 14th day of May

A. D. 1987 , before me, a Notary Public in and for said County, personally came the above named

     Harvey J. Wender and Della J. Wender, husband and wife

    12   who are personally known to me to be the identical persons whose names
            affixed to the above instrument as grantors , and they have
            acknowledged said instrument to be their voluntary act and deed.
    SEAL   **WITNESS** my hand and Notarial Seal the date last aforesaid.
                 Judy M. Selling Notary Public.
    My commission expires on the 8th day of July A. D., 1989

FIGURE 4.2 A general warranty deed.

an "X" for his or her mark in the presence of witnesses. If the property is owned by a corporation, the deed is signed by its authorized officer(s) and the corporate seal is placed on the deed.

The deed illustrated in figure 4.2 is a warranty deed, vesting entire title to the grantee. This deed is for joint tenancy ownership, which will be explained under deeds in this chapter. The numbers on the deed designate the following:

1. The sellers' names appear conveying the property. Their names must be exactly as they appeared when they took title. The marital status of the grantors is stated as well.
2. The amount the real property is selling for. While we have used the actual amount, it is legal to merely put a token amount such as; "$1.00 and other valuable consideration."
3. The clause of conveyance must be present in all deeds. In this deed it states that the seller will "grant, bargain, sell, convey and confirm" the property to the buyer.
4. The buyer's names, along with their marital status.
5. The complete legal description of the property.
6. State documentary stamps (in states where used).
7. This paragraph enumerates any limitations that exist in the conveyance of the property, and includes the loan assumption clause if a loan is being assumed.
8. This is the joint tenancy clause, vesting entire rights in the survivor.
9. The habendum clause defines the quantity of the estate being granted to the grantees and is referred to as the "to have and to hold" clause.
10. Signatures of the grantors—exactly as shown at number 1.
11. Signature of witness.
12. The acknowledgment of the document by the notary public. In this instance, the real estate agent was a notary public, and so she witnessed the owners' signatures to the deed.

State Documentary Stamps

Title transfer tax   When title to real property is transferred, the state may collect a tariff in the form of *state documentary stamps*. The cost of state documentary stamps varies from state to state, with some states charging no revenue from the sale of real property. Generally, they are paid by the grantor and the amount is stamped on the deed by the Register of Deeds at the time the instrument is recorded. In Nebraska, the stamps are based on the rate of $1.50 per $1000.00 or any part thereof. Thus, if a property sells for $10,000.00, the state would collect $15.00 worth of stamps. If a property sold for $10,500 it would be necessary to add another $1.50 to the $15.00.

In the deed shown in figure 4.2, the purchase price of the property located at 1040 Clear Street was $84,000. At the rate of $1.50 per $1,000.00, the grantors would pay documentary stamp fees of $126.00 (at number 6).

Types of Deeds

The following deeds are the most commonly used:

Warranty deed   • The *general warranty deed* conveys the highest and most complete ownership in real estate. The grantors of a general warranty deed guarantee the title against the whole world. They are telling the grantee that it is free and clear of all liens and that they are relinquishing all rights through themselves, their heirs, and even their predecessors. A sample of a warranty deed is shown in figure 4.2. The warranties that a grantor conveys in a general warranty deed include:

1. *Covenant of seizin:* The grantors declare they are in full possession of the interest granted.
2. *Quiet enjoyment:* No one will evict the grantee with a prior title.
3. *Freedom from encumbrances:* There will be no liens or unpaid taxes on the interest unless specifically noted in the deed. (For example, a grantee might agree to assume an existing mortgage.)
4. *Further assurances:* Insures good title and that if there should be any faults found in the deed, the grantor will correct them.
5. *Right to convey:* Guarantees possession and title.

• In the *special warranty* deed the grantors guarantee the title through themselves and their heirs, but not their predecessors. Basically, the grantors are giving the same guarantee as in a general warranty deed but they are covering the time only since they owned interest in the property. The period of time covered represents the only difference from a general warranty deed. *Special warranty*

• A *grant deed* contains warranties as in a warranty deed but they are created by the grantors themselves. The grantors imply that they warrant the deed and that they have not previously conveyed the real property to another. The warranty includes encumbrances made while the grantors owned it but not those made during another's ownership. As in the special warranty deed, the grantors warrant only their ownership. *Grant deed*

• A *bargain and sale deed* is similar to the quitclaim deed in that it contains no warranties. However, in this deed the grantors do acknowledge that they have an interest in the real property. The grantees must have the title searched to be absolutely certain that they are receiving a good and marketable title. *Bargain and sale*

The words of conveyance usually will state, "grant, bargain, and sell," or "grant and release" implying that the grantor holds title to the property. If the deed contains covenants against the grantor's acts (which can be added to the deed) then it has the same validity as a special warranty deed.

• The *quitclaim* deed gives no warranties to the grantee. The grantors may not have clear title and may be conveying only the interest they have in the property. The grantors "quit their claim" and the grantee receives whatever interest the grantors have. This deed is often used to remove a cloud on the title, which is a partial interest in real property. It is also used to correct defects in a title, such as an incorrect description or an error in the spelling of a grantor's name. *Quitclaim deed*

Special purpose deeds are used to comply with certain legal purposes. They include the trust deed, sheriff's deed, tax deed, correction deed, executor's deed, guardian deed, cession deed and director's deed. *Special purpose deeds*

• A *deed of trust* is not merely a deed but is a deed to secure payment of a debt. Not only does it convey title but it is held in trust by a third disinterested party for the benefit of the lender. Further explanation of this type of deed can be found in the chapter on financing, since the main function of a deed of trust is to secure a note.

• The *sheriff's deed* transfers real estate sold at a public sale, usually the result of a foreclosure on a judgment or a mortgage. There are no warranties or representations with this deed since the sheriff is acting on behalf of the public.

• A *tax deed* transfers real property that has been sold by the government because taxes have not been paid. As with the sheriff's deed, there are no warranties.

• A *correction deed* (sometimes referred to as a reformation deed or a deed of confirmation) is used to correct an error such as a mistake in the spelling of a name, an inaccuracy in the legal description of a property, or some omission. The grantor must correct the mistake if he gave a covenant of further assurances (as with a warranty deed). The correction deed must conform to the requirements of a legal document; usually a quitclaim deed is used.

• The *executor's deed* is issued by an executor of an estate upon the sale of the deceased person's real property. The deed is executed under court approval and carries no warranty other than against the executor's acts. Unlike other deeds, the executor's deed must state the full purchase price.

• The *guardian's deed* issued to convey a minor's interest in real property, passes title carrying the covenant that neither the guardian nor the minor have encumbered the property.

• A *cession deed* is given by the subdivider when he dedicates the streets in the subdivision to the county or city. All street rights (and the obligation of maintenance) are transferred to the appropriate unit of government.

• A *director's deed* is used when a public agency sells surplus land.

TAKING TITLE TO REAL PROPERTY

When taking title to real property, ownership may be described as joint tenancy, tenancy in common, concurrent ownership, tenancy by the entirety, severalty ownership, or multiple ownership. (See figure 4.3 for a diagram of different types of ownership and figure 4.4 for a list of the form of ownership allowed in each state.)

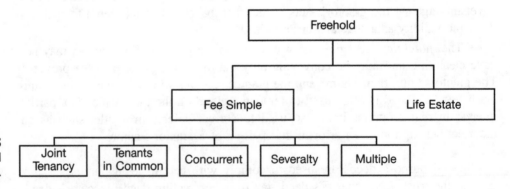

FIGURE 4.3
Different types of real property ownership.

Joint Tenancy

Title with right of survivorship Joint tenancy is ownership by two or more persons with the right of survivorship. This must be clearly stated in the deed; otherwise tenancy in common may be assumed in some states. Joint tenancy means that when one of the owners dies, the

	Tenancy in Common	Joint Tenancy	Tenancy by the Entirety	Community Property
Alabama	X	X		
Alaska	X	X	X	
Arizona	X	X		X
Arkansas	X	X	X	
California	X	X		X
Colorado	X	X		
Connecticut	X	X		
Delaware	X	X	X	
District of Columbia	X	X	X	
Florida	X	X	X	
Georgia	X			
Hawaii	X	X	X	
Idaho	X	X		X
Illinois	X	X		
Indiana	X	X	X	
Iowa	X	X		
Kansas	X	X		
Kentucky	X	X	X	
Louisiana				X
Maine	X	X		
Maryland	X	X	X	
Massachusetts	X	X	X	
Michigan	X	X	X	
Minnesota	X	X		
Mississippi	X	X		
Missouri	X	X	X	
Montana	X	X		
Nebraska	X	X		
Nevada	X	X		X
New Hampshire	X	X		
New Jersey	X	X	X	
New Mexico	X	X		X
New York	X	X	X	
North Carolina	X	X	X	
North Dakota	X	X		
Ohio	X			
Oklahoma	X	X	X	
Oregon	X		X	
Pennsylvania	X	X	X	
Rhode Island	X	X	X	
South Carolina	X	X		
South Dakota	X	X		
Tennessee	X	X	X	
Texas	X	X		X
Utah	X	X		
Vermont	X	X	X	
Virginia	X	X	X	
Washington	X	X		X
West Virginia	X	X		
Wisconsin	X	X	X	
Wyoming	X	X	X	

FIGURE 4.4 Forms of ownership allowed in each state.

surviving joint tenant(s) obtain the property. In joint tenancy all the joint tenants must have the same

1. *Time*—the interest must be acquired at the same time.
2. *Title*—all joint tenants must receive their interest through a single deed.
3. *Interest*—the rights of the owners must be equal.
4. *Possession*—all owners must have equal rights of possession.

Joint tenancy is generally only used by family members because of the right of survivorship. If parties own property under joint tenancy, when one dies, the other receives the property; however, the value of the entire property would be subject to estate taxes twice. Because of possible tax consequences such as these it has become increasingly important for people to seek counsel when taking title. In joint tenancy ownership, if one of the parties dies the unity of ownership continues. For example, if three individuals own a property in joint tenancy and one of the parties dies, the remaining two parties still own the property in joint tenancy receiving the deceased person's share under the right of survivorship.

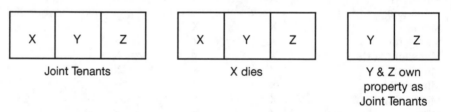

Conversely, if one of the three parties *sold* his share to another the joint tenancy would cease to exist between the three parties. The remaining two owners would be joint tenants, but the new owner would be a tenant in common.

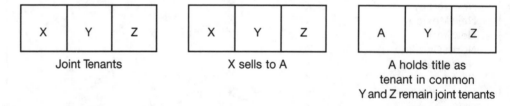

Advantages of joint tenancy ownership:

1. Probate expenses may be eliminated.
2. The surviving joint tenant automatically succeeds to the title immediately.
3. Estate held in joint tenancy would not be subject to debts incurred by the descendant.

Disadvantages of joint tenancy ownership:

1. The descendant's heirs will not inherit the property.
2. A joint tenant relinquishes his or her right to will his or her share of the property.
3. It may create tax problems.
4. It does not replace the need for a will.

Tenancy in Common

Tenancy in common is ownership by two or more persons without the right of survivorship. If one of the owners dies, his or her interest reverts to his or her heirs or devisee and not to the surviving tenant in common. Each owner has an undivided interest in the whole. That is, one person can't designate ownership of the south side of the lot and the other owner the north side; they own the whole with an undivided interest. This is true in all types of ownership. However, each person's share need not be equal; one tenant-in-common owner could own two-thirds of the value of the whole, while the other owns one-third. In addition, one owner may sell his or her interest without the consent of the other owner so that, unlike joint tenancy, title may be taken at different times.

Without right of survivorship

Tenancy by the Entirety

Tenancy by the entirety can only be held by husband and wife. As with joint tenancy, it vests entire rights in the surviving spouse. Neither the husband or wife can convey the property without the consent of the other. Not all states recognize tenancy by the entirety. While it provides for automatic survivorship, it can establish inheritance tax problems and should not be used as a replacement for a will. In states that recognize tenancy by the entirety, the deed generally will need to specifically state this fact.

Ownership by husband and wife

Historically under English common law, the wife was considered a "part" of her husband with no separate rights in property. Thus, as a "single unit" the tenancy by the entireties gave him absolute control. However, the laws today recognize a wife's rights and benefits as equal to a husband's and states that use tenancy by the entireties acknowledge this. Should the couple divorce, tenancy by the entireties automatically ceases to exist and the parties become tenants in common.

Concurrent ownership is held by two or more persons, as in joint tenants and tenants in common.

Severalty Ownership

Severalty ownership is the sole ownership of a property by one person. Do not think of the term as implying several, but look at the first five letters, *sever*, the person's ownership is "severed" from all others.

Severalty ownership

While a married person may own property in severalty, most states will require the spouse to sign away any marital rights upon the sale of the property.

In law, a corporation is a legal person and as such takes title to property in severalty.

There are advantages in sole ownership of real property. The individual makes the decision when to buy or sell and on what terms. Unlike concurrent ownership, s/he has total control. Needless to say, with that control goes all responsibility of maintenance and care.

Community Property

In the eight states* that recognize community property laws, ownership of property acquired by either husband and wife during the marriage is considered *community property*. They are considered to have contributed equally to the marriage and thus any property they purchase will be equally shared. This is true even if one of the spouses does not work outside the home.

*Arizona, California, Idaho, Louisiana, Nevada, New Mexico, Texas, and Washington.

Property held prior to the marriage does not apply and is considered separate property. Property that is acquired AFTER marriage by inheritance or gift is also excluded from community property. If one of the parties purchased property with separate funds, this too would be excluded.

Community property states allow the spouse to devise by will his or her portion of the estate to anyone he or she chooses to name. In the states of California, Idaho, Nevada, New Mexico and Washington, if no will is left, the deceased person's estate reverts to the surviving spouse. However, in Arizona, Louisiana, or Texas, the heirs of the deceased would be the beneficiary.

Partition

Partition A **co-owner** of real property may *partition* to terminate the shared ownership. If the co-owners have not voluntarily agreed to the dissolving of the estate one co-owner can partition and the courts will conduct a compulsory division of the land. If it is not feasible to actually divide the land, a sale will be ordered and the proceeds split in accordance with each owner's share. A co-owner may demand partition regardless of the amount of his share.

In addition to the individual and concurrent forms of ownership, group ownership is held by business enterprises. Partnerships, corporations, syndications, and trusts hold real estate for business purposes.

Partnership

A *partnership* is formed when two or more people join together in a business venture for the purpose of making a profit. The partnership will operate under its own name or in the name of the owners. If operating under a trade name—for example, XYZ Partnership—the property will be held in severalty since a partnership is considered by law as a single entity. If held in the names of the individual owners, title would be held as tenants-in-common or joint tenancy.

Legal Life Estates

Legal life estates are established by dower, curtesy and homestead laws as a result of marriage. While many states have abolished dower and curtesy rights and have initiated statutory laws as substitutions, other states still maintain many features of old English Common Law. The underlying reason for curtesy and dower rights are to legally protect property rights of a surviving spouse.

Dower is the right a wife has to her husband's estate at the time of his death. Since this right does not materialize until death, it is *inchoate* or incomplete. This law guarantees the wife a minimum of a one-third interest in her husband's estate, protecting her against any creditor's claims or acts by her husband to disinherit her.

Dower rights further protect the wife since the husband cannot sell real property without her consent. The wife must relinquish her rights by signing the deed.

Curtesy represents the husband's life interest in any of his deceased wife's property. However, many states require that a child have been born to the marriage in order for curtesy rights to take effect. The wife also has the option to will her property to another and defeat the curtesy rights. As with dower rights, all states require that the husband sign any deed affecting title to property held by the wife.

The family's place of residence is classified as their **homestead.** Most states have enacted homestead laws to exempt the home from a forced sale due to liens and judgments by creditors. It is protection for the family in the event of a financial disaster, conceived primarily to benefit dependents.

States that have established homestead laws require that the real estate is the family's permanent residence. Additionally, the property may have to be filed as a homestead at the county courthouse. States vary in the requirements of establishing a homestead. Some states will designate a single person as fulfilling the term family. Each state determines the amount to be exempt. For example, if the law exempts $10,000 from debts, upon the sale and satisfaction of any taxes due, mortgages and mechanics liens, the owner would receive the first $10,000 with the remainder applied towards other outstanding debts.

Most homestead laws were legislated when much of the country was rural and the laws served as protection for the farmer and his family. Some states exempt a certain amount of farm land, as 160 acres. Today the amount is often times less than the farmer's debts.

While the homestead exemption benefits the owner to a degree, there are some claims that are not exempt. They include

1. real estate taxes
2. real estate special assessments
3. real estate mortgages
4. mechanics liens

SUMMARY

This chapter discusses the ownership of real property, which includes defining the estates, interests, deeds, and title held in real property.

A freehold estate conveys the maximum interest available under the law. The owner can dispose of the property as he wishes and it is inheritable by his heirs upon his death. A life estate gives the holder the right of possession and use of the land for his or her lifetime. A less than freehold estate gives possessary or controlling interest in the real estate for a definite period of time as stated in the lease.

To enable you to thoroughly understand the instrument that conveys title to real property, considerable space has been allotted to the explanation of the deeds. The contents of the deed are very important. If a deed lacks a description of the property, the conveyance clause or consideration, the names of the parties, or the grantors' signatures, it is invalid. Proper execution of the deed must be carried out and delivery made for title to pass.

There are several types of deeds, with different interests acquired in each. A general warranty deed (sometimes simply referred to as a warranty deed) conveys the greatest quality of interest. It clearly spells out the covenants the grantor warrants and promises. In a special warranty deed, the grantor only warrants the title since he took possession. A bargain and sale deed confirms that an interest is held by the grantor, but he *is not* warranting that interest; and in a quitclaim deed *no* warranties are given, as the signer only gives whatever interest he has. If I gave you a quitclaim deed to the Brooklyn Bridge, you would receive exactly the interest I have, which is zero.

When taking title to real property, the grantee may hold interest by means of joint tenancy, tenancy in common, severalty, tenancy by the entireties, or multiple ownership. Since laws vary from state to state, careful consideration should be given as to how the person wishes to take title. While many married couples automatically think they should hold title by joint tenancy, this may not always be wise; the property is subject to inheritance tax upon the death of the first partner and *again* upon the survivor's death.

Multiple ownership has become increasingly popular. Since inflation has caused property to increase greatly in value, many people are interested in acquiring investment property. Unable to finance a purchase alone, they pool their funds with others. Investments and their tax benefits are covered in the chapter on investments.

KEY WORDS AND CONCEPTS

Co-ownership: Two or more parties own an undivided interest in the same property.

Curtesy: Interest a husband has in his wife's estate.

Deed: A written instrument that transfers ownership of real property.

Dower: Rights a wife has in her husband's estate.

Freehold estate: An estate in real estate that conveys fee simple title, or grants the maximum interests for an indefinite amount of time.

Grantee: The purchaser of real property.

Grantor: The owner and seller of real property.

Habendum clause: The "to have and to hold" clause, which defines the quantity of the estate the grantor is deeding to the grantee.

Homestead: The place of residence of a family; in some states a portion of the homestead is exempt from creditors' claims.

Instrument: A document or a written statement.

Less than freehold estate: An estate that lasts for a definite period of time.

Life estate: Interest in real estate limited to the lifetime of the life tenant.

Livery of seizin: Transfer of possession.

Real property: Property that is immobile and permanent in nature.

Record: To give public notice.

State documentary stamps: A state tax placed on the sale of real property.

Tenancy by the entirety: Real property held in joint tenancy by husband and wife.

Title: Evidence of ownership in real property.

REVIEW QUESTIONS

1. The essential ingredients of a deed include(s)
   a. the signatures of the grantees and grantors
   b. words of conveyance
   c. recordation
   d. all of the above

2. If Charlie Brown purchases a property and receives title from the grantor by a quitclaim deed
   a. Brown does not receive clear title
   b. Brown receives whatever title the grantor had
   c. Brown can force the grantor to correct any title defects
   d. all of the above

3. The responsibility of recording a deed lies with
   a. the state
   b. the county
   c. the grantor
   d. the grantee

4. Deed restrictions are considered to be
   a. general liens
   b. escheat
   c. an encumbrance
   d. enforceable only by the property owner

5. Property held in joint tenancy, upon the death of one of the tenants, would pass to
   a. the state
   b. the owner's heirs
   c. the spouse
   d. the surviving joint tenant

6. A life tenant can do all of the following with her interest except
   a. sell
   b. lease
   c. bequeath
   d. mortgage

7. A warranty deed guarantees against all except
   a. the grantor's heirs
   b. easements of record
   c. mortgage
   d. a judgment creating a lien

8. Susan Jones lists her home with Sam Suresell and indicates that she wishes to deliver the deed that best protects her when she passes title. Ms. Jones will convey title by means of
   a. a quitclaim deed
   b. a warranty deed
   c. a special warranty deed
   d. a grant deed

9. Henry Dudd subsequently views the Jones home and decides to make an offer to purchase the property. He informs his agent, Diane Dealquick, that he wants the deed that will give him the most assurance of receiving a clear title. Ms. Dealquick suggest
   a. a quitclaim deed
   b. a warranty deed
   c. a special warranty deed
   d. a grant deed

10. After much negotiation, Jones and Dudd agree that Jones will deliver a deed that assures good title through her time of ownership only. The deed agreed upon was
    a. a quitclaim deed
    b. a warranty deed
    c. a special warranty deed
    d. a grant deed

11. A deed that is executed by the grantor several days before it is delivered is
    a. invalid and not enforceable
    b. valid as long as it is recorded
    c. valid upon delivery
    d. invalid if not recorded within ten days

12. For a deed to be recorded it must contain
    a. the signatures of the grantors and grantees
    b. valuable consideration
    c. both of the above
    d. neither of the above

13. For a deed to be conveyed, it must be
    a. signed
    b. accepted
    c. acknowledged
    d. recorded

14. The deed(s) of conveyance an owner of real estate may use to voluntarily transfer his right, title, or interest in real estate include
    a. warranty deed
    b. sheriff's deed
    c. both of the above
    d. neither of the above

15. Two friends jointly purchase a property. To protect their heirs, they should take title in
    a. joint tenancy
    b. severalty
    c. life estate
    d. tenancy in common

16. The "to have and hold" clause in a deed is represented by the
    a. consideration
    b. acknowledgment
    c. words of conveyance
    d. habendum

17. Tenancy by the entirety may exist between
    a. family members only
    b. any two parties of legal age
    c. both of the above
    d. neither of the above

18. Joel Smith and Mark Jones lived together in a home they purchased. Joel dies in an automobile accident. Mark now owns the property in severalty. Joel and Mark had title to the property as
    a. tenants by the entirety
    b. joint tenants
    c. tenants in common
    d. owners in severalty

19. What is the primary purpose of a deed?
    a. transfer of title
    b. proof of ownership
    c. recordation
    d. legal evidence

20. For a deed to be considered valid, it must
    a. contain an adequate description of the property
    b. be acknowledged
    c. be recorded
    d. be drawn on any day but Sunday

21. The covenant of quiet enjoyment refers to
    a. occupancy
    b. ownership
    c. the prevention of interference by other parties
    d. the absence of liens on the property

22. Marcia Moore had a life estate to which her daughter was named remainderman. Ms. Moore leased the property for five years. Three years later, she passed away and the daughter decided to cancel the lease.
    a. The lease was totally void from the beginning.
    b. The terms of the lease prevailed.
    c. The lease was void upon the death of the life tenant.
    d. The lessee can sue for damages if evicted.

The Orderly Process of a Sale

This section begins the explanation of the orderly process of the sale, beginning with an introductory chapter on Contract and Business Law to enable the reader to develop an understanding of the various contracts used in real estate transactions. Once this foundation has been laid, this segment of the text follows the orderly process of the sale in the natural sequence of events in listing and selling a property.

Throughout this section, a single property has been used as an example to give continuity to the procedures involved in a transaction.

Chapter 6 explains the role of the real estate brokerage firm and its relationship to the seller when listing a property for sale. The listing contract is explained and the various types of listings are described.

Chapter 7 builds upon Chapter 6, dealing with locating the buyer to purchase the property. The offer to purchase is written after the buyers are given an estimate of the costs involved. A step-by-step analysis of the agreement is covered with an explanation of rejections and counter offers. The role of the real estate agent in representing the buyer and seller is explained and defined.

Chapter 8 covers the role of financial institutions since most real estate sales are financed, and gives a background of the lending institutions and the loans they issue.

Chapter 9 further develops an understanding of finance by explaining the mortgage and deed of trust, the financing instruments used by the lending institutions. The many varied types of mortgages available complete the chapter.

Chapter 10 completes this section with the closing of the transaction. The responsibilities of the real estate firm (or the escrow company), the lender, and the title company are all covered. The many forms used in closing a sale are shown, concluding with the buyer's and seller's closing statements and the broker's trust account balance sheet.

Contracts and Business Law | 5

Since contracts are an essential part of real estate transactions and we could not do business without them it is necessary to fully understand contract law. This chapter will take you through the "making of a contract" explaining all the elements and legal requirements of a valid and binding contract.

The contracts most frequently used in real estate are the listing and purchase agreements, leases, installment contracts, options, escrow agreements, and mortgages. Their use is an everyday occurrence for the real estate agent and subsequent chapters will cover each in detail.

CONTRACTS

A **contract** is a voluntary agreement between two or more parties to perform (or abstain from performing) a legal act on which they have had a "meeting of the minds." In other words, they agreed on the subject matter of the contract. In this legally enforceable agreement, the parties are bound to the conditions of the contract.

Contract

Contracts may be implied or expressed, oral or written. An **implied contract** is neither written nor explicitly stated orally, but is created by an act of the party. Most people enter into implied business contracts every day when they ask for a cup of coffee at a restaurant, take public transportation to work, or make a purchase at a store. The implication is that they will pay for these services and purchases. (These implied contracts are not enforceable.)

Implied contract

An **expressed contract** may be written or oral. A purchase agreement will be in writing and specifically spell out the intentions of the parties. A lease may be oral or written; tenants taking possession of the premises show their expressed consent to occupy and pay rent for the apartment. The landlord expresses consent by permitting the party to move into the apartment.

Expressed contract

A **bilateral contract** embodies the promise on the part of both parties to the contract. In a purchase contract the offeror (buyer) promises to buy and the offeree (seller) promises to sell. A lease is another example of a bilateral contract; the lessee (tenant) agrees to pay rent and the lessor (landlord) to give possession.

Bilateral contract

A **unilateral contract** is the promise on the part of one party to complete an act. In a listing contract the owner lists the property and agrees to pay the agent a commission upon the sale. The agent naturally hopes to sell the property and earn a commission, but the contract does not bind him or her to do so. Likewise, in an option contract the optionor agrees to sell the property to the optionee, but the optionee is not bound to purchase.

Unilateral contract

ELEMENTS OF A CONTRACT

A valid contract requires certain basic elements and qualities:

1. *Offer and acceptance* (A meeting of the minds on the subject matter.)
2. *Consideration* (Good or valuable exchange.)
3. *Capacity of the parties* (The parties must be capable of entering into a contract.)
4. *Legality of the object* (The contract must be for a legal purpose.)
5. *Contract in writing and signed* (When required by law.)

Upon fulfillment of these five conditions a valid and binding agreement is "contracted."

Offer and acceptance

The concept of **offer and acceptance** means that the parties have agreed by mutual consent to the terms of a contract. For example, in the purchase agreement the buyer (offeror) agrees to purchase the property on the terms stated. If the seller (offeree) signs the contract, s/he agrees to the terms offered and both parties are obligated to abide by the contract. The terms of the contract must be precise and clearly defined. If they are not specified in detail so that each party understands the terms, mutual agreement does not exist.

Consideration

The **consideration** must be evident in all contracts, indicating a mutual exchange of promises. This consideration must offer a benefit or a detriment. One party is giving and the other receiving. In the example of a purchase agreement the buyer agrees to purchase the property for a stated price and upon acceptance by the seller a transaction has been agreed to. The earnest deposit the buyer places with the broker shows his good faith in wanting to perform according to the terms of the contract but is not the consideration that makes a valid contract. In the event the buyer should decide not to perform, the earnest money may be dispersed to the seller as liquidated damages, which will be covered later in Chapter 7.

Good consideration

A promise must be accompanied by consideration from one party to another to be enforceable. You may have heard the term *good and valuable* consideration. *Good consideration* is recognized by law when an *act* is given for consideration. You hire a nursery to trim your trees on the promise that upon completion of the act you will pay the agreed upon fee. Another example, "A" promises to sell his condominium to "B" for one half its market value if "B" marries "A's" daughter. If "B" marries the daughter, "A" must fulfill his promise since the act was carried out. In this situation, "A's" daughter had other plans for her life so the transfer did not take place. Nevertheless, "A" wanted his daughter to have the property so he deeded it to her for "love and affection," which meets the legal requirement of consideration.

Valuable consideration

The vast majority of contracts carry *valuable consideration* in the form of money. One party agrees to sell property to another for a stated price; in other words, one gives money and the other relinquishes property for the monetary consideration.

Capacity of the parties

The law is emphatic in stating who is able and who is not able to enter into a contract. To be capable of entering into a contract, one must be able to understand what the contract contains and to carry out its terms. A person not of legal age may rescind a contract; however, the person who accepts the minor's contract is still bound to the terms of the contract. In most states the age of majority is 18 years. This law provides protection for minors since they may not be able to understand contract terms. The minor must request release from the contract while still a minor or within a reasonable time period after reaching majority. Failure to rescind the contract makes it valid. A guardian may act for a minor in the event the minor had received property (as through inheritance) and it was deemed in the best interest of the minor that the property be sold.

A mentally incompetent person cannot enter into a contract since s/he is not responsible for his or her actions. An insane or mentally retarded person must have someone appointed by law to act on his or her behalf.

Some states have extended the law to include intoxicated persons or persons high on drugs. If property was sold to someone knowing he or she was intoxicated and unable to make a sound judgment, the party to the contract may ask the courts to annul the contract.

The purpose of the promise in a contract must be a lawful one. One could not enter into a legal contract with someone to burn down a house, irrespective of the consequences, as it could not be legally completed or enforced. *Lawful object*

If one party to a contract is not at fault then the courts will intervene to avenge the injured party. An example, Evans purchased a property and opened a delicatessen only to be closed down because zoning laws did not permit the space to be used for a commercial purpose. Evans can rescind the purchase contract upon proof that the property was sold under false pretense.

All states have enacted a statute of frauds requiring that certain contracts be in writing in order to be enforceable. These statutes of frauds protect against fraud and perjury. The document must be signed by the party or parties against whom enforcement would be sought. In lieu of a legal document, a written memorandum such as a series of letters and telegrams would suffice. The memorandum must describe the property and contain the names of the parties, conditions and terms of the sale, and signatures of the party (or parties) against whom compliance is sought. *Contract written and signed*

While some state statutes do not require a lease of less than a year to be in writing, it is far wiser to have it written than to rely on oral evidence.

Parol Evidence Rule

The **parol evidence rule** forbids the admittance of any prior verbal or written evidence to vary or add to the terms of a written instrument. If the contract has been properly written, there is no valid reason to introduce such evidence. The parol evidence rule helps eliminate fraudulent claims. One particular point to remember is that the execution of a written contract, whether the law requires it to be written or not, supersedes all the negotiations and stipulations that preceeded or accompanied the execution of the instrument. Thus, if the buyer tells the broker that s/he wants the drapes to remain with the house, but this was not put into the purchase agreement nor transmitted to the seller and the seller signed and accepted the contract as written expecting to remove the drapes, the buyer could not bring in the oral statement that preceeded the written document. In this instance, the agent was remiss in not placing it in the contract and the buyer was negligent in not reading the contract carefully before signing it.

Executory and Executed Contracts

A contract that has not been completed is an **executory contract;** performance has not taken place. A purchase agreement in which the seller has not yet transferred title is an example of an executory contract. Upon title passing, the contract has been **executed,** that is; the terms of the agreement have been carried out. Execution of a contract simply refers to the fact that it has been signed, thus executed. When a party signs a deed, he executes the document.

Dual Contracts

When real estate is sold or purchased it is illegal to have **dual contracts** between buyer and seller, with each contract containing a different price so that the buyer can obtain a larger loan from a lender. Such a dual contract, written for the purpose of obtaining a larger loan from the lender, would subject the agent to a fine or revocation of his license. Nor could the agent declare to the lender that the earnest deposit was greater than it truly was, or delay in depositing the earnest money so it appears that the purchaser has more assets than he does.

VALIDITY OF CONTRACTS

A contract may be valid, void, voidable, or unenforceable.

The **valid contract** complies with all the requirements of contract law. It exists when all parties agree to the terms of an enforceable contract. It has been contracted with all the essential elements previously discussed in this chapter and is legally binding and enforceable.

A contract is **void** when entered into for an illegal purpose, having no legal force or validity. A void agreement is in effect, no contract.

A contract is **voidable** when one person may cancel his or her promise, for example, if the party is a minor. The contract is a valid act but may be rescinded by the minor.

An **unenforceable** contract appears to be valid but cannot be enforced. It may not be in writing in accordance with the statute of frauds and consequently cannot be enforced by court action.

Misrepresentation　　Misrepresentation and fraud can make a contract unenforceable. **Misrepresentation** is an erroneous statement made without the intention to deceive, but with an effect on the finalization of the contract. This does not include a mere expression of opinion. However, if a statement is made with the intent to induce a party to a contract, the person making the statement is liable. The defrauded party may rescind the contract or collect money damages. In the case of a sale, if the seller withholds a pertinent fact that has an effect on the property value, the buyer may retain the property but sue the seller for any difference between the actual value and the purchase price. Courts have ruled against agents if they knew or should have known about a material defect and withheld the information from the purchaser.

Fraud　　**Fraud** is an outright attempt to cheat someone. If a false statement is knowingly made as to a material fact, and if the other party relies upon that statement and suffers damages, fraud has been committed. A seller shows his or her property, and when asked if the home is on public sewer responds affirmatively even though this was a deliberate misstatement of fact. After the sale is consummated, the purchaser learns that the house has a septic system. The actions of the seller constitute fraud. Had the seller honestly believed the property was on sewer it would be a mistake and the contract would be voidable.

Latent and patent defects　　If a defect is hidden from the view of the purchaser (for example, defective plumbing), it is known as a **latent defect** and must be revealed to the intended purchaser. However, if a defect can be seen, it is a **patent defect** and the buyer must observe it for himself. A large crack on a dining room wall can be seen and the purchaser can examine the defect. If the agent has any thought that the buyer would not notice the defect, then it should be pointed out to the buyer.

Duress　　The contract must be entered into by the free will of all parties. To force someone to perform against his or her will is unlawful constraint. Any contract entered into under *duress* would not be valid. To threaten someone by force is referred to as menace. If a person is under *undue influence* when signing a contract, it is voidable by the signer.

Performance of Contract

The contract terms should state when the performance of the contract is to transpire. Purchase contracts call for a set date upon which the closing of the sale will take place; leases state the length of the lease and the date of termination. If a contract does not contain a date, the act should be performed within a reasonable time. The type of contract will determine the defining of reasonable time.

Assignment of a Contract

Since all contracts are assignable, unless it specifically states to the contrary, the assignor (holder of the contract) may assign his or her rights to the assignee (receiver of the contract). If a purchaser assigns his or her rights in a purchase agreement to a third party, the assignee would have all the rights, privileges, and obligations that the buyer had under the contract terms. The terms of the contract must be fulfilled as they were stated. If a contract requires an obligation that is personal (as with a listing contract), it is not assignable without the consent of the seller. If a renowed artist is contracted to paint a portrait he cannot assign another artist to complete the painting.

The terms of a contract may also be completed by **novation.** Novation requires the substitution of a new contract for the existing contract. When an existing loan is assumed by a purchaser, the original contracting party is released from the obligation and the balance of the debt is the responsibility of the new purchaser. This is true if all the terms of the mortgage, such as the interest rate, remain the same. For example, John Blair contracts with Joe Bright for the removal of snow from Blair's property for the winter months of November through March for $XX. In December Joe Bright moves to another state but Jim Jones is willing to carry out the contract as written. This substitution of names is novation.

Novation

DISCHARGING OF CONTRACT

When terms of the contract have been fulfilled the contract is completed or discharged. If performance has not taken place, the contract has been breached unless the parties have agreed to cancel. Under the following conditions complete performance has failed to take place:

1. *Damage to the property:* If the property is destroyed (as by fire, tornado, or a hurricane) prior to performance, the contract may be cancelled.
2. *Death:* If the contract cannot be completed by another equally capable of performing the act, it will be discharged. For example, a renowed portrait artist with a unique painting style dies; the party who employed the artist justifiably may cancel the contract. However, in the situation of a purchase agreement, if the buyer dies, his or her estate can be held responsible to complete the terms of the contract.
3. *Rescission of the contract by mutual agreement:* All parties involved decide to rescind the contract.

4. *Partial performance:* The parties agree to terminate the contract before completion. A designer is contracted to redecorate a house, but after a portion is completed decides to cancel the contract because the homeowner is displeased.

Laches

Laches is delay or negligence in asserting one's legal rights; the party has waited too long to complain. The statute of limitations sets a time limit within which one may claim his or her legal rights. This time limit varies widely between states. If the party does not exercise this right within that time, s/he waives the claim. For example, a house constructed on a vacant lot may not have a wood shake roof as was stipulated in the covenants of the subdivision. The neighbors must bring action within the required time or lose their legal right to insist upon compliance.

If one of the parties to the contract has failed to carry out conditions of the agreement, a *breach* is committed. A tenant decides to move, but has six months remaining on the lease. If the tenant defaults on paying the remainder due s/he has breached the contract.

SPECIFIC PERFORMANCE

Specific performance is a remedy in a court of equity compelling the defendent to carry out the terms of the contract. A decree of specific performance may be brought by the injured party, demanding that the defendent perform the promise made or pay damages for losses suffered. When a party brings such a suit, he agrees to abide by the decree of the court.

In the purchase of a property if the buyer does not go through with the purchase the seller may take recourse in one of the following actions:

Sellers' recourse

1. The seller may rescind the contract and release the buyer from any obligation.
2. The seller may retain the earnest money as liquidated damages.
3. The seller may resell the property and sue the buyer for the difference if s/he takes a loss on the second sale.
4. The seller may sue for the balance of the purchase price.

The usual procedure is to retain the earnest money, dividing it equally between the brokerage firm and the seller (if this is written in the listing agreement). The mechanics of a legal suit are involved and lengthy, and the seller usually favors placing the property on the open market again for a sale.

If the seller refuses to transfer the property to the buyer in accordance with the contract the buyer has a choice of the following remedies:

Buyers' recourse

1. The buyer may agree to rescind the contract and receive back as liquidated damages any earnest deposit s/he placed with the broker.
2. The buyer may sue for specific performance in an effort to force the seller to perform.
3. The buyer may bring action for money damages against the seller. For example, if the buyer purchases another property with the expectation of moving into the new premises and suddenly finds she will not be able to take possession, this could result in the cost of two moves if she is forced to seek temporary housing until she locates and closes on the purchase of a substitute house.

OPTION

An **option** is a contract granting the exclusive right to buy for a limited time. In an option, time is of the essence. The optionee (prospective purchaser) takes the option and the optionor (owner) gives the option. Again, this contract must be in writing to be enforceable and must contain a consideration (dollar value) to be valid. If the optionee does not wish to carry out his option, s/he forfeits the consideration. The optionor retains all the rights of ownership during the term of the option. The optionee is not entitled to any rents or benefits; s/he has only the exclusive right to buy. If the option expires and the parties choose to renew the option, an additional consideration is necessary. The optionee may also assign the option to another. An option is a unilateral contract since it embodies a promise on the part of only one person, the optionor. The differences between an option and a purchase contract are:

1. An option gives the right to buy to the purchaser, who may or may not choose to exercise that right.
2. A purchase contract is an offer to purchase a real property; if accepted by the seller, it becomes a binding contract.

UNIFORM COMMERCIAL CODE

The *Uniform Commercial Code* has been adopted by most states, requiring that personal property sold in excess of $500.00 be recorded in writing. The creditor can then file a financial statement containing a detailed description of the merchandise at the recorder's office. This alerts any subsequent mortgagees and purchasers that a lien exists and protects the creditor in the event the debtor defaults on payments. The supplier can repossess the personal property and remove it from the real estate. The Uniform Commercial Code covers conditional sales contracts, pledges and chattel mortgages and personal property sales including stocks and commercial paper.

The bulk transfer law is regulated under the Uniform Commercial Code and prevents the merchant from selling out his stock, pocketing the proceeds, and leaving creditors unpaid. It further disallows the debtor selling business trade fixtures that have not been paid for without informing the creditors of the impending sale.

COMMONLY USED CONTRACTS

The contracts used most frequently in real estate transactions are:

1. *Listing contract:* The employment contract between the seller and the brokerage firm (Chapter 6).
2. *Purchase agreement:* The contract between the buyer and seller (Chapter 7).
3. *The option contract:* Used to reserve the right to purchase a property.
4. *Lease:* Between the tenant and landlord (Chapter 12).
5. *Property management contract:* Between the property manager and the owner (Chapter 13).
6. *Mortgage:* Between the owner (mortgagor) and the lender (mortgagee) (Chapter 9).
7. *Land contract:* An installment sale contract between vendee (buyer) and vendor (seller) (Chapter 8).

While there are other contracts used, the above will be covered in depth in succeeding chapters. The diagram below explains the position of the parties involved in contracts.

Contracts	Buyer	Seller (owner)
purchase agreement	grantee	grantor
land contract	vendee	vendor
option	optionee	optionor
lease	lessee	lessor
assignment	assignee	assignor
mortgage	mortgagee (lender)	mortgagor
offer	offeror	offeree

You will note that in the first six contracts the buyer is the "ee" (he gets, receives, to him it goes); the mortgagee is not "buying" the property but is buying the loan. The exception is offeror and offeree; the owner in this case is the *offeree*. The listing contract is not included in the above since the seller (grantor) is only granting *permission* to the real estate firm to sell the property. The firm is not taking title; they have merely received an employment contract to offer the property for sale.

SUMMARY

The essential elements in the making of a contract include the offer and acceptance, consideration, capacity of the parties, legality of the object, and the contract being in writing and signed by the parties to the contract.

A contract is either implied by an act or expressed, orally or in writing. The statute of frauds requires that contracts must be in writing to be enforceable. The written contract leaves no doubt as to the intention of the parties.

The unilateral contract obligates only *one* of the parties whereas in the bilateral contract *both* parties must perform according to the terms of the contract.

A contract in which performance has not taken place is an executory contract, as a purchase agreement. The contract is binding when the seller accepts the buyer's offer, but completion does not occur until later. Upon finalization of a contract, it is said to be executed: the terms have been carried out.

A valid contract meets all the requirements of law, whereas a void contract has no legal force. A contract is voidable if one of the parties can cancel, as a minor. A contract may have the appearance of being valid but is unenforceable.

When misrepresentation or fraud is involved, the contract may be set aside. Misrepresentation is the act of giving misinformation with no intent to commit fraud. However, the person giving the incorrect information is responsible and if s/he is a licensed agent may be subject to losing his or her license. Fraud is done deliberately in an effort to obtain someone's consent to enter into the contract.

Any defect that cannot be seen by a prospective purchaser is a latent defect and must be revealed to the buyer if it is known. A patent defect is in plain view and need not be pointed out.

Contracts are assignable unless they specifically state otherwise. All obligations pass to the assignee and the contract must be performed as it was written. Assumable mortgages are transferred to the purchaser by novation, the new owner taking over the responsibility of paying the loan.

Sometimes contracts are not completed, either due to destruction of the property, death, or partial performance. If one of the parties defaults there are remedies for the injured party.

The most commonly used contracts in real estate transactions (listing and sales contracts, mortgages and leases) will be covered in detail in following chapters.

KEY WORDS AND CONCEPTS

Bilateral contract: A contract involving promises on the part of both parties, as in a purchase agreement.

Capacity of parties: All parties must be legally capable of entering into the contract.

Consideration: The value one party is giving another, the mutual exchange of promises.

Contract: An agreement between two or more parties in which they have a "meeting of the minds."

Dual contract: Two separate contracts between buyer and seller, each with a different purchase price, designed to obtain a larger loan from a lender.

Executed contract: Terms of the contract have been carried out.

Executory contract: Performance has not taken place.

Expressed contract: Clearly states the contract terms.

Fraud: A statement made with the intent of deceiving.

Implied contract: The act constitutes agreement to a contract.

Latent defect: A material defect hidden from view.

Lawful object: The contract itself must be for a lawful purpose.

Misrepresentation: An erroneous statement made that affects the contract.

Novation: The substitution of a new obligation for an existing one.

Offer and acceptance: Parties agree to the terms of the contract.

Option: Right to buy within a specified time at a stipulated price.

Patent defect A defect obvious to the viewer.

Parol evidence rule: Prior verbal or oral evidence does not change the written document.

Rescind: Revoke; to annul or cancel, as a contract.

Unenforceable contract: A valid contract that is not enforceable.

Unilateral contract: A promise on the part of one party in a contract, as in an option.

Valid contract: A contract in which both parties agree to the terms of an enforceable contract.

Void contract: A contract entered into for illegal purposes.

Voidable contract: A contract that can be terminated by one of the parties, or that is capable of being void.

REVIEW QUESTIONS

1. A contract based upon the following would be capable of being voided by the injured party:
   a. error
   b. undue influence
   c. fraud
   d. all of these

2. A latent defect is best described as
   a. a defect that the prudent buyer can see
   b. an old defect
   c. a defect that is hidden from view
   d. a breach of contract by the seller

3. Which of the following persons cannot be held to a contract?
   a. a minor
   b. an unmarried woman
   c. an elderly person
   d. a widow or widower

4. The difference between an option and a purchase agreement is
   a. the option gives the right to buy; the purchase contract, if accepted by the seller, is a binding contract to buy.
   b. the option need not be in writing, but the purchase contract must be in writing.
   c. the option is always in favor of the optionee, while the purchase contract favors the grantee.
   d. the option is a bilateral contract, while the purchase agreement is a unilateral contract.

5. If an optionee fails to exercise his or her option within the stated time
   a. he may sue the optionor for the consideration
   b. he may automatically renew the option if he puts down another consideration
   c. he forfeits the consideration
   d. the purchase is automatically confirmed

6. The important object in the offer and acceptance of a contract is
   a. the good intent of both grantee and grantor in fulfilling the contract
   b. A "meeting of the minds" on the subject matter of the contract
   c. the capability of each party entering into the contract
   d. the legality of the contract

7. Rescission of a contract most nearly means
   a. all goes back to the way it was before the contract
   b. ratification of the contract
   c. affirmation of the contract
   d. none of the above

8. Meeting of the minds refers to
   a. the consummation of the contract
   b. the consideration
   c. the offer and acceptance
   d. the closing of the transaction

9. The term *contractual ability* refers to
   a. the contract containing all of the covenants needed to make it legal
   b. the attorney having the ability to draw the contract
   c. the capability of two people to enter into a written agreement
   d. the legality of the contract

10. All of the following are essential to a valid contract, except
    a. consideration
    b. duress
    c. offer and acceptance
    d. legality of object

11. If the purchaser assigns his interest in the property while the contract is still pending, realizing a profit
    a. the seller receives the profit
    b. it cancels the contract
    c. the broker receives the profit
    d. the original purchaser receives the profit

12. A contract between a competent and an incompetent party can be voided by
    a. the incompetent
    b. the competent
    c. both of the above
    d. neither of the above

13. A unilateral contract
    a. embodies a promise on the part of both parties
    b. binds only one party to the contract terms
    c. is voidable by the maker
    d. has been executed by all parties

14. The substitution of a new contract for an existing contract is
    a. execution
    b. breach of contract
    c. specific performance
    d. novation

15. Upon the default of a contract, all of the following are remedies to the injured party, except
    a. specific performance
    b. retain the earnest deposit as liquidated damages
    c. execution of the contract
    d. rescission of the contract

The Brokerage Firm: Listing the Property

6

The real estate brokerage firm lists the property and when a prospective buyer signs the offer to purchase and it is accepted by the seller, a binding contract exists. Once the financing has been secured, the closing of the transaction takes place.

In this chapter the agency relationship between the seller and the brokerage firm is explained, along with the obligations of the parties and the actual listing of the property.

THE BROKERAGE FIRM

As in most industries and professions, specialization has emerged in the field of real estate. The most familiar of these specialized services is provided by the real estate brokerage firm. The complexity of the laws dealing with the sale and transfer of land makes it difficult for the average citizen to handle the entire operation him- or herself. Real estate brokerage firms serve the public by listing and selling the property of others. To provide this service, it is necessary to have a license to sell real estate, a privilege granted by the real estate commission or regulatory agency of each state. All fifty states have statutes governing real estate brokerage; therefore, to maintain a license, a high degree of professionalism is required.

SALESPERSON AND BROKER

Licensing the agent

There are two types of real estate licenses: the *salesperson's* and the *broker's*. A salesperson is a licensed individual who has complied with the regulations set forth by the real estate commission or the regulatory agency in his or her state and has subsequently become licensed to sell the property of others for a fee. The salesperson must always be under the jurisdiction and supervision of a broker. A broker will have fulfilled additional qualifications before being issued a broker's license. The broker may conduct real estate business under his or her own name or a trade name; s/he may be in partnership with another broker or be part of a corporation. In some states, if s/he works under the employ of another broker, s/he is referred to as an associate broker. Chapter 18 covers in greater detail license law regulations.

Generally speaking, privately owned real estate agencies may be involved in the listing, selling, exchanging, optioning, leasing, managing, building, appraising, or buying of real estate. They may sell new and existing residential properties, bare land, farms, commercial, or industrial properties. Many firms have a separate department to handle the leasing and management of clients' income property. Others subdivide and develop land to erect homes, apartments, shopping centers, and office buildings. Many real estate agents also appraise property on a fee basis. The license law of most states requires that to appraise for a fee, the individual must be a broker. In a few states the law requires a separate appraiser's license. Insurance is sold in connection with some real estate offices, supplying buyers with protection on their newly purchased properties.

Anyone deciding to make real estate his or her profession can look forward to interesting and varied experiences. The large sums of money involved in the purchasing of real property demand close supervision of each licensee by state real estate commissions. However, professionalism, experience, and knowledge are just as important as state licensing requirements. For the prospective sales representative, expertise and professionalism are essential ingredients for a successful career in real estate.

Need for a Professional

Why hire a broker? While the law permits a property owner to sell his or her own home, the owner will soon become aware of the many complex details that are involved in the marketing of real estate. To begin with, the owner must determine the value of the property. The owner's concept of the worth of the property may be influenced by sentimental attachments and by the costs of maintenance and additions made over the years, but for an accurate valuation the owner should also be familiar with the current real estate market and the trends of buying.

The owner must next attract the right sales prospects—people who are ready, willing, and able to buy, not just those who are curious to see what the interior of the home looks like. The real estate salesperson will qualify customers in advance, ensuring that only those who are definitely prospective buyers will be shown the house.

A property owner is at a disadvantage when it comes to tactfully questioning the buyer's financial status in order to qualify the buyer for the purchase of the property. Hours may be spent showing the home to prospects who cannot afford to purchase it. A vital cog in almost every real estate transaction is the financing. What types of loans are available to the buyer? What are the current interest rates? Should the purchaser buy under FHA? Can s/he qualify for VA financing? Would a conventional loan or land contract better suit the buyer's needs?

The owner must also know how to prorate such items as property taxes, the insurance (if the policy is to be assumed by the purchaser), and the interest on the existing loan if it is to be assumed. Real estate salespersons are specialists in their field since they deal in such transactions every day. Sales ability is learned and perfected through specialized practice and training.

THE AGENCY RELATIONSHIP

The creation of an **agency** occurs when one party appoints another to act on his or her behalf in transacting business with a third party. The agency law has evolved from common practices (common law) and from legislated law.

In the instance of a listing, the owner of the property is known as a **principal** and the agency is created between the broker and the principal. A **fiduciary** relationship exists between the broker and the principal, meaning the principal has faith, trust, and confidence in the agent hired. The broker represents the owner and derives authority from the owner for the specific purpose of negotiating a sale. When the broker has accomplished this purpose, his or her authority ends. In many states verbal listings are not enforceable. The law of agency dictates the obligations to be performed by each party. The **listing contract** is a specific agency; that is, the broker or agent is employed for a particular purpose.

This fiduciary relationship requires that the agent

1. Cannot receive any undisclosed profit from the transaction unknown to the principal.
2. Must obey all lawful requests issued by the principal and as outlined in the contract.
3. Is acting for the principal and cannot represent another without the knowledge of both parties (dual agency).
4. Owes his or her principal loyalty and disclosure of material facts that may affect the value of the property, such as a proposed change in zoning that would increase the value of the property.
5. Accounts for all money coming into his possession.
6. Does not reveal information that would be detrimental to the broker's negotiating power—such as that the seller is forced to sell for financial reasons or that s/he is willing to take less than the asking price. The agent must honor the confidentiality of his or her principal.

The agency also places certain responsibilities upon the principal:

1. all pertinent facts or hidden (latent) defects must be disclosed to the agent, and
2. the agent must not be hindered by acts of the principal in efforts to transact a sale.

The agent and his or her principal also have a duty to the third party, the purchaser. The agent must be honest and fair with the buyer and under no circumstances conceal any defects. Fair representation must be made.

Special agent

The real estate agent is a *special agent,* meaning that the agent is limited to producing a buyer for the principal as stated under the terms of the listing contract. A *general agent* would possess more latitude and could literally "speak" for the principal. The general agent would be given power of attorney to represent the principal, who would outline the framework under which the principal wants the agent to act, as in buying and selling investment properties.

Independent contractors

Real estate firms generally do not pay their agents a salary. They work as *independent contractors* and are responsible for their own expenses. Agents are paid strictly on the basis of production; when a sale is finalized they receive a percentage of the total commission earned. Unlike the requirements in paying salaried employees, the broker does not need to withhold social security tax and income tax on commission paid to independent contractors.

A written contractual agreement should be entered into between the broker and agent to safeguard the broker in the event of an IRS investigation. The broker cannot pay any of the agents' expenses, such as entertainment costs, license and trade membership fees, or automobile expenses. Since the agent is not an employee, the broker cannot make it mandatory that the agents attend sales meetings or require office hours.

Briefly:

Employee	Independent Contractor
1. receives a salary	1. receives no minimum salary
2. broker must withhold social security, income tax and unemployment tax from salary	2. agent pays taxes
3. broker can require set hours for agent	3. sets own hours
4. broker can pay extras (as fees for agents)	4. pays for all expenses—receives no extra compensation

OBTAINING THE LISTING

It is important for the real estate firm to secure listings since they represent the merchandise the company has to offer for sale. The salesperson will seek these listings through relatives, friends, neighbors, business associates, and acquaintances. The agent may also develop a "listing farm." That is, the agent will select a certain neighborhood of homes where a reasonable turnover in ownership is expected and actively "farm" the area. Many agents prepare newsletters with information on household tips, recipes, financing trends, current interest rates, and data on recent sales in the area and deliver them to homeowners in the selected neighborhood. By calling on the homeowners in person, by telephone, and by mail the salesperson will become known to the owners.

When a property owner calls a brokerage firm to list his house, he is naturally anxious to obtain top dollar for the property. The agent will determine the property value by comparing it to similar properties that have recently sold and properties currently offered for sale. In some areas of the country this is referred to as a *comparable market analysis*. The salesperson follows a series of steps in the preparation of the market analysis, which would typically be

1. Measuring the house for square footage (the listing worksheet in the appendix, figure A-32, is an excellent format).
2. Comparing the subject property with recent sales and with competition on the market similar in square footage and style (see appendix figure A-29). The multiple listing service is an excellent means for easily locating the sold properties. If the MLS service is computerized and the firm has a computer, the salesperson can pull up comparable sold listings.
3. Some agents use the estimate of reasonable value form (Figure A-30).
4. A proceeds to seller form on page 66 informs the seller what his proceeds will be from the sale, a most important document.
5. A listing contract as shown on page 68.
6. Several well written ads to show the seller how he intends to market the property.

This packet of information is presented to the sellers with the expectation of obtaining the listing. A professional approach such as this lends credence to the salesperson's ability to successfully market the home.

THE LISTING CONTRACT

The listing contract must be signed by all the owners of the property, as it constitutes employment of the agent. Once the broker has accepted the listing, s/he is responsible to the principal and cannot delegate this authority to another. This does not necessarily mean s/he will not cooperate with other brokers, but the responsibility for making appointments for showing of the property, for negotiating agreements of sale with the owners, and for closing the transaction generally rests with the listing agent.

The listing agent must ask the principal what personal property, if any, will remain with the property. The agent can then include the items on the listing contract. An example might be draperies custom made for a particular room; the owners may decide it will facilitate a sale to leave them.

If the owners have an attached fixture, which is rightly real property, that they do not want to leave, it should be removed and replaced prior to any showings of the property. For example, Aunt Harriet may have given the owners the crystal chandelier in the dining room as a wedding gift. Removing it will prevent the problem of a buyer seeing the chandelier and insisting it must stay if he purchases the home.

In addition, it is of great importance that at the time the property is listed that the listing agent clearly explain to the sellers all costs involved in the sale of the real property. The agent should never assume that the sellers understand their obligations and costs concerning the sale, but should always enumerate them clearly. The "Proceeds to Seller" form (see figure 6.1) should be completed by the real estate agent at the time of listing, giving the sellers an estimate of what they will net after all costs.

The listing contract itself allows the real estate firm to review listed properties at a glance. If a purchaser calls on a particular property, all the pertinent and accurate data are readily accessible on the contract and this eliminates errors that could arise if this information were not readily available. Listing contracts vary in different areas of the country; some states allow verbal listings, but in many states the law requires listing contracts to be in writing to be enforceable. In these states, the contract must also be signed by the parties to be charged or held to the agreement in order to be legally enforceable.

The listing contract should contain

1. A description of the property,
2. The amount of commission to be paid,
3. The expiration date, and
4. The signature of the party or parties to be charged.

There are four types of listing contracts. Each differs in the degree of responsibility and the legal rights assigned to the broker.

Exclusive Right to Sell

The **exclusive right to sell** contract gives the real estate firm the sole right to act as agent for the sellers. Should the principals find a purchaser during the term of the listing, they are obligated by the contract to pay a commission. Appointments for showings of the property by other firms generally are made through the listing firm, as they are the firm responsible to the seller.

Greatest security for broker

NAME___Harvey and Della Wender___ DATE___3-10-87___

ADDRESS___1040 Clear Street___ PHONE___313-0234___

LEGAL DESCRIPTION___Lot 8, Block 1, Confusion Hill___

PROJECTED SALE PRICE___$85,500___

PROCEEDS TO SELLERS

	VA	FHA	PMI	CONV.	ASSUMP.
Balance 1st Mortgage	45,320.10	45,320.10	45,320.10	45,320.10	45,320.10
Record Release	3.25	3.25	3.25	3.25	
Title Ins/Abstract (½ cost of title insurance)	159.63	159.63	159.63	159.63	159.63
Documentary Stamps	126.00	126.00	126.00	126.00	126.00
Discount Points (currently 2 % VA, FHA)	1,710.00	1,560.00			
Termite Inspection	25.00				
Prepayment Penalty			-0-	-0-	-0-
Special Assessments	-0-	-0-	-0-	-0-	-0-
Brokerage fee 7%	5,985.00	5,985.00	5,985.00	5,985.00	5,985.00
Sale Price	85,500.00	85,500.00	85,500.00	85,500.00	85,500.00
Less Costs (as shown above)	53,331.98	53,156.98	51,596.98	51,596.98	51,623.73
Net to Seller	32,168.02	32,343.02	33,903.02	33,903.02	33,906.27

Existing escrow account is returned to sellers when property is refinanced. Taxes and interest are prorated.

Existing escrow account is retained by lender and assigned to buyers when loan is assumed.

THIS IS AN ESTIMATE

A-1 Real Estate Company

Judy M Selling
Agent

Harvey J Wender
Seller

Della J Wender
Seller

FIGURE 6.1 A proceeds to seller form.

In the exclusive right to sell contract (shown in figure 6.2), the numbered sections outline the contract terms as follows:

• *Section 1* states the expiration date of the listing, and the street address and legal description of the property. It also states the offering price and the terms of sale.

• *Section 2* states the commission to be paid and the terms under which the sellers agree to pay the broker. These conditions include the following:

a. If an offer is made by a bona fide purchaser during the term of the listing for the listed price or any other price or terms the sellers agreed would be acceptable;

b. If the sellers unfairly hinder showings of the property;

c. If the sale cannot close due to liens, judgments, or suits pending against the property;

d. If a sale is made due to the agent's efforts or advertising during the listing or within a specified number of days of the expiration date.

• *Section 3* states that if the purchaser forfeits the earnest money deposit, it will be divided equally between owner and agent after the agent's expenses have been deducted.

• *Section 4* explains that if termite damage is found and was known about by the owners prior to closing a sale, the owners will carry full responsibility.

• *Section 5* says that the owners agree to provide either an abstract that has been brought to date or a title insurance policy and that the owners agree to correct any defects in the title. On this contract, the owners will give a warranty deed. The possession date is stated. The owners also agree that a "for sale" sign and a lock box may be placed on the property.

• *Section 6* lists the owners' signatures and the real estate agent's signature.

• *Section 7* gives a description of the property, room sizes, loan information and other data pertinent to the listed property.

The exclusive right to sell contract gives the real estate firm the sole right to act as agent for the sellers. Should the principals find a buyer during the term of the listing, they are obligated by the employment contract to pay a commission to the brokerage firm. Appointments for showings of the property by other firms generally are made through the listing firm, as they are responsible to the seller. The exclusive right to sell listing is the most popular listing since the firm that lists the property receives a commission regardless of who sells the property.

Exclusive Agency

Other types of listing contracts

Under the terms of the **exclusive agency** contract only one firm is hired to sell the property, but the owners retain possession to sell the property themselves without paying a commission to the firm. If the broker is what is called the *procuring cause* in the transaction, the owner would be liable for the commission; that is, if the brokerage firm caused the sale to happen, as by introducing the buyers to the property.

With this type of contract, problems may arise as to whether the listing broker actually was instrumental in introducing the purchaser to the property. A buyer may see the sign in the yard, stop and visit with the owner and subsequently purchase the home directly from the owner. In this case, the broker's "for sale" sign was the

LISTING CONTRACT   Date March 10, 1987

1. We hereby agree to list and offer for sale our property hereafter described and give you the sole and exclusive right to and including June 10, 1987 to sell _____ 1040 Clear St. Legal Lot 8, Block 1, Confusion Hill Subdivision together with attached fixtures for the sum of $ 85,500 , upon the following terms: loan assumption, cash, conventional

2. I agree to pay you a cash commission of 7 % of the gross sales price, with minimum commission of $ 2000.00 , (whichever is greater) said commission to be payable under any of the following conditions:

    A. If a sale is made, or a purchaser found, who is ready, willing and able to purchase the property before the expiration of this listing, by you, myself, or any other person, at the above price and terms or for any other price and terms I may agree to accept.
    B. If you are unfairly hindered by me in the showing or attempting to sell said premises within the listed period.
    C. If you are prevented in closing the sale of this property by existing liens, judgments, or suits pending against said property.
    D. If I make a sale of said premises to any one due to your efforts or advertising done under this listing within 90 days after the expiration date. This property is offered without respect to race, color, national origin or religion.

3. In case of the forfeiture, by a prospective purchaser, of any earnest money payment, upon the within described property, said earnest money, after expense incurred by you has been deducted, shall be divided one-half to the owners and one-half to the agent.

4. I hereby represent that to the best of my knowledge, information and belief there are no termites in the buildings on the real estate hereinbefore described, and if termites are found in said buildings and it is known that such condition existed prior to the time of the closing of the sale thereof, I hereby agree to indemnify you and hold you harmless from any and all loss, damage or expense to which you may be subjected arising in connection therewith.

5. I agree to furnish either a complete abstract certified to date of sale showing merchantable title or a Title Insurance Policy, to complete said sale and to pay any expense incurred in perfecting the title in case it is found defective, and convey within 30 days from date of sale, the property by warranty deed, or none other executed by all persons having any interest therein, and clear of all encumbrances except no exceptions
    Possession to be given 90 days after closing.
    For Sale sign and Lock Box permitted.
    We hereby accept the above listing and agree to the above terms. Receipt of a copy of this agreement is hereby acknowledged.

6. A-1 Real Estate Company
    Real Estate Company

    By _Judy M Selling_
          Agent

    Harvey J. Wender Owner
    Husband

    Della J Wender Owner
    Wife

    1040 Clear Street   Address

    Telephone Residence 313-0234 Business 313-0003

7.
Address	1040 Clear St.	Legal	Lot 8, Block 1, Confusion Hill Subdivision		
Style	ranch	Occupant	owner	Age	7
Rooms	6	Possession	negotiable		
Bedrooms	3	Mtg	Ready S & L	Mtg. Bal	45,320.10
Baths	1 - 3/4	Type Mtg	FHA	Int	10 %
2 Car Garage	attached	Payment	547.68	Taxes	yes Ins yes
Lot Size	85 x 110	2nd Mtg	----	Taxes 19 87	$ 1550.00
Square Ft.	1770 Main 2nd Fl	Fin B	420		

Living Room	20 x 15	Fireplace	one	Dishwasher	X
Dining Room	12 x 13	Exterior	wood	Disposal	X
Kitchen	10 x 12	Roof	comp.	Range/oven	X
Family Room	-----	Heat	FA Gas	Power Humid	X
Rec Room	28 x 15	Central Air	yes	Grade School	William Elem.
Bedroom	10 x 12	Fencing	chain link	Jr. High	Carter Jr. High
Bedroom	12 x 11	Paving	X	High School	Carter High
Bedroom	12 x 15	Water	X	Sewer	X
Bedroom		Gas	X	Elec	X

FIGURE 6.2 An exclusive right to sell listing contract.

procuring cause and the owner would be responsible for paying the broker's fee. However, the broker may be reluctant to spend money on advertising and promoting the property knowing that if the owner finds a buyer before the broker, the broker will not receive a commission.

Open Listing

An **open listing** is open to any number of agents the sellers wish to employ. The sellers are obligated to pay a commission only to that broker who successfully produces a buyer ready, willing, and able to purchase the home. If the owners sell it themselves, they need not pay anyone a fee. Generally under an open listing, owners will not allow signs on the property and agents will be less enthusiastic in trying to find a buyer. An agent will be reluctant to advertise a property on which s/he is not protected should a sale result.

Open listings are not always in writing and while the owner may feel "everyone will be working to sell it," the opposite is usually true. The brokers are more inclined to spend their time and money on properties for which they will be assured a return on their investment when a sale occurs.

Net Listing

In a **net listing** a property is listed at an agreed-upon net price and the broker receives the excess over and above the net listing as his commission. Net listings are illegal in some states and frowned on by other real estate regulatory agencies, as they can easily lead to disputes and misunderstandings.

California real estate law requires that the broker give to the seller in writing before the seller signs the contract (1) the exact sale price, and (2) broker's total earnings.

A net listing may be an exclusive right to sell, an exclusive agency, or an open listing.

The rate of the professional service fee depends upon the contract, as there is no set commission. To set commission rates would be a violation of federal and state anti-trust laws. The fee is negotiable between the seller and the real estate firm. The commission is payable under the following terms:

Payment for services

1. The broker must produce a buyer who is ready, willing, and able to buy.
2. The broker must be able to prove his or her performance (with a signed listing).
3. The sale must be consummated.
4. If the sale is terminated by the seller's refusal to close after accepting the offer, the fee must still be paid to the broker.

Terminating the Listing

By mutual consent between the principal and the brokerage firm, a listing may be terminated. Upon entering into the listing contract, the seller agrees not to hinder the agent in his or her endeavors to show the property. If the principal simply decides to break the contract for no valid reason, the brokerage firm, under the terms of the contract, has a right to sue for damages. Conversely, the real estate firm must spend time on marketing the property and make an earnest effort to locate prospective purchasers. If no such effort is made, ample reason to terminate the listing would exist. Should either of the parties die, the listing would be cancelled. If the property is destroyed by fire, tornado, or other natural cause, cancellation of the listing would become effective.

Expiration of time   At the end of the listing term, the listing expires, unless the parties agree to extend the employment contract. Most states require that written listings state a specific time period. Automatic extensions which state that the contract will continue until either party gives written notice to terminate the listing are generally not recognized. However, many times owners will relist the property with the same broker if they are satisfied with the servicing of the listing. Market conditions may have prevented a sale within the listed time frame.

MULTIPLE LISTING SERVICES

Cooperation among brokers   A multiple listing service (MLS) is not a different type of listings, but an organized exchange of real estate listings conducted by a group of brokers, usually members of a real estate board. A standard multiple listing form is used by the members, who turn all their listings in to a central service bureau, and from there they are distributed to all members. According to the bylaws of the organization, all members can sell the listings and the commission earned on a sale is divided accordingly. In this type of service, the brokerage firms cooperate on the sale of the properties; a single dwelling has not only the members of one agency working on its sale, but all of the firms belonging to the MLS exchange, thus exposing the property to more customers. If for any reason the owner does not want his property in the MLS exchange, a signed waiver will protect the listing broker.

If a salesperson does not have a property among his or her own company's listing that meets the requirements of a prospect, the multiple listing service broadens the chances for making a sale. Many large MLS services publish the listings in a book form, distributing them to the members on a weekly basis.

Computer terminals are another service made available by MLS. Salespersons can search the computer for new listings on a daily basis and thus enhance their ability to locate properties for their prospects. Not only may the sales office have a terminal, but personal computers may be available to the individual in small carrying cases, providing instant access wherever the agent may be.

Some services have a *broker load* system where the listing is loaded into the computer from the broker's office, thus shortening the time to make the listing available to all members.

Most MLS services will require that new listings be turned in for processing within a limited time frame, such as 48 hours. A penalty may be imposed upon members who fail to comply with the time requirement for processing the listing.

REAL ESTATE ASSOCIATIONS

Trade organizations   A real estate board is a voluntary organization whose membership is comprised of persons engaged in some phase of the real estate business or who are directly or indirectly interested in real estate. Most boards maintain an affiliate classification of membership that is open to lending institutions, title and abstracting companies, and others whose duties or interests are related to real estate.

The purpose of a real estate board is to promote good ethics among its members, promote the enactment of legislation for the protection of property rights and interests, and secure the benefits of united efforts for its members. The board upholds fair practices and generally endeavors to professionalize the industry.

Members of the local real estate board also belong to the state association. The salesperson or broker who resides in areas where no local board exists is a member-at-large of the state association. Yearly conventions are held by the members where ideas are exchanged and new concepts within the industry are discussed. Educational seminars are always an important part of the conventions.

The Realtor®

The National Association of Realtors (NAR) is the parent organization of the state boards and is headquartered in Chicago, Illinois. Its membership is composed of members of local boards and state associations. Anyone belonging to the organization can refer to him- or herself as a **Realtor®**, a registered trademark that can only be used by NAR members. The NAR has set forth a strict code of ethics to which all members must adhere.

Under the umbrella of NAR are numerous affiliate organizations that offer a wide range of educational opportunities. The American Institute of Real Estate Appraisers (AIREA) offers an appraisal designation after the completion of courses that include demonstration appraisals and examinations. Other affiliates specialize in property management (IREM), sales techniques (RNMI), office management courses for brokers (IREM), and leadership training courses (WCR). Table 6.1 lists the affiliates and the designations available. With specialization becoming more prevalent in real estate, the availability of these courses is an important reason to belong to the National Association of Realtors®.

A *realtist* is a member of a group of brokers known as the National Association of Real Estate Brokers. The association is basically composed of minority brokers who banned together in 1947 to promote improved housing in the areas they serve.

SUMMARY

The first step in the sale of real property is to make the property available to prospective buyers. The owner can offer it for sale him- or herself or arrange to be represented by a real estate salesperson. If the owner hires an agent, there are four types of listings to consider. The exclusive right to sell gives the real estate firm the sole right to act as the agent of the owner, while the exclusive agency listing allows the owner an opportunity to sell it himself. The open listing is used by the owner if s/he desires to list with more than one agency. The net listing sets the dollar amount that the seller wants to *net* from the sale with the agency receiving the excess.

Most real estate agents insist upon the exclusive right to sell contract, since they spend time and money obtaining a sale for the owner. The agency is paid *only* when they produce a buyer who meets the terms that the owner agreed to in the listing. It is thus understandable that their services are worthy of a contract that protects their interests.

The multiple listing service is the vehicle used by real estate companies to make known to other firms the data on their listings. This method encourages cooperation among companies since all agents are aware of the property's availability.

The National Association of Realtors® is the parent organization to state and local real estate boards. These voluntary associations help promote good ethics among their members and generally endeavor to professionalize the industry.

Table 6.1 Affiliate memberships of the NAR.

	Affiliate	Function	Designation	Requirements
AIREA	American Institute of Real Estate Appraisers	Provides educational courses and publications on appraising	MAI—Member of the Appraisal Institute RM—Residential Member	Completion of courses plus practical experience, demonstration appraisals, examinations
ASREC	American Society of Real Estate Counselors	Provides educational courses pertaining to counseling on real estate problems	CRF—Counselor of Real Estate	Experience, professionalism, education
FLI	Farm and Land Institute	Provides educational programs in sale of land and farms, developing land, management and land syndication	AFLM—Accredited Farm and Land Member	Educational courses, experience, examination
IREF	International Real Estate Federation, American Chapter	Promotes worldwide understanding of real estate and of its members	none	Member of a local board of Realtors interested in real estate on an international level
IREM	Institute of Real Estate Management	Promotes educational programs on property	AMO—Accredited Management Organization ARM—Accredited Residential Manager CPM—Certified Property Manager	Experience, education, examinaton
RNMI	Realtors National Marketing Institute	Promotes educational courses and materials	CRB—Certified Residential Management Broker CRS—Certified Residential Specialist CCIM—Certified Commercial and Investment Manager	Education, experience, GRI courses, five courses for CRB
SIR	Society of Industrial Realtors	Promotes educational programs in industrial properties	SIR—Society of Industrial Realtors	Experience and education
RESSI	Real Estate Securities and Syndication Institute	Promotes education in marketing securities and real estate syndication	none	Member Realtor with interest in syndication or real estate securities
WCR	Women's Council of Realtors	Educates women in residential brokerage training seminars and leadership training	LTG—Leadership Training Graduate	Active member of WCR

KEY WORDS AND CONCEPTS

Agency: The relationship created between principal and broker when the property is listed.

Agent: One who represents another; the employee of the principal.

Consummate: Conclude, bring to completion, as in the finalization of a sale.

Exclusive agency: The real estate firm has an exclusive listing, but the owner may sell it himself and not pay a commission.

Exclusive right to sell: The brokerage firm has the sole right to offer the property for sale.

Fiduciary: Involving confidence and trust, as in the relationship between agent and principal.

License: A personal privilege and right that is not transferable.

Listing contract: Authorization to search for a buyer for a specific property.

Multiple listing service: A group of brokers that pools their listings and cooperates to sell any listing of a member firm.

National Association of Realtors®: A trade organization that promotes fair and ethical practices among its members.

Net listing: Property listed at an agreed-upon net price the seller wishes to receive with any excess going to the agent as his commission.

Open listing: A nonexclusive listing available for sale to any number of brokers, with a commission paid to the selling firm.

Principal: The person who hires a real estate brokerage firm to sell his property; one of the main parties to a transaction.

Realtor®: A coined trade name used by persons who belong to the National Association of Realtors.

REVIEW QUESTIONS

1. An agency relationship is created between a principal and a real estate broker by a
   a. purchase agreement
   b. listing contract
   c. both of the above
   d. neither of the above

2. A real estate salesperson must
   a. always be under the employ of a broker
   b. never refuse to accept a listing
   c. both of the above
   d. neither of the above

3. An exclusive right to sell listing contract
   a. gives the broker a commission based on an agreed price the seller wishes to net, with the broker receiving the excess over the agreed amount.
   b. makes the brokerage firm exclusive agent for a stipulated period of time.
   c. both of the above
   d. neither of the above

4. Under the terms and conditions of an open listing
   a. the owner may sell the property without paying a commission to the listing broker.
   b. the listing is given to any number of brokers the seller wishes to hire, with a commission going only to the selling firm.
   c. both of the above
   d. neither of the above

5. It is mandatory that a listing contract
   a. have a termination date.
   b. be signed by the purchasers.
   c. both of the above
   d. neither of the above

6. Under the rules of a multiple listing service
   a. only the firm who has the listing may show the property.
   b. all members of the MLS cooperate in selling the property.
   c. both of the above
   d. neither of the above

7. The term Realtor® is a coined word:
   a. available for use only by members of the multiple listing service.
   b. used only by members of the National Association of Realtors®.
   c. both of the above
   d. neither of the above

8. Which of the following represents a standard agency relationship?
   a. buyer and seller
   b. seller and salesperson
   c. seller and broker
   d. buyer and salesperson

9. A real estate broker is
   a. appointed by the property owner to act for and in his stead in the sale of his property.
   b. not responsible for his salesperson's actions.
   c. a fiduciary to the property owner.
   d. both a and c

10. The most desirable type of listing for a real estate broker is
    a. open listing
    b. net listing
    c. exclusive right to sell listing
    d. exclusive listing

11. An owner gave an open listing to Firms X and Y. Firm X sells the property to a buyer to whom Firm Y had previously shown the property. The commission was
    a. earned by Firm X.
    b. earned by Firm Y.
    c. split evenly between X and Y.
    d. arbitrated by the Board of Realtors.

12. If an owner sells her own home on which you have an exclusive agency
    a. you receive no commission.
    b. you receive a full commission.
    c. you receive half commission.
    d. you receive 40 percent.

13. Which is the closest to a multiple listing?
    a. cooperative
    b. net listing
    c. exclusive agency
    d. exclusive right to sell

14. Mr. Jennings lists his house with Ms. Walls, a real estate salesperson employed by the A-1 Real Estate Company. The agency exists
    a. between Jennings and Walls.
    b. between Jennings and the A-1 Real Estate Company.
    c. both a and b are correct
    d. neither a nor b is correct

15. The least protection a broker has is with a(n)
    a. exclusive agency
    b. open listing
    c. exclusive right to sell
    d. multiple listing

16. The brokerage firm receives the excess over and above a specified sales price in a(n)
    a. net listing
    b. gross listing
    c. open listing
    d. exclusive listing

17. Broker X has an exclusive agency on a property that he learns has been sold by Broker Y. Broker Y receives a full commission. Broker X should
    a. request half commission from Broker Y.
    b. request full commission from Broker Y.
    c. request full commission from the owner.
    d. realize no commission is due him.

18. The exclusive right to sell listing contract can be terminated by
    a. mutual consent
    b. by the seller if the broker is not working on the property
    c. both of the above
    d. neither of the above

19. An owner of real property wishes to sell the property and not pay a commission. Under which type of listing(s) would this be possible?
    a. exclusive right to sell
    b. exclusive agency
    c. open listing
    d. both a and b
    e. both b and c

20. The law of agency is between
    a. principal and brokerage firm
    b. broker and salesperson
    c. both of the above
    d. neither of the above

21. Sally Wells obtains 2 listings; one is an open listing from owner A and the other is an exclusive listing from owner B. After one week A and B, who had previously visited about their properties, decide to exchange their real estate. Sally Wells will obtain the following:
    a. a commission from A and B
    b. a commission from A
    c. a commission from B
    d. no commission

22. What happens when a principal sells his home under an exclusive right to sell listing?
    a. The broker receives no commission.
    b. The broker receives a commission on the gross sales price.
    c. A broker receives half the commission ordinarily due him.
    d. none of the above

23. The only way a seller could terminate an exclusive agency is if
    a. a buyer is introduced by an outside broker.
    b. a buyer is introduced by the seller.
    c. both of the above
    d. neither of the above

24. Which of the following listings is least likely to be defined as a percentage of the sale price?
    a. open listing
    b. net listing
    c. exclusive agency
    d. exclusive right to sell

25. A licensed broker brings a buyer and seller together. The buyer later finds out he is being transferred. The buyer goes to the seller and they agree to rescind the contract. The broker involved
    a. gets to keep the earnest deposit as liquidation damage.
    b. gets a full commission from the seller.
    c. both of the above
    d. neither of the above

Marketing and Selling Real Property

7

Having listed a property for sale, the real estate broker then performs the function for which he or she was employed—finding a buyer. Usually the broker advertises the property in the newspaper and places a "for sale" sign on the premises to bring responses from prospective purchasers. In addition, the sales representatives check their lists of prospects to see if the new listing will meet anyone's requirements. If the firm belongs to a multiple listing service, it immediately sends the listing information to the bureau for processing. Open houses (holding the house open for inspection) are another means of attracting would-be buyers.

THE PURCHASE AGREEMENT

The salesperson will have prequalified the buyers prior to showing them properties to determine the price range they could qualify to purchase. When a prospective buyer makes the decision to purchase a particular property, the salesperson completes an *estimated buyer's figures* form (see figure 7.1). These costs will vary across the country and between lenders. It gives the buyer a clear picture of what money will be needed to close the loan and what the monthly payments will be. With the buyer's approval of the estimated costs, a purchase agreement is then written. In some parts of the country this document is referred to as an *offer and acceptance* or a *deposit receipt*.

Upon acceptance, the agreement is a *contract* and, according to the statute of frauds in most states, must be in writing to be enforceable. While the writing of the contract is generally done by the selling agent, some states require that since a contract is a legal document, the actual writing of the offer to purchase must be done by an attorney. In this instance, after the buyers have selected the house they desire to purchase, the licensee directs them to an attorney. The presentation of the offer to the seller will still be the listing agent's responsibility.

Offer to Purchase

The offer-to-purchase contract shown in figure 7.2 (pages 80–81) contains the following information:

- *Section A* states the date the offer to purchase was signed, along with the street and legal address of the property. Any personal property included in the sale is written in this section of the agreement.

ESTIMATED BUYER'S FIGURES

Property Address **1040 Clear Street**   Price **$84,000**

Tentative Closing Date **May 15, 1987**   Mortgage Balance **$67,200**

CLOSING COSTS

Initial Investment	16,800.00
Credit Report	35.00
Appraisal	150.00
Termite Inspection	50.00
Title Insurance/Abstract	227.00
Survey	45.00
Recording Fees	25.00
_1_ % Loan Origination	672.00
___ % Discount Points	0
___ % VA Funding Fee	0
___ % PMI Insurance (1 year)	0
Pro-rated Interest	280.00
Miscellaneous Lenders Fees	
on line fee	45.00
underwriting fee	75.00

TOTAL --   **$18,404.00**

ESCROW

1 year Hazard Insurance	300.00
2 Months Hazard Insurance	50.00
7 Months Taxes	904.17
2 Months PMI Ins/FHA 245 Ins	0

TOTAL --   1,254.17   1,254.17

Estimate of Total Costs:	19,658.17
Less Earnest Deposit	2,000.00
Approximate Amount needed to close transaction	17,658.17

ESTIMATED MONTHLY PAYMENT

Principal and Interest @ ___10 %	=	590.02
Hazard Insurance (1/12)	=	25.00
Taxes (1/12) $1550.00/year	=	129.17
PMI (1/12) /FHA 245 1/2%	=	0

TOTAL -MONTHLY INVESTMENT   744.19

We understand that above figures are approximate and the approximate amount needed.

Harvey J Wender	4-8-87	_Della J Wender_	4-8-87
Purchaser	Date	Purchaser	Date

FIGURE 7.1   By _Judy Selling_
               Sales Associate

- *Section B* stipulates that the owners will convey good title, free of all liens (unless the buyers are assuming an existing mortgage). The sellers further agree that any existing indebtedness against the property will be paid.
- *Section C* sets forth the purchase price and the amount of the earnest deposit. The balance of the purchase price will be paid according to the type of financing checked in Section D.
- *Section D* contains four choices: the buyers may either (1) pay cash, (2) assume the existing mortgage, (3) obtain a new loan, or (4) request a land contract.
- *Section E* contains any additional conditions of the agreement that need to be clarified.
- *Section F* provides for proration of taxes.
- *Section G* states that the buyers have inspected the premises and agree to accept the property in its present condition. The sellers agree to maintain all the component parts in working order. The sellers further state they will be responsible for any loss to the property until title is conveyed. If any termite damage is found, they promise to pay for repairs.
- *Section H* states the contract is binding upon the parties and their heirs and assigns. The purchasers sign the agreement.
- *Section I* is the statement of receipt for the earnest deposit and the time allowed for the owners to accept the offer. The real estate company's name and address are also stated.
- *Section J* shows the signatures of the accepting owners and of the witness.
- *Section K* is signed by the buyers to show that they received a copy of the accepted contract.

Presenting the Offer

When the offer to purchase is written, a copy is given to the offeror (purchaser) as a receipt. The agent then takes the offer to the offeree (seller) for formal acceptance. Generally it is the listing agent who contacts the seller to present the offer. If the seller agrees to *all* the conditions of the offer, he or she signs the acceptance. In figure 7.2 at section J, the sellers accepted the offer as written.

When the terms of the contract are agreed upon, a copy is left with the seller and the agent notifies the buyer that the offer was accepted and gives the buyer a copy of the signed contract. In our sample purchase agreement at section K, the buyers sign that they have received a copy of the sellers' acceptance.

An offer may be rescinded at any time prior to its acceptance so it behooves the agent to deliver the accepted contract promptly.

Counter Offers

To alter *any* portion of the offer nullifies the entire agreement. If the seller does not accept the terms s/he may elect to make a counter offer. Any counter offer revokes the previous offer and is replaced with a new contract. A counter offer is *not* a

(This is a legally binding contract. If not understood, seek legal advice.)

PURCHASE AGREEMENT

April 8 19*87*

A

I, the undersigned Purchaser, hereby agree to purchase the property described as follows:
Address *1040 Clear Street*
Legal Description *Lot 8, Block 1, Confusion Hill Subdivision,*
including all fixtures and equipment permanently attached to said premises. The only
personal property included is as follows: *living room drapes*

B

Subject, however, and on condition that the owner thereof has good, valid and marketable
title, in fee simple, and said owner agrees to convey title to said property to me or my
nominees by warranty deed or *none other* free and clear of all liens,
encumbrances or special taxes levied or assessed, except *no exceptions*
This offer subject to all building and use restrictions, utility easements not exceeding
10 feet in width abutting the boundary of said property, and covenants now of record.
Seller agrees to pay any assessments for paving, curb, sidewalk or utilities previously
constructed or now under construction but not yet assessed.

C

I agree to pay for same *Eighty-four thousand & %oo*—($ *84,000.00*) DOLLARS, on the
following terms: $ *2000.oo* deposited herewith as evidence by your receipt attached
below. Balance to be paid only as shown in following paragraphs *3, 5, 6* :

D

#1 CASH
Balance of $_____ to be paid in cash or by certified check at time of delivery of
deed, no financing being required.

#2 LOAN ASSUMPTION
I agree to assume and pay existing mortgage balance in favor of _____
in the approximate amount of $_____ and pay the balance in cash or by certified
check at the time of delivery of deed; it being understood that present mortgage terms
call for stated interest rate of _____ % per annum and payments of $_____ per _____.
Said payment includes _____. Stated interest on existing
loan to be prorated to date of closing. I agree to reimburse the Seller for the amount in
the escrow reserve account which is to be assigned to me.

#3 CONDITIONAL UPON LOAN
Balance of $ *82,000* to be paid in cash or by certified check at time of delivery of
deed, conditional however, upon my ability to obtain a loan, to be secured by first mortgage,
or deed of trust, on above described property in the amount of $ *67,200* . Said loan to
be VA____, FHA____, CONVENTIONAL *X* , P.M.I._____, or VA/FHA_____, with terms
providing for stated interest not exceeding *10* % per annum, and monthly payments of
approximately $ *590.02* plus taxes and insurance. Loan origination fee/service fee
to be paid by purchaser. I agree to make application for said loan within 10 days of
acceptance of this offer. I hereby authorize you to negotiate for a loan on the above
basis and I agree to sign all papers and pay all costs in connection therewith.

#4 LAND CONTRACT
Balance to be evidenced by land contract with present owner, providing for additional cash
payment or certified check of $_____ at time of execution of the contract, and remainder
$_____ to be paid in monthly payments of $_____, or more, which monthly
payments shall include stated interest at the rate of _____% per annum computed monthly on
the unpaid portion of the principal. All other terms and conditions of the land contract
to be as mutually agreed.

E

#5
possession no later than May 15, 1987

F

#6 TAXES
All real estate taxes shall be pro-rated as of date of possession *May 15, 1987* .

G

This offer is based upon my personal inspection or investigation of the premises and not
upon any representation or warranties of condition by the Seller or his agent. Seller
agrees to maintain, until delivery of possession, the heating, air condition, water heater,
sewer, plumbing and electrical systems and any built-in appliances in working conditions.

Any risk of loss to the property shall be borne by the Seller until title has been conveyed
to the Purchaser. In the event, prior to closing, the structures on said property are
materially damaged by fire, explosion or any other cause, Purchaser shall have the right to
rescind this agreement, whereupon Seller shall then refund to Purchaser the deposit made
hereunder. Purchaser, except for V.A. loan, agrees to pay the cost of a termite inspection
of the house and attached structures, and Seller agrees to pay for any treatment or repair
work found necessary. If repairs are found to be needed for issuance of termite warranty,
upon completion of repairs, Purchaser agrees to accept said treated real estate.

FIGURE 7.2 A purchase agreement or contract.

This offer is binding upon both parties and the heirs and assigns of said parties.

WITNESS:

H

Judy M. Selling _Kurt K. Kindly_ , Purchaser

Susan A. Kindly , Purchaser

Address _328 Harbor Lane_ Phone _333-0193_

I

RECEIVED FROM _Kurt K. Kindly + Susan A. Kindly_
the sum of _two thousand and no/100_ ————— ($ _2000.00_) DOLLARS (by _check_)
to apply on the purchase price of the above described property. In the event the above
offer is not accepted by the owner of said property within the time hereinafter specified,
or that in the event there are any defects in the title which cannot be cured as specified
above, the money hereby paid is to be refunded. If purchaser fails to consummate the
purchase, the owner may, at his option, retain said money hereby paid as liquidated
damages for such failure to carry out said agreement of sale, subject to the terms of the
listing agreement.
This receipt is not an acceptance of the above offer, it being understood that the above
proposition is taken subject to the written approval and acceptance by the owner on or
before _10 pm on April 9, 1987_

445 Homestead Ave. _333-3004_ _A-1 Real Estate_
OFFICE ADDRESS PHONE # REAL ESTATE COMPANY

J

ACCEPTANCE:

April 9 , 19 _87_

We agree to the above stated terms and will deliver possession and title and perform according
to this contract. _We agree to pay A-1 Real Estate Company a cash fee
of 7% of the sale price_

Judy M. Selling _Harvey J Wender_
WITNESS SELLER

Della J Wender
SELLER

K

Receipt of executed copy of this instrument is acknowledged this _9th_ day
of _April_ 19 _87_.

Kurt K. Kindly
Susan A. Kindly
BUYERS' SIGNATURES

FIGURE 7.2, continued

partial acceptance since an acceptance cannot be conditional. However, the counter
offer can be dated and signed by the owner and the time limit for acceptance of this
new offer be stated. The buyer can now agree to the new terms or decide against
purchasing the property.

When an offer is countered, the property is available for another offer, whether
from the original offeror or from another party. If the seller counters an offer and
meanwhile another offer from a second party is presented to the seller, s/he may

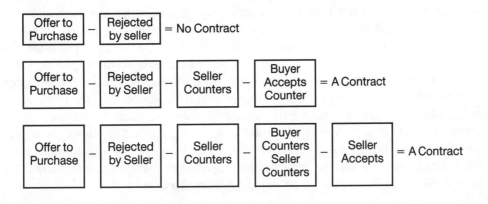

FIGURE 7.3

accept the second party's offer and cancel the counter offer to the first party (assuming the first party did not act upon and accept the counter). Time is of the essence and a "would be" buyer may lose the property s/he is attempting to purchase by negotiating terms and price. Conversely, the buyer may save money in such negotiating tactics.

Earnest Deposits

The **earnest deposit** is the amount of money that the purchaser gives to the broker at the time the agreement to purchase is written. It "binds" the contract and demonstrates the good intent of the purchaser. In some states the earnest deposit is referred to as *hand money* or a *binder*. This earnest money deposit must be placed in the broker's trust account upon acceptance of the offer. It is credited to the buyer's total payment at the time of closing. If the offer is not accepted, the earnest money is returned to the would-be purchaser.

The amount of the earnest money is not set by law, though in some areas it is common practice to ask for five or ten percent of the purchase price as a deposit. The size of the deposit should be sufficient to show the seller that the buyer's offer is sincere. However, in the final analysis the seller determines what s/he will accept. The buyer's money will be forfeited should the buyer default on the contract because the seller has taken the property off the market and may have missed an opportunity to sell it to someone else. Many states require the broker to receive in writing the forfeiture of the funds if the buyer decides not to complete the contract. Although the funds are entrusted to the broker's care, s/he must not make decisions as to their dispersal without written permission. In the case of the buyer defaulting, not only would the buyer agree in writing to relinquish the earnest deposit, but the seller would agree in writing to accept the deposit as liquidated damages. If the property later sells for less, the seller has been compensated for the difference.

Some brokers have a statement in their listing contract that in case of the forfeiture by a prospective purchaser of any earnest money deposit, after expenses incurred by the broker are deducted, the money is divided one-half to the owners and one-half to the agent.

Trust Accounts

In most states a broker must maintain a **trust account** in the firm's name in a bank located in the state where the broker is doing business. All money coming into the possession of the broker must be kept in this trust account, unless there is written agreement to the contrary, until the transaction has been consummated or terminated. This includes earnest deposits, down payments, and security deposits on leased property. Many states require a separate trust account for the processing of sales and another trust account for rents received from the managing of rental properties. Each deposit must be separately identified in the trust account records, and the broker shall not be entitled to any part of the money as a commission until the finalization of the sale. Most states require the trust account to be a non-interest bearing checking account. However, if a substantial earnest deposit is given and the closing is scheduled for a time months later, the buyer may desire his or her deposit to be earning interest. In such a situation, with *written* approval of both buyer and seller, the broker will place the deposit in an interest bearing account.

The trust accounts are audited in most states, generally on an annual basis. If the books reveal any discrepancies, the broker's license could be in jeopardy. It is the broker's duty to safeguard the funds of others in all transactions.

Lease Options

Another means of purchasing property is by leasing with an option to buy. The option permits the lessee to purchase the property within a set period of time at the price and terms defined in the lease option agreement. The lessee must execute his or her right to buy within the time frame stated in the lease option or the right is forfeited. If s/he elects to perform on the option agreement, a purchase agreement will be completed as in a regular sale. If the tenant chooses not to perform, either the lease will be renewed or the property owner can place the property on the open market for sale.

The use of the lease option generally occurs when financing terms are not advantageous to the purchaser or the seller is having difficulty finding a buyer for a particular property. It permits someone to lease the property and later make the decision to buy or not. In some instances the property owner may allow a portion of the rent to apply towards the down payment. If the property has not appreciated in value, the seller may be eager to apply the rent towards the purchase price. Conversely, the lessee may not be as eager to purchase it if similar properties can be bought for less.

Right of First Refusal

A tenant may wish to rent a property with the **right of first refusal** to purchase. This allows the tenant the right to match any offer that the property owner may receive. It does not obligate the renter to perform, but gives him or her an advantage in having the first right to buy. This could prove to be a disadvantage to the owner as prospective purchasers may shy away from offering to buy when aware that the tenant holds a previous right to meet any offer presented to the owner.

Equitable Interest

Once the offer is accepted by the owner, the buyer has an equitable interest in the real estate. The seller is still the title holder of record until the closing of the transaction but the buyer has what is known as **equitable title.** The seller must perform in accordance with the signed contract and now holds title in name only.

The question may arise: can the buyer assign the contract to another? As stated in the chapter on contracts, unless it specifically states to the contrary, the buyer has the rights to transfer the equitable interest. However, the assignee must perform according to the terms of the contract. In some instances the buyer may have been acting as a "strawman"—that is, his or her offer was made with the intent of transferring the contract prior to the closing. In this case, the true buyer may have wanted to remain anonymous until the seller accepted the terms of the offer.

Assignment of contract

Most contracts, including options, leases, mortgages, and land contracts, are *assignable* unless they specifically state to the contrary. However, if the contract is for a personal right, as in a listing contract, the assignor would need the consent of the seller.

Bill of Sale

Occasionally a purchase offer for real property will include personal property. While a deed is used to transfer the real property, a bill of sale is used when chattel (personal property) is sold. The bill of sale transfers the goods.

Marketable Title

The owner is responsible to deliver good and marketable title to the buyer. It must be free of any defects, liens, and encumbrances. The only time an existing mortgage remains against the property would be when the purchaser is assuming the loan.

Uniform Commercial Code

Chattel sales The Uniform Commercial Code (UCC) has been mandated in varying degrees in all fifty states in an effort to make laws covering chattel (personal property) sales uniform. The law covers any conditional sales contracts and chattel mortgages, including stocks and commercial paper. It covers the sale of personal property and only relates to real estate when fixtures are involved. If a chattel is purchased and financed, the financial statement can be filed at the recorder's office. If subsequently the chattel is not paid for, the creditor can repossess it from the property.

Bulk transfers are also regulated by the Uniform Commercial Code. This act covers the transfer of a large amount of inventory or material. The merchant cannot sell out his or her stock and keep the money, leaving creditors unpaid. Any buyer of the merchandise is required by UCC to receive an inventory of the goods from the seller along with a list of creditors. The buyer must then give notice to any creditor that a sale is pending. The induction of bulk transfers takes place if a business is sold or if it is liquidated.

REPRESENTING THE SELLER

The listing agent represents the seller by virtue of the contract between them. Is he or she then also able to represent the buyer? In the past few years much discussion has ensued over whom the *selling* broker represents. The majority of buyers feel that the selling broker is their agent since s/he is showing them properties, writing and presenting offers on their behalf, and seemingly caring that they purchase the property that best fulfills their needs. Buyers have been led to believe that the selling agent was representing them at "no fee." They may have confided to the agent that the price offered is not their final bid for the property. Does the agent relay this to the seller? Where does the agent's loyalty lie?

In accordance with license laws and the listing contract the selling agent is obligated to work for the best interest of his or her client, the seller. All parties need to be informed who is the client and who is the customer. The **client** is the person who is represented by another and the **customer** is one who purchases a commodity. While the selling agent represents the seller, he or she does owe the buyer true disclosure of all the facts concerning the property. The buyer is entitled only to fair treatment, while counseling and confidentiality are owed to clients under the contract.

Broker cooperation in showing each other's listings has always meant a sharing of the commission between firms. The selling agent is considered a subagent of the listing broker and thus owes his loyalty to the seller. The listing broker handles the closing through his trust account, paying a percentage to the firm that sold the property and acted in the capacity of a subagent.

To avoid confusion and misunderstanding of who the selling agent represents, some states are enacting into law that a disclosure must be made to the buyer that the selling agent is representing the seller because of the existence of the listing contract. *When* this disclosure is made is the critical issue. *Who* the agent represents should be revealed to the buyer or seller at the first meeting, ideally before the first showing of the property is made. Early disclosure minimizes any alleged undisclosed dual agency. Needless to say, it should appear in the offer-to-purchase agreement. However, by the time the buyers are ready to enter into a contract they have already confided in the agent. Considering this, oral or written transmission would be deemed necessary early on in the relationship. A recent regulation adopted by the State of Colorado requires verbal disclosure at the time the agent agrees to search for a property to show the purchaser, but in no event later than the first showing. Written affirmation of the previous disclosure must be in the purchase agreement. In 1985 Minnesota adopted a similar law and other states are either studying the problem or have enacted disclosure statements into law.

BUYER'S AGENCY

Can the buyers hire a real estate broker to represent them exclusively? Referred to as a *buyer's agency,* the purchaser can enter into an agreement with an agent to represent his or her interest only: the agent's fee would be paid by the buyer. The agent will give the buyer his complete loyalty, working strictly for the buyer's best interest.

Buyer hires broker

In the buyer agency situation, the buyer requests a broker to locate a specific property, agreeing to pay a flat fee or a percentage of the purchase price. Buyer agency is generally used more for locating specific commercial building than for a home search.

While the selling agent represents the seller, the agent owes the buyer true disclosure of all the facts concerning the property. New accountability for real estate agents was raised when suit was brought by the Eastons over structural problems of a home they purchased 25 miles east of San Francisco, California. Two months after the Eastons bought their $250,000 hillside ranch home the land began to buckle and creep. Years of litigation followed that broadened to include not only the previous owner but also three real estate companies and two contractors. The lawsuit raised the question of whether the real estate brokers were financially liable if they sell a defective property, *even* if they were unaware of the problem at the time of the sale. Both the trial court and the California Supreme Court decided the agent *was* negligent and had been obligated to investigate the property. Previously it was considered sufficient that the agent disclose facts s/he *knew* about the property. The landmark Easton case reached beyond this and stated it was the selling broker's responsibility to discover and disclose that there may be a problem on a property. The courts awarded the Eastons in excess of $200,000 in damages, which was largely covered by insurance held by one of the real estate firms.

Agent responsibility to customer

The case resulted in California legislation that requires a seller to complete a standardized disclosure form. The form has a checklist of inspections of potential problem areas such as settling, landfill areas, septic tanks, room additions that were non-code, and appliances (see figure 7.4). The California law states that a broker's responsibility is limited to areas that are accessible for visual inspection. A real estate broker is *not* expected to be a specialist in areas such as engineering and architecture, or land faults and soil compaction.

NCR (No Carbon Required)   **SELLER'S PROPERTY DISCLOSURE STATEMENT**   Page 1 of 2
(Including the main structure and any outbuildings)

PROPERTY ADDRESS _____

SELLER'S NAME _____

1. TITLE AND ACCESS

   a. Is the property currently leased? _____ If so, when does the lease expire? _____ Does the lessee have an option to extend the lease? _____
   b. Does anyone have a first right of refusal to buy, option, or lease the property? _____ If so, who: _____
   c. Do you know of any existing, pending or potential legal actions concerning the property or the Homeowners Association? _____
   _____
   d. Are there any bonds, assessments, or judgements which are either liens upon the property or which limit its use? _____
   e. Do you own real property adjacent to, across the street from, or in the same sub-division as the subject property? If yes, please describe: _____
   _____
   f. Do you know of any encroachments, easements, licenses, boundary disputes, or third party claims affecting the property (rights of other people to
   interfere with the use of the property in any way)? _____ If so, explain: _____
   _____
   g. Are you aware of any pending real estate development in your area (such as condominiums, planned unit developments, subdivisions, or property for
   commercial, educational, or religious use)? _____
   h. Do you experience any excessive noises, for example airplanes, trains, trucks, freeway, etc.? _____
   i. Are you aware of any other conditions that could affect the value or desirability of the property? _____
   _____

2. LAND

   a. Does the property have any filled ground? _____ If so, is the house built on filled or unstable ground? _____
   b. Do you know of any past or present settling or soil movement problems on the property or on adjacent properties? _____ If so, have they resulted in
   any structural damage? _____ What was the extent of damage? _____
   _____
   c. Do you know of any past or present drainage or flooding problem on your property or adjacent properties? _____ If so, explain on separate sheet.
   Is there water standing on the property after rainfall? _____ Any active springs? _____
   d. Is the property in a designated flood zone? _____
   e. Is the property in a "Special Studies Zone" as provided by the Alquist-Priolo Geological Hazard Zones Act? _____
   f. Are you aware of any past or present problems with driveways, walkways, patios, or retaining walls on your property or adjacent properties due to
   drainage, flooding, or soil movement (such as large cracks, potholes, raised sections)? _____ If so, please describe: _____
   _____

3. STRUCTURAL DISCLOSURES

   a. **Do you know of any structural additions or alterations, or the installation, alteration, repair, or replacement of significant components of the
   structures upon the property, completed during the term of your ownership or that of a prior owner ☐ with, ☐ without an appropriate
   permit or other authority for construction from a public agency having jurisdiction?** _____ **☐ Explanation attached.**
   b. Approx. age of structure: _____ Do you know of any condition in the original or existing design or workmanship of the structure that would be
   considered substandard? _____ If so, please explain: _____
   c. Are you aware of excessive settling, slanted floors, large cracks in walls, foundations, garage floors, driveways, chimneys, or fireplaces? _____ If so,
   explain: _____
   d. Are you aware of any structural wood members, including mudsills, being below soil level? _____
   e. Is crawlspace, if any, below soil level? _____
   f. Do you know of any inspection reports, surveys, studies, notices, etc. concerning the property? _____ If so, please list each one, even if you have
   already made them available _____
   g. Date of last structural pest control inspection? _____ By whom? _____
   h. Do you prefer a pre-sale structural pest control inspection? _____
   i. Date of last City/County mandatory inspection report? _____
   j. Have you any Notice(s) of Violations relating to the property from any City, County or State Agencies? _____ If so, please explain: _____
   _____
   k. Do you know of any violations of government regulations, ordinances, or zoning laws regarding this property? _____ If so, explain: _____
   _____

4. ROOF, GUTTERS, DOWNSPOUTS

   a. Type of roof: ☐ Tar and Gravel, ☐ Asphalt Shingle, ☐ Wood Shingle, ☐ Tile, ☐ Other _____ Age of roof: _____
   b. Has roof been resurfaced? _____ If so, what year? _____ Is there a guarantee on the roof? _____ For how long? _____ By whom? _____
   c. Has roof ever leaked since you owned the property? _____ If so, what was done to correct the leak? _____
   _____
   d. Are gutters and downspouts free of holes and excessive rust? _____
   e. Do downspouts empty into drainage system or onto splash blocks? _____ Is water directed away from structure? _____

5. PLUMBING SYSTEM

   a. Source of water supply: ☐ Public, ☐ Private Well. If well water, when was water sample last checked for safety? _____ Result of test: _____
   b. Well water pump: _____ Date installed: _____ Condition: _____ Sufficient water during late summer? _____
   c. Are water supply pipes copper or galvanized? _____
   d. Are you aware of below normal water pressure in your water supply lines (normal is 50 to 70 lbs.)? _____
   e. Are you aware of excessive rust stains in tubs, lavatories and sinks? _____
   f. Are you aware of water standing around any of the lawn sprinkler heads? _____
   g. Are there any plumbing leaks around and under sinks, toilets, showers, bathtubs, and lavatories? _____ If so, where? _____
   _____
   h. Pool: Age: _____ Pool Heater: ☐ Gas, ☐ Electric, ☐ Solar. Pool Sweep? _____ Date of last inspection: _____
   By whom? _____ Regular maintenance? _____
   i. Hot Tub/Spa: _____ Date of last inspection: _____ By Whom: _____
   j. ☐ City Sewer, ☐ Septic Tank: ☐ Concrete, ☐ Redwood. Capacity: _____ Is septic tank in good working order? _____

6. ELECTRICAL SYSTEM

   a. 220 Volt? _____
   b. Are there any damaged or malfunctioning receptacles? _____
   c. Are you aware of any damaged or malfunctioning switches? _____
   d. Are there any extension cords stapled to baseboards or underneath carpets or rugs? _____
   e. Does outside TV antenna have a ground connection? _____
   f. Are you aware of any defects, malfunctioning, or illegal installation of electrical equipment in or outside the house? _____
   _____

Seller's Initials [_____] [_____]   (CONTINUED ON PAGE 109.2)

FORM   109.1   (4-86)   COPYRIGHT © 1986, BY PROFESSIONAL PUBLISHING CORP. 122 PAUL DR. SAN RAFAEL, CA 94903   **PROFESSIONAL PUBLISHING**

FIGURE 7.4

7. HEATING, AIR CONDITIONING, OTHER EQUIPMENT

a. Is the house insulated? _____ _____

b. Type of Heating System: _____

c. Is furnace room or furnace closet adequately vented? _____

d. Are fuel-consuming heating devices adequately vented to the outside, directly or through a chimney? _____

e. Date of last inspection of Heating Equipment: _____ By whom: _____

f. Solar heating: _____ In working order? _____

g. Air Conditioning: _____ Date of last inspection: _____ By whom: _____

h. Does Fireplace have a damper? _____

i. Provision for outside venting of clothes dryer? _____

j. Approximate age of water heater: _____ Capacity: _____ Is your water heater equipped with temperature pressure relief valve, which is a required safety device? _____

k. Electric garage door opener: _____ Condition: _____ Number of controls: _____

l. Burglar alarm: _____ Make: _____ In working order? _____ Owned: _____ Leased: _____ Rented: _____

m. Smoke Detectors: _____ How many? _____ ☐ 110 V, ☐ Battery. In working order? _____

n. Lawn Sprinklers: _____ Automatic clock: _____ In working order? _____

o. Water softener: _____ In working order? _____

p. Sump pump: _____ In working order? _____

q. Are you aware of any of the above equipment that is in need of repair or replacement or is illegally installed? _____

8. BUILT-IN APPLIANCES

a. Are you aware of any built-in appliances that are in need of repair or replacement? _____ If so, which: _____

9. PERSONAL PROPERTY INCLUDED IN THE PURCHASE PRICE

a. The following items of personal property are included in the purchase price: _____
_____

b. Are there any liens against any of these items? _____ If so, please explain: _____

10. HOME PROTECTION PROGRAM

a. Do you want to provide a Home Protection Program at your expense? _____

11. CONDOMINIUMS

a. Please check availability of copies of the following documents: ☐ CC&Rs, ☐ Condominium Declaration, ☐ Association Bylaws, ☐ Articles of Incorporation, ☐ Subdivision Report, ☐ Current Financial Statement ☐ Regulations currently in force.

b. Does the Condominium Declaration contain any resale restrictions? _____

c. Does the Homeowners Association have the first right of refusal? _____

d. Please check occupancy restrictions imposed by the association, including but not limited to: ☐ Pets, ☐ Storage of Recreational Vehicles or Boats on driveways or in common areas, ☐ Advertising or For Sale signs, ☐ Architectural or decorative alterations subject to association approval, ☐ Others: _____

e. In case of a conversion, have you an engineer's report on the condition of the building and its equipment? _____

f. Monthly/annual association dues:$ _____ What is included in the association dues? _____

g. Has your association notified you of any future dues increases or special assessments? _____ If so, please give details _____
_____

h. Are all dues, assessments, and taxes current? _____

i. Has there been a Notice of Default filed against your property? _____ If yes, please explain: _____

j. I shall provide a statement from the Condominium Homeowners Association documenting the amount of any delinquent assessments, including penalties, attorney's fees, and any other charges provided for in the management documents to be delivered to Purchaser. _____

k. Security: ☐ Inter-com, ☐ Closed circuit TV, ☐ Guards, ☐ Electric gate, ☐ Other: _____

l. Parking: Does each unit have its own designated parking spaces? _____ How close to unit? _____ Is space ample? _____ Guest parking? _____

m. Sound proofing adequate? _____ Are there noisy trash chutes? _____ Bond guaranteeing completion of common area and facilities? _____ Property Management Co. _____

12. NEWLY CONSTRUCTED RESIDENCES

a. Is deposit held in trust fund? _____

b. Bond guaranteeing completion of unit? _____

c. Is builder a member of Home Builders Association?_____ Is Home Owners Warranty (HOW) available? _____

d. Will carpets, draperies, and appliances be identical to those shown in model unit? _____

e. Please list expiration dates of warranties covering appliances and equipment: _____
Final Inspection date:_____ Occupancy Permit date:_____ Contractor:_____ License_____

13. OWNERSHIP

a. Are you a builder or developer? _____

b. Are you a licensed real estate agent? _____

c. Have all persons on the title signed the listing agreement? _____

d. Please list all persons on the title who are not U.S. citizens: _____

e. Are you aware of anything else you should disclose to a prospective purchaser? _____ If so, please explain (use addendum if necessary):_____
_____

The foregoing answers and explanations are true and complete to the best of my/our knowledge and I/we have retained a copy hereof. I/we herewith authorize _____ , the agent in this transaction, to disclose the information set forth above to other real estate brokers, real estate agents, and prospective purchasers of the property.

Dated: _____ Seller: _____ Seller: _____

I/we acknowledge receipt of this SELLER'S PROPERTY DISCLOSURE STATEMENT, including additional explanations, if any, attached hereto.

Dated: _____ Purchaser: _____ Purchaser: _____

I am satisfied with the above SELLER'S PROPERTY DISCLOSURE STATEMENT.
Dated: _____ Purchaser: _____ Purchaser: _____

I am NOT satisfied with the above SELLER'S PROPERTY DISCLOSURE STATEMENT and herewith rescind my offer to purchase above property.

Dated: _____ Purchaser: _____ Purchaser: _____

I reserve the right to have the property inspected by the following professional(s) _____
and to submit a copy of the inspection report(s) to Seller's agent on or before _____ .

Dated: _____ Purchaser: _____ Purchaser: _____

FIGURE 7.4, continued

Errors and omission

Because of the Easton case, other lawsuits followed and brokers are concerned that it may result in frivolous claims. Many have purchased malpractice insurance, commonly referred to as **errors and omission insurance.** For an annual premium the broker is defended should a claim be filed against him. The state of Kentucky enacted legislation mandating such insurance. Some real estate companies are being denied errors and omission insurance if they are involved in more than listing and selling real property since additional risks are incurred if the company is in property management, construction, or land development. While the insurance rates are high, the trend towards consumerism has propelled brokers to insure against unhappy buyers. A case in point was a problem that resulted when the purchaser of an acreage was alarmed several months after the sale by the sight of a backhoe digging a trench across his property. He learned the adjoining property owners had been given an easement by the past owner to tap into his well. The easement was never recorded so the buyer had no knowledge of its existence. The seller declared he had told the agent about the easement, but the agent had no recollection of the conversation. Fortunately, attorneys for the errors and omission insurance company defended the broker and his agent.

BUYER'S WARRANTIES

Home Buyer's Insurance

Insurance on new construction

Home buyer's insurance is available in many areas of the country for the purchaser's protection. If it is a newly constructed home the builder may insure the house under the Home Owners Warranty Corporation, referred to as the HOW program. A ten year warranty plan, the insurance covers defects in material, faulty workmanship, and structural problems. If a major defect should arise the buyer is protected against costly repairs.

Home Warranty Insurance

Insurance on existing property

Home warranty insurance is also available on existing homes. The policy may be purchased by the buyer or seller and covers such items as heating, air conditioning, electrical, plumbing and appliances. They generally carry a deductible amount and coverage on some items may be excluded.

If insurance is not available, some buyers may request an inspection on such major items as heating and air conditioning as a contingency of the purchase agreement. Pre-inspections by qualified service representatives or home inspection agencies assure the buyer that the items in question are in workable order.

SUMMARY

The procedures for carrying out the terms of a purchase contract are complicated, so the salesperson must take care in handling his or her responsibilities as an agent of the seller. In addition to diligence, the act of negotiating is important to the finalization of the contract. As a professional salesperson, the agent must weigh the value of each offer when presenting it to the seller. If a small item in the offer is countered by the seller, it voids the entire offer and the seller may lose a potential buyer.

To safeguard the purchaser's deposit the real estate firm is required by law to place the earnest deposit in its trust account after the offer is accepted. This must be done within the time stipulated in the license law of each state. The money is not withdrawn from the trust account until finalization of the sale. Many states have examiners audit trust accounts to assure that they are maintained as the law mandates.

In recent years new emphasis has been placed on the question of whom the selling broker represents. Many buyers erroneously feel the salesperson is *their* agent, due in part to the relationship that is formed in the process of hunting for a suitable home. Greater responsibility for clarification rests with the salesperson and consequently some states are requiring a disclosure statement in the purchase agreement revealing whom the salesperson is representing.

A dual agency exists if the salesperson represents both the buyer and the seller. Since formalities are not required to create an agency relationship, the selling agent must take care in not implying with his conduct that he is representing the buyer. A buyer's agency can be formed between the buyer and the selling agent, but this must then be disclosed to the seller and seller's agent.

A subagency relationship exists when a salesperson shows the property of another broker and is thus bound by the agency relationship of the listing broker.

KEY WORDS AND CONCEPTS

Bill of sale: Transfers personal property.

Buyer's agency: The buyer employs an agent to represent him exclusively.

Client: Person represented by another.

Counter offer: Offer is not accepted and a counter is presented.

Customer: Purchaser of a commodity, in real estate sales normally the buyer.

Earnest deposit: Amount given at time the purchase agreement is written to show the good intent of the buyer.

Equitable interest: Interest of purchaser upon acceptance of the offer by the owner.

Errors and omission insurance: Carried by the broker as protection against claims.

Home buyer's insurance (HOW): A 10 year warranty on new construction covering defects in workmanship, materials or structural problems.

Home warranty insurance: Available on existing homes as protection on major repairs on items such as heating and air conditioning.

Lease options: Lessee has exclusive right to purchase the property for the terms and price agreed upon within a set time period.

Purchase agreement: An offer to buy real property; if accepted by seller, it becomes a binding contract.

Right of first refusal: The holder has the right to accept or reject any offer received on the property. Usually held by a tenant.

Trust account: A broker's bank account reserved for funds entrusted to him that belong to others.

REVIEW QUESTIONS

1. A broker's trust account is used
   a. for the deposit of earnest money only.
   b. in lieu of a general account.
   c. for the deposit of money, belonging to others, that comes into his possession.
   d. to compensate the broker for expenditures.

2. A seller's counter offer would be included in which of the following?
   a. an amended listing contract
   b. an amended offer to purchase
   c. both a and b
   d. neither a nor b

3. If the purchaser assigns her interest in the property while the contract is still pending, realizing a profit
   a. the seller receives the profit.
   b. it cancels the contract.
   c. the broker receives the profit.
   d. the original purchaser receives the profit.

4. Ms. Jones hires A-1 Realty to sell her house and explains to agent Judy Jewel the reason she wants to sell is that the house has a faulty sewer system. Jewel does not include this information on the listing agreement. The property is sold by salesperson Paul Parker of another real estate firm, who looked only at the listing agreement. Who has placed their license in jeopardy?
   a. Judy Jewel
   b. Paul Parker
   c. both a and b
   d. neither a nor b

5. To whom must a copy of the accepted purchase agreement be delivered?
   a. buyer
   b. seller
   c. both of the above
   d. neither of the above

6. Funds deposited in a trust account that will ultimately belong to the broker
   a. cannot be used by the broker until the sale is consummated or terminated.
   b. may be transferred to the broker's business account if one of the parties to the contract has agreed in writing.
   c. both a and b
   d. neither a nor b

7. A lessee has the right as specified in the lease contract to purchase the property because of
   a. a lease clause
   b. the right of first refusal
   c. a reversionary clause
   d. a transfer clause

8. The person who hires another to represent him is known as
   a. a customer
   b. a client
   c. a broker
   d. an agent

9. An offeror may withdraw his offer until
   a. the closing date.
   b. the deed is recorded.
   c. the contract is signed.
   d. he is notified that his offer has been accepted.

10. When a contract for the sale of real estate is signed by the purchaser and the seller, the purchaser acquires
    a. equitable title to the property
    b. legal title to the property
    c. both a and b
    d. neither a nor b

11. The amount and type of earnest deposit required is determined by
    a. seller
    b. buyer
    c. law
    d. broker

12. A sales agent has a listing on a property and has just written a purchase agreement. The agent could do the following:
    a. tell the seller the highest price the buyer is willing to pay.
    b. tell the buyer the lowest offer the seller will accept.
    c. both a and b
    d. neither a nor b

13. A salesperson should prepare all of the following for the purchaser who wants to make an offer on a property, except
    a. an estimate of the buyer's closing costs.
    b. an estimate of the monthly principal, interest, taxes and an insurance payment.
    c. an offer to purchase agreement.
    d. a right of first refusal document.

14. If personal property is included in the sale of real property, the following document is used:
    a. purchase agreement
    b. bill of sale
    c. lease option
    d. none of the above

15. John and Janice Jones hire Bill Williams to locate a home for them in the exclusive Fairmont district. After searching for a home that fits the requirements of the Joneses, Williams locates a property listed with ABC Realty. An agreement to purchase is written and accepted by the sellers. Bill Williams fee will be paid by
    a. John and Janice Jones
    b. the sellers
    c. ABC Realty
    d. all of the above

16. All of the following are essential to an agreement to purchase contract, except
    a. purchase price
    b. description of the property
    c. buyer's and seller's signatures
    d. mortgage assumption

17. The sale price of a property and the amount of the earnest deposit are all determined by
    a. state law
    b. negotiation
    c. Real Estate board
    d. the broker who has the property listed

18. When a salesperson represents both the buyer and the seller, the relationship is referred to as
    a. dual agency
    b. subagency
    c. buyer agency
    d. broker's agency

Lending Institutions and Loans | 8

We refer to the business enterprise whose purpose it is to make available various kinds of financing as the *money market*. Most of the funds used for financing real estate are savings from firms and individuals who deposit their money in return for interest earned on their savings. The lending institutions are called *financial fiduciaries* and as such they are responsible to safeguard the funds entrusted to them by their depositors. These lending institutions and the loans they originate are covered in this chapter.

Until recently, bankers did not search for customers, but waited for business to come to them. The borrower considered himself lucky to get the loan. Not so today. In today's competitive world of real estate finance it takes more than low rates and discount points to obtain business. When the real estate agent sells a property, s/he guides the borrower to a loan officer whose service and knowledge assist in providing a smooth closing for the customer.

In the 1970s most agents took their business to the savings and loan institutions where interest rates were relatively constant from month to month and discount points were almost nonexistent. Then in the mid to late 1970s, deposits left the savings and loans for the higher interest rates provided by the money market funds. The process whereby funds left the savings and loans to go to the higher paying money markets is called **disintermediation.** This left savings and loan institutions with insufficient reserves to make real estate loans and the home borrower was forced to seek funds on Wall Street and compete with industry and government for the limited savings available for lending. Interest rates were now determined by the market place and loans had to be sold on a **secondary mortgage market** to investors, often at a discount from face value. The situation led to the birth of a new multimillion dollar industry called mortgage banking. Mortgage bankers originate new loans and package them in million dollar pools. These pools form collateral for mortgage backed securities which are sold to investors through an auction process. In this chapter you will learn where the money for home mortgages comes from, why we must now pay discount points, and the roles played by various financial institutions, along with Fannie Mae, Ginny Mae, and Freddy Mac to provide a source of mortgage money for home buyers.

SOURCES OF FINANCE

Savings and Loans

Savings and loan associations are no longer the primary source of home financing: their role has changed greatly in the past decade. During the early 1980s they were caught with long term mortgages at seven to eight percent while existing market rates were running twelve to sixteen percent. They needed to replace these loans with adjustable rate loans where the rate would move up or down with current market conditions. This type of loan places the burden of future interest rate increases squarely on the shoulders of the borrower. Consequently, savings and loans now only lend on short term, three to five years, or adjustable rate mortgages (ARM) loans from their own vaults. Recently we have seen a trend wherein large savings and loans buy or form their own mortgage banking operations that originate long-term, fixed-rate real estate loans and sell these loans on the secondary market to investors such as insurance companies, pension and trust funds, and large corporations.

The history of the savings and loan associations dates back to January 1, 1831. In Frankford, Pennsylvania, a borough of 2,000 near Philadelphia, six men met to discuss forming a "building club." Modeled after a building society formed fifty years earlier in Birmington, England, the organization was named the Oxford Providence Building Association. Thirty-seven members made regular deposits into a common fund, and when each contributor had purchased a home, the Oxford Providence Club was dissolved. Five months after the association was formed, in May of 1831, they had collected sufficient funds to grant their first loan. Comly Rich was the highest bidder, paying $10 for a $375 loan. The two-story, 450 square foot frame home that he purchased with the loan still stands in Philadelphia.

FIGURE 8.1
The Philadelphia home built with the first loan made by a savings and loan in the United States.

In the years to follow many such organizations were patterned after the club. Groups of people purchased shares of stock from which they would later be able to borrow. It was necessary that each association collect enough money to have the funds available to make these loans. The borrower not only pledged his home, but also his shares as collateral. Today, the borrower at a savings and loan association does not have to be a depositor.

As housing needs increased, the expansion of savings and loans grew. By the time of the 1929 stock market crash, there were more than 12,000 savings and loan associations in the United States.

Following the Great Depression years, legislation was enacted to provide protection to depositors. The Federal Home Loan Act of 1932 required reserve funds from which the savings and loans could draw. The Homeowners Act of 1933 established a system for federal chartering of savings and loan associations. In 1934, the National Housing Act created the Federal Housing Administration (FHA), which provides federal insurance on home mortgages, and the Federal Savings and Loan Insurance Corporation, which insures the savings of depositors in savings and loans for up to $100,000.

A savings and loan association must be state or federally chartered to operate. *Federal charters* The Federal Home Loan Bank Board gives the charter to associations that are owned by their depositors. The requirements of a federally chartered savings and loan are:

1. It must be a member of the Federal Home Loan Bank System.
2. It must be owned by its depositors (borrowers are asked to sign a membership card).
3. It must carry Federal Savings and Loan Insurance Corporation insurance.
4. The loan-to-value ratios are regulated (up to 95 percent of appraised value with a thirty-year term available).
5. The maximum amount of a loan is regulated.
6. The ratio of home loans to other types of loans is regulated.
7. A maximum interest payable to depositors is set, with greater interest on time certificates since the funds are assured to be on deposit for a longer time.

The requirements of a state-chartered savings and loan are: *State charters*

1. It must be owned by depositors or by corporations owned by stockholders.
2. It need not be federally insured, but it is subject to audit (it must be privately insured).
3. It need not belong to the Federal Home Loan Bank System.

Insurance Companies

Life insurance companies have funds available to invest in real estate and are heavy *Other loan sources* investors in mortgage backed securities sold on the secondary mortgage market. Their large amounts of cash available from insurance premiums need to be invested to provide for future cash needs.

Insurance firms favor investment in larger apartment complexes and commercial loans greater than one million dollars and are the biggest suppliers of funds for large mortgages on apartment complexes, commercial buildings, and shopping centers. Since they are not concerned with quick liquidity, they often enter into an equity position in the projects they finance. Referred to as *participation* financing, it affords them greater returns on the investment.

Commercial Banks

Commercial Banks generally serve the community in short-term (three to five year), high-yield loans such as automobile and household loans. Their funds for long-term real estate loans are limited to adjustable rate mortgages.

These banks also make short-term construction and home improvement loans. They may also grant interim financing, called a *bridge loan*, to fill the gap if a purchaser buys a home prior to selling an existing one.

Trust Funds

Commercial banks have trust departments that manage and supervise real estate holdings and properties of clients. The money held in trust funds is placed there for the benefit of a third party. Their fiduciary position includes acting as executor for estates, guardians for the estates of minors, and serving as trustees for individuals and corporations. They are known for their conservative approach since their responsibility is to safeguard the property entrusted to them. Little of this money is used for residential loans; it is usually placed in large commercial investments or some of it may be used to purchase mortgage-backed securities.

Mutual Savings

Primarily located in the eastern section of the United States, mutual savings banks favor long-term investments since they are basically savings institutes. Preferring a low-risk position, they generally finance real estate only in the near vicinity. They are also quite diversified in their investment approach; they buy stocks, bonds, and government securities. Mutual savings banks have no stockholders, so all earnings after operational costs are met are returned to depositors as interest earned.

Credit Unions

Credit unions were founded by individual firms as savings programs for their employees, with regular payroll deductions taken from each participating employee's check. Many people feel this is a painless way to save, since most people don't miss money they never receive. Credit unions usually pay a higher rate of interest and offer lower interest rates to employees wishing to borrow money. Credit unions generally do not make many long-term real estate loans, but normally limit their funds to home improvement and personal property loans. Some credit unions are providing long-term, fixed-rate loans for their members and selling them to the Credit Union National Association (CUNA), much like mortgage bankers sell to the secondary market.

Pension Funds

The purpose of a pension fund is much like that of the Social Security program; it offers a forced savings program for its contributors. Pension funds are deducted from employees' salaries and held in trust until retirement when they are paid out in monthly sums. This cash requirement dovetails nicely with the homebuyer's need for money. Most pension funds are used for corporate and government stocks and bonds or mortgage-backed securities (MBS) that are generally purchased from the secondary market. Dividends are passed on to the subscribers to increase their retirement savings as inflation continues to climb.

Mortgage Bankers

Selling the mortgage   **Mortgage bankers** originate mortgages and then sell the loans to investors, through the secondary market. They assume the risk of underwriting the loans and may have to buy the loan back if it does not meet Fanny Mae standards. Funds are sometimes committed from the investors prior to the mortgage banker's original loan. Serving as an intermediary, the mortgage banker earns his income from origination fees and service fees for collecting monthly payments and handling foreclosures. The origination fee will generally be one percent of the loan amount with the servicing fee generating an income of one-half a percent to one percent of the monthly payment.

Home loans are originated in what is referred to as the *primary mortgage market*. The borrower visits the mortgage banker and requests a loan on the property being purchased. The originator of the loan packages the loans and sells them on the secondary market to investors in million dollar blocks. The mortgage banker services the loan.

How loans are made

Mortgage Brokers

The primary purpose of the **mortgage broker** is to locate lenders and borrowers and bring them together, much as the real estate broker brings together buyers and sellers of property. The mortgage broker does not lend his own money nor does he service (collect payments or handle foreclosures) the loan. For his efforts, the mortgage broker earns a placement fee, usually a percentage of the loan. He must locate sources for loans as he finds the borrowers. The mortgage banker must take care in placing loans so that no high-risk loans affect his credibility.

Mortgage Correspondents

A *mortgage correspondent* is an agent for the lender, placing the loan for the borrower. S/He usually services the loan for the lending institution and receives a fee for doing so. The mortgage broker and the mortgage banker are both mortgage correspondents.

GOVERNMENT REGULATIONS ON LOANS

The federal government has enacted legislation that requires credit arrangers to comply with certain laws.

The Truth-in-Lending Law

Truth in lending is a federal law enforced and administered by the Federal Reserve. Regulation Z, as published by the Board of Governors of the Federal Reserve System, implements the act. As part of the A-1 Consumer Protection Act, truth in lending became effective July 1, 1969. However, the Act was simplified and refined and in October of 1982 the Truth-In-Lending Simplification and Reform Act (TILSRA) became law.

The law requires that disclosure of the true annual percentage rate (APR) be made to the borrower within three days of the loan application. The APR shows the result of up-front finance charges made by the lender on the note rate. A disclosure statement form is used to disclose hidden finance charges to the borrower and allows the borrower to compare one lender's loan with a competitor. In the past, lenders may have advertised low rates and then charged the borrower large fees "up front" on the day of closing, increasing the lenders' yield on the loan. Now lenders must calculate the APR utilizing the *net* loan proceeds and disclose this to the borrower (see figure 8.2). The finance charges include all costs the consumer must pay either directly or indirectly (such as discount points, private mortgage insurance, loan fees, and interest paid in advance). Designed to protect the consumer, Regulation Z requires the lender to reveal in writing where the borrower's money is going through a "good faith" estimate. This disclosure must be given at the time of the loan application. The disclosure must include the following:

Disclosure of loan costs

1. The date the finance charge commences
2. The annual percentage rate

FEDERAL TRUTH IN LENDING DISCLOSURE STATEMENT

Creditor:

Borrower(s):

Account Number:

ANNUAL PERCENTAGE RATE The cost of your credit as a yearly rate	FINANCE CHARGE The dollar amount the credit will cost you	Amount Financed The amount of credit provided to you or on your behalf	Total of Payments The amount you will have paid after you have made all payments as scheduled
%	$	e $	$

Your payment schedule will be:

NUMBER OF PAYMENTS	AMOUNT OF PAYMENTS	WHEN PAYMENTS ARE DUE
	$	

Variable Rate: ☐ If checked, this is a variable rate loan. The interest rate may increase during the term of this transaction if the index increases. The index used is the weekly average yield on United States Treasury securities adjusted to a constant maturity of ___ year(s). The interest rate may not increase more than ___ every ___ year(s), and there is ___ limit in the maximum interest rate. Any increase will take the form of higher payment amounts. If the interest rate increases by .25% in ___ year(s), then your regular payments will increase to $ ___ ☐ If checked, the interest rate may not increase more than ___ % every ___ year(s). ☐ If checked, the interest rate will not increase above ___ %.

Demand Feature: ☐ If checked, this obligation has a demand feature.

Insurance: You may obtain property insurance from anyone you want that is acceptable to First Union Mortgage Corporation. ☐ If checked, you can get the insurance from First Union Mortgage Corporation and you will pay $ ___ for 12 months coverage.

Security: You are giving a security interest in:
☐ property being purchased   ☐ property located at

Late Charges: If a payment is late, you will be charged ___ % of the payment.

Prepayment: If you pay off early, you ☐ may ☐ will not have to pay a penalty. You ☐ may ☐ will not be entitled to a refund of part of the finance charge.

Assumption: Someone buying your house ☐ may ☐ may, subject to conditions ☐ cannot be allowed to assume the remainder of the mortgage on the original terms.

See your contract documents for any additional information about nonpayment, default, any required repayment in full before the scheduled date, prepayment refunds and penalties and assumption policy.

e means an estimate

FIGURE 8.2

3. The number of monthly payments
4. The date payments are due
5. Any pay-off penalties
6. Charges made in case of late payment or default
7. Sufficient description of the property
8. The total finance charges

This law applies to all arrangers of credit, including savings and loan associations, commercial banks, mortgage brokers, and finance companies. It extends to the broker only if s/he sells three properties within a nineteen month period by way of contract for deed. Assumptions of existing mortgages and contracts from creditors must also adhere to the law. While the real estate agent and mortgage broker bring the consumer and the lender together, they are not considered as "arrangers" of credit since they do not finance the sale themselves.

Exemptions to the Truth-in-Lending Act include

Exempt from truth-in-lending

1. Business loans
2. Commercial loans
3. Loans to corporations and partnerships
4. Installment loans with four or less installments
5. Loans where no finance charges are made

For some types of loans, such as refinances or home improvement items, the borrower may cancel the loan up until midnight of the third working day after the applicant signs the loan note. However, with the loans that real estate salespeople help secure for their customers (such as a first mortgage or first trust deed), the buyer does not have the three day "cooling off" period. On a refinancing of a person's residence, though, the three day period does apply.

Regulation Z of the act further determines the advertising of credit terms, a condition with which the real estate industry must comply. It is permissible to advertise the annual percentage rate (APR) and the price of the property. However, if further mention of credit terms is stated, all of the terms must be disclosed. No advertisement may say simply, "7 percent mortgage" or "no down payment" unless all other terms are mentioned in the advertisement. In a mortgage assumption, the advertiser can state the rate of finance charge without any other disclosure, but the finance charge must be stated as an annual percentage rate; that is, "assume 10 percent mortgage" is wrong, but "assume 10 percent annual percentage rate mortgage" or "assumable loan" is right. If any credit terms are stated, then the price, down payment, and the amount of the mortgage must be set forth, together with the amount, the due dates, the number of payments, and the annual percentage rate. An advertisement that mentions price alone is beyond suspicion.

Advertising guidelines

The penalty for not complying with the Truth-in-Lending Law when advertising is enforced by the Federal Trade Commission and includes

1. Criminal liability of a fine of up to $5000 and one year in jail or both.
2. Civil liability to the mortgagor, who must file his or her complaint within one year. This liability shall not exceed $1000 and costs.
3. The arranger of credit may eliminate any fines by complying with the law within fifteen days after notification.

Truth-in-lending penalties

RESPA

RESPA prevents kickbacks

As of June 20, 1975, the Real Estate Settlement Procedures Act (RESPA) became effective. This act was intended to provide the purchaser and seller with regulated and standardized procedures in closing a federally related sale. Because of the many complaints from lenders and real estate brokers concerning the involved implementation of the act, it was modified in June of 1976.

RESPA's main thrust is to eliminate any kickbacks that might occur through referrals by closing agents or attorneys for particular title companies. It also prevents the seller of the property from insisting that the purchaser buy title insurance from a specific title company.

The act further limits the amount of tax and insurance escrow that the lender can require the borrower to pay in advance. Only one-sixth of the amount due in a one-year period, commencing at the settlement date, may be collected. This amount will adequately cover the lender by the taxes and insurance due date but will not leave more than necessary (one-sixth of the amount due in a one year period) in the reserve account.

When applying for a loan, the mortgagor can expect the following:

Escrow amount limited

1. An information booklet from HUD explaining RESPA
2. The lender's use of the Uniform Settlement Statement as required by HUD (see chapter 9)
3. The receipt of a good-faith estimate of closing costs at loan application
4. The right to inspect the Uniform Settlement Statement one day prior to settlement

Disclosure of closing costs

A good-faith estimate of closing costs has been substituted for the repealed twelve-day Advance Disclosure of Settlement Costs. The good-faith estimate must be supplied by the lender at the time of the loan application. When a good-faith estimate cannot be provided, a range of charges must be supplied. HUD encourages but does not require estimates of loan-related fees.

The settlement statement must be made available to the borrower at or prior to the settlement except when

1. The secretary of HUD exempts the above requirements in a particular locality, or
2. The borrower has waived the requirement, in which case the statement shall be mailed or delivered at the earliest practical date.

The Uniform Settlement Statement is virtually unchanged from the original RESPA Disclosure Statement. The new statement, however, has been revised to eliminate references to advance disclosure and truth in lending.

LOANS

FHA

The **Federal Housing Administration** (FHA) has been in existence since 1934. Prior to that time, most borrowers in need of home financing were dependent upon banks to renew short-term (generally five-year) loans. During the Great Depression of the 1930s, many banks closed or could not renew loans. The debtor lost his property and any equity he had acquired.

The FHA was created after the depression to create construction jobs, stimulate the housing industry, and help Americans obtain good quality, affordable housing. FHA has been a boon to housing financing because

1. they established a set of standards concerning the construction and appraisal of property to qualify for FHA insurance;
2. they set up new standards for qualifying buyers for mortgage insurance;
3. they initiated the long term mortgage, thereby providing lower monthly house payments so more Americans could own their own home; and
4. the above innovations made it possible to sell mortgages through a national clearing house, later to be called the secondary mortgage market.

The FHA does not make loans; it insures loans made by approved lenders. The FHA offers protection to the lender in the event of foreclosure. If the borrower defaults on the loan, the lender may foreclose and the FHA will repay the lender's loss, if any.

Effective September 1, 1983, FHA changed the Mortgage Insurance Premium *MIP* (MIP) payment program and began requiring collection of mortgage insurance for the loan at the time the loan is made rather than payments over the life of the loan. In the event the loan is paid off prior to the term, the unused portion of the MIP is refunded to the borrower. FHA offers several options to the borrower, including the financing of the MIP, or it may be paid at the closing by either the buyer or the seller. For example, the premium is 3.8 percent if financed for a 30 year loan. If the complete MIP premium is paid in cash at closing, a person other than the buyer (such as the seller, parents, etc.) may pay all or a portion of the premium.

Let's assume on the purchase of a $60,000 home the MIP is added to the loan:

Down payment:	3% of $25,000	= $ 750.00	
(see discussion	5% of $35,000	= 1750.00	
below of FHA		$2500.00	required down
down payment)			payment

Loan Amount:	$60,000 − $2,500	= $57,500 loan
Add MIP:	$57,500 × 3.8% (MIP)	= $ 2,185 MIP
	$57,500 + $2,185	= $59,685 loan

Adding the MIP has increased the loan by $2,185, but it provided the purchaser the opportunity to obtain housing with a minimum down payment. A problem that surfaces is that adding the MIP and closing costs to FHA loans results in a loan greater than the value of the property.

FHA loans are based either on the acquisition cost (purchase price plus the FHA allowable closing costs) or on the FHA appraised value, whichever is lower.

The Federal Housing Administration requires the loan to be paid back in periodic *Discount points* payments, both principal and interest. The loans are generally issued for 15 or 30 years, with insurance and taxes included in the monthly payment. Lenders may vary as to their requirements in making an FHA loan. Discount points are charged if the borrower wants a below current market interest rate. It is permissible to charge either the seller or the buyer for points if it is disclosed in the purchase agreement.

FHA down payment
FHA insures loans only for one- to four-family housing. The FHA section 203B program under Title II requires a minimum down payment with the maximum loan based on local market conditions which vary across the nation. If the acquisition value is less than $50,000, the purchaser is only required to put 3 percent down. If the home is less than one year old and not built under FHA specifications, the minimum down payment is 10 percent. FHA does not permit secondary financing on a new loan and the home must be purchased as the buyer's residence to obtain the maximum financing. If a note is taken as a down payment, it will result in a fine or prison sentence for the agent. This program was designed for households that have sufficient income but lack sufficient savings to make a large down payment.

Since some builders were adding excessive financing costs to the price of their new homes, FHA felt it necessary to limit the amount of dollars the seller could contribute to the buyer as an enticement to buy the home. The maximum seller contribution for an FHA loan is 5 percent of the sales price. If the contribution exceeds 5 percent then the FHA mortgage is reduced dollar for dollar of excess contribution.

The buyers must have from their own funds the down payment and prepaid expenses. The seller can pay the closing costs or they may be added to the FHA mortgage. It is possible for the source of buyer's funds to be from a gift letter. The gift letter must be from a relative or an employer.

Controlled ceiling removed
Until November of 1983, the government controlled the amount of interest the lender could charge on FHA loans. However, because of spiraling interest rates in the late 1970s and early 1980s, lenders were reluctant to loan out money at lower rates than they could receive on conventional loans. The alternative was to charge enormous discount points which meant the seller was generally asked to pay them. This in effect meant the seller was taking less for his or her home after deducting the cost of paying the points.

Eliminating the controlled ceiling on the FHA loan allows the borrower to "shop" rates for his loan. The rate will adjust or float with the market and either the buyer or seller can pay the points. The rate will be determined by discount points paid. The lower the rate the higher the points. Rate and points may be locked in for a set period of time from the date of the loan application, or they may float and lock in at any time prior to submitting to FHA.

A break from the traditional 30 year mortgage is the FHA adjustable loan. The advantages include the fact that it is available at a lower initial interest rate and with reduced points.

A typical guide used by a mortgage banker issuing FHA loans is

1. income qualifications for PITI, maintenance, and utilities should not exceed 38 percent of the *net monthly income*; and
2. total *debt ratio* should be no more than 58 percent.

The gross monthly income, less federal taxes, equals the net monthly income. The total debts considered by the lender are

Income qualifications
1. social security payment (7.15%)
2. state taxes
3. proposed principal, interest and taxes
4. proposed maintenance and utilities

5. all recurring debts over 10 months in length

6. child care if both spouses work and they have pre-school children

While most FHA loans are under the 203 program, variations from the original FHA plan have developed to fill the needs of buyers.   *Subsidized FHA plan*

• The FHA 235 program subsidized lower and moderate income families by reducing their monthly payments through a government subsidy. However, at the current time these loans are no longer available.

• The FHA 245 program requires a somewhat larger down payment than a 203B but offers a graduated payment plan which permits the borrower to begin payments at a substantially lower interest rate with a gradual increase the first four to five years of the loan. The 245 program is designed to assist buyers who initially need low monthly payments to qualify and whose income is expected to grow in the next four to five years. Since interest that occurred in the first year equals more than the payments, the outstanding principal balance increases, resulting in what is called *negative amortization*. That is, the debt increases over time instead of decreasing. At the end of 5 years the maximum mortgage is reached and the debt will begin to decline just as a regularly amortized real estate loan.

• FHA loans are available for non-owner occupied purchasers but the maximum loan can be no more than 85 percent of what an owner occupant could receive. If the monthly payment greatly exceeds rental income then the loan amount may be lowered. Also, if an investor has more than seven units, FHA may elect not to make additional loans to him.

FHA loans are assumable by the purchaser of a home carrying an FHA loan.   *FHA loans assumable*
However, the owner is responsible for the loan that he allows to be assumed unless a *release of liability* is granted by the lender and FHA. If the approval of the lending institution is gained, this release form relieves the original borrower of any liability. This substitution of liability to a new debtor is termed *novation*. Effective December 1, 1986, all FHA loans contain the provision requiring that any subsequent purchaser of the property must pass a credit check and qualify for the payment prior to title passing or the acceleration clause would be invoked causing the loan to be due on sale. This applies to loan assumptions within 2 years of the date of the loan. If an assumption takes place prior to this time to an unqualified buyer it will be grounds for accelerating the note. A means of getting around this limitation would be to sell on a land contract with a two year balloon.

FHA loan assumptions become extremely popular when interest rates are high. Not only is the interest lower, but the cost of originating a new loan is bypassed. Since the loans have generally been in force for a number of years and the owners equity has built up, a larger down payment will be necessary. However, since it is not a new loan the purchaser can borrow some of the down payment from the seller. The purchaser must be realistic in what amount he can allot to his monthly house payment. The guidelines set down by lenders are a wise plan for any buyer assuming an existing loan. Also, the larger the down payment the less risk the seller has of foreclosure.

FHA Title I

The FHA Title I Act authorized the FHA to insure lending institutions against losses   *FHA home improvement*
on loans made to finance repairs and improvements to existing structures and to   *loans*

build new structures for nonresidential use. FHA liability is limited to 90 percent of the loss on individual loans and to 10 percent of all such loans made by the institutions. The borrower must have a satisfactory income and credit record. S/He must own the property or have a lease expiring not less than six months beyond the maturity of the loan. The loan may not exceed $5000 or have a maturity greater than seven years and thirty-two days. The lender pays an insurance charge on each loan made. This revenue, plus recoveries on defaulted notes, is sufficient to make the program self-supporting and establish a substantial reserve for paying off losses.

VA Loans

VA loans require no down payment

The Veterans Administration designed the **VA loans** (often referred to as GI loans) for veterans who qualify under the law. A minimum of 181 days active service during World War II, the Korean War or the Vietnam War with an honorable discharge is required to obtain a VA loan. This eligibility is valid until used and extends to widows and widowers of veterans who died on active duty if they have not remarried.

Unlike FHA loans, there is no charge to the veteran. VA loans are for 15 or 30 years duration and the Veterans Administration guarantees the loan for 60 percent of the sale price or $27,500, whichever is less. If there is a default on a guaranteed loan, the government reimburses the lender for his loss up to the amount of the VA guarantee (veterans eligiblity). The maximum loaned depends upon the lending institution, with most lenders stopping at $110,000 with no money down. The maximum loan, regardless of down payment, is $135,000. In order to sell a VA loan on the secondary market, it can not exceed a 75 percent loan-to-value ratio. The veteran must occupy the property and there is no prepayment penalty.

VA loans guaranteed

The veteran must secure a *Certificate of Eligibility* and sign a statement that says he or she intends to occupy the home. No down payment is required by the government. When the loan is paid off, the veteran's eligibility will be fully restored. If the loan is assumed by another veteran who substitutes his eligibility, with release of liability, the veteran will be given entitlement again. The lending institution may charge a set fee determined by the VA to the buyer who assumes the loan. It must be remembered that the federal government fixes the interest rates on VA loans, so that when the rate is lower than the market discount points will be charged to equalize the yield. Unlike FHA loans, discount points must be paid by the seller. VA loans vary considerably, reaching a high of 17.5 percent in 1981 and down to 8.5 percent in 1987.

The VA funding fee is one percent of the mortgage amount and may be paid by buyer or seller. It may also be added to the mortgage amount. If the veteran is disabled, the funding fee is waived. The veteran must occupy the home as his residence, as the VA loan cannot be used for income property (except in the case of a loan assumption).

With both FHA and VA loans, an escape clause is a mandatory part of the purchase agreement and is signed by both seller and buyer. If the lender does not appraise the property for the purchase price, the purchaser need not carry through with the purchase. If he agrees to buy the property, the difference between the purchase price and the appraisal will be renegotiated between the buyer and the seller.

Farmers Home Administration

The *Farmers Home Administration* (FmHA) was established in 1946 to make and insure loans to farmers for construction or repair of farm homes and farm buildings.

The FmHA is available for loans in towns and rural areas of up to 20,000 in population. In addition to the property location, borrowers must demonstrate limited income record and a need for housing. The loans are reviewed periodically and payments are increased as the borrower's income rises.

Private Mortgage Insurance

A great boost to the housing industry in the early 1960s, the *Mortgage Guarantee Insurance Corporation (MGIC)* of Milwaukee, Wisconsin introduced a mortgage that allowed borrowers to obtain homes with a minimal down payment. New houses not built under FHA and VA requirements could now be purchased with a minimum 10 percent down payment. Discount points were charged, but could be paid by either the buyer or the seller. A one-half of one percent insurance premium is paid by the borrower for the first year, and one-quarter of one percent from then on, on the mortgage amount. Other private mortgage insurance followed and in 1971 they were approved by the Federal Home Loan Bank. PMI accounts for a large percentage of loans, requiring only 5%-10% as a down payment.

PMI insurance

Similar to FHA, the PMI insures its lenders but only for the top 20 or 25 percent of the loan. After the loan is paid down to the insured amount, the insurance premium can be eliminated.

Conventional Loans

The lender of a **conventional loan** is not government insured, nor is the loan guaranteed by the federal government. The lending institution sets its own requirements and policies. If a borrower requests a shorter-term loan with a larger down payment, the lender may decrease the interest rate, depending on the availability of funds. Conventional loans require a minimum of 20 percent down.

Private Loans

Private loans are often used when the credit of the borrower is not extrememly good. Usually a private loan has a higher interest rate since there is a greater risk involved. A buyer may not have sufficient down payment or income to qualify for a loan so that a private lender is needed. With the rise of home mortgage interest rates, the position of lender has become attractive to individuals with the capital.

Land Contracts

Variously referred to as **land contracts**, land sales contracts, installment sales contracts, or contracts for deed, these financing arrangements are contracts to buy wherein the seller finances the purchaser. In this type of contract, the seller takes the role of lender. Historically, land contracts are used in the sale of vacant land since lenders do not categorize bare land as property that is eligible for loans. Land contracts are also used if the property is not readily salable and would not qualify for a long-term loan, if the purchaser has insufficient funds for a minimum down payment or an unstable income, or if the seller does not want all the equity immediately but prefers to receive a regular monthly income from the land contract. In the tight-money period of the late 1970s and the early 1980s, land contracts were often the only means of obtaining financing.

Vendor retains title

In a land contract sale, the vendor (seller) retains legal title to the real property with the vendee (buyer) receiving the equitable title. While the vendee does not become the owner of record, he has the right to use, possess, and transfer the

Vendee receives equitable interest

property. Customarily, the purchaser pays the insurance and maintenance expenses. Upon fulfillment of the terms of the contract, the deed is delivered to the vendee. If the vendee fails to live up to the terms of the contract, the vendor may terminate the contract and recapture the property. Many purchasers are concerned about the risks involved in land contracts since title is retained by the seller. However, the seller would have to go through the normal foreclosure procedures of his or her particular state if the vendee defaulted. The greatest potential risk of a land contract would be claims brought against the vendor during the term of the contract that could prohibit the vendee from obtaining clear title.

Qualifying the Buyer

Some of the factors underwriters consider when qualifying the borrower include:

1. credit report
2. job stability and ability to meet future debt retirement
3. cash equity invested
4. bonus (Must be verified.)
5. second job (These are usually short term so lenders are strict.)
6. child support payments (Lender takes into account that it may not be received.)
7. overtime pay (It must be consistent and substantiated.)
8. bankruptcy (Lenders consider if action was made to repay creditors, if 2 or 3 years have passed, and if applicant has a good credit history since the bankruptcy. They also consider if there was a valid reason for bankruptcy.)
9. installment debts (Usually a factor if for 10 or more months; credit cards carefully scrutinized.)
10. total debt ratio (Should not exceed 41 percent for VA loans.)

THE SECONDARY MORTGAGE MARKET

The **secondary mortgage market** refers to the resale of mortgages by the primary lender. The choice of resale affords lenders an opportunity to dispose of their inventory enabling them to obtain new funds and make new mortgages. The original lender continues to service the loan and receives a fee for this service.

FNMA

The **Federal National Mortgage Association (FNMA),** dubbed Fannie Mae, was created by the government to stimulate the housing market. Originally chartered in 1938 as a government agency, it was primed with ten million dollars. FNMA purchased loans from commercial banks providing the banks with new funds to lend. Revised as a federal agency in 1954, FNMA was acquired from the department of HUD by the private sector in 1968 and is now owned by stockholders and the stock is traded on the New York stock exchange. It is called a quasi-government enterprise because the board of directors must get government approval before issuing bonds and making other financial decisions. Fulfilling its role as a "warehouse" for loans, FNMA buys, sells, and services loans. Fannie Mae is now the mortgage industry leader in defining standards in underwriting loans and appraising property for one- to four-family dwellings.

GNMA

Government National Mortgage Association (GNMA), called Ginny Mae, was established in 1968 and is operated by the Department of Housing and Urban Development (HUD). Ginny Mae receives the funds to purchase loans from the sale of long term bonds on Wall Street. These bonds are often purchased by insurance companies, pension and trust funds, and mutual fund/money market funds. Ginny Mae's purpose is to provide housing and to stabilize mortgage money. The GNMA provides reduced interest rates to lower-income home purchasers.

FHLMC

The **Federal Home Loan Mortgage Corporation (FREDDIE MAC)** is under the control of the Federal Home Loan Bank Board. It was created to buy loans from savings and loan associations, much the same way FNMA initially bought loans from commerical banks.

MBS

The secondary mortgage market affects everyone involved in real estate financing—builder, seller, borrower, lender, agent, broker, and investor—particularly in residential transactions.

Figure 8.3 explains where the money for home mortgages comes from and why we now have to pay discount points to obtain the funds for our mortgages.

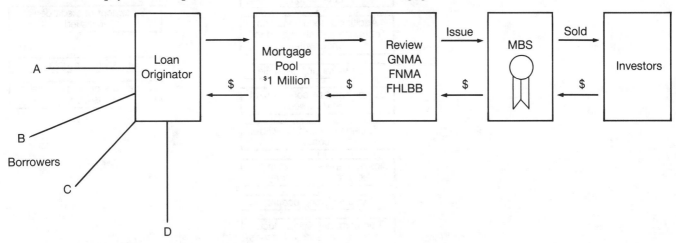

FIGURE 8.3 Secondary mortgage market.

The loan originator is the institution that takes the loan application and gets the loan approved and closed. It can be a bank, savings and loan, mortgage broker, or mortgage banker. After the loans are closed, they are placed in a mortgage pool with an aggregate amount of one million or more. All the loans in the mortgage pool must be homogeneous; that is, they must have the same rate and the same term.

The mortgage pools are then reviewed for compliance with applicable regulations and are then approved by Fannie Mae, Ginny Mae, or Freddie Mac. A *mortgage backed security (MBS)* is then issued and auctioned to investors such as insurance companies, pension and trust funds or money market funds. The proceeds from the sale, after commissions and discount points are subtracted, are then sent to the originator to be lent out again for new mortgages. The average life of a MBS is 12 years; by then most of the loans have been paid off when the property was sold, or refinanced.

FLOW OF ORIGINATION

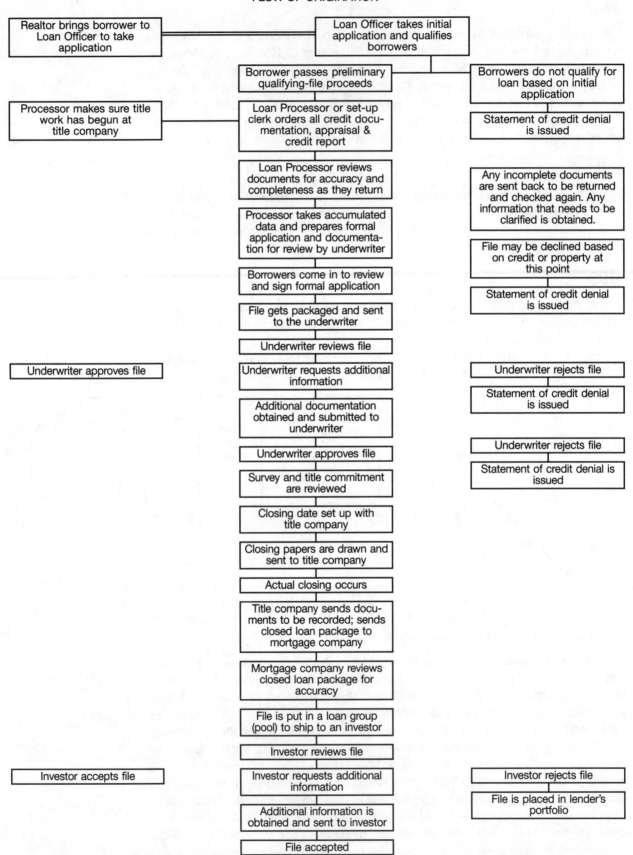

FIGURE 8.4 The cycle of a loan, from application to sale of the loan to the secondary market.

The lower the interest rate of the MBS, relative to the current money market, the higher the discount. For example; if a MBS containing 30 year mortgages with an average rate of 9 percent is being auctioned when the current market rate (as determined by long term treasury bills and bonds) is 10 percent, then investors will only pay 94 cents on the dollar because they could buy T-bills with no risk for 10 percent. This discount of 6 cents on the dollar or 6 points is collected from the borrower or the seller at closing.

As much as 3 months may elapse between the time the borrower signs the note at closing and the time the MBS is sold on the secondary market. Mortgage bankers and brokers often play the market, betting that they can sell the mortgage 3 months later at a profit. This is a high risk game and millions of dollars are at stake. It is akin to playing Russian Roulette with 3 bullets in the chamber.

SUMMARY

The backbone of the housing industry, the savings and loan institutions, have historically provided the bulk of the funds for one to four family homes. Dating back to the original "building club" of the early nineteenth century, the idea of saving money in savings and loan institutions has spread tremendously. Today the borrower does not need to be a depositor in a savings and loan to obtain a loan. Mortgage bankers have taken their place as a large supplier of home loans.

Because of inflation, great changes within the savings and loan industry have occurred. Some of the more important factors to be remembered include:

1. Savings and loans institutions hold portfolios of thirty year loans that average out at interest rates much below the current rates.

2. The interest the savings and loan pay depositors must be great enough to lure savers to continue to deposit their funds. The interest paid on passbook savings is no longer federally regulated, but higher interest can be given on certificates of deposit, which are issued for three, six or twelve months or several years. The competition for these funds comes from money market funds that pay high interest rates and allow the savers to withdraw the money at any time. Money market rates fluctuate with the daily market. Also in competition for individual savings is the federal government with its treasury bills and private industry which also goes to Wall Street for funds.

Mortgage brokers help join lenders and borrowers, but do not service the loans. Government regulations on lending are outlined by Regulation Z and the Real Estate Settlement Procedures Act. The government is also active in insuring loans through the FHA and VA programs. Conventional loans, private loans, and land contracts may also be obtained to finance mortgages.

The secondary mortgage market involves the resale of mortgages. The FNMA, GNMA, and FHLMC all serve to provide a stable market for mortgages.

As a result of the dilemma of the savings and loan industry in the late 1970s and early 1980s, they found that traditional thirty-year mortgages were not sound financing instruments in inflationary times and switched to adjustable rate mortgages in lieu of fixed rates. A move to shorter term loans has been seen, with the 15 year mortgage becoming increasingly popular due to the interest saved when compared with 30 year loans. Chapter 9 will further explain the changes that have taken place in the mortgage market.

KEY WORDS AND CONCEPTS

Conventional loans: Not guaranteed or insured; the lender generally requires a larger down payment.

Fannie Mae (FNMA): Federal National Mortgage Association; purchases loans from qualified lenders.

Disintermediation: Funds are shifted to higher yielding markets.

Federal Housing Administration (FHA): Insures loans made by qualified lending institutions.

Freddie Mac (FHLMC): Federal Home Loan Mortgage Corporation; acts as a secondary market for loans of member banks.

Ginny Mae (GNMA): Government National Mortgage Association; provides housing by giving reduced interest rates to lower-income purchasers

Land contract: Seller finances purchaser and retains title; purchaser obtains equitable title.

Mortgage banker: Lends money and subsequently sells the loan to long-term investor and retains servicing the loan.

Mortgage broker: Brings together the lender and borrower, does not service the loan.

PITI: Principal, interest, taxes, and insurance; one monthly payment is made on an amortized loan.

Private mortgage insurance (PMI): Insurance on conventional loans that have less than 20 percent down payment.

Secondary mortgage market: Resale of existing mortgages by the primary lender.

VA loans: Available for veterans who qualify under the law; guaranteed by Veterans Administration.

REVIEW QUESTIONS

1. Money for FHA financing is provided by
   a. any governmental agency
   b. FDIC
   c. any qualified lending institution
   d. the Federal Housing Administration

2. The Federal Housing Administration is actively engaged in
   a. planning houses
   b. building houses
   c. purchasing land
   d. none of the above

3. In order to make financing for homes available, the best source of secondary mortgage money is
   a. the seller taking a second mortgage
   b. the Federal National Mortgage Association
   c. insurance companies
   d. the Federal Housing Administration

4. The following are true regarding a federally chartered savings and loan:
   a. It must be a member of the Federal Home Loan Bank System.
   b. It need not be federally insured.
   c. Deposits are insured up to $100,000.
   d. Both a and c are true.

5. In securing a residential loan
   a. a down payment is made when obtaining a FHA loan.
   b. no down payment is made on a VA loan unless the selling price of the home is greater than the appraised value.
   c. Both a and b are true.
   d. Neither a nor b are true.

6. The following facts are true concerning VA loans:
   a. a VA loan on a four-plex cannot exceed fifteen years.
   b. a buyer must pay the difference between the amount the VA appraises the home for and the purchase price.
   c. a VA loan can be assumed by a nonveteran.
   d. all of the above

7. The mortgagor who has a VA loan on his or her property
   a. can sell the property and allow the loan to be assumed by a person who is not a veteran.
   b. can transfer the loan to a new home he or she is purchasing.
   c. both of the above
   d. neither of the above

8. In securing a loan on a home
   a. through VA, the buyer must occupy the home as a residence.
   b. through FHA, the buyer must occupy the home as a residence.
   c. both of the above
   d. neither of the above

9. The largest source of money for home mortgages on single-family housing is
   a. savings and loan institutions
   b. banks
   c. insurance companies
   d. the secondary market

10. The maximum amount guaranteed by the government on any VA loan is
    a. the same as on an FHA loan
    b. $27,500
    c. 50 percent of the purchase price
    d. $60,000

11. The Veterans Administration
    a. insures loans
    b. guarantees loans
    c. sells loans
    d. both a and b

12. The private corporation that buys federally insured or guaranteed mortgages for resale is
    a. FNMA
    b. GNMA
    c. MGIC
    d. FDIC

13. When a purchaser of real estate assumes the seller's existing loan
    a. he buys out the lender's equity.
    b. he becomes responsible for the repayment of the debt along with the original borrower.
    c. the original borrower is relieved of responsibility for repayment of the debt.
    d. none of the above

14. Conventional loans are
    a. never insured
    b. insured by FHA
    c. not insured by the federal government
    d. guaranteed

15. If the original owner was released when his loan was assumed, this substitution of liability is known as
    a. novation
    b. satisfaction
    c. release
    d. reversion

16. In an FHA loan, discount points are paid by
    a. the buyer
    b. the seller
    c. buyer and seller
    d. buyer or seller

17. The following would be true of a VA loan:
    a. The buyers may pay more than the appraised value.
    b. If the buyer fails to receive VA financing, his deposit must be returned.
    c. both of the above
    d. neither of the above

18. A young couple wants to buy a home. Their income is low, but will increase greatly in the next few years. They will apply for
    a. an FHA 203
    b. a conventional insured loan
    c. an FHA 245
    d. FNMA

Financing

9

One of the most important cogs in any real estate transaction is the financing. Since the purchase of a home is the largest investment the average person enters into, almost everyone needs to finance at least a portion of the purchase price. Without adequate financing the sale can be lost.

When interest rates for real estate mortgages escalated to all-time highs in the late 1970s and early 1980s it caused financiers to develop many new creative financing techniques. The traditional financing practices gave way to innovative methods. Many of these practices remain with us today even though interest rates are lower.

This chapter explains interest rates, the various clauses found in notes and mortgages, and the different types of mortgages.

INTEREST RATES

Interest is rent for the use of money. The interest rate depends upon many complex economic factors, including

Renting money

1. The risk involved in making the loan;
2. The business outlook for the future; and
3. The market rate for alternate investments such as Treasury Bonds: if there are fewer buyers for bonds then the points and rates must increase. This is a simple application of the law of supply and demand.

Since investors are in business to make a profit, they require a certain rate of return on their investments. Under the free market system in the United States, the market rates of interest are not set by the government, but by auction process. The only rates set by law are the interest rates on VA loans.

Amortization

The most common means of repaying a mortgage is by making equal payments that gradually reduce the balance of the loan within a stated period of time. The equal payment includes a portion for interest and a portion for principal, which reduces the unpaid balance. Basically, **amortization** is the liquidation of a financial obligation on the installment basis. For example, on a $60,000 loan at 12 percent interest for 30 years, the interest and principal payment would be $617.40 monthly. After the first payment, the balance due would be figured as follows:

$60,000 *loan amount*
× .12 *interest rate*
$7,200 *yearly interest*

Equal payments over loan period

$600 *monthly interest* = $7,200 *for 12 months*

$617.40 *principal and interest payment*
600.00 *first month's interest*
$ 17.40 *towards principal*

$60,000.00
− 17.40
$59,982.60 *balance due after first payment*

As this example shows, the debt is reduced by $17.40 the first month. Since the borrower pays each month on the unpaid balance due, a larger amount is attributed to the principal reduction each month. Some lending institutions require that monthly mortgage payments not only include the principal and interest (known as P and I) payment, but one-twelfth of the yearly taxes and insurance also. This *Impounding funds* amount is kept in an *escrow* or reserve account from which the lender pays the taxes and insurance as they become due. The lender is then assured protection on his investment, for if the dwelling burns down it is covered by insurance. Similarly, the taxes are paid so there will be no tax foreclosure sale.

The following equation demonstrates the calculation of a PITI (Principal, Interest, Taxes, and Insurance) payment. To the $617.40 payment on a $60,000 loan at 12 percent interest, add one-twelfth of the $2,200 yearly tax and one-twelfth of the $360 yearly insurance premium.

$617.40 *P&I*
183.33 *Taxes*
30.00 *Insurance*
$830.73 *Total PITI monthly payment*

A departure from the traditional 30 year mortgage is the 15 or 20 year fixed rate loan. One advantage is that it is available at a lower interest rate and with reduced discount points. The following illustrate the difference in interest paid on 15, 20, and 30 year mortgages.

A. $50,000 loan for 30 years at 10% interest
$439.00 P&I × 360 payments = $158,040.00
158,040 − $50,000 loan = $108,040 interest paid

B. $50,000 loan for 20 years at 10% interest
$483.00 × 240 payments − $115,920.00
$115,920 − $50,000 loan = $65,920 interest paid

C. $50,000 loan for 15 years at 10% interest
$537.50 × 180 payments = $96,750.00
$96,750 − $50,000 loan = $46,750 interest paid

Equal Monthly Payments to Amortize a Loan of $1000

Years	8.00%	8.50%	9.00%	9.50%	10.00%	10.50%	11.00%	11.50%	12.00%
1	86.99	87.22	87.46	87.69	87.92	88.15	88.39	88.62	88.85
2	45.23	45.46	45.69	45.92	46.15	46.38	46.61	46.85	47.08
3	31.34	31.57	31.80	32.04	32.27	32.51	32.74	32.98	33.22
4	24.42	24.65	24.89	25.13	25.37	25.61	25.85	26.09	26.34
5	20.28	20.52	20.76	21.01	21.25	21.50	21.75	22.00	22.25
6	17.54	17.78	18.03	18.28	18.53	18.78	19.04	19.30	19.56
7	15.59	15.84	16.09	16.35	16.61	16.87	17.13	17.39	17.66
8	14.14	14.40	14.66	14.92	15.18	15.45	15.71	15.98	16.26
9	13.02	13.28	13.55	13.81	14.08	14.36	14.63	14.91	15.19
10	12.14	12.40	12.67	12.94	13.22	13.50	13.78	14.06	14.35
11	11.42	11.69	11.97	12.24	12.52	12.81	13.10	13.39	13.68
12	10.83	11.11	11.39	11.67	11.96	12.25	12.54	12.84	13.14
13	10.34	10.62	10.90	11.19	11.48	11.78	12.08	12.38	12.69
14	9.92	10.20	10.49	10.79	11.09	11.39	11.70	12.01	12.32
15	9.56	9.85	10.15	10.45	10.75	11.06	11.37	11.69	12.01
16	9.25	9.55	9.85	10.15	10.46	10.78	11.10	11.42	11.74
17	8.99	9.29	9.59	9.90	10.22	10.54	10.86	11.19	11.52
18	8.75	9.06	9.37	9.68	10.00	10.33	10.66	10.99	11.32
19	8.55	8.86	9.17	9.49	9.82	10.15	10.48	10.82	11.16
20	8.37	8.68	9.00	9.33	9.66	9.99	10.33	10.67	11.02
21	8.21	8.53	8.85	9.18	9.51	9.85	10.19	10.54	10.89
22	8.07	8.39	8.72	9.05	9.39	9.73	10.08	10.43	10.78
23	7.94	8.27	8.60	8.93	9.28	9.62	9.98	10.33	10.69
24	7.83	8.16	8.49	8.83	9.18	9.53	9.89	10.25	10.61
25	7.72	8.06	8.40	8.74	9.09	9.45	9.81	10.17	10.54
26	7.63	7.97	8.31	8.66	9.01	9.37	9.74	10.10	10.47
27	7.55	7.89	8.24	8.59	8.95	9.31	9.67	10.05	10.42
28	7.47	7.82	8.17	8.52	8.88	9.25	9.62	9.99	10.37
29	7.40	7.75	8.11	8.47	8.83	9.20	9.57	9.95	10.33
30	7.34	7.69	8.05	8.41	8.78	9.15	9.52	9.91	10.29

FIGURE 9.1
Amortization chart.

Equity

The equity an owner has in property represents the difference between the value and the mortgage. A $60,000 property with a $50,000 mortgage represents a $10,000 equity for the owner. As the principal is paid off through the monthly amortized payments, the equity increases. In the early years of the mortgage, the equity build-up is gradual. Since the payments are on the unpaid balance this equity increases as the loan is paid off.

Usury

If interest is charged or accepted by a money lender in excess of the amount allowed by law, it is considered *usury* and is illegal. Usury laws are not federal laws, but are set by state statutes. With the unprecedented rise of interest rates during the early 1980s many states placed a moratorium on their usury laws since many were originally lower than the national market for mortgage money. During the first three months of 1980, Congress placed a suspension order on all state usury laws. Designed to protect the borrower from paying excessive interest rates, the usury laws may indeed be a symbol of the past.

Illegal interest

Discount Points

Discount points are charged by money lenders to increase the yield on the money lent to the borrower. Originally, discount amounts were based on the quality of the property, market conditions, and the ability of the purchaser to borrow and repay. Today the amount is determined by market conditions.

Percentage charges made on new loans

If yields on mortgage loans are lower than other investments, funds will be drawn away from the home mortgage market and money for home mortgages will become scarce and more expensive. The fixed rate mortgage lender has to determine the cost of doing business and allow for a reasonable profit to arrive at the yield needed to make the sale of a mortgage at a given discount economically sound.

One discount point is equal to one percent of the loan amount. Thus, if a lender charges two discount points on a $30,000 loan he will be receiving 2 percent of $30,000 or $600. This is received at the time the loan originates. While most loans are paid off before the thirty-year maturity, a general rule is that each discount point lowers the note rate by one-eighth of one percent. So the two discount points in the example would lower the interest rate by one-fourth of one percent. As the interest rate increases, the discount points are lower until you reach the market or "par" rate at which no points are charged.

Do not confuse discount points with the origination fee. The origination fee is paid by the borrower to the lender for the originating and processing of the new loan and is generally an additional one percent of the loan.

Loan-to-Value Ratio (LTV)

Percentage loaned by lenders

The lender makes a loan on the property for a proportionate value of the real estate. If the property appraises for $40,000 and the purchaser is putting 20 percent down, the loan-to-value ratio will be 80 percent of the $40,000 or $32,000. Needless to say, the greater the loan-to-value ratio is, the greater the risk involved for the lending institution since the down payment represents the borrower's equity. Mortgages are made as high as 95 percent LTV; however, the borrower must have excellent credit to qualify.

THE MORTGAGE

A mortgage is an instrument which pledges the property as collateral for a debt. There are two parties to the mortgage, the mortgagee and the mortgagor. The *mortgagee* is the person or lender to whom the mortgage has been given as security (the creditor). He can assign his interest to another.

Security pledged on a note

The *mortgagor* is the owner (debtor) of the property put up as security. He has all the rights of ownership, but must live up to the terms of the mortgage. The mortgage is usually determined by terms of payment and satisfaction: in real estate financing, the borrower signs a *note* in which he promises to pay a certain amount of money at a certain rate. He also gives the creditor a mortgage that pledges the property as security for the loan. This pledge gives the lender security while permitting the mortgagor use of the property. If the borrower does not make the payments as agreed, it gives the creditor the right to seize and sell the property through foreclosure to satisfy the debt. Thus, the mortgagor is not paying on a mortgage but on a note! A mortgage note is a negotiable instrument and as such can be bought or sold.

The mortgage contains certain covenants that the mortgagor makes to the mortgagee, as shown in figure 9.2:

• *Section 1* sets forth the owners' names, the amount of the loan, the lender's name, and the street address and legal description of the property.
• In *Section 2*, the mortgagors affirm that they have title to the property.

MORTGAGE

KNOW ALL MEN BY THESE PRESENTS: That Kurt K. Kindly and Susan A. Kindly, husband and wife   (hereinafter called the Mortgagors) in consideration of the sum of

1   Sixty-seven thousand two hundred and no/100------- Dollars ($ 67,200.00) loaned to Mortgagors, do hereby grant, bargain, sell and convey unto READY SAVINGS AND LOAN ASSOCIATION of Big Red, Nebraska, (hereinafter called "Ready"), its successors and assigns, the following described real estate, situated in the County of, Kent, State of Nebraska, to-wit:

Lot Eight (8) Block One (1) Confusion Hill Subdivision

2   Said Mortgagors hereby covenant with said Ready, its successors and assigns, that Mortgagors are lawfully seized of said premises, that they are free from encumbrances, and that they will forever warrant and defend the title to said premises against the lawful claims of all persons whomsoever.

Provided, nevertheless, these presents are upon the following conditions:

That whereas this mortgage shall secure any additional advances, with interest, which may, at the option of Ready, be made by Ready to the under-signed Mortgagors or their successors in title for any purpose, at any time before the release and cancellation of this mortgage, but PROVIDED, HOWEVER, at no

3   time shall the aggregate principal amount secured by this mortgage, being the amount due at any time on said original note and any additional advances made, exceed an amount equal to 110 percent of the amount of the original note, but in no event shall said note exceed the maximum amount permitted by law.

If the said Mortgagors shall pay or cause to be paid the said sums of money

4   when due, as set forth in said note, then this mortgage shall be null and void; otherwise, to be and remain in full force and effect;

(a) If default should be made: in any of the payments due on said note, and any other note for additional advances made, as therein agreed to be made for three months, or

(b) In keeping the improvements on said premises insured against loss by reason of fire, lightning, and other hazards included in extended coverage insur-ance in an amount not less than the unpaid balance of said mortgage loan, in a company or companies acceptable to Ready Savings & Loan, the original of such policy or policies to be held by Ready Savings & Loan, and with a mortgage clause attached to said policy or policies, in favor of Ready; or

(c) In the payment of taxes and assessments levied upon said premises, or on this mortgage, before they are delinquent; or

(d) If there is any change in the ownership of the real estate mortgaged herein, by sale, either outright or by land contract, or by assignment of any interest there-on or otherwise;

then, in any of the above set-forth events, the whole indebtedness hereby secured shall, at the option of Ready Savings & Loan, immediately become due and payable without further notice.   The amount due under said note and any other note for ad-ditional advances made shall, from the date of the exercise of said option, bear interest at the maximum legal rate per annum, and this mortgage may then be fore-closed to satisfy the amount due on said note, and any other note for additional

5   advances, together with all sums paid by Ready Savings & Loan for insurance, taxes, assessments and abstract extension charges, with interest there on from the date of payment at the maximum legal rate.

PROVIDED, further, that in the event that default occurs, Ready shall be en-titled to the immediate possession of the premises above described, together with all rents, proceeds and issues arising out of the premises, and may in its discre-tion use the rents so far as it deems necessary for the purpose of making repairs upon the premises and for payment of insurance premiums, taxes and assessments upon such premises, and for necessary expenses incurred in renting said premises and collecting rent therefrom, and to apply same on said note and any notes evi-

6   dencing future advances hereunder until the indebtedness secured is fully paid; and for such purposes, the undersigned does hereby sell, assign, set over and trans-fer unto Ready all of said rents, proceeds and incomes including any land contract payments due mortgage owners or any other incomes of any type whatsoever from said property to be applied on the notes above-described, but said Ready shall in

FIGURE 9.2 A mortgage instrument.

no case be liable for the failure to procure tenants, to collect rents, or to prosecute actions to recover possession of said premises.

The Mortgagors hereby agree that if Ready either voluntarily or involuntarily becomes or is made a party any suit or proceeding relating to the hereinbefore described real estate, or to this mortgage or said note or notes, other than a foreclosure instituted by Ready, Mortgagors will reimburse Ready for all reasonable costs incurred in said suit or proceeding. The Mortgagors further agree that if the hereinbefore described real estate or any part thereof be condemned under the power of eminent domain, or is otherwise acquired for a public use, the damages awarded, the proceeds for the taking, and for the consideration for such acquisition to the extent of the full amount of the remaining unpaid indebtedness secured by this mortgage, be, and they hereby are, assigned to Ready and shall be paid forthwith to Ready to be applied on account of the last maturing installments of such indebtedness.

Dated this ____15th____ day of ____May____, 19 _87_.

IN THE PRESENCE OF:

7

Ruth A. Masterson   _Kurt K Kindly_
Name

8   _Susan R Kindly_

FIGURE 9.2, continued

- *Section 3* explains that the mortgage is an open-end mortgage and that Ready Savings and Loan will loan, at its option, additional money not to exceed 110 percent of the original note. (A section on open-end mortgages appears later in this chapter.)

- *Section 4* is the defeasance clause which states that the mortgage is defeated when the debt is paid in full; That is, when the mortgagors have abided by the terms of the mortgage and the debt has been paid, the rights that the mortgagee held to take the property if the terms were not met have been defeated. However, if the mortgagors do not repay the debt as scheduled in the mortgage, they lose the property to the lender, and their opportunity to defeat the clause is lost. The section further states that the mortgagors must (a) make payments as they are due, or the lender can call the mortgage due and payable. The mortgagors also covenant that (b) they will keep insurance on the property for not less than the loan amount, with the lender conamed as beneficiary. Finally, they agree that (c) the taxes must be kept current and (d) if the property is sold, the note is due and payable.

Note due upon sale

- *Section 5* reconfirms that the mortgage will be foreclosed upon if any of the items under section 4 are violated. Known as the *alienation clause*, it allows the lender to call the balance due and payable upon the sale of the property. It is commonly referred to as the *due-on-sale* clause. This protects the lender in the event that interest rates have risen since the loan was originally placed. If the purchaser desires to assume the existing mortgage, the lender can raise the interest rate. Some states passed into law mandatory compulsion on the part of the lender to permit conventional loan assumptions. However, in July 1982 the federal Supreme Court ruled that federally chartered savings and loan associations can enforce the due-on-sale clause, thus superseding the state law.

The news media related the ensuing pandemonium that took place in the states where sales were being consummated on the basis of the state's law. At this writing, the only loans that are assumable without exception are FHA and VA loans.

"Call" clause

- *Section 6* says that if the owner does default in payment, the lender can immediately take possession of the premises. This clause, called the *acceleration* clause, is recited in deeds of trust, mortgages, and land contracts. It permits the lender or creditor to declare the entire sum due and payable upon certain default by the debtor. The legality of the *call clause*, as it is commonly known, has been upheld for loans issued by federally chartered savings and loans.

This section also provides the lender protection in the event that the mortgagor rents the property and fails to make the mortgage payment. Referred to as an *assignment of rents* clause, this provision states that the mortgagee can notify the tenants that the mortgage is in default and future rents shall be paid to the mortgagee. The lender in this case is called the *mortgagee in possession.*

• *Section 7* helps protect the lender's rights by stating that if the mortgagor is involved in a lawsuit and it results in expenses to the lender, the mortgagor will pay all costs. This section further states that the mortgagee will be first in line for payment if the property should be taken by the government. (The right of the government to take property by condemnation is called the right of eminent domain.)

• *Section 8* includes the date and the witness and mortgagor signatures.

OTHER MORTGAGE CLAUSES AND CONDITIONS

The Subordination Clause

The *subordination* clause states that the rights of the mortgage holder shall be secondary to subsequent encumbrances. This agreement provides that the mortgage lien will be second in priority to any specific existing lien or future liens. Since the risk involved to the lender is greater, interest rates on such mortgages are usually higher. For example, imagine that a purchaser of an $80,000 parcel of land puts down $50,000 and requests the seller to take a first mortgage of $30,000 with a subordination clause. The buyer needs a $250,000 mortgage to erect an office building. The lender of the $250,000 insists on being first in priority, even though this mortgage is technically a second mortgage. Thus, the subordination clause in the first mortgage clears the path for the buyer to obtain the $250,000 mortgage.

Interests of holder are secondary

The Prepayment Penalty Clause

The prepayment penalty clause permits the mortgagee to charge a penalty to the borrower if the loan is paid off prior to its maturity. The prepayment penalty protects the mortgagee in the event that interest rates decrease; the borrower will not refinance at a lower rate if he must pay a penalty to do so.

The Assumption Clause

If a loan is assumed by a new owner, the *assumption clause* in the deed says that the buyer is obligating him- or herself to pay off the loan. This transfers the responsibility onto the buyer. In case of default, the lender will expect the new owner to fulfill his or her promise. If he or she fails to do so, the original owner will still be liable since his or her name is on the promissory note. However, if the seller obtains a release of liability from the lender, the seller's obligation ends when the title is transferred. If the clause in the deed states that the buyer is purchasing the property "subject to the existing loan," the buyer acknowledges the existing loan but is not personally responsible for it.

Buyer assumes existing mortgage

THE NOTE

The Promissory Note

The promissory note (see figure 9.3) has no prepayment penalty. If the mortgagor pays the note off before its due date, he is not charged any fee for prepaying the amount borrowed. This is important to the borrower since the average person changes residence every seven years due to employment transfers, changes in family size, or other personal reasons. The following descriptions match the corresponding letters on figure 9.3:

Elements of a note

a. Shows the amount of the sum borrowed, along with terms for payment.

b. Allows the lender to charge one-twelfth of the yearly taxes and insurance along with the principal and interest payment. Referred to as an *escrow*, this assures the lender that the property will not go into tax foreclosure and that it will be kept insured.

c. Provides for a late charge penalty.

d. Provides that if the borrower does not keep his promise to pay, this acceleration will allow the lender to demand immediate payment on the unpaid balance.

e. Provides that if the borrower defaults in his payment, the lender's costs of collecting will be borne by the borrower.

f. States that the borrower has the option to prepay the note.

g. Provides for all the signers (also known as makers) of the note to be jointly responsible for repayment.

h. States that the note is secured by mortgage.

Deed of Trust

Holding the deed of trust

A *deed of trust* is a conditional deed to secure money for the payment of a debt. There are three parties to the instrument. The borrower transfers the property to a trustee, who holds it for the benefit of the lender. Remember, the purpose of a trust deed is to borrow money. Widely used in most parts of the country, a trust deed is considerably easier to foreclose on than a mortgage. In a deed of trust the trustee has the power of sale in the event the trustor (borrower) defaults. This shortens the time of foreclosure because a public trustee is authorized by law to hold foreclosure sales when a default execution releases the trust deed. If the trustee is not an authorized public trustee, the law states the foreclosure must proceed through the courts in the same manner as a routine mortgage foreclosure. See *deed of trust* in appendix, pages 307-310.

There are three parties to a deed of trust:

1. The *trustor*: the owner or borrower

2. The *trustee*: a public trustee; the disinterested third party

3. The *beneficiary*: the lender

NO PREPAYMENT PENALTY

M O R T G A G E   N O T E

PRINCIPAL NOTE
(Nebraska)

Big Red   , **Nebraska**

Date May 15, 1987

FOR VALUE RECEIVED, the undersigned ("Borrower") promise(s) to pay to the order of

Ready Savings & Loan, 8250 Alert Dr., Big Red, NE   ("Lender"), the principal sum of sixty-seven thousand two hundred and no/100 ----------------Dollars (67,200) with interest on the unpaid principal balance from the date of this Note, until paid, at the rate of ten percent

(10 %) percent per annum. Principal and interest shall be payable at READY SAVINGS AND LOAN, 8250 Alert Drive, Big Red, Nebraska 68222,   or such other place as the Note holder may designate, in consecutive monthly installments of five hundred ninety and

a   02/100-----Dollars (US $ 590.02), on the first day of each month beginning July 1 , 1987. Such monthly installments shall continue until the entire indebtedness evidenced by this Note is fully paid, except that any remaining indebtedness, if not sooner paid, shall be due and payable on July 1, 2017 . In the event the first installment due date is sixty (60) days after date of this note, interest on the unpaid balance shall be paid as accrued on the first of each month.

b   In addition to the payment of principal and interest, the Borrower also agrees to pay monthly installments sufficient to anticipate the payment of taxes, insurance premiums and similar items which shall accrue against or in connection with the mortgaged real estate, and agree to pay such items to said Lender and agree that such payment may be held by the Lender and commingled with other funds and the Lender's own funds and the Lender may pay such items from its own funds, and the Lender shall not be liable for interest or dividends on such funds.

c   The Borrower shall pay to the Note holder hereof a late charge of 5 percent of any monthly installment of principal and interest not received within 15 days after the installment is due.

d   If any monthly installment under this Note is not paid when due and remains unpaid after a date specified by a notice to Borrower, the entire principal amount outstanding and accrued interest thereon is then in default and shall at once become due and payable at the option of the Note holder. The date specified shall not be less than thirty days from the date such notice is mailed. The Note holder may exercise this option to accelerate during any default by Borrower regardless of any prior forbearance.

e   This Note shall bear interest after default at the rate of eleven (11) percent per annum until paid, whether the same becomes due by the exercise of the option provided for herein, or by the lapse of time according to its terms. Should suit be commenced to collect this Note, or to foreclose the mortgage securing the same, a reasonable attorney's fee shall be allowed and shall become a part of the judgment or decree rendered.

f   Borrower may prepay the principal amount outstanding in whole or in part. The Note holder may require that any partial prepayments (i) be made on the date monthly installments are due and (ii) be in the amount of that part of one or more monthly installments which would be applicable to principal. Any partial prepayment shall be applied against the principal amount outstanding and shall not postpone the due date of any subsequent monthly installments or change the amount of such installments, unless the Note holder shall otherwise agree in writing.

g   Presentment, notice of dishonor, and protest are hereby waived by all makers, sureties, guarantors and endorsers hereof. The Note shall be the joint and several obligation of all makers, sureties, guarantors and endorsers, and shall be binding upon them and their successors and assigns.

h   This Note is given for actual loan on the above amount, and is secured by a mortgage of even date herewith, which is a first lien on certain Real Estate described therein, in Kent County, Nebraska.

i **Property Address:** 1040 Clear St., Big Red, Nebraska

k *Ruth A Masterson*

j *Kurt K Kindly*
               Borrower

Susan A Kindly
               Borrower

FIGURE 9.3 A promissory note.

TYPES OF MORTGAGES
Open-End Mortgages

Rights to borrow additional money

An **open-end mortgage** allows the mortgagor to extend the amount of the loan. The loan company has the option of advancing additional money to the borrower at a later date. The borrower may not have taken the full amount he could have requested at the time the mortgage was initiated, or the loan may have been paid down enough for the borrower to borrow more. However, the terms of the mortgage can be changed by the lender if the borrower requests more money. For example, ten years ago a borrower obtained a $30,000 open-end mortgage on his new home. Inflation has since added $10,000 to the original value of the home; furthermore, the mortgage is now reduced to $26,000. The lending institution agrees to loan an additional $4,000 to the borrower for remodeling. The loan is back to $30,000 and the time period of the loan is extended.

Package Mortgages

The *package mortgage* is very often used in the financing of new homes since it expressly includes built-in appliances and any such equipment that may be offered for sale with a new home. This may include carpets, drapes and furniture. While a loan on a new house may not be specifically defined as a package mortgage to the borrower, in essence it is.

Blanket Mortgages

Covering several properties with a single mortgage

When more than one piece of property is under a single mortgage it is referred to as a **blanket mortgage**. Developers of subdivisions often use this type of mortgage and then obtain partial releases as they sell off individual lots. A partial release clause is included in the mortgage so specific lots can be released as they are purchased. The lender requires a specified amount to be paid on the mortgage before allowing the release of the lots.

A real estate agent may be approached by an individual who desires to purchase a new home but currently owns another home. If his equity is sufficient, a blanket mortgage could be placed on the two properties. When the first home is sold it would be released from the loan.

Open Mortgages

An *open mortgage* is an overdue mortgage that has not yet been foreclosed on. The mortgagee can request payment when this type of mortgage has reached its maturity and is due. The name is derived from the fact that the mortgage is open for payment.

Balloon Payment

Larger final payment

If a loan does not amortize out at the due date, the total unpaid sum is paid in a **balloon payment**; that is, the final payment is much larger than the regular monthly payment. In some situations the mortgagor may only make interest payments, with the full amount of the principal due at an agreed-upon time. Balloons are used when the lender does not want his money lent out for a long period of time.

The mortgage is generally a three-to-five-year fixed loan with an amortization schedule of fifteen to thirty years. The mortgage holder is under no obligation to refinance the loan. The borrower must find other means of financing when the balloon payment is due.

Purchase-Money Mortgages

In a *purchase-money mortgage* the seller takes back a mortgage as part of the purchase price in a transaction. In some cases the buyer may not have sufficient funds to purchase the property; by means of a purchase-money mortgage the transaction is consummated. It can be a wise investment for sellers if they do not need all the cash from the sale. The interest may be greater than the interest the money would earn in a bank. Purchase-money mortgages may be first or second liens.

Seller holds mortgage

Second Mortgages

A *second mortgage* pledges the owner's equity in the real estate with the property as collateral. It is second in priority to the first mortgage in case of default. Since it represents a greater risk to the lender, a higher rate of interest is required. Sometimes a seller of real estate will *carry back* a second mortgage to help finance the new owner. If a buyer has limited cash to invest in a home, he may assume the balance of the existing mortgage, make a down payment, and obtain a second mortgage for the money needed to make up the remainder of the purchase price. The actual interest rate is a combination of the old lower rate and the new second mortgage rate. The combined rate is generally lower than the current market on the total amount borrowed. Generally the combined loan-to-value ratio of both first and second mortgages should be less than 80 percent LTV.

Second in priority

Junior Mortgages

A *junior mortgage* is subordinate to any other mortgage; the holder agrees to subordinate his interest to any existing mortgage. The junior mortgage may be second, third, or even fourth in priority. In case of default by the borrower, the first mortgagee would collect on the debt before the junior or second mortgagee. If the first mortgage is paid off, then the second mortgage would become first in priority.

Construction Loan

Construction loans are used as interim financing; money is advanced in installments as progress on construction is made. Payouts are usually limited to 80 percent of the loan until final inspection is made. The borrower must own the lot before construction begins. This type of mortgage is advantageous to the borrower because he pays interest only on the amount advanced. The lender disburses principal only upon inspection and when the security has been improved. As a high-risk loan, a construction loan generally does not extend beyond three years.

Interim financing

Direct-Reduction Mortgages

Direct-reduction mortgages are synonymous with amortizing budget mortgages; they are straight mortgages as used in FHA, VA and conventional loans.

Term Mortgages

Not commonly used, *term mortgages* are for specified periods of time and demand full payment at the end of those periods. They are not amortized and are issued for only short periods of time, usually three to five years. Builders sometimes use term mortgages since there are no monthly payments and their money is not tied up. The borrower's credit must be extremely good to obtain this type of loan.

Wraparound Mortgages

Two mortgages on one property

The *wraparound mortgage* allows the buyer to purchase with a small down payment and the added benefit of a low interest rate first mortgage. The seller received all of his or her cash at the time of closing. The lender wraps new money around an existing assumable loan. If in the future the borrower has the cash available s/he could pay off the new money and resort back to the original, low-interest mortgage.

Wrap mortgages are used when interest rates are high, allowing the buyer to take advantage of the lower rate existing mortgage without having to come up with a large down payment as in the case of a loan assumption. The following example will clarify the use of the wrap mortgage.

Assume a sale price of	$80,000
FHA 1st mortgage of	50,000 8½%
Seller's equity	30,000

The buyer does not have $30,000 to invest; her savings are only $16,000. The seller refuses to carry back a second mortgage because he needs all his equity to purchase another home. The dilemma is solved by the lender who makes wrap loans. The buyer will obtain an 80 percent loan of $64,000:

$50,000	*at 8½% rate (existing 1st mgt.)*
14,000	*at 16% rate (current rate)*
64,000	*wrap mortgage*

The $64,000 will be paid back over the same time period as remain on the first mortgage. Assume the existing first mortgage is 5 years old, then the amortization of the wrap mortgage will be 25 years. The composite interest rate is determined from an interest table provided by the lender (see figure 9.4). The composite rate depends on the following variables: the rate of the existing mortgage and the percentage or amount of new money needed. In our example, the borrower is obtaining:

$$\frac{14,000 \ new \ money}{50,000 \ existing \ loan} = 28\% \ new \ money$$

Looking at figure 9.4, entering the chart with 28 percent (round up to 30%) new money on the left, over across the page to the 8½ percent column for the existing mortgage and the composite rate is 10.75 percent. This rate is higher than the existing first mortgage of 8½ percent, but far less than the present mortgage rate of 16 percent.

The buyer is pleased because she receives a less-than-market-rate loan that has only 25 years remaining instead of 30 years for a new loan; and if in the future she has $14,000 she can pay off the new money and resort back to the underlying first mortgage of $50,000 at 8½ percent.

The seller is pleased because he receives all his money at closing and does not need to carry back a second mortgage. The lender who made the wrap loan is pleased because he is lending money at the current 16 percent rate. The only loser is the lender who holds the existing first mortgage of 8½ percent on his books. The buyer would make one monthly payment to the wrap lender of $615.74, plus taxes and insurance ($64,000 at 10.75% for 25 years). The wrap lender makes the PITI payment to the original lender. In the event that the new money is paid off, the wrap lender drops out of the picture and the borrower makes her payment directly to the original lender. Wrap mortgages are available up to 95 percent LTV.

Existing Mortgage Rate

Amount of new money to be disbursed, stated as % of existing loan, remaining balance	7.00%	7.25%	7.50%	7.75%	8.00%	8.25%	8.50%	8.75%	9.00%	9.25%
5%	7.75	8.00	8.25	8.25	8.50	8.75	9.00	9.25	9.50	9.75
10%	8.25	8.25	8.50	8.75	9.00	9.25	9.50	9.75	10.00	10.25
15%	8.50	8.75	9.00	9.25	9.50	9.50	9.75	10.00	10.25	10.50
20%	9.00	9.25	9.25	9.50	9.75	10.00	10.25	10.25	10.50	10.75
25%	9.25	9.50	9.75	10.00	10.00	10.25	10.50	10.75	10.75	11.00
30%	9.75	9.75	10.00	10.25	10.25	10.50	10.75	11.00	11.00	11.25
35%	10.00	10.00	10.25	10.50	10.50	10.75	11.00	11.25	11.25	11.50
40%	10.25	10.50	10.50	10.75	10.75	11.00	11.25	11.25	11.50	11.75
45%	10.50	10.75	10.75	11.00	11.00	11.25	11.50	11.50	11.75	12.00
50%	10.75	10.75	11.00	11.25	11.25	11.50	11.50	11.75	12.00	12.00
55%	11.00	11.00	11.25	11.25	11.50	11.75	11.75	12.00	12.00	12.25
60%	11.25	11.25	11.50	11.50	11.75	11.75	12.00	12.00	12.25	12.50
65%	11.25	11.50	11.50	11.75	11.75	12.00	12.25	12.25	12.50	12.50
70%	11.50	11.75	11.75	12.00	12.00	12.25	12.25	12.50	12.50	12.75
75%	11.75	11.75	12.00	12.00	12.25	12.25	12.50	12.50	12.75	12.75
80%	11.75	12.00	12.00	12.25	12.25	12.50	12.50	12.75	12.75	13.00
85%	12.00	12.00	12.25	12.25	12.50	12.50	12.75	12.75	13.00	13.00
90%	12.00	12.25	12.25	12.50	12.50	12.75	12.75	13.00	13.00	13.25
95%	12.25	12.25	12.50	12.50	12.75	12.75	13.00	13.00	13.25	13.25
100%	12.50	12.50	12.50	12.75	12.75	13.00	13.00	13.25	13.25	13.50
110%	12.50	12.75	12.75	13.00	13.00	13.25	13.25	13.25	13.50	13.50
120%	12.75	13.00	13.00	13.00	13.25	13.25	13.50	13.50	13.50	13.75
130%	13.00	13.00	13.25	13.25	13.50	13.50	13.50	13.75	13.75	13.75
140%	13.25	13.25	13.25	13.50	13.50	13.75	13.75	13.75	14.00	14.00
150%	13.25	13.50	13.50	13.50	13.75	13.75	13.75	14.00	14.00	14.25
160%	13.50	13.50	13.75	13.75	13.75	14.00	14.00	14.00	14.25	14.25
170%	13.75	13.75	13.75	13.75	14.00	14.00	14.00	14.25	14.25	14.25
180%	13.75	13.75	14.00	14.00	14.00	14.25	14.25	14.25	14.50	14.50
190%	14.00	14.00	14.00	14.00	14.25	14.25	14.25	14.50	14.50	14.50
200%	14.00	14.00	14.25	14.25	14.25	14.25	14.50	14.50	14.50	14.75

FIGURE 9.4 Wraparound mortgage rate.

ALTERNATE MORTGAGE PLANS

Most of the alternate financing available is very new and is an outgrowth of the tight money market and high interest rates of the 1980s. With the rapid rise of interest, the housing market went into a slump. Innovative financing techniques were developed by lenders and real estate agents to keep homes affordable.

Variable-Rate Mortgages (VRM and ARM)

The *variable-rate mortgage* offers protection to the mortgagee since it allows the mortgagee to vary the interest in the future. The interest rate may move up or down depending on the current costs of funds (called an *index*), usually the one year T-Bill. Thus, with a variable-rate mortgage the yield to the lender may be kept close

Rates that vary

Sales Price (or appraised value if lower) .... $_____

Mortgage Request $_____ + Sales price = _____% Loan to Value

Existing Mortgage $_____ Existing Rate _____%

FHA or VA: _____ Yes _____ No (No 245's)

Remaining Term on Existing Mortgage _____ Years _____ Months

Round up to next full year: _____

Total WRAP Mortgage Request .... $_____

Less: Balance of Existing Mortgage .... $_____

New Money Required .... $_____

The New Money Required + Existing Mortgage = _____%

Please Note: The interest rate on a WRAP loan is the direct function of:

1. the percentage of new money loaned relative to the existing loan balance

2. the spread between the rate of the existing loan and the rate of the yield required on the new money.

The REALTOR must rely upon their loan officer for the proposed interest rate on each WRAP application, since the yields are determined by the current money market conditions. The REALTOR should contact their loan officer after completing the above information.

_____

Proposed Interest Rate: _____

Proposed Payment:

Total WRAP Mortgage amount $_____

Principal and Interest $_____

Taxes $_____

Hazard Insurance $_____

FHA MIP (if applicable) $_____

TOTAL PAYMENT $_____

FIGURE 9.5
Worksheet for a
Wrap Mortgage.

to market interest rates. The lender adds a profit margin to the index which varies from one to three percent. If the rate is increased, it does not necessarily mean that the monthly payments will be increased; however, in this case there is the possibility of negative amortization. Another solution to avoid increased payments is that the life of the loan can be extended up to a maximum of one-third of the original term. The time will not be extended, however, to a point that would reduce the payments.

Reverse-Annuity Mortgages (RAM)

In the *reverse-annuity mortgage* (RAM), retired home owners can receive payments from the equity they have acquired in their homes. The lender pays a net amount over a specified period of time or until a stated event such as death or the sale of the property. This means that the loan increases, an exact reverse of the normal procedure of reducing the debt. If the owners sell the home, their equity will naturally be less. Spendable income may be more important than accumulated wealth to the retirees and the RAM can provide an income stream or a lump-sum payment.

Collecting payments from lenders

Rollover Mortgages

Lenders use a medly of names for the rollover mortgage. Variously referred to as a renegotiable rate mortgage (RRM), adjusted rate mortgage (ARM), or an adjustable interest mortgage (AIM), the rollover mortgage has a set loan rate for a specified short period of time, one to five years, after which it must be renegotiated. These loans are popular at times of high interest because the first few years are below market rates. The unpaid balance is refinanced, or rolled over, every one to five years.

Adjustable rate mortgages

When mortgage rates rose to an all-time high in 1981 and 1982, the rollover became popular since lenders offered them for less than current rates. For example, lenders could issue a three year rollover for 14 percent when fixed-rate mortgages were 16 percent because they knew they could renegotiate the mortgage in three years to reflect changes in economic conditions. In a rollover loan, the borrower must be notified ninety days prior to the expiration date, giving the borrower time to check with other lenders for better terms. If the borrower does not act, the loan is automatically extended with payments made according to the new schedule. Increase and decrease schedules are set by the Federal Home Loan Bank Board. Interest rate changes are governed by a national index based on the average contract interest rate charged on new mortgages for existing houses across the country.

FNMA Rewrites

The FNMA (Fannie Mae) rewrite is used to obtain a new loan, generally at a lower-than-market interest rate if the property has an existing mortgage carried by the Federal National Mortgage Association.

Graduated-Payment Plans (GPM)

In the graduated-payment plan (GPM), the monthly payment begins at a lower-than-normal rate and increases as the borrower's income increases. This plan allows the borrower to obtain housing and pay the current interest as he can afford to. Also referred to as the Flexible Loan Insurance Program (FLIP), the GPM is a relatively simple procedure. The payments are individually tailored to the buyer's needs by carefully analyzing the buyer's assets and projected income. The payments level off to the full payment any time up to ten years after the loan is made. In the meantime, negative amortization occurs. A good example of the GPM is the FHA 245 loan.

Shared-Appreciation Mortgages (SAM)

Lender shares profit　With the *shared-appreciation mortgage* (SAM), the borrower agrees to share future benefits with the lender in exchange for a fixed, below-market interest rate. The future appreciation percentage is known as *contingent interest*, since the money due the lender is dependent upon the property's appreciation in value. The prearranged percentage can reach a maximum of 40 percent of the net appreciated value of the mortgaged property, payable when any one of the following occurs:

1. The house is sold
2. The loan is paid off
3. Ten years have passed

If the property is not sold within the ten-year period, most SAMs would require that the buyer pay the lending institution a percentage of the appreciation due. The SAM program is useful in high-growth areas where home values are likely to escalate in the future. The lender can qualify more buyers because of the lower payments and at the same time receive a potentially higher rate of return than on a fixed-rate mortgage. The lender guarantees the borrower that refinancing is available.

Temporary Buydown

The *temporary buydown* is a mortgage differential allowance program that permits the seller of the property to place a percentage of his sale proceeds at closing with the lender in an escrow account. This money is used to reduce the effective interest costs and monthly payments for the first two or three years of the loan. The buyer makes the offer-to-purchase contingent on the seller establishing a mortgage differential account for the purchaser, in the purchaser's name, at the time of closing. The account will have sufficient funds to effectively reduce the purchaser's monthly payment to reflect a lower interest rate for the first few years of the purchaser's loan. The buyer will still be signing the note and mortgage at the current interest rate. In essence, the seller is prepaying interest for the buyer. The differential will be established in a savings account in the purchaser's name with the lender who makes the loan.

3-2-1 Buydowns

The 3-2-1 buydown program offers the buyer 3 percent off the first year's rate, 2 percent off the second year's rate, and 1 percent off the third year's rate. It can be used on VA, PMI, or conventional mortgages. The maximum FHA seller subsidy is 5 percent. The eligibility of the borrower may be obtained by using the higher fixed rate if the one- or two-year term is used instead of three years. The lower "bought down" payment may generally be used for ratios and eligibility if the three-year buydown term is chosen. Using a buydown permits the purchaser to qualify at a lower income level or afford a more expensive property than without the buydown.

Blend Mortgages

The *blend mortgage* is like a wrap mortgage except that if the new money is paid back, the borrower can not revert back to the original first mortgage. It is a "blend" between the existing mortgage rate on the property and current market rates. The purchaser assumes the existing mortgage at a renegotiated rate. For example:

Sale price	$90,000
20% down payment	18,000
New mortgage	$72,000

The existing mortgage is $36,000 at 10 percent. Q-T Savings and Loan will increase the 10 percent by one-half of one percentage point to 10½ percent. The purchaser needs another $36,000, which will be loaned at the prevailing rate of 18 percent. The two rates will then be blended for a total rate of $72,000 at 14½ percent.

Growing Equity Mortgage (GEM)

In today's market the *growing equity mortgage* (GEM) is similar to a graduated-payment mortgage without negative amortization and considered second in popularity to the fixed-rate mortgage. GEM's monthly payment for the first year is identical to the traditional fixed-rate mortgage. However, monthly payments increase each year with this increase applying to the principal. This provides for a shorter payment period of 10 to 15 years as opposed to the traditional 25 to 30 year loan. The buyer must be able to afford these increased payments and have a desire to build his equity faster. The advantage of this loan is the borrower saves interest over a 30 year loan and pays back with inflated dollars.

Reduction of the principal is accomplished with the use of curtailments. *Curtailments* are usually predetermined annual percentage increases in the monthly payments that are applied directly to the principal balance of the loan, generally a seven percent per year increase in payment. Since these curtailments are applied directly to the loan balance, the mortgage will be paid off at almost twice the rate of a fully amortized 25 year mortgage.

Many growing equity mortgages also provide a temporary buydown option. The buydown amount is placed in a pledged account and used to reduce monthly payments in the early years of the loan.

INSTRUMENTS RELATIVE TO FINANCING

An *estoppel certificate* is an instrument executed by the mortgagor as to the validity of the full mortgage debt. In other words, it declares the exact balance of the debt to the new owner of the mortgage. It is sometimes called a *certificate of no defense* or a *declaration of no set off*. When a mortgage is assigned by the mortgagee to the new owner of the mortgage, the mortgagee must issue an assignment. The person to whom the mortgage is assigned (the assignee) acquires title and interest in the mortgage and note.

Declaring the full balance of a note

A *satisfaction piece* or a mortgage release is an instrument for recording and acknowledging full payment of an indebtedness that is secured by a mortgage. It means "satisfied in full." It is recorded to show the debt has been paid.

A *pledge* is money kept on deposit with the lending agency. It is held as security for a debt until the extra amount loaned to the purchaser is paid off. The pledge is an interest-bearing account but is technically a "frozen" asset that cannot be removed

Pledge held as security

until the amount specified on the loan is paid. For an example of a pledge, consider a young couple wishing to purchase a home. They have the required down payment, but are short in qualifying for the loan. A second party could put up the necessary amount in a pledge account with the lender.

An *escrow agreement* is used by the parties to a contract to carry out the terms of the agreement. The parties involved appoint a third party to act as escrow agent. This agent should be a disinterested party who will not benefit in any way.

An example: you have just purchased a new home but at the time of closing the carpet has not been installed. The lending institution will hold a sufficient sum back from the builder until the carpet is in place, at which time the escrow fund will be released to the builder. Another example is the loan that requires monthly payments that include not only the principal and interest payment, but one-twelfth of the annual taxes and insurance. This tax and insurance payment accumulates in an escrow account so the lender can pay the taxes and insurance premium when they are due.

FORECLOSURES, JUDGMENTS, AND LIENS

Nonpayment of debt

A *foreclosure* is a court action to cut out the right to *equity redemption* the debtor or owner has in the property. In some states after a decree of foreclosure has been entered under certain conditions, the mortgagor may obtain a court order postponing the foreclosure sale. The courts give the mortgagor a statutory period within which to redeem the property, and if s/he fails to do so, s/he loses the property. This right is known as the *right of redemption*. If the mortgagor has considerable equity in the property, the courts may order the property sold.

Rights of the debtor

The sheriff auctions foreclosed property on the steps of the court house in order to get market price. The mortgagee will always bid for the property at the balance due on the mortgage, plus penalties and legal fees. If a bid is made by a third party for a higher amount than the morgagee's bid, the mortgagor will receive the amount above the existing costs.

The foreclosure procedure was originally designed to allow the farmer sufficient time to harvest crops before losing the right to redeem. These same lengthy foreclosure procedures are a disadvantage to the lender on residential property. The delayed time period of foreclosure (set by state statute) permits the debtor to stay on without making payments or caring for the property.

The *title theory* evolved from the days when the rights of the mortgagee were primary. If the borrower defaulted on the loan, the mortgagee could dispossess him without notice and all the equity the borrower had built up was forfeited. Today the states that adopted the title theory of real estate finance have modified the law so that the borrower has the right of redemption. This gives the debtor a reasonable time after default to redeem the property.

The *lien theory*, used by most of the states, acknowledges that the borrower retains his legal rights in the property, with the mortgagee having equitable rights. This means that the borrower keeps possession and title in his property while the lender must follow the state's legal foreclosure procedures.

Some states have a modified plan of either the title or the lien theory whereby the lender does not have to wait until foreclosure to obtain possession of the property. Title is not turned over, however, until the statutory redemption period has ended.

If the mortgagee does not receive the full amount due him upon the foreclosure sale, he has the right to enter a *deficiency judgment* against the mortgagor. For example, if the owner has a mortgage balance due of $12,000 and the property brings only $10,000, the mortgagee may request the courts to file a deficiency judgment for the $2,000 balance due.

The hold or claim one person has upon another as security for a debt or charge is known as a **lien**. In most states, a general contractor may file a mechanics lien for work completed on property but not paid for. The lien must be filed within a specified time after the work has been completed. General liens are so termed because they are held against all the real property of the debtor. Examples of general liens would be income tax liens or judgments.

Placing liens on property

A *moratoriam* is the legal right to delay meeting a money obligation. The lending institution must agree to permit the mortgagor to delay his payment.

Lis pendens means suit pending; it is public notice that a suit is filed against a specific property that may affect the right to ownership of land.

SUMMARY

The many terms and types of mortgages and mortgage clauses relevant to the financing of real estate are covered in this chapter. New creative financing programs surfaced due to the rising cost of home financing and the shortage of funds to lend. Since our population dictates that the market for housing will not diminish, the need for making housing affordable for this generation and generations to follow is imperative.

Among the many creative financing techniques developed in the search for funds is the renegotiable rate mortgage. This mortgage allows the lender the option of raising or lowering the interest rate after three, four or five years. There is a strong indication that many new loans will be renegotiable or variable.

Since most loans written after the mid 1970s have alienation clauses that call the mortgage due and payable upon the sale, the blend mortgage is being successfully implemented. The lender that holds the existing mortgage gives the new buyers a loan at a rate that is higher than the existing rate but less than the current market rate. This gives the lender a better yield and the buyer lower-than-normal interest.

There have been many changes in the mortgage market. The savings and loan industry had been the mainstay of the one-to-four family home mortgages, and its continuance could only be assured by using renegotiable mortgages. However, with the lowering of interest rates in the mid 1980s, less need for innovative mortgage plans exist. Today, the mortgage banker provides most of the fixed rate mortgages. It is not unusual for borrowers to select 15 and 20 year term mortgages instead of the traditional 30 year in an effort to save interest.

KEY WORDS AND CONCEPTS

Amortization: The liquidation of a financial obligation on the installment basis.

Balloon payment: A final payment on a mortgage that is larger than the previous payment.

Blanket Mortgage: A single mortgage covering more than one piece of property.

Deed of trust: An absolute deed to secure payment of a debt.

Discount points: A percentage charge on the amount of the loan.

Equity: The value of a property above liens and mortgages.

Interest: Rent for the use of money.

Lien: The hold or claim of one person against another for a debt.

Moratorium: The legal period of delay for meeting a money obligation.

Mortgage: The pledge that secures the lender's investment; the mortgage accompanies the note.

Mortgagee: The lending institution receiving payments on the loan.

Mortgagor: The owner of the real property; the debtor.

Open-end mortgage: A mortgage with a clause that permits the mortgagor to borrow additional money without changing the terms of the mortgage.

REVIEW QUESTIONS

1. When monthly payments made on a loan are amortized over a period of years
   a. it liquidates the debt on an installment basis.
   b. the payments include both principal and interest.
   c. both of the above
   d. neither of the above

2. Discount points are charged by lending institutions
   a. to make the loan more favorable to the lender.
   b. to help the mortgagor with his down payment.
   c. both of the above
   d. neither of the above

3. Under the terms of the mortgage, the mortgagor
   a. has all the rights of ownership.
   b. can automatically assign the mortgage to another.
   c. both of the above
   d. neither of the above

4. If the mortgagor defaults on the note
   a. he or she is given a six-month grace period
   b. the mortgage becomes due and payable.
   c. both of the above
   d. neither of the above

5. An open-end mortgage is favorable to the mortgagor because
   a. the loan cannot be paid off ahead of time.
   b. more than one piece of property can be under a single mortgage.
   c. both of the above
   d. neither of the above

6. An assignment of rents allows the mortgagee to take possession
   a. when the mortgage is assigned to another.
   b. when the mortgagor defaults in meeting his payments on rental property.
   c. both of the above
   d. neither of the above

7. A second mortgage taken on real property
   a. has precedence over the first mortgage.
   b. is subordinate to any previously issued mortgage on the property.
   c. both of the above
   d. neither of the above

8. The advantage of a deed of trust for a mortgagee is that
   a. the title is held in trust and the property can be sold by a public trustee if the borrower defaults on her payments.
   b. no second mortgage can be made on the property.
   c. both of the above
   d. neither of the above

9. Who signs the note that goes along with the mortgage?
   a. mortgagor
   b. mortgagee
   c. both of the above
   d. neither of the above

10. The lender in a mortgage arrangement is the
    a. mortgagee
    b. trustee
    c. both of the above
    d. neither of the above

11. Abigail Jones purchases a home for $55,000. She puts 20 percent down with the balance to be paid over twenty years at 14 percent interest. Her monthly principal and interest payments are $547.36. What is the amount of interest paid the first month?
    a. $547.36
    b. $513.33
    c. $34.03
    d. $540.00

12. What is the approximate amount of interest paid on the loan at its maturity?
    a. $131,366.40
    b. $87,366.40
    c. $76,366.40
    d. $6,568.32

13. The repayment of principal and interest within a specified time is characteristic of a(n)
    a. delinquent loan
    b. amortized loan
    c. accelerated loan
    d. equalized loan

14. The clause in a mortgage that allows the mortgagee to declare the entire sum due upon default by the mortgagor is
    a. the escalator clause
    b. the acceleration clause
    c. the forfeiture clause
    d. the termination clause

15. The type of mortgage that encompasses more than one property is
    a. a package mortgage
    b. a wraparound mortgage
    c. a blanket mortgage
    d. a net mortgage

16. A loan used for interim financing is
    a. a land contract
    b. a VA loan
    c. a variable loan
    d. a construction loan

17. An act performed by a creditor to receive payment on a loan is called
    a. redemption
    b. escrow
    c. foreclosure
    d. assignment

18. To charge interest in excess of the amount allowable by law is
    a. truth in lending
    b. discount points
    c. rent
    d. usury

19. Which mortgage allows the mortgagor to extend the amount of the loan?
    a. an open mortgage
    b. a blanket mortgage
    c. an open-end mortgage
    d. a wraparound mortgage

20. A note, as opposed to a mortgage, is a
    a. lien
    b. personal obligation
    c. second mortgage
    d. judgment

21. On a $45,000 loan at 13 percent interest for thirty years, the interest and principal payment is $497.79. After the first payment, the loan balance would be
    a. $44,502.21
    b. $44,989.71
    c. $44,990.00
    d. $44,500.00

22. Which permits the seller to subsidize the buyer's interest so that the first few years require lower payments from the buyer?
    a. Open-end mortgage
    b. Temporary buydown
    c. Blanket mortgage
    d. Balloon payment

23. Which clause in a mortgage allows the mortgagee to collect rents directly from a tenant when the mortgage is in default?
    a. Mortgagee in possession
    b. Foreclosure clause
    c. Possession by law
    d. Acceleration clause

24. Jane Stree sold her property for $120,000. The buyer put $25,000 down and Jane took a note back for $95,000, agreeing to transfer title when the note is paid. Jane holds a(n)
    a. Land contract
    b. Second mortgage
    c. Interim loan
    d. Purchase money mortgage

25. Mortgages and deeds of trust have in common the
    a. number of parties
    b. redemption clause
    c. both a and b
    d. neither a or b

Closing Statements | 10

We have covered the listing, marketing, and financing of real property. The final step in the sale is the closing of the transaction. At this point, title is transferred to the purchaser.

The procedure for closing the sale will vary from state to state. When a sale is handled by a real estate company, the buyer and seller rarely meet. The real estate agent writes the offer with the buyer and presents it to the seller for acceptance (Chapter 7). Once the seller signs the contract, the agent puts into motion the procedures for closing the sale. The sale may be closed through escrow or by the real estate company. This chapter explains both procedures; however, the example of Kurt and Susan Kindly buying a home from Harvey and Della Wender that has been followed in Part Two will use the settlement procedures as handled by a real estate company.

ESCROW CLOSING

In some states, the process of title closing is concluded by an escrow agent and is referred to as an **escrow closing**. The escrow agent is a disinterested third party who handles the closing procedure for the buyer and seller. His obligation commences when he receives the buyer's earnest deposit and places it in a trust account. The deed and all papers relating to the sale are delivered to the escrow agent. He then follows the exact instructions outlined in the purchase contract between the buyer and seller. The escrow agent collects the funds from the buyer, gives the buyer the deed, and disperses the proceeds to the seller. Escrow closings are most often handled by attorneys, title insurance companies, or the escrow departments of lending institutions.

Organizing the closing

SETTLEMENT

The **settlement** or **closing procedure** is the most commonly used method of closing the sale. The real estate broker prepares closing statements which are presented to the purchaser and seller when the sale is finalized. The closing statements itemize debits (costs) and credits (assets) incurred in the purchase and sale of the property.

Since we have followed in our examples the sale of the property located at 1040 Clear Street, we will now follow the closing procedure from the time the purchase agreement was accepted by the seller to the final culmination of the sale.

If the purchaser needs a loan (the cash buyer is very rare), the real estate agent sets a loan application appointment with the lending institution. A copy of the purchase agreement is given to the lender. In addition to the information regarding the property, the lender will complete a loan application on the borrower, inquiring as to income, employment record, assets, and liabilities (see figure 10.1).

Fees are collected from the borrower to cover the cost of the credit report and property appraisal. In compliance with the RESPA act, if the loan is federally related, the lender must furnish the borrower with a HUD information booklet and an estimate of the closing costs on the HUD Uniform Settlement Statement (see figure 10.2).

The lending institution follows a series of preliminary steps prior to setting the closing dates. The lender

The loan application

1. *Immediately orders a credit report.* The credit report reveals the borrowers' past record in paying debts. If they have been slow or delinquent in payments, the lender takes this into consideration when evaluating the risk involved in issuing them a loan.

2. *Orders an appraisal.* The lender's appraiser inspects the property to ensure that the purchase price is not more than the property's market value.

3. *Obtains verification of employment from the borrower's employer.* (See figure 10.3.) A borrower's employment record should indicate that s/he has been regularly employed and, preferably, possesses a marketable job skill. If the borrower's work is seasonal, s/he may have difficulty in meeting a monthly payment obligation. Lenders usually like to see no more than a quarter of the borrower's monthly gross income used for housing. The number and ages of dependents the borrower must support is also taken into consideration. If the buyer's spouse is employed, it is credited to their ability to repay the loan.

Since the Federal Equal Credit Opportunity Act has been in force, the lender cannot discriminate as to race, marital status, sex, or age. Today a single woman or an older person can purchase a home, provided they meet the requirements of sufficient income, good credit rating, and employment stability.

4. *Obtains verification of bank deposits.* (See figure 10.4.)

5. *Obtains Survey.* Mortgage bankers require surveys since they may later sell the mortgage. (See figure 10.5.)

6. *Prepares settlement statement for borrower.*

If the credit report reveals no adverse information—that is, if the borrower's employment is verified as stated in the loan application, if the bank verifies his deposits, and if the lender's appraiser values the property at the purchase price—the lender informs the broker they are ready to proceed with the closing.

The real estate firm is responsible for

1. Seeing that the present loan is paid off if it is not being assumed by the purchaser. The holder of the mortgage issues a pay-off letter (reduction certificate) stating the exact mortgage balance.

2. Obtaining the sellers' signatures on the deed.

3. Obtaining a general lien waiver in which the seller attests that there are no unpaid debts against the property.

4. Ordering a wood infestation report certifying that there is no damage.

Loan Number..

Term in Years..

Rate of Interest.......................................

Date Judgment Searched........................

Date Judgment O.K.........By...................

Monthly Loan Payment.................$....................

Monthly Tax Payment....................$....................

Monthly Hazard Ins. Payment........$....................

Monthly FHA Ins. Payment............$....................

Monthly Life Ins. Payment............$....................

....$....................

TOTAL MONTHLY PAYMENT....$....................

LOAN APPLICATION

LOAN APPLICATION

Applicant_Kurt K. Kindly_ Age_33_ Ever Divorced? Yes ☐ No ☒ Any Judgment? Yes ☐ No ☐

Co-applicant_Susan A. Kindly_ Age_32_ Wife ☒ Other_____

Number of Dependent Children_2_ Ages_4,2_ Currently Renting? Yes ☒ No ☐ Monthly Rental $_450.00_

Applicant's Address_11250 Cherry Blossom Lane_ Home Phone_330-1532_ Business Phone_330-5300_

Applicant's Employer_Great Western Engineers_ Address_356 Central Ave._

Type of Business_Engineers_ Occupation_Engineer_ How Long_8_yrs. at $_2750_per month

Previous Employer_Village Engineers_ How Long_2_yrs.

Co-applicant's Employer_Facto Art Inc._ Occupation_artist (part-time)_ How Long_6_yrs. at $_600_per month

Other Income (Source)_____ at $_____per month

Life Ins. in Force $_50,000.00_ Amt. Wanted $_0_ Total Income $_3350.00_per month

H & A Ins. in Force $_0_ Amt. Wanted $_0_

ASSETS		LIABILITIES		
			Payment	Balance
Cash (Where Deposited)_Community Bank_	$_578.00_	Installment Loans		
Ready Savings & Loan	$_9000.00_	Auto	$_57.00_	$_1500.00_
Earnest Money: (Has been Deducted Above)	$_2000.00_	To Whom_Nifty Credit Union_		
Stocks and Other Securities:		Furniture	$_45.00_	$_180.00_
C.D. Ready S&L.	$_5,000.00_	To Whom_Big Red Furniture Co._		
C.D. Community Bank	$_5,000.00_		$_____	$_____
Cash Value of Life Insurance	$_0_		$_____	$_____
U.S. Savings Bonds	$_0_		$_____	$_____
Real Estate:		Mortgages: (To Whom)		
Subject (address)_____	$_____		$_____	$_____
Other:_____	$_____		$_____	$_____
_____	$_____		$_____	$_____
_____	$_____		$_____	$_____
Auto: Make(s)_Ford_ Yr._81_Datsun Yr._79_	$_11,900.00_	Other Liabilities	$_____	$_____
Other Assets_____	$_____	_Visa Card_	$_45.00_	$_300.00_
Household Goods	$_10,000.00_		$_____	$_____
TOTAL ASSETS	$_43,278.00_	TOTAL LIABILITIES	$_147.00_	$_1980.00_

Credit References_Nifty Credit Union, Visa, Big Red Furniture Co., Master Charge_

Purpose of Loan_home for occupancy_

Will there be a second mortgage?_no_ Amount $_____ Payment per Month $_____ To Whom_____

PROPERTY ADDRESS_1040 Clear Street, Big Red, Nebraska_

Legal Description_Lot 8, Block 1, Confusion Hill Subdivision_

Lot Size_85x110_

Date Purchased_April 8_ Price Paid $_84,000.00_ Cash ☐ Land Contract ☐

Will property be occupied by applicant? ☒ Tenant ☐ Monthly Rental $_____ For Sale ☐ Sale Price $_____

Existing Construction ☒ Improvements Since_____

_____Cost $_____

Proposed Improvements_____Cost $_____

New Construction ☐ Contractor_____ Cost of Lot $_____ Cost of Construction $_____

Current Taxes $_1550.00_ Delinquent $_no_ Any Unpaid Specials $_no_

Present Encumbrances: 1st Mortgage $_43,320.10_ Held by_Ready Savings & Loan_

Land Contract or 2nd Mortgage $_0_ Held by_____

Title Holder_Harvey & Della Wender_ Occupied by_Owner_ Phone_313-0234_

Have you ever had a loan with us before? Yes ☐ No ☒ When?_____ Address_____

Have you applied any place else for this loan? Yes ☐ No ☒ If yes, give result_____

Big Red, Nebraska_April 9_,19_87_ _Kurt K. Kindly_

Witness:_Ruth A. Masterson_ _Susan A. Kindly_

FIGURE 10.1 A completed loan application.

DATE April 9, 1987

LOAN OFFICER Ruth Masterson

GOOD FAITH ESTIMATE
OF SETTLEMENT COSTS

The following Good Faith Estimate of Closing Costs is made pursuant to the Real Estate Settlement Procedures Act (RESPA). These figures are only estimates and the actual charges due at settlement may be different.

L. SETTLEMENT CHARGES	PAID FROM BORROWER'S FUNDS AT SETTLEMENT	PAID FROM SELLER'S FUNDS AT SETTLEMENT
800. ITEMS PAYABLE IN CONNECTION WITH LOAN		
801. Loan Origination Fee 1 %	672.00	
802. Loan Discount %		
803. Appraisal Fee to		
804. Credit Report to Big Red Credit Bureau	12.50	
805. Lender's Inspection Fee	55.00	
806. Mortgage Insurance Application Fee to		
807. Assumption Fee		
808. FHA/VA Inspection Fee to		
900. ITEMS REQUIRED BY LENDER TO BE PAID IN ADVANCE		
901. Interest from 5-15-87 to 6-1-87 @ $ 24.26 day x 15 days	364.00	
902. Mortgage Insurance Premium for mo. to		
903. Hazard Insurance Premium for 1 yrs. to Bleecher Ins. Co. (185.00)	*	
1000. RESERVES DEPOSITED WITH LENDER FOR		
1001. Hazard Insurance 2 mo. @ $32.50 /mo.	65.00 *	
1002. Mortgage Insurance mo. @ $ /mo.		
1005. Annual Assessments mo. @ $ /mo.	*	
1006. Real Estate Tax 5 mo. @ $129.17 /mo.	645.83 *	
1100. TITLE CHARGES (Refer to Note #1)		
1102. Abstract or Title Search to		
1103. Title Examination to	55.00	
1104. Title Insurance Binder to		
1107. Attorney's Fees to		
(includes above items No.:)		
1108. Title Insurance to	159.63	159.63
(includes above items No.:)		
1109. Lender's Coverage $ 67,200		
1110. Owner's Coverage $ 84,000		
1200. GOVERNMENT RECORDING AND TRANSFER CHARGES		
1201. Recording Fees: Deed $ 3.25 ; Mtg. $ 3.25 ; Rel. $ 3.25	6.50	3.25
1203. State Tax/Stamps: Deed $ 126.00		126.00
1300. ADDITIONAL SETTLEMENT CHARGES		
1301. Survey to		
1302. Pest Inspection to		
1304. Warranty Inspection Service to		
1400. TOTAL SETTLEMENT CHARGES	2035.46	288.88

*Optional estimates if information available. This form does not cover all items you will be required to pay in cash at settlement, for example, deposit in escrow for real estate taxes and insurance. You may wish to inquire as to the amount of such other items. You may be required to pay other additional amounts at settlement.

NOTE #1—SECTION 1100 TITLE CHARGES
Listed below are providers of certain required services. The charges or range indicated in the Good Faith Estimate above are based upon the corresponding charge of the below designated providers.

Line Number   . . . .
Service Provided   . . .
Providers Name   .
Address and   . .
Telephone Number   . . .

We (do) (do not) have a business relationship with the above provider.   We (do) (do not) have a business relationship with the above provider.   We (do) (do not) have a business relationship with the above provider.

I (would) (would not) desire to inspect H.U.D.-1 (Settlement Statement) during the business day immediately preceding the date of settlement. (Completed as to those items which are then known.)

WAIVER—HUD #1 SETTLEMENT STATEMENT. I waive the right to the delivery of the completed form before or at the settlement. Complete form will be mailed or delivered as soon as practical after settlement.

Signature

Form 679 (Rev. 1-77)

FIGURE 10.2 HUD uniform settlement statement.

FHA FORM No. 2004 G
Revised 4/63

Form approved.
Budget Bureau No. 63-R267.5.

REQUEST FOR VERIFICATION OF EMPLOYMENT

1. NAME OF APPLICANT

Kurt K. Kindly & Susan A. Kindly

2. FHA Case No.
(when available)

3. ADDRESS OF APPLICANT

11250 Cherry Blossom Lane

INSTRUCTIONS: Initiated by Mortgagee and forwarded to Applicant's Employer for completion and return.

Name and Address of Applicant's Employer

Great Western Engineers
356 Central Ave.
Big Red, Nebraska

To Employer:

An application has been made by the above-named applicant for a mortgage loan to be made by this institution and insured by the Federal Housing Administration. The confirmation requested is to be forwarded to us for the confidential use of ourselves and the Federal Housing Administration.

The Applicant's signed statement contains the following:

"The Commissioner and Mortgagee may verify the statements contained herein by communicating with any firm or institutions named in this statement."

4. Date	5. Mortgagee
April 9, 1987	Ready Savings and Loan

EMPLOYER'S VERIFICATION

6. Present position	7. Length of employment	8.	PRESENT RATE OF PAY*	
engineer	8 years		HOURLY	ANNUAL

Name and Address of Mortgagee

Ready Savings and Loan
8052 Alert Drive
Big Red, Nebraska

	HOURLY	ANNUAL
	$	$ 33,000

ADDITIONAL COMPENSATION—ACTUAL AMOUNTS RECEIVED PAST 12 MONTHS

Overtime	$
Commissions	$
Bonus	$

* If applicant is in military service please report income on a monthly basis as follows:

Base pay $————quarters and subsistence $ ————flight or hazard duty allowance $ ————

9. Probability of continued employment   excellent

10. Other remarks

Dependable employee, knowledgable and exacting in his work.

The above is furnished you in strict confidence in response to your request

11. Date	12. Signature of employer
April 11, 1987	_K. M. Happy, Manager_

FIGURE 10.3 A lender's request for verification of the borrower's employment.

FHA FORM NO. 2004-F Rev. 12/75
VA FORM NO. 26-8497a Rev. 12/75

Form Approved
OMB No. 63R-1062

VETERANS ADMINISTRATION
AND
U. S. DEPARTMENT OF HOUSING AND URBAN DEVELOPMENT
FEDERAL HOUSING ADMINISTRATION
REQUEST FOR VERIFICATION OF DEPOSIT

INSTRUCTIONS: LENDER – Complete Items 1 through 7. Have applicant complete Items 8 and 9. Forward directly to bank or depository named in Item 1.
BANK or DEPOSITORY – Please complete Items 10 through 13. Return directly to lender named in Item 2.

PART I — REQUEST

1. TO: (Name and Address of Bank or other Depository)	2. FROM: (Name and Address of Lender)
Community Bank 8130 Birch Tree Road Big Red, Nebraska	Ready Savings and Loan 8052 Alert Drive Big Red, Nebraska

3. I certify that this verification has been sent directly to the bank or other depository and has not passed through the hands of the applicant or any other interested party. *Ruth A. Masterson* Signature of Lender	4. Title: Loan Officer	5. Date: April 9, 1987
		6. FHA or VA Number:

7. STATEMENT OF APPLICANT:

7A. Name and Address of Applicant:

Kurt K. and Susan A. Kindly
11250 Cherry Blossom Lane
Big Red, Nebraska

7B. TYPE OF ACCOUNT	BALANCE	ACCOUNT NUMBER
Checking	$ 578.00	A–21850
Savings	$	
Certificate of Deposit	$	

8. I have applied for a mortgage loan and stated that I maintain account(s) with the bank or other depository named in Item 1. My signature below authorizes that bank or other depository to furnish the lender named in Item 2 the information set forth in Part II. Your response is solely a matter of courtesy for which no responsibility is attached to your institution or any of your officers.

Kurt K. Kindly
Signature of Applicant

7C. TYPE OF LOAN	BALANCE	ACCOUNT NUMBER
Secured	$	
Unsecured	$	

9. Date: April 9, 1987

PART II — VERIFICATION

10A. Does Applicant have any outstanding loans? ☐ YES ☒ NO (If YES, enter total in Item 10B.)	CURRENT STATUS OF ACCOUNTS:		

10B. TYPE OF LOAN	MONTHLY PAYMENT	PRESENT BALANCE	11A. Is account less than two months old? (If YES, give date account was opened in Item 11B)	Checking	Savings	Cert. of Deposit
				☒ YES ☐ NO	☒ YES ☐ NO	☒ YES ☐ NO
			11B. Date the account was opened.	1–78		11–85
Secured	$	$	11C. Present Balance.	$ 572.40	$	$ 5,000.00
Unsecured	$	$	11D. Is account other than individual, e.g., Joint or Trust? (If YES, explain in Remarks)	☒ YES ☐ NO	☐ YES ☐ NO	☐ YES ☐ NO
10C. Payment experience: ☐ Favorable ☐ Unfavorable (If Unfavorable, explain in Remarks.)			11E. Is account satisfactory?	☒ YES ☐ NO		

12. REMARKS:

The above information is provided in response to your request.

13A. Signature of Official of Bank or other Depository: *Charles K. Dooley*	13B. Title: Vice-president	13C. Date: April 21, 1987

THIS INFORMATION IS FOR THE SOLE PURPOSE OF ASSISTING THE APPLICANT IN OBTAINING A MORTGAGE LOAN.

RETURN DIRECTLY TO LENDER

☆U.S. GOVERNMENT PRINTING OFFICE: 1977—765-033/64

FIGURE 10.4 A lender's request for verification of the borrower's bank deposits.

Project No. _13130_   Location _1040 Clear St._

Field Notes:

Found all iron pipe as shown, using SE corner, Lot 1 Old Home estates and NE corner Lot 6 Confusion Hill Subdivision. Established A12' offset line. Checked remaining distance around survey.

LAND SURVEYOR'S CERTIFICATE

I hereby certify that this plat, map, survey or report was made by me or under my direct personal supervision and that I am a duly Registered Land Surveyor under the laws of the State of Nebraska.

Legal Description:

Lot 8, Block 1 in Confusion Hill Subdivision, An Addition to the City of Big Red, Kent County, Nebraska, as Surveyed, platted and recorded.

Plat to scale showing tract surveyed with all pertinent points.

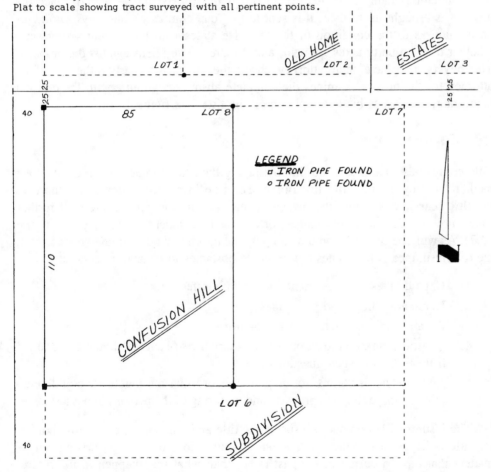

Signature of Land Surveyor

Date Received: *April 16, 1987*

Official Address: *Yards, Measure & Associates, Inc.*
11421 Goldenrod Lane, Big Red, NE

Bldg. Permit No.:

FIGURE 10.5
A certificate of survey.

5. Ordering the abstract to be extended or seeing that title insurance is obtained. Either the abstract to the property will be brought up to date or title insurance will be issued.

6. Completing closing statements for the buyer and seller.

ABSTRACTS

The division of land from the time of the original land grant to the present time is explained in an abstract of the property. An *abstract* is a condensed history of the title. It reveals the "chain of title," listing all the previous owners of the land, along with any instruments affecting the title. The term instrument refers to a deed, mortgage, or any legal paper that has been acknowledged (sworn to under oath) and recorded in the office of the Register of Deeds.

Searching the title   If an abstract is used, a title search is performed by a bonded abstractor and extended, or brought up to date. The abstractor lists any additional instruments recorded against the property since the current owner took title. The abstract does not guarantee good title; it merely lists the instruments of public record. However, the abstractor is liable if an item of record is overlooked in the search. Once the abstract is brought up to date, it is sent to the loan company's attorney, who gives an opinion as to the condition of the title. He states who the current owners are, whether their property taxes are paid, and if there are any liens against the property. The buyers also have their attorney check the abstract to certify the title. The attorney for the buyers examines the complete abstract beginning with the original land grant, and issues his own opinion on the title (see figure 10.6).

TITLE INSURANCE

Insuring good title   Title companies guarantee good title by having the title searched, as in the abstract method, and by issuing **title insurance**. The title insurance policy states the date the **title search** was made, the owner's name, and the property address. It further states any recorded liens, mortgages, or easements against the property (see figure 10.7). As with the title opinion drawn up by the attorney who examined the abstract, the title insurance policy states any possible obstacles to clear title, such as

1. Unpaid taxes or assessments not of public record.
2. Unrecorded liens and mortgages.
3. Repair work completed but not paid for.
4. Questions on exact locations of boundary lines (a survey should be obtained if there are any such questions).
5. Any interest or claims not of public record that the purchaser could determine by inspecting the property and inquiring of the persons in possession.

The insurer (title company) inspects the title and validates it to the title holder; the title policy is a contract of indemnity against loss or damage arising out of matters that have occurred in the past rather than what may happen in the future. There are many possible causes of title defects that are not disclosed by examination. If the claim, lien or defect has never been recorded it will not appear of record. Title insurance protects against such undisclosed and hidden risks. This could include defects that invalidate titles, such as forged deeds, illegal acts of trustees, guardians or attorneys, or false claims of ownership. A human error in copying, in recording, or the destruction of records could occur.

Righteous, Righteous & Caveat
Attorneys At Law
321 Legal Drive
Big Red, Nebraska 68102

May 12, 1987

Kurt K. & Susan A. Kindly
11250 Cherry Blossom Lane
Big Red, Nebraska

Dear Mr. & Mrs. Kindly:

We have carefully examined Abstract of Title to the property described as:

Lot 8, Block 1, Confusion Hill Subdivision,
city of Big Red, Kent County, Nebraska

consisting of plat and 103 entries last certified to October 10, 1978, at 8:00 a.m. by Title Services, Inc.

We find the fee simple title to said real estate as of that date to be vested in Harvey J. Wender and Della J. Wender, husband and wife as joint tenants, subject only to the following:

1. A mortgage to Ready Savings and Loan Association dated October 13, 1980 in Book 1670 at Page 314 in the original sum of $47,500.

2. The restrictions shown in the deed at entry 163 regulating the size of any dwelling which may be erected in the addition giving the utility companies the right to install and maintain their lines along the rear lot lines.

3. The first half taxes are paid, in the sum of $775.00. There are no special assessments.

You are required to take notice of the rights of any persons in possession of the premises. Also, whether or not any labor has been performed or materials delivered on the premises within the last four months which might result in a lien. Also as to whether any special improvements have been planned or commenced which might later result in special taxes against the property.

Yours truly,

I. M. Righteous

IMR:rm

FIGURE 10.6
An attorney's abstract opinion.

SCHEDULE A
Date of Policy
May 15, 1987
at 2:30 P.M.

POLICY NUMBER		AMOUNT	PREMIUM
O-121756-ram		$67,200	$319.20

1. Name of Insured

   Ready Savings and Loan

2. The estate or interest in the land described in this Schedule and which is encumbered by the insured Mortgage or Deed of Trust is:

   Fee Simple Title

3. The estate or interest referred to herein is at Date of Policy vested in:

   Kurt K. Kindly and Susan A. Kindly, husband and wife

4. The Mortgage or Deed of Trust herein referred to as the insured Mortgage or Deed of Trust, and the assignments thereof, if any, are described as follows:

   Mortgage from Kurt K. Kindly and Susan A. Kindly, husband and wife to Ready Savings and Loan to secure $67,200,   dated May 15, 1987 and recorded May 16, 1987 in Book 2210 at Page 295, Mortgage Records.

5. The land referred to in this policy is described as follows:

   Lot 8, Block 1 in Confusion Hill Subdivision, an Addition to the City of Big Red, Kent County, Nebraska, as Surveyed, platted and recorded.

SCHEDULE B - PART I

This policy does not insure against loss or damage by reason of the following:

1. Rights or claims of parties in possession not shown by the public records.

2. Easements, or claims of easements, not shown by the public records.

3. Discrepancies, conflicts in boundary lines, shortage in area, encroachments, and any facts which a correct survey and inspection of the premises would disclose and which are not shown by the public records.

4. Any lien, or right to a lien, for services, labor, or material heretofore, or hereafter furnished, imposed by law and not shown by the public records.

5. General taxes paid for first ½ year. Special taxes or assessments now assessed or levied, but payable in future installments: None certified to the office of the County Treasurer at date hereof.

6. Protective Covenants dated March 27, 1975, filed April 3, 1972 in Book 379 at Page 709 of the Miscellaneous Records of Kent County, Nebraska, shall run with the land for a period of twenty-five years. A five foot (5) easement across and along the rear and side boundary lines of each of said lot is hereby reserved for the construction, maintenance, operation and repair of electric and communication lines and for the erection of poles thereon, with privilege of access thereto.

SCHEDULE B - PART II

In addition to the matters set forth in Part 1 of this Schedule, the title to the estate or interest in the land described or referred to in Schedule A is subject to the following matters, if any be shown, but the Company insures that such matters are subordinate to the lien or charge of the insured mortgage upon said estate or interest: None.

FIGURE 10.7
A title insurance policy.

Issued at __Big Red, Nebraska_____ Countersigned by _G.B. Goodwin_
Authorized Signatory

Title insurance policies are divided into four main classes. A *leasehold* policy insures and protects the interests of a lessee under the terms and conditions of the lease as it would pertain to that property.

Types of title insurance policies

An *easement policy* is used to insure easement interests of the insured over or across a particular parcel of real estate. The two types most commonly issued are the owner's policy and the mortgagee's policy.

An *owner's policy* is issued to the property owner to insure good title. The policy guarantees the owner of real property against any title loss or damages suffered as a result of liens or defects in title that were not revealed when the examination of the title was made. Title insurance rates are not paid annually as with other types of insurance; the coverage runs indefinitely. That is, the insured will be protected against claims based upon the insured warranty of title to successors in interest. However, if the property is sold, the new owners would want to obtain a policy to cover their interest, since the owner's policy in not transferable. The owner's policy is issued for the full purchase price of the property.

Owner's policy

The *mortgagee's policy* is issued to the holder of the mortgage because of his or her interest in the property created by the mortgage. The mortgagee's only concern is to provide security for the loan, so the policy is for the loan amount only. The mortgagee's policy protects the investor for the term of the mortgage. If the mortgagee assigns the loan to someone who does not see the property, the title insurance eliminates any risk of survey problems. The policy is reassigned by the lender upon sale of the loan.

Mortgagee's policy

The American Land Title Association (ALTA) is a group of approximately 2,000 land title companies who have banned together to promote professional standards and ethics among their members. While some members are both abstractors and title insurance agents, other members only offer one service.

THE TORRENS SYSTEM

Robert Torrens was the originator of the *Torrens System* of title registration. Adopted in Australia in 1857, this system requires that application for title be made by the landowner. A petition requesting registration of the title is filed by the owner in the county where the land is located. A notice is published in the newspaper that a hearing will be held before a court of law. All known parties having an interest in the real estate are sent copies of the publication. Once the hearing takes place, the court mandates that the owner has good and merchantable title. The title is registered and the certificate of title reveals the owner of record and any encumbrances against the title. Similar to the method used in car registration, this system negates the need for a title search when the property is sold. While approximately ten states recognize its use, lack of public acceptance has limited more active use of this system.

Registering the title

OTHER PREREQUISITES TO CLOSING

Termite Inspection

In many states a termite and wood infestation inspection is a standard part of the purchase agreement. Our purchase agreement (see figure 7.2 at section G) states "that except for a VA loan the purchaser agrees to pay the cost of a termite inspection of the house and attached structure with the seller agreeing to pay for any treatment or repair work found necessary. If repairs are found to be needed for issuance of termite warranty, upon completion of repairs, the purchaser agrees to accept said treated real estate."

As stated in the subject contract, the inspection cost is generally paid for by the purchasers, except in the case of VA financing, when the cost must be borne by the seller. If the inspection reveals damage, the seller is responsible for the repair.

Structural Inspection

In some areas of the country, structural inspections are required to be performed by qualified inspectors, with the stipulation being made a part of the offer to purchase. Whether the structure is built on solid ground and the soil properly compacted is of concern to agents and buyers of homes situated on slopes, hillsides, and newly excavated areas where the soil has been moved considerably. This was the problem faced by the Eastons in the landmark case where the California courts awarded damages to them because of structural problems that arose when the land began to buckle and slide. A standardized disclosure form is now used in California with a checklist of inspections for potential problem areas. (See figure 7.4.)

Appliance Inspection

Across the country there are insurance plans that buyers and sellers may purchase that warrant appliances against defect. The policy may cover electrical, plumbing, heating, air conditioning, and major appliances. This provides protection to the buyer in the event that a costly defect occurs after the sale. Some of the insurers require that an inspection be made prior to issuing the policy.

Homeowner's Insurance

For anyone purchasing a home and obtaining a mortgage, lending institutions require the mortgagor to carry homeowner's insurance. This protects the lender's interest in the property should loss or damage to the premises occur. The borrower must give proof of fire and extended coverage by presenting an insurance binder to the mortgagee at the time the loan is closed. The lender will be named on the policy along with the homeowner and if damage occurs the checks will be made out jointly to the lender and borrower.

There is a variety of coverage available to the homeowner, ranging from Homeowner 1 (HO-1) to Homeowner 5 (HO-5). The HO-5 policy is the more comprehensive plan covering all possible types of perils, excluding only such catastrophies as earthquakes, floods, war, settling and cracking.

Lien Waivers

To insure the buyers that there are no unpaid liens against the property, the real estate firm may request that the sellers sign an affidavit attesting to the fact that there are no unpaid bills that could result in a lien against the property (see figure 10.8). This affidavit is called a **lien waiver**.

THE REAL ESTATE TRANSACTION

The Purchase and Loan

Let's review the total transaction to date. In Chapter 6, the property owned by Harvey J. Wender and Della Wender at 1040 Clear Street was listed by the A-1 Real Estate Company. A purchase agreement was written (Chapter 7) and the property was purchased by Kurt K. Kindly and Susan A. Kindly on April 8, 1987.

AGREEMENT

TO: _____ Kurt K. and Susan A. Kindly _____

This is written evidence to you that there are no unpaid bills for material or labor furnished for the construction and erection, repairs or improvements of building located at _____ 1040 Clear Street _____
LEGALLY DESCRIBED AS:

Lot 8, Block 1 in Confusion Hill Subdivision, an addition to the city of Big Red, Kent County, Nebraska

We further represent that there have been no public improvements affecting the property prior to date of the purchase contract that would give rise to a special property tax assessment against the property after the date of closing.

We further agree to fully indemnify you against any and all possible payment or expense of legal action in regard to mechanic's liens that may be filed upon the above described premises as a result of any improvements made or caused to be made by us prior to our surrendering possession to you.

This agreement is executed with and forms a part of the sale of the above described premise and is given in addition to the conveyance of the premises in consideration for the conveyance and forms a complete agreement by itself for any action thereon.

Harvey J. Wender
Harvey J. Wender

Della J. Wender
Della J. Wender

STATE OF NEBRASKA)
) SS
COUNTY OF KENT)

Subscribed in my presence and sworn to before me this _15_ day of __May__, 19 _87_ .

Judy M Selling

My Commission expires: ___July 8, 1990___

FIGURE 10.8
A completed lien waiver.

The Kindlys gave A-1 Real Estate Company a $2,000 earnest deposit and signed for an 80 percent loan at 10 percent interest for 30 years. The taxes for the first one-half have been paid by the Wenders. The Kindlys will take possession upon closing and all prorations will be figured as of that date.

Prorations

All prorated items paid in arrears will appear as debits to the seller and credits to the buyer. **Prorations** are calculated on the basis of a thirty-day month.

The purchase contract in Chapter 7 indicates that certain items will be prorated at the time of settlement. Expenses such as taxes, rent, interest, and escrow deposits will be divided according to who received the benefits. If the taxes are paid in advance, as in our transaction, the sellers will receive the portion back that they did not use. Had the taxes been unpaid, the sellers would pay for the time the property was in their possession. Prorating is further explained with examples in the chapter covering real estate math.

THE PURCHASER'S SETTLEMENT STATEMENT

The buyer's closing costs   Figure 10.9 shows a purchaser's settlement statement:

1. On the **debit** side, the first item shown is the purchase price. Since the buyers owe this amount, it appears as a *cost* to them.
2. The Kindlys deposited $2,000 as earnest money at the time they entered into the purchase contract. Since it was paid in advance and held in the broker's trust account, it now appears as a **credit** on the settlement statement.
3. The buyers requested an 80 percent loan on the cost of the property. Since the purchase price is $84,000 and the buyers are making a 20 percent down payment, the loan is in the amount of $67,200. All mortgages are *always a credit* to the purchaser.
4. Title insurance will be purchased at a cost of $319.26. This cost will be equally divided between the buyer and seller, representing a $159.63 debit to the buyer. (Keep in mind that some areas of the country may charge the entire fee to either the seller or the buyer.)
5. Bleecher Insurance Company will issue a homeowner's policy for $390.00 per year, effective upon the closing date. The year's premium is payable at the time of issuance, since insurance is *always* payable in advance.
6. The property taxes are paid for the first half of 1987, so the buyer will be charged for the amount prepaid by the seller. As per our listing contract in chapter 6, the total annual taxes are $1,550. This breaks down to $129.17 per month. Since closing and possession are set for May 15th, the buyers are charged for one and one-half months of taxes.
7. The columns *must balance*. By adding the credits and subtracting the total from the debits, we find the buyer will need $15,543.38 in the form of a certified check at the time of closing.

THE LENDER'S SETTLEMENT STATEMENT

The lender's closing statement   The lending institution will also have a settlement statement for the borrower. In compliance with the Real Estate Settlement Procedures Act, they use a standard form as shown in 10.10. The costs will vary from region to region and may also

A-1 REAL ESTATE
1104 Homestead Avenue
Big Red, Nebraska

PURCHASER'S CLOSING STATEMENT

NAME Kurt K. and Susan A. Kindly   DATE 5/15/87

ADDRESS   1040 Clear Street, Big Red, Nebraska

	Debit	Credit
Purchase Price	**1** $84,000.00	$
Earnest Deposit		2,000.00 **2**
First Mortgage-Ready S & L		67,200.00 **3**
Title Insurance ($\frac{1}{2}$ cost)	159.63 **4**	
Bleecher Ins. Co. (1 yr. Prem.)	390.00 **5**	
Prorated Taxes ($1550 @ $1\frac{1}{2}$ mo. 5/15/87 - 7/1/87	193.75 **6**	
Balance due from Purchaser		15,543.38 **7**
Totals	$84,743.38	$84,743.38

FIGURE 10.9 A purchaser's settlement or closing statement. In compliance with license law, the purchaser receives a copy of the settlement statement at the time of closing. A copy is also given to the lending institution as required by the Real Estate Settlement Procedures Act, and the broker keeps a copy in his or her file.

vary between lenders in a given location. Since the A-1 Real Estate Company is closing the transaction, the *only* collection made by the loan company will be under J, number 103—$2,341.46. These costs are the lender's charges in connection with placing the loan.

The statement reveals the following:

1. The borrowers' names.
2. The sellers' names.
3. The lending institution.
4. The property address.
5. The name of the settlement agent.
6. The place of settlement.
7. The date the sale is being closed.
8. The sale price (J is the borrower's summary and K is the seller's).

HUD-1 Rev. 5/76

Form Approved
OMB NO. 63-R-1501

A.	B. TYPE OF LOAN
U. S. DEPARTMENT OF HOUSING AND URBAN DEVELOPMENT SETTLEMENT STATEMENT	1. ☐ FHA 2. ☐ FmHA 3. ☒ CONV. UNINS. 4. ☐ VA 5. ☐ CONV. INS. 6. File Number: 1007-70 7. Loan Number: 007 8. Mortgage Insurance Case Number:

C. **NOTE**: *This form is furnished to give you a statement of actual settlement costs. Amounts paid to and by the settlement agent are shown. Items marked "(p.o.c.)" were paid outside the closing; they are shown here for informational purposes and are not included in the totals.*

D. NAME OF BORROWER:	E. NAME OF SELLER:	F. NAME OF LENDER:
Kurt K. Kindly and [1] Susan A. Kindly	Harvey J. Wender and[2] Della Wender	Ready Savings & Loan[3]

G. PROPERTY LOCATION:	H. SETTLEMENT AGENT:	I. SETTLEMENT DATE:
1040 Clear Street[4] Big Red, Nebraska	Ready Savings & Loan[5] PLACE OF SETTLEMENT: 8052 Alert Drive[6]	May 15, 1987[7]

J. SUMMARY OF BORROWER'S TRANSACTION		K. SUMMARY OF SELLER'S TRANSACTION	
100. GROSS AMOUNT DUE FROM BORROWER:		**400. GROSS AMOUNT DUE TO SELLER:**	
101. Contract sales price [8]	84,000.00	401. Contract sales price [8]	84,000.00
102. Personal property		402. Personal property	
103. Settlement charges to borrower (line 1400) [9]	2,341.46	403.	
104.		404.	
105.		405.	
Adjustments for items paid by seller in advance		*Adjustments for items paid by seller in advance*	
106. City/town taxes to		406. City/town taxes to	
107. County taxes to		407. County taxes to	
108. Assessments to		408. Assessments to	
109. Real Estate Taxes 5-15 to 7-1 [17]	193.75	409. Real Estate Taxes 5-15 to 7-1	193.75
110.		410.	
111.		411.	
112.		412.	
120. **GROSS AMOUNT DUE FROM BORROWER**	86,535.26	420. **GROSS AMOUNT DUE TO SELLER** [26]	84,193.75
200. AMOUNTS PAID BY OR IN BEHALF OF BORROWER:		**500. REDUCTIONS IN AMOUNT DUE TO SELLER:**	
201. Deposit or earnest money [18]	2,000.00	501. Excess deposit (see instructions)	
202. Principal amount of new loan(s)	67,200.00	502. Settlement charges to seller (line 1400) [27]	6,168.88
203. Existing loan(s) taken subject to		503. Existing loan(s) taken subject to	
204.		504. Payoff of first mortgage loan [28]	45,320.10
205.		505. Payoff of second mortgage loan	
206.		506.	
207.		507.	
208.		508.	
209.		509.	
Adjustments for items unpaid by seller		*Adjustments for items unpaid by seller*	
210. City/town taxes to		510. City/town taxes to	
211. County taxes to		511. County taxes to	
212. Assessments to		512. Assessments to	
213.		513.	
214.		514.	
215.		515.	
216.		516.	
217.		517.	
218.		518.	
219.		519.	
220. **TOTAL PAID BY/FOR BORROWER** [19]	69,200.00	520. **TOTAL REDUCTION AMOUNT DUE SELLER** [29]	51,488.98
300. CASH AT SETTLEMENT FROM/TO BORROWER		**600. CASH AT SETTLEMENT TO/FROM SELLER**	
301. Gross amount due from borrower (line 120)	86,535.26	601. Gross amount due to seller (line 420)	84,193.75
302. Less amounts paid by/for borrower (line 220)	(69,200.00)	602. Less reductions in amount due seller (line 520)	51,488.98
303. CASH (☐ FROM) (☐ TO) BORROWER [20]	17,335.26	603. CASH (☒ TO) (☐ FROM) SELLER [30]	32,704.77

Amt. paid to agent at closing   15,543.38
Amt. due to lender at closing   1,791.88
Total ----------------------- 17,335.26

FIGURE 10.10 The lender's settlement statement.

–2–

L. SETTLEMENT CHARGES		PAID FROM BORROWER'S FUNDS AT SETTLEMENT	PAID FROM SELLER'S FUNDS AT SETTLEMENT
700. TOTAL SALES/BROKER'S COMMISSION based on price $ @ % =			
Division of Commission (line 700) as follows:			
701. $ 5880 to A-1 Real Estate			
702. $ to			
703. Commission paid at Settlement		**21**	5,880.00
704.			
800. ITEMS PAYABLE IN CONNECTION WITH LOAN			
801. Loan Origination Fee 1 %		672.00	
802. Loan Discount %	**10**		
803. Appraisal Fee to			
804. Credit Report to Big Red Credit Bureau		12.50	
805. Lender's Inspection Fee		55.00	
806. Mortgage Insurance Application Fee to			
807. Assumption Fee			
808.			
809.			
810.			
811.			
900. ITEMS REQUIRED BY LENDER TO BE PAID IN ADVANCE			
901. Interest from 5-15-87 to 6-1-87 @ $ 24.27 /day x 15 Days	**11**	280.00	
902. Mortgage Insurance Premium for months to			
903. Hazard Insurance Premium for 1 years to Bleecher Ins. Co.	**12**	390.00	
904. years to			
905.			
1000. RESERVES DEPOSITED WITH LENDER			
1001. Hazard insurance 2 months @ $ 32.50 per month		65.00	
1002. Mortgage insurance months @ $ per month			
1003. City property taxes months @ $ per month	**13**		
1004. County property taxes months @ $ per month			
1005. Annual assessments months @ $ per month			
1006. Real Estate Tax 5 months @ $129.166 per month		645.83	
1007. months @ $ per month			
1008. months @ $ per month			
1100. TITLE CHARGES			
1101. Settlement or closing fee to			
1102. Abstract or title search to			
1103. Title examination to		55.00	
1104. Title insurance binder to			
1105. Document preparation to			
1106. Notary fees to	**14**		
1107. Attorney's fees to			
(includes above items numbers;			
1108. Title insurance to Protection Title Company		159.63	**22** 159.63
(includes above items numbers;			
1109. Lender's coverage $ 67,200			
1110. Owner's coverage $ 84,000			
1111.			
1112.			
1113.			
1200. GOVERNMENT RECORDING AND TRANSFER CHARGES			
1201. Recording fees: Deed $ 3.25 ; Mortgage $ 3.25 ; Releases $ 3.25	**15**	6.50	**23** 3.25
1202. City/county tax/stamps: Deed $; Mortgage $			
1203. State tax/stamps: Deed $; Mortgage $			**24** 126.00
1204.			
1205.			
1300. ADDITIONAL SETTLEMENT CHARGES			
1301. Survey to			
1302. Pest inspection to			
1303.			
1304.			
1305.			
1400. TOTAL SETTLEMENT CHARGES (enter on lines 103, Section J and 502, Section K)		**16** 2,341.46	**25** 6,168.88

NM-148b
(Rev. 7-76)
ACKNOWLEDGED: Buyer *Kurt K Kindly* Seller *Judy M Selling* Date _____

HUD-1

FIGURE 10.10, continued

Proceeding through the borrower's transaction (section J):

9. Total costs are brought forward from section L (numbers 10 through 15).

10. This column shows the loan **origination fee** charged by the lender—the $672.00 charge represents one percent of the $67,200 loan the borrowers are receiving. The lender's appraisal fee is $55.00 and the credit report is $12.50.

11. The lender will charge interest on the loan from the settlement date to the next month. The closing date is May 15, so interest is charged from that date to June 1. Many lenders do not request a payment until the following month (in this case, July 1) so the interest will always be one month in arrears. When the borrowers make their July 1 payment, they would then be paying the June interest. The loan of $67,200 times 10 percent interest equals $6720 interest per year. This amount, divided by twelve months, equals $560.00; fifteen days (one-half month) equals $280.00.

12. One year's hazard insurance is collected from the borrowers.

13. **Reserves** will be needed if the lender is going to establish a reserve account and collect monthly taxes and insurance along with the principal and interest payments. Some lenders prefer to escrow these items to assure their payment. The yearly insurance premium is $390.00. The lender will need that amount when the policy is due next May. Since the payments will not begin until July 1, the lender will be short two months, so $65.00 will be charged the purchaser at the time of the closing so that the full $390 will be in the account when the premium is due.

    The same procedure will be applied to the taxes. The date when taxes are due and payable will determine the amount needed for the reserve account. Assuming the second-half taxes are due and payable August 1, the lender will require five months escrow. Since the yearly taxes are $1,550.00 there must be $645.83 in the reserve account. In the event that the taxes or insurance are subsequently increased, the monthly payments will be raised accordingly.

14. The title charge will differ between lenders (and between various areas of the country), so all of the items in this section are pertinent to this particular settlement. If the settlement was handled by an attorney, title company, or escrow agency, these expenses would be noted here. Since the lenders are placing a new loan on the property, they are also servicing the customer by handling the closing transaction. The attorney fees are $55.00, and one-half of the title costs (159.63) are charged to the borrower.

15. The recording fees include $3.25 for recording the buyer's deed and another $3.25 for recording the buyer's mortgage (line 1201).

16. The gross amount due from the borrower is entered here, and carried back to number 9 (line 103).

17. The buyer's costs are credited to the seller. In this instance, the seller **prepaid** taxes. So the buyer will reimburse the seller for them.

18. The borrowers are credited with their earnest deposit and the loan that will be issued.

19. The total of the credits to the borrower is entered here.

20. The difference between line 120 (costs) and number 19 (line 220–credits) is recorded.

Upon closing with the buyer, the deed will be passed to the lender, who will record the deed (see figure 10.11) and the mortgage (figure 9.2).

Now let's proceed through the seller's transaction:

21. If two brokerage firms had been involved in the sale, one firm listing the property and another firm selling it, the division of commission would be shown. In this instance, A-1 Real Estate handled both the listing and the sale.

22. The sellers are charged half of the title insurance.

23. The sellers are charged $3.25 for release of their mortgage.

24. The state documentary stamps are generally paid by the sellers and will vary from state to state. In Nebraska, they are payable on the full sales price at $1.50 per $1,000 ($1.50 times $84,000 equals $126.00).

25. The total charged to seller.

26. The selling price of $84,000 is shown at number 8 of the seller's summary. This figure, added to the $193.75 tax credit, is brought down to number 26.

27. The settlement charges due from the seller are brought forward from number 25 (line 1400).

28. The amount still due on the first mortgage, which will be paid off, is listed.

29. The costs in numbers 27 and 28 are totalled.

30. The balance due to the seller is entered. This sum must balance with the real estate firm's statement (see figure 10.12).

THE SELLER'S SETTLEMENT STATEMENT

Now let's proceed to the analysis of the seller's statement. When the real estate broker delivers the proceeds from the sale to the seller, he also presents the **closing statement**, showing all disbursements. These include:

The seller's proceeds

1. The selling price (a **credit** to the owner).

2. The mortgage balance of $45,320.10, which appears as a **debit** since it is *owed* by the seller.

3. The cost of the release of the mortgage. This is filed at the County Courthouse to prove the mortgage has been paid in full and is no longer a lien on the property.

4. The state documentary stamps, as explained in Chapter 1, are based on the rate of $1.50 per $1,000 of the sale price. This rate will vary from state to state, and is most generally paid for by the grantor.

5. The cost of one-half of the title insurance is $159.63.

6. The prorated taxes are a credit, since the first half are paid and the buyers will reimburse the owner for them from the time they take possession. Keep in mind that the person who has the use of the property will be expected to pay the taxes.

7. The brokerage fee of 7 percent is based on the gross sales price of $84,000, so we debit the seller $5,880.00.

8. The amount of $32,704.77 is the sum due the seller as proceeds from the sale. This figure was arrived at by totalling the credit side, which shows the

NO. 342—WARRANTY DEED, VESTING ENTIRE TITLE IN SURVIVOR.   OMAHA PRINTING COMPANY

KNOW ALL MEN BY THESE PRESENTS, That

Harvey J. Wender and Della J. Wender, husband and wife, **1**

in consideration of Eighty Four Thousand and no/100 ($84,000.00)----- **2** ---------- DOLLARS
in hand paid, do hereby grant, bargain, sell, convey and confirm unto **3**

Kurt K. Kindly and Susan A. Kindly, husband and wife **4**

as **JOINT TENANTS,** and not as tenants in common; the following described real estate, situate in the County of
Kent   and State of Nebraska, to-wit:

Lot Eight (8), Block One (1), in Confusion Hill
subdivision, an Addition to the City of Big Red, **5**
Kent County, Nebraska, as surveyed, platted
and recorded.

STATE
DOCUMENTARY **6**
STAMPS
126.00

together with all the tenements, hereditaments, and appurtenances to the same belonging, and all the estate, title, dower,
right of homestead, claim or demand whatsoever of the said grantors , of, in or to the same, or any part thereof,
subject to covenants, restrictions and easements of record, all regular taxes and
subsequent taxes and assessments. **7**

**IT BEING THE INTENTION OF ALL PARTIES HERETO, THAT IN THE EVENT OF THE DEATH OF
EITHER OF SAID GRANTEES, THE ENTIRE FEE SIMPLE TITLE TO THE REAL ESTATE DESCRIBED
HEREIN SHALL VEST IN THE SURVIVING GRANTEE. 8**

TO HAVE AND TO HOLD the above described premises, with the appurtenances, unto the said grantees as
JOINT TENANTS, and not as tenants in common, and to their assigns, or to the heirs and assigns of the survivor of
them, forever, and we the grantors named herein for ourselves **9** and our heirs, executors, and
administrators, do covenant with the grantees named herein and with their assigns and with the heirs and assigns of
the survivor of them, that we are lawfully seized of said premises; that they are free from incumbrance except
as stated herein, and that we the said grantors have good right and lawful authority to sell the same, and
that we will and our heirs, executors and administrators shall warrant and defend the same
unto the grantees named herein and unto their assigns and unto the heirs and assigns of the survivor of them, forever,
against the lawful claims of all persons whomsoever, excluding the exceptions named herein.

IN WITNESS WHEREOF we have hereunto set our hands this 14th day of
May   A. D., 1987   *Harvey J. Wender*
                                           (Harvey J. Wender)
In presence of   *Della J. Wender* **10**
Judy M. Selling **11**   (Della J. Wender)

STATE OF NEBRASKA,   }
County of Kent   } ss.   On this 14th day of May
A. D. 1987 , before me, a Notary Public in and for said County, personally came the above named
Harvey J. Wender and Della J. Wender, husband and wife

12 who are personally known to me to be the identical persons whose names
affixed to the above instrument as grantors , and they have
acknowledged said instrument to be their voluntary act and deed.

SEAL   **WITNESS** my hand and Notarial Seal the date last aforesaid.
Judy M. Selling Notary Public.
My commission expires on the 8th day of July A. D., 1990

FIGURE 10.11
A warranty deed.

A-1 REAL ESTATE
1104 Homestead Avenue
Big Red, Nebraska

SELLER'S CLOSING STATEMENT

NAME _____ Harvey J. and Della Wender _____ DATE_5/15/87_

ADDRESS_____ 1040 Clear Street, Big Red, Nebraska _____

	Debit	Credit	
Selling Price	$	$84,000.00	1
Title Insurance	159.63		5
State Documentary Stamps $1.50 per 1,000	126.00		4
Mortgage Release	3.25		3
Balance of First Mortgage Ready S & L	45,320.10		2
Prorated Taxes ($1550 @ 1½ mo. 5/15/87–7/1/87)		193.75	6
Professional Services Fee (7%)	5,880.00		7
Balance due to Seller, Proceeds from sale	32,704.77		8
Totals	$84,193.75	$84,193.75	

FIGURE 10.12
The seller's
closing statement.

$84,000 sale price and the tax proration of $193.75, and subtracting the debit column from the credits.

At the time the new loan (for the buyers) closes with the lending institution, the broker gives the lender a copy of the seller's closing statement. Real estate firms need to maintain accurate records, so a ledger sheet revealing the disbursements from the trust account is also included (see figure 10.13).

A-1 REAL ESTATE COMPANY
TRUST ACCOUNT BALANCE SHEET

Wender, H.

Kindly, K.

1040 Clear Street, Big Red, Nebraska

Date	Name	Ck#		Credit	Balance
4/09/87	Kurt A. Kindly and Susan A. Kindly		$	$ 2,000.00	$ 2,000.00
5/15/87	Balance due from K. Kindly			15,543.38	17,543.38
5/15/87	Proceeds from Ready Savings and Loan			21,876.65*	39,420.03
5/15/87	Best Title Company	441	319.36		39,110.77
5/15/87	Bleecher Insurance Co.	442	390.00		38,710.79
5/15/87	Register of Deeds	443	126.00		38,584.77
5/15/87	H. Wender and D. Wender Proceeds from Sale	444	33,704.77		5,880.00
5/15/87	A-1 Real Estate Co.	445	5,880.00		–0–

The balance sheet from A-1 Real Estate Company Trust Account records is completed as shown. This ledger sheet shows the receipts and disbursements for this sale.

*The proceeds from Ready Savings and Loan to A-1 Real Estate represent the difference between the existing loan of $45,320.10 and the new loan of $67,200, minus the $3.25 deduction to record the release of the old mortgage.

The last check written will be to the real estate company for their brokerage fee due. It will be placed in the firm's business account and from there will be paid to the salesperson(s) involved in the listing and sale of the property.

FIGURE 10.13 A trust account balance sheet.

SUMMARY

This chapter furnishes invaluable information on the closing of the transaction. The steps taken prior to the actual closing are reviewed, with the lending institution's responsibility defined. Numerous documents used in the preparation of the closing are included. The closing statement the lender completes for the buyer as required by federal law is evaluated step by step.

The real estate firm's obligation in preparing the settlement statement is reviewed, with a detailed accounting for both buyer and seller.

KEY WORDS AND CONCEPTS

Closing statement: An accounting of costs and credits to buyer and seller upon finalization of the sale.

Credit report: A statement of the purchaser's credit rating; reveals his or her past performance in paying debts.

Credits: Assets; something with worth or value.

Debits: Costs; charges against a buyer or seller.

Lien waiver: A statement signed by the sellers affirming they have no unpaid debts against the property.

Origination fee: A finance fee paid to the lender by the borrower.

Prepaids: Items paid in advance, such as taxes and insurance.

Prorations: Dividing costs between buyer and seller.

Reserves: Funds impounded by the lender to pay for taxes and insurance when they become due.

Title insurance: Insures the title against defects occurring before the policyholder took title.

Title search: An examination of public records to determine if there are any defects in the title.

REVIEW QUESTIONS

1. At the time of the closing, any prepaid taxes would be considered a
   a. credit to the buyer
   b. credit to the seller
   c. debit to the seller
   d. none of the above

2. The mortgage release is charged to
   a. the seller
   b. the buyer
   c. the loan company
   d. the seller's agent

3. The HUD Settlement Statement is best defined as
   a. a means of establishing the prorations of a closing.
   b. a means of regulating the real estate closing.
   c. a summary of charges to be paid by the borrower and the seller at the closing of a sale.
   d. a means of prohibiting the finder's fee.

4. Before the closing, the lender does all of the following except
   a. obtaining verification of the borrower's employment.
   b. ordering an appraisal on the property.
   c. obtaining the sellers' signatures on the deed.
   d. ordering a credit report on the borrower.

5. The cost of recording the deed is charged to
   a. the seller
   b. the buyer
   c. both of the above
   d. neither of the above

6. The most accurate definition of a closing statement would be
   a. the reconciliation of credits and debits to the buyer and seller.
   b. the proration of credits due the brokerage firm.
   c. the establishment of the brokerage fee due from the purchaser.
   d. the establishment of all expenses due to the lender from the purchaser.

7. The following charge(s) are usually the responsibility of the buyer:
   a. the insurance premium
   b. state documentary stamps
   c. both of the above
   d. neither of the above

8. The most commonly used method of closing a sale is
   a. escrow agent
   b. escrow closing
   c. settlement closing
   d. buyer's agent

9. The brokerage fee is charged to
   a. the buyer
   b. the seller
   c. the lender
   d. both a and b

10. A reserve held by the lender to pay for taxes and insurance when due is called the
    a. closing statement
    b. proration
    c. earnest deposit
    d. escrow

11. At closing, the settlement statements show
    a. how much the buyer pays at closing.
    b. how much the seller is to receive as proceeds from the sale.
    c. both a and b
    d. neither a nor b

12. In the settlement statement for the sale of a house, all of the following are credited to the buyer except
    a. the purchase price
    b. the down payment
    c. the earnest deposit
    d. the purchase-money mortgage

13. A copy of the closing cost statement should go to
    a. buyer and seller
    b. the recorder's office where the deed is being held
    c. both of the above
    d. neither of the above

14. A closing takes place and the seller is delinquent $572 on his taxes. This would show on the statement as a
    a. debit to the seller
    b. credit to the seller and debit to the buyer
    c. credit to the buyer
    d. credit to the seller

15. Mr. Smith's property tax is $948.00 per year and is paid semiannually January 1st and July 1st. He sold the property to Ms. Huff, and closing took place August 1. The settlement would show
    a. Mr. Smith will have to pay $553.00
    b. Mr. Smith will be credited $79.00
    b. both a and b
    d. neither a nor b

16. Beverly Buyer purchases a house for $35,000. She deposits 10 percent on the contract and acquires a 75 percent loan. The lender charges her a 1 percent origination fee. How much money will Ms. Buyer need at closing?
    a. $5512.50
    b. $5250.00
    c. $5750.00
    d. $9012.50

17. When an existing mortgage is assumed by the buyer, it appears as a
    a. credit to the seller
    b. credit to the buyer and the seller
    c. credit to the buyer, debit to the seller
    d. debit to the buyer

Answer questions 18–21 from the following information.

On May 10, 1983, Jane Sellum, a broker for A-1 Realty, listed Harry Brown's house for $82,950 for a period of ninety days. The commission is to be 7 percent of the gross sales price with 30 percent for the listing agent. Taxes of $1,320 per year are paid and the $302 insurance for one year was paid March 20. Agent Isaac Blake with ABC Realty sold the property July 6 for $81,000, with an August 20 possession date.

18. What commission does the listing agent earn?
    a. $1741.95
    b. $1701.00
    c. $5806.50
    d. $4105.50

19. The prorated tax amount is
    a. $843.40
    b. $953.40
    c. $476.67
    d. $513.33

20. The taxes would appear on the closing statement as a
    a. debit to the buyer
    b. credit to the seller
    c. credit to the buyer
    d. both a and b

21. If the buyer assumes the existing insurance policy, the prorated amount will be a
    a. credit of $125.81 to seller
    b. credit of $176.19 to seller
    c. debit of $125.81 to seller
    d. none of the above

Other Aspects of Real Estate Ownership

PART THREE

Condominiums, Townhouses, and Cooperatives

11

New life styles have emerged, and along with them have come new variations of home ownership. While shelter used to be limited mostly to either home ownership or apartment rental, many new options have appeared in the housing market. The single-family home with its picket fence and rose hedge has been the traditional American dream, but it is being replaced across the country by a new mode of living. The growing trend is to **condominium** ownership. The word *condominium* is derived from the Latin words meaning "for exercising domain with others." Condominium ownership is the individual ownership of a single-family unit in a multifamily structure or group of buildings, together with joint ownership of common areas. It is a way of life, not just a type of building or living complex. A condominium can be a townhouse, a duplex, a four-plex, a high-rise structure, an office or a commercial building. This form of group ownership provides the owner with individual and absolute title to his own living space, just as in a single-family home. Along with receiving a deed to the property, he owns an undivided interest in the common areas of the property.

CONDOMINIUMS

Condominium ownership was created by a special real estate law that allows individual ownership within a larger estate. The owner of the development files a master deed and a declaration of the *condominium regime* along with the plot and plans of the area to be developed. A property that was previously a single traditional estate is thus divided into a number of units within a common area. Recognized in all fifty states, the Horizontal Property Act allows for ownership of a specific unit of space that differs from traditional ownership of property with rights to the surface, subsurface, and air space above the property. The individual unit is not complete without an undivided interest in the whole area.

Single ownership within a master deed

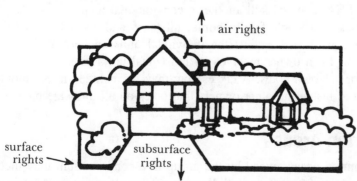

air rights

surface rights

subsurface rights

As we learned in Chapter 3 on land descriptions, property boundaries are established by surveying a particular parcel of land. By relying on previously established reference points, the boundaries are staked out and recorded. As the sketch indicates, the boundaries are defined and the individual has ownership of that area into the earth's surface and up into the sky above her ground lot. The condominium owner

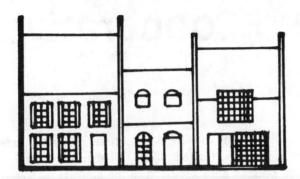

may also own space in the sky and beneath the earth's surface if she owns a duplex or townhouse. In a high-rise type of condominium, in lieu of having title to a piece of land on the earth's surface, ownership is created that allows the individual a cubic unit of space. This space is called an apartment **air lot.** According to this horizontal

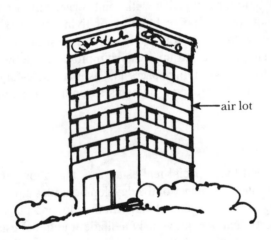

property division, the individual owners of these cubes of space also have ownership in the common areas. The purchaser obtains a mortgage on terms agreeable to him or to her and is liable for only his or her own mortgage, not for any default of other owners in the condominium unit. One owner may have paid cash while another may have an FHA loan and still another a conventional loan.

Just as in a single-family home, all taxes and special assessments on a condominium are levied against the individual units and not against the whole condominium. Each owner receives an individual tax assessment and is liable solely for his or her own taxes. A tax escrow may be included in the monthly mortgage payment to insure the other owners that taxes on all units are paid.

Common Areas

Areas jointly owned   The **common areas** owned by the group in a condominium may include the land, the exterior surfaces of the buildings, roofs, yards, driveways, stairways, and any special features such as swimming pools and tennis courts. Sharing the monthly cost of maintenance and repair of the common area with the other residents tends to reduce expenses since costs are divided by the group. Another attraction of condominium living is freedom from lawn care, snow removal, and exterior maintenance. This carefree life-style, which eliminates outside maintenance chores for the owner and makes added recreational facilities available, draws many people to the condominium way of life. Many condominiums offer such special amenities as tennis courts, swimming pools, and putting greens.

Bylaws

The condominium declaration states the covenants, restrictions, and conditions of the condominium regime. The **bylaws** provide for an **owners' association** to administer the affairs of the common elements and facilities. This gives the individual a greater voice in these matters. It also allows the association board to levy charges against individual owners for the maintenance of the common areas. If monthly assessments are not paid by an individual, the bylaws provide for the legal enforcement of placing a lien against the delinquent owner's unit.

Owners' association

Assessments

Each unit in a condominium is assessed according to the ratio of that unit to the total condominium units. If one owner has 1,000 square feet, his unit will be assessed for less than an owner with 1,500 square feet. Some states require that a definite formula be followed regarding this ratio. It may be by value, by living area, by market price, or in equal shares.

Due to high land costs and growing construction costs, more living space can generally be obtained in a condominium for the same number of dollars invested. Many condominium residents feel they have the best of two worlds; the advantages of ownership and the benefits of apartment living. The owner has the security of apartment living and the tax benefits of home ownership. Paying for a condominium is also much more appealing than collecting rent receipts, because the buyer has an opportunity to build up equity. Renting provides no deductions for income tax purposes, while the condominium owner may deduct the interest on his mortgage payments and his property taxes.

Carefree ownership

TOWNHOUSES

There is no legal difference between a high-rise condominium building and **townhouse** units. The townhouse is a form of condominium construction. It is an individual unit joined to another unit by a common wall. The land beneath the unit is sometimes deeded to the townhouse owner and not included as part of the common area. The townhouse resembles the single-family home since the units do not have neighbors above or below. However, land costs are saved since the units can be clustered together.

COOPERATIVES

In **cooperative** ownership of an apartment unit, the apartment owner buys shares of stock in the corporation (or partnership or trust) that holds title to the entire building. The purchaser of a cooperative apartment is thus a shareholder in a corporation whose principal asset is a building. Owning stock in the corporation allows

Owning shares of stock in real estate

the purchaser to occupy a specific unit in the building; she occupies the unit, but she does not own it, since her interest is considered to be personal property. A nonprofit corporation holds title to the property with the shareholders owning the stock.

The shareholder is responsible for his pro rata share of the corporation expenses, which include real estate taxes, maintenance, mortgage payment, and other miscellaneous costs. The owner can deduct his proportion of taxes and interest charges on the mortgage for income tax purposes only if 80 percent of the cooperative's income is derived from tenant owner rentals.

CONDOMINIUMS VS. CO-OPS

There are many fundamental variances between a cooperative and a condominium. A condominium owner takes out an individual mortgage depending on her needs, and she is responsible only for her own mortgage. There is no blanket mortgage on the building. A co-op has a single mortgage on the entire building. If one stockholder defaults, then the other owners are liable, or risk losing their investments.

While the condominium owner has absolute title to his unit, in a co-op, the entire corporation owns the building and the shareholder holds shares in the corporation, giving him a **proprietary lease** for the shares owned. Since a single mortgage covers the entire building, an owner who decides to sell his shares may find that the buyer cannot obtain financing on the individual unit. The shares he is purchasing will have to be paid for in cash, through a personal loan, or through an installment contract from the seller. Cooperative shareholders may be quite selective in allowing buyers to purchase shares. They participate in the operation of the co-op, as do the condominium owners.

TIME SHARING

Joint ownership of a unit

Time sharing is a new concept of ownership in real estate whereby several purchasers buy an undivided interest in the property, with each party holding the right to use the property for a certain time period. Time sharing attracts buyers who want condominiums to use only for vacations. These buyers purchase the units with others, lured by the idea that the property's appreciation will build an equity for them along with giving them the enjoyment of a vacation home. Mainly used in resort areas, time sharing allows each owner a fixed or floating time period to use the accommodations. A reservation system or rotation system for use may be set up. If six owners purchased a unit, they would each have two months of the year to use it. It would be important to establish in the agreement who would take the responsibility for caring for the property and the provisions for sale if one party decides to divest of his interest.

All of the owners in a time-sharing arrangement share the expenses, mortgage payments, and taxes. The costs of maintenance, upkeep of the recreational facilities, furniture replacement, maid service, and management must be taken into consideration by the purchasers. Each owner has input in controlling expenses through the owners' association.

A long-term lease form of time sharing has also been developed. A whole unit or a portion of a unit in a hotel or apartment house is sold to individuals who have several weeks a year to use the space. The lessee shares in the maintenance and management costs of operating the building.

VACATION LICENSES

While there are many legal structures for a time-share plan, they basically can be grouped into two broad areas: (1) buying an *ownership* interest in the real estate, or (2) buying the *right to use* a living space for a specified period of time without actually owning an interest in the real property. This **vacation license** gives the purchaser the right to use a particular unit for a designated period of time. According to the terms of the contract, most licenses to use cannot be sold for profit. These contracts state that the unit cannot be leased to another in compliance with federal and state laws, so the license cannot be interpreted as a security.

Buying future vacations

In vacation areas that are overbuilt with condominiums, interval ownership has provided developers with a means of selling units. Although there may not be enough individual buyers for each unit, under this system a purchaser can buy one week for a period of ten to fifty years. Thus, the developer can sell the unit fifty times over, usually reserving two weeks a year for maintenance. In some instances, the unit will revert back to the developer at the end of the specified time.

The return on selling vacation licenses is much greater to the developer than selling single condominium units. For example, if the unit would normally sell for $90,000 but is instead sold for fifty weeks at $4,000 a week, the sale price is now $200,000. One of the selling points to the buyer is the increasing cost of rentals; future vacations are purchased at today's prices. Maintenance fees, however, are reassessed to each vacation-license holder each year.

Time-share ownership has been recognized by hotel chains, and two-week luxury cruises are now offered to purchasers for as long as twenty years. The idea of buying a vacation for the future at today's prices may well become the new American dream.

EXCHANGE PROGRAMS

One of the most evident objections to time sharing is the idea of vacationing at the same time and same place year after year. Exchange programs are alleviating this concern: the owner swaps time with another owner at another resort. Resorts across the country are forming exchange groups between their owners, so the owner of a time-sharing plan in California could swap for equal time in Florida. As the concept of time sharing spreads, exchange companies are being formed across the world to meet the needs of their members. For certain membership dues, an individual owner may join such a group and make application to use a unit in another resort.

Swapping use

Leisure time is on the increase. If the average person does not want or cannot afford a second home, a time-share program may be the answer.

SUMMARY

Although the traditional dream of middle-class Americans has been to own a single-family home, other types of housing have surfaced to accommodate the need for shelter, especially in areas where land is scarce, as in high-employment centers. The large metropolitan cities have seen the concepts of condominium and townhouse ownership spreading. In fact, so many apartment houses have been converted to condominiums that some cities have placed moratoriums on future conversions. In some sections of the country, the trend toward condominiums has reduced rental units to a point where adequate rental housing is in jeopardy.

Many times the conversion units have just had "cosmetic" face lifts, perhaps by replacing paint and carpeting. Depending on the age of the structure, the purchaser may be buying a unit that will soon need a new furnace, an air conditioner, and appliance replacements. It behooves the purchaser of a conversion unit to carefully examine these component parts.

Because so many condominium units are available in vacation areas such as ski resorts and regions near water, the developers in these areas have sold units on a time-share basis. Still others have sold vacation licenses where the purchaser buys only the right to use the unit for future vacations. These licenses are sold on the premise that housing costs will continue to escalate, and that the purchaser can save money by buying future vacations at today's prices.

When purchasing a cooperative, the buyer receives shares or stock for which he obtains the right to possession of a unit. Since the building is taxed as a single, whole unit and necessary assessments are divided proportionally among the owners, the solvency of the investment depends to a great degree upon the other shareholders. Some exclusive buildings are sold as cooperatives so the owners can select their buyers carefully. In essence, these owners can "tactfully" discriminate on who they wish to have as neighbors.

The varied choices on the types of housing available today literally offer something for everyone. Many authorities feel that traditional single-family home ownership will before long be a remnant of the past.

KEY WORDS AND CONCEPTS

Air lot: A "cube of space" individually owned in a high- rise unit.

Bylaws: Condominium rules that outline the covenants, restrictions, and conditions of the regime.

Common elements: Common areas such as yards, stairways, and pools that are jointly owned by condominium owners.

Condominium: Individual ownership of a single unit in a multiunit structure or group of buildings, with joint ownership of common areas.

Cooperative: Ownership of shares or stock in a corporation for which the individual obtains a proprietary lease.

Owners association: Individual condominium owners who group together to administrate the affairs of the common elements and facilities.

Proprietary lease: The right of a co-op shareholder to occupy a unit.

Time sharing: An arrangement whereby several purchasers own a property in which they share the use for specified periods of time.

Townhouse: A form of condominium construction; individual units joined by common walls.

Vacation license: The right to use a particular unit for a specified period of time.

REVIEW QUESTIONS

1. In a condominium development, decisions regarding repairs or improvements to the common areas are made by
   a. individual tenants
   b. the owners' association
   c. a board of governors
   d. the Real Estate Commission

2. What type of ownership does a condominium owner hold?
   a. fee simple
   b. estate in trust
   c. estate in rescission
   d. group ownership

3. Under the condominium type of ownership
   a. individual units are mortgaged separately.
   b. a blanket mortgage covers the regime.
   c. only common areas are mortgaged.
   d. none of the above

4. Individual fee ownership of a single unit in a multifamily structure is characteristic of
   a. a cooperative
   b. a condominium
   c. time-sharing
   d. all of the above

5. The following statement(s) are true regarding condominium ownership:
   a. Failure of an owner to pay taxes on his condominium creates a lien on his unit only.
   b. The entire condominium regime is responsible for any tax default.
   c. A tennis court in a condominium project is a common element.
   d. The condominium owner owns stock or shares in the project.
   e. More than one of the above are true.

6. Concerning the tax liability of a condominium owner and a co-op owner
   a. each is individually responsible for his own taxes.
   b. a co-op owner is individually responsible for his taxes.
   c. a condominium owner is individually responsible for his taxes.
   d. neither is responsible for taxes.

7. The amenities of condominium ownership may include
   a. no exterior maintenance
   b. reduced maintenance and repair expenses in group ownership
   c. income tax deductions on interest payment
   d. all of the above

8. The difference between a condominium and a townhouse is
   a. only condominium owners may have fee simple title.
   b. condominiums are high-rise structures.
   c. townhouses have no common areas.
   d. the form of construction.

9. The time-sharing plan of ownership is best explained as
   a. a condominium owner shares his individual unit.
   b. several purchasers own a property and share in its use.
   c. an easy payment plan is used in purchasing a condominium.
   d. none of the above

10. The "cube of space" owned in a high-rise condominium is called
    a. a space lot
    b. an air lot
    c. a tax lot
    d. an apartment lot

11. The owner of a condominium shares in all of the following, except
    a. a unit deed
    b. a master deed
    c. a proprietary lease
    d. the bylaws of the owners' association

12. In a cooperative apartment complex, each unit owner is individually responsible for
    a. the building insurance
    b. paying her own taxes
    c. both a and b
    d. neither a nor b

13. A time-sharing estate is an example of
    a. severalty ownership
    b. a leasehold estate
    c. a nonfreehold estate in a condominium
    d. the right to exclusive use for a specified time each year

14. Which of the following statement(s) about a unit in a condominium building is (are) correct?
    a. It is eligible for title insurance as a separate piece of property.
    b. It can be individually mortgaged.
    c. both of the above
    d. neither of the above

15. In which of the following must the owners or occupants in a building be stockholders of the corporation that owns the building?
    a. a cooperative apartment house
    b. a condominium building
    c. both of the above
    d. neither of the above

16. The horizontal property regime refers to
    a. set-backs from the perimeter of a property
    b. condominium ownership
    c. homestead laws
    d. cooperatives

17. Which fee would a condominium owner least likely be expected to pay?
    a. a recreation fee
    b. a condo maintenance fee
    c. a stock transfer fee
    d. a hazard insurance fee

Leases | 12

Many individuals need to use real property but don't need or desire absolute ownership. For the segment of our population that is nomadic in nature, the desire and need for permanent ownership is not of primary concern. In fact, because many households are headed today by younger and older people, the population age distribution favors apartments. Many students living away from home, young adults working in cities, retired people, and newly married couples not certain of permanency in a locality prefer to rent until they establish definite residency. It must also be remembered that the continued trend of climbing construction costs and interest rates price many people out of home ownership.

Commercial rentals are also needed by small businesses without the cash flow required to purchase land and erect buildings. The rights and conditions imposed by a lease are discussed in this chapter.

THE LEASE

A **lease** is a contract between a **lessee** (tenant) and a **lessor** (owner) of real property. *Conveying the use* Two examples of leases are shown in figures 12.1 and 12.2. A lease contract between *of real property* two parties can also be considered a conveyance in that it gives the right of possession to the tenant, for which he pays the owner rent. This conveyance is referred to as a **demise,** or the conveyance of an estate under lease. In the lease, the words "grant, demise, and let" give the lessee the right of possession.

Upon expiration of the lease, the lessor again gains possession of the property. The lessor has a reversionary interest in the property while it is under lease. In other words, it will revert back to her when the lease terminates.

LEASEHOLD INTERESTS

As mentioned in Chapter 4, a lease is a less than freehold estate in that it is set for *Interests under lease terms* a definite period of time. The rights granted by a lease constitute a *leasehold interest*. Leasehold estates can be classified into four main types:

1. *Tenancy for years*. This estate is for a definite or fixed period of time as agreed to between the lessee and the lessor. The main characteristic of this lease is that it must have a stated expiration date. The term of a *lease for years* may

actually be less than a year, perhaps only for a week or a month. Upon the termination of a lease for years, the tenant must vacate and surrender possession of the property.

2. *Periodic tenancy.* This type of estate is for a specified period to period, such as a month-to-month, or year-to-year agreement. There is no set termination date, as the lease is automatically reviewed at the end of each period. If one of the parties wishes to cancel the lease, notice to quit must be given to the other party. A tenancy from month-to-month usually requires a thirty-day notice prior to the due date of the next month's rent to cancel the lease.

3. *Tenancy at will.* This nonfreehold estate at will provides for either the lessee or the lessor to terminate the agreement whenever they so desire. Most states require the party to give proper notice to terminate the lease. If one of the parties dies, the tenancy at will is automatically terminated.

4. *Tenancy at sufferance.* A tenant who remains in possession of the premises after his lease has expired has a tenancy at sufferance. The tenant stays in possession without consent of the landlord and is referred to as a holdover tenant. The tenant has a possessory interest in the land only because he has stayed past the expiration date, so technically he no longer has an estate in land; he has the lowest estate one can have in a leasehold estate. The lessor may evict the lessee or may decide to accept him according to the terms of the previous lease. If the landlord does not evict him, a periodic estate will be created.

LEASE CONTENTS

Provisions in a lease While the lease states the names of the parties and describes the property, it should also stipulate the terms and conditions of the agreement.

1. *Duration of the lease.* The commencement and termination dates of the lease should be set forth. If the lease is renewed, a new agreement should be written.
2. *Rent.* The amount of rent to be paid should be stipulated, along with the time and place payment is to be made.
3. *Possession, maintenance, and improvements.* Any conditions imposed upon the lessee and any exceptions to the lessee's rights should be enumerated.
4. *Liability of the parties.* The person held responsible for injuries resulting from conditions of the premises should be included.
5. *Transfer by the lessee.* It is to the lessee's benefit to have a clause of transfer in the lease.
6. *Special covenants, conditions, and provisions.* Any special rights and privileges of the parties should be included in the lease.

TERMINATION OF A LEASE

The lease term ends A lease may be terminated under the following conditions:

1. *Expiration of the lease.* When the term of the lease expires, the tenancy understandably ends. Usually a written notice must be given by the party desiring

to terminate the lease, especially under the terms of a tenancy at will or a periodic tenancy. A tenancy for years expires at the termination time stated in the lease so no notice need be given. In a tenancy at sufferance, the tenant has overstayed the lease term so it may be terminated at any time.

2. *Agreement between the parties.* By mutual agreement, the landlord and tenant can sever the lease. The lessee surrenders the lease and the lessor accepts the terms. This is referred to as **surrender and acceptance.** *Severing a lease*

3. *Breach of condition.* If either the lessee or lessor breaks the terms of the lease, a breach has been committed and the injured party may cancel the lease.

4. *Eviction of the lessee.* The lessee may be evicted through either actual eviction or constructive eviction.

 a. *Actual eviction.* The tenant is dismissed from the premises by the lessor. The tenant may have stayed over after the expiration of the lease (as a holdover tenant), or she may have failed to live up to the terms of the lease (for example, failure to pay rent).

 b. *Constructive eviction.* A lessee may break the terms of the lease if the owner violates the covenants or terms of the lease and interferes with the quiet enjoyment of the lessee. If the owner fails to maintain the property according to the terms of the lease, the tenant may break the lease under constructive eviction.

LEASE PROVISIONS

Leases for one year or less do not need to be in writing; however according to the statute of fraud in most states, if the lease is for more than one year, it must be in writing. In lieu of a written lease, the fact that the lessee takes possession is sufficient to affirm his acceptance of the lease and delivery by the lessor.

Rent is payable in advance, in money, chattel, labor, or provisions. The lessee has the right to enjoy the use of the property as specified in the lease, without interruption or invasion by the lessor or another.

An *option clause* allows the lessee the right to renew the lease upon the expiration date. The lessee may not be certain at the time s/he enters into the lease agreement if s/he will want to remain past the initial term of the lease. For example, a real estate broker may decide to open a second office. If she rents the branch office with an option, the option will allow her the choice of continuing or discontinuing business at the new location. *Various lease clauses*

A **tax participation clause** is an agreement in a lease whereby the lessee agrees to pay all or a stated portion of any increase in real estate taxes on the leased property. If a lessor's taxes increase $1,000 over the year and he has five tenants leasing equal square footage, each tenant's rent would rise $200 for the year. A tax participation clause is often used on office or commercial rentals. It offers the owner protection against rising costs of ownership.

The term **distraint** refers to the owner's right, pursuant to a court order, to seize the lessee's personal property if the lessee is in arrears (is behind) in his rent.

While improvements to the leased property by the lessee usually become the property of the lessor upon termination of the lease, *trade fixtures* become real upon being affixed to the leased premises and are generally removable by the tenant. Trade fixtures could include such items as display cases or shelves installed by the tenant.

Assigning a lease to another

When an unexpired portion of the lease is reconveyed to and accepted by the lessor, it is termed **surrender and acceptance.** If the lessee abandons the demised property without the owner's acceptance, he remains liable for the lease.

When one **assigns** a lease, s/he is giving the remainder of the lease over entirely. The lessee may assign his or her interest unless the terms of the lease expressly state otherwise.

The assignee (new lessee) obtains all the rights and interests that the assignor possessed. If the assignee does not live up to the terms of the lease, the assignor will be held responsible until he or she is released by the owner.

When a property is sold and there are existing leases on the premises, the leases are *assigned* to the new owner and are binding to the purchaser of the property.

When a lessee **sublets** the property, he retains a portion of the lease, or a portion of the premises. The lessee may sublet a room or the entire property for a limited time and then take over the lease at a later date.

Obligations of the Parties

Tenant responsibilities and rights

The *Uniform Landlord and Tenant Act* in force in many states lists the obligations of the parties to a lease. If the lease does not clearly indicate who is responsible for the conditions of the premises, this act clarifies the responsibility.

Basically, the tenant is required to keep the property clean and in good condition with the exception of the expected normal wear and tear through use. He is held responsible for destroying or damaging the premises. Garbage and other wastes must be disposed of in a clean and safe manner. The tenant must not disturb other tenants or nearby neighbors and is expected to conform to the law concerning occupation of the property.

The landlord, in turn, must comply with the minimum housing codes and keep the premises in good repair and safe to live in unless otherwise provided in the lease. The tenant may prefer to perform certain repairs in lieu of part of the rental payment. This may be done if an agreement is reached between the landlord and tenant. The landlord must also see that all electrical, plumbing, and other facilities are in good repair. S/he basically provides a habitable dwelling. It is understood the tenant will have quiet enjoyment; that is, the use of the property without interruption or invasion by the lessor or another.

Security Deposits

A **security deposit** is often required when the lessee takes possession of the property. This deposit is refundable upon expiration of the lease, providing the property has not been materially damaged.

In most states the landlord cannot request more than one month's rent as a security deposit. This deposit must be returned, with deductions for any repairs itemized, within a reasonable time after the tenant vacates and requests the refund.

TYPES OF LEASES

Leases generally fall into the following categories:

Extra lease expenses

The **net lease** requires the tenant to assume all or a portion of the property expenses normally paid by the owner, leaving the rent *net* to the lessor. Many long-term commercial and industrial leases are *triple net* leases. This type of lease places the responsibility of *all* the expenses upon the tenant, including taxes, repairs, maintenance, insurance, and generally even exterior maintenance. The triple net lease has a special appeal to the institutional lessor, such as a college or insurance company, as such a lessor would desire to avoid repairs and management concerns.

The **percentage lease** is based on a flat fee plus a percentage of the gross income received by the tenant doing business on the premises. Several factors must be considered in a percentage lease. The base rent may be low, but a percentage of the business income must be paid to the lessor. If the business income exceeds the lessee's expectations, the rent is subsequently increased. The percentage should be at a rate that permits the lessee to obtain a reasonable profit and provides him or her with an incentive to gain additional volume.

In the **straight, gross** or **flat lease,** the lessee makes periodic payments of rent over a fixed period of time. The lessee's responsibility is limited to the rental payment. This lease may have a renewal option and may provide for an escalator clause to accommodate increased costs. An example of a flat lease would be a farm lease or house lease as shown in figures 12.1 and 12.2.

The **ground lease** is used when a parcel of unimproved land is leased, usually for a long period of time. If the owner doesn't wish to sell the land and has no plans to build on it, a ground lease may be the answer. The tenant agrees to erect a building, so it is desirable for him to have a long-term lease. It should remain fixed for a specified period of time. Renegotiation of rent is normally based on current market value of the land.

Leasing bare land

An example of a place where ground leases might be used is on home sites in a recreational area. A provision in the lease generally stipulates the disposition of the improvements at the termination of the lease. The reversionary interest may revert to either the lessee or the lessor.

The *oil and gas lease* gives the lessee the right to explore on the land of the lessor. A flat rent is usually paid, and if oil or gas is discovered, the landowner receives royalties.

The *sandwich lease* develops when there is a sublease. The lessor is on the "top layer," the lessee is in the middle, and the sublessee is on the "bottom layer."

The *reappraisal lease* protects the owner by requiring periodic reappraisals of the value of the leased property. A long-term lease usually is reevaluated every five years. If the property has increased in value, the rent is increased by the percentage called for in the original lease. If the value has decreased, the rent will likewise decrease.

Sale and leaseback occurs when real property is sold on the condition that it is leased back to the seller. The seller's money is released and available for inventory or reinvesting. He need not seek another place to rent since he will be leasing back the property he sold. In addition, the rental payments are deductible from the seller's income tax. The sale and leaseback arrangement is desirable for the buyer also, since she has a guaranteed tenant and may deduct depreciation on the structure from her taxable income.

Seller rents back property

The *graduated lease* is also referred to as a *stepped-up lease,* as it provides for a series of graded step-ups in the rent at stated intervals. This type of lease is

THIS AGREEMENT, Made and entered into this   day of ,

by and between

party of the first part, and

party of the second part, WITNESSETH, That the said party of the first part has this day leased unto the party of the second part the following described property, situated in the County of   and State of   to wit:

The   quarter of section   , in Township   , Range   of the P.M., together with the   buildings and improvements thereon from the   day of   , 19   to the   day of   , 19   and the said second party, in consideration of the leasing of the above premises, hereby covenants and agrees with the said party of the first party to pay the said party of the first part as rent for the same as follows, to-wit:

AND IT IS FURTHER EXPRESSLY AGREED between the parties hereto that the said party of the first part should   deem it necessary may, at the cost and expense of the party of the second part, employ men and equipment to go upon said premises and cultivate the crops and harvest them or to do anything that is necessary to promote their growth or save them at any time before they are in the granaries, the whole expense of the same to be a lien upon said second party's share of said crops.
AND IT IS FURTHER EXPRESSLY AGREED by the party of the second party that   will carefully protect all buildings, fences and improvements of every kind that are now on said premises or that may be erected thereon during the continuance of this lease; that   will promptly at the expiration of the term herein granted yield up possession of said premises, without notice, unto the party of the first part, in good repair.
AND IT IS FURTHER AGREED that the party of the first part and   agents may go upon said premises at any time to inspect the same or to make improvements thereon and to plow for future crops and to sow small grain in corn and stubble ground in the fall before the expiration of this lease.
AND IT IS FURTHER AGREED by the party of the second part that   will not sub-let nor in any manner release any part of the described premises without the consent of party of the first part.
   The covenants herein shall extend to and be binding upon the heirs executors and administrators of the parties to this lease.

   Signed this   day of   , 19

   Witness   --(SEAL)

   -----------------------------------   --(SEAL

   -----------------------------------   --(SEAL)

   -----------------------------------   --(SEAL)

FIGURE 12.1 An example of a lease.

THIS AGREEMENT Witnesseth: That I or we, _____

_____

_____

have this day rented to_____

_____

_____

in the present condition thereof, the premises known as;_____

_____

_____

_____

for the period of _____

from the _____day of _____, 19____, on the following terms and

conditions, to-wit: for the use and rent thereof the said lessee, hereby promises

to pay the lessor, or to his, her or their order _____

_____Dollars

per _____for the whole time above stated, and to pay the same _____

_____on the _____of each _____; that lessee
will not sub-let or allow any other tenant to come in with or under him, her or
them without the written consent of said lessor; that lessee will repair all injuries or damages done the premises during his, her or their occupancy, or pay for the
same; that all of his, her or their property, whether subject to legal exemption,
or not, shall be bound and subject to the payment of rents and damages thereof; that
lessee will comply with all city ordinances, will take good care of the buildings
and premises, and keep them free from filth, from danger or fire, and will keep the
side-walks free from ice and snow and the house and premises shall be kept clean.
If in default of the payment of rent for a period of _____days after the same
is due, lessee will at the request of said lessor quit and render to lessor the
peaceable possession thereof; but, for this cause, the obligation to pay shall not
cease; and finally at the end of lessees term, lessee will surrender to the said
lessor, his, her or their heirs and assigns, the peaceable possession of said demised premises with all the keys, bolts, latches and repairs, if any, in as good
condition as the same was received, the usual wear and tear.

The said lessor reserves the privilege of entering and showing above property

to prospective renters during the last thirty-day period of this lease or for any

other reasonable purpose at any time._____

_____

_____

_____

_____

_____

IN WITNESS WHEREOF the parties hereto have subscribed to two copies hereof, one

to be retained by each party.

Dated this _____ day of _____, 19____.

Lessor _____   Lessee _____

Lessor _____   Lessee _____

FIGURE 12.2
A second example
of a lease.

advantageous to the lessee because it can start at a lower rental and increase as the business matures (figure 12.3).

An *index lease* calls for periodic increases or decreases in rent. This change is locked into some national index, such as the cost-of-living index.

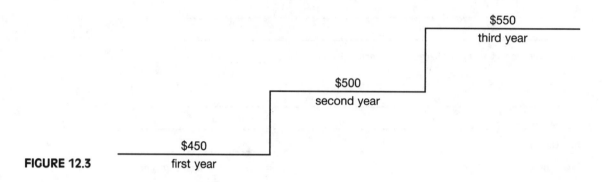

FIGURE 12.3

An *air lease* gives the right to occupy the space of another over a designated property. A restaurant built over a freeway and elevated walkways that connect buildings across streets are examples of property under air leases.

SUMMARY

Since not all people own real property, a segment of the population leases housing or business space from investors. The lease is a contract that must be in writing, under most states' statutes, if it is for more than a year. The lessee (tenant) rents from the lessor (owner). The tenant has a less than freehold (nonfreehold) estate in the property of the landlord. Under the terms of the lease the lessee has the right to the property for the time period stipulated in the lease.

The four major leasehold interests include the *estate for years,* which is for a specified time period; the *periodic lease,* which is for an indefinite period with no stated termination date; the *tenancy at will,* which allows for either the lessee or the lessor to decide the length of the lease; and the *tenancy at sufferance,* which occurs when the tenant has stayed past the lease term and becomes a holdover tenant. The lease should define the time period, the amount of rent, the liability, possession, and responsibilities of each party.

If the lessee violates the terms of the lease, the lessor may institute proceedings for *actual eviction* of the tenant. If the lessor does not maintain the property in a livable manner, the lessee can abandon the property under the terms of *constructive eviction.*

For commercial tenants who lease space for a business, leases vary. Many owners request the tenant pay a portion of the expenses under a *net lease* arrangement. These expenses may include repairs, tax escalations, insurance, and maintenance. *Percentage leases* are often imposed upon retail merchants, requiring them to pay a flat fee plus a percentage of their profits based on the volume of business they transact.

There are specific leases to cover houses, apartments, farms, office buildings, retail stores, commercial and industrial tracts. Each type of lease is specially designed to cover the rights and privileges of lessor and lessee of the property.

KEY WORDS AND CONCEPTS

Assignment of lease: An agreement to give over the entire balance of the lease.

Demise: The conveyance of an estate under lease.

Distraint: Legal seizure of goods.

Ground lease: A lease on unimproved land.

Lease: A contract whereby the owner gives the use of the property to the tenant upon payment of rent.

Lessee: The person to whom the use of the property is given by a lease.

Lessor: The owner of property rented to another.

Net lease: A lease whereby the lessee agrees to assume all or a portion of the expenses normally paid by the owner.

Percentage lease: A lease whereby the lessee pays a flat fee plus a percentage based on the volume of business transacted on the premises.

Reversionary interest: The future interest an owner has in leased property.

Security deposit: A deposit made to assure the performance of an obligation, such as a lessee gives to a lessor.

Sublet: To lease from the original lessee for a portion of the unexpired balance of the term.

Surrender and acceptance: The cancellation of a lease by the mutual consent of lessor and lessee.

Tax participation clause: A lease clause whereby the tenant assumes a proportionate share of an increase in property tax.

REVIEW QUESTIONS

1. When the lessee assigns his lease to another
   a. he gives up the remainder of the lease.
   b. he retains a portion of the lease.
   c. he terminates his lease with the lessee.
   d. none of the above

2. When a property is sold
   a. leases automatically expire.
   b. leases are assigned to the new owner.
   c. a lessee can break the terms of her lease.
   d. none of the above

3. Demise refers to
   a. the death of a grantor
   b. a gift by will
   c. interest by decree
   d. an estate of lease

4. What is the lowest estate one can have
   a. tenancy at will
   b. tenancy at sufferance
   c. tenancy for years
   d. fee simple title

5. Which lease calls for periodic changes in the amount of the lease fee?
   a. a graduated lease
   b. a percentage lease
   c. a gross lease
   d. a net lease

6. A percentage lease refers to
   a. a straight lease.
   b. a lease with a sliding scale whereby the rent gradually increases.
   c. a minimum base rent plus a percentage of the volume of sales.
   d. a flat fee that diminishes over a period of years.

7. Who is the final tenant on a sale and leaseback?
   a. the buyer
   b. the seller
   c. the optionor
   d. the optionee

8. A lease that requires the tenant to pay all or a stated portion of the expenses is a
   a. gross lease
   b. flat lease
   c. percentage lease
   d. net lease

9. When the premises reach a physical condition in which the tenant is unable to occupy them for the purpose intended, the situation is legally recognized as
   a. actual eviction
   b. constructive eviction
   c. surrender and acceptance
   d. income conversion

10. All of the following are necessary in a lease except
    a. the names of the parties
    b. a description of the property
    c. a renewal option
    d. the rent and terms of the lease

11. If a lessor dies, the lease is
    a. cancelled
    b. renegotiated
    c. unchanged
    d. liable for breach of contract

12. In a net lease arrangement, a lessee may be liable for
    a. utilities
    b. depreciation
    c. both of the above
    d. neither of the above

13. Cancellation of a lease by mutual consent of the lessor and lessee is called
    a. assignment of the lease
    b. renegotiation of the lease
    c. surrender and acceptance
    d. none of the above

14. The tenant has the least interest in a(n)
    a. estate at will
    b. periodic tenancy
    c. estate for years
    d. tenancy at sufferance

15. The reversionary interest is owned by
    a. the mortgagor
    b. the life tenant
    c. the grantee
    d. the lessor

16. A lease may best be described as
    a. an option
    b. consideration
    c. a contract
    d. assignable

17. A lessee may terminate a lease by
    a. assignment
    b. moving prior to termination date and not paying the remaining balance due
    c. constructive eviction
    d. subletting

18. A person renting an apartment would most likely have what type of lease?
    a. gross
    b. net
    c. percentage
    d. graduated

19. Lois and Larry Grub were renting a house and Lois died two months before the lease expired. There was no automatic renewal clause in the lease. Larry is uncertain about renewing the lease, but he paid the next month's rent after the expiration date. He is now considered a
    a. tenant at will
    b. tenant in common
    c. tenant at sufferance
    d. tenant for years

20. The lease that would be least affected by death is
    a. tenancy at sufferance
    b. tenancy for life
    c. estate for years
    d. periodic estate

21. A lessor, when he or she executes a lease
    a. gives possession to the tenant.
    b. implies that the property is fit for use.
    c. both a and b
    d. neither a nor b

22. A landlord-tenant relationship would be which of the following?
    a. at will
    b. severalty
    c. tenancy by entireties
    d. a freehold estate

Property Management | 13

In most states a real estate license is required to manage the real property of another. Real estate firms specializing in the sale of investment properties often operate a management department to supervise their clients' investments. A property manager is employed to take over the management responsibility for the owner. By applying knowledge and expertise, the manager tries to produce the greatest net return possible for the investor. He or she is responsible to protect the clients' investments. The property manager has a **fiduciary** relationship with the principal, and the agreement between them should clearly define the agent's duties and authority.

THE NEED FOR MANAGEMENT

Many investors have busy schedules that allow little spare time for the problems of management. These owners prefer to turn the responsibility of their investments over to capable management specialists who often are able to bring them greater profits. Investment syndicates, composed of a number of individuals who band together to purchase investment properties, also need management firms to administrate their investments, and absentee owners are becoming more prevalent and need the reliable services of management companies to care for their investments.

Managing property as a career

A property manager may specialize in just one type of property. Since there are vast differences between properties, an expert in apartment management may not necessarily be as knowledgeable in managing farm properties, shopping centers, or office buildings.

Property management may involve

1. Single-family residences or duplexes
2. Apartment complexes
3. Office buildings
4. Commercial buildings
5. Shopping centers
6. Farms

It is clear that the requirements of these properties would vary greatly.

Farm Management

A farm management company provides complete services for the farmland owner. Concerned with assuring the owner maximum returns from his or her land, a farm management specialist analyzes the farm to evaluate its production potential.

Land conservation methods   One of the first steps is to take an inventory of the farm's soil and physical resources. The management service will also evaluate the farm's conservation practices, with the proper use of waterways and/or terrace construction, and maintenance. The farm may be adaptable to irrigation and might therefore produce a greater return for the tenant and the owner. If the soil is wet, it may be necessary to complete a tilling program to carry water away from wet areas and thus provide more land for farming or to make the area less prone to flooding and therefore produce a higher-yielding crop. The farm manager also takes preventive measures to eliminate as much soil erosion as possible.

Crop rotation prevents the exhaustion of the land's natural minerals. Crop planning also includes cost-efficient fertilizer and weed-control programs. If a management service can purchase pest controls, seed, and fertilizer in co-op quantities, savings can be passed on to the owners.

The professional farm manager is responsible for the selection of the best tenant possible. Lease terms may be on a share crop, cash rent, guaranteed bushel, or net lease basis.

Methods of selling crops   By keeping abreast of the many marketing techniques available, the manager is able to offer suggestions on handling the sale of the crop to maximize profits. This may include deferred payment, price-later contracts, cash sales or hedging.

Farm accounting   Finally, the farm manager maintains accurate records on the farm's production to improve the returns of the farm. Complete accounting is provided for the landowner, with completely audited financial statements listing expenses paid and income received from the farm. The farm management firm reviews proper insurance programs and makes recommendations to the landowner. The firm reviews real estate taxes, pays them and then incorporates the data into the financial statements. The managers prepare annual summaries for the landowners for use in their income tax preparation.

Apartment Rentals

Among an apartment complex manager's concerns are securing and retaining tenants, collecting rents, advertising, providing cleaning and maintenance services, and keeping financial records and accounts.

Selecting tenants   Investigating the prospective tenant's credit record and present employment should be standard procedure. Obtaining references from past landlords gives additional assurance of the tenant's stability. Exercising care in screening applicants results in fewer vacancies and less collection loss.

Proper maintenance and quick attention to tenant complaints means content occupants who tend to remain longer. When vacancies do occur, a careful analysis of the most effective way to advertise is important. If pets and children are not allowed, it will eliminate many vain telephone calls to place this information in the ad. If the complex caters to young singles, an indication of this in the advertisement will eliminate inquiries from older applicants.

Office Space

Need for compatible tenants   Managing leased office space is another specialty requiring careful analysis of the prospective tenants in a given building. If all the tenants create excessive traffic, the available parking area may prove insufficient. While accounting firms, attorneys, and small businesses may not need an abundance of parking space, a physician or dental clinic could mean considerable traffic. The needs of the tenants must be carefully considered if the property manager expects to do justice by the owner.

Large office buildings, especially high-rise structures, require supervision of the considerable staff needed for the operation and maintenance of the building. Trained specialists such as electricians, engineers, and purchasing agents must be supervised by trained management. The personnel needed for the accounting system alone is considerable. Cleaning, security, and maintenance usually require round-the-clock attendance to the property.

Commercial Buildings

Shopping centers

Strip centers generally consist of a single building with four to twelve bays conveniently located and with easy access to and from the main area. The larger **neighborhood shopping centers** may be made up of several buildings grouped together with fifteen or more retail bays. **Regional centers** house several nationally recognized stores such as Sears, Wards, and Penney's with a broad mix of other shops. Many times these stores are all under one roof and offer seating facilities in a central mall for the weary shopper. Some regional centers have skating rinks to occupy youngsters while their parents shop. Any such amenities in the center enhance it in the eye of the shopper.

A commercial manager needs to understand the type of tenant best suited to the particular center. A prospective tenant may desire a clause in the lease that disallows competition from a similar store. To place several beauty salons, dress shops, or book stores in a small neighborhood center may result in insufficient volume for any of the businesses. Since many shopping areas are rented on a percentage basis, it would also be disastrous for the owner.

Many shopping bays have heating and air conditioning ducts above suspended ceilings that could conduct smells across to adjoining spaces. A restaurant specializing in fish or fried foods next door to a dress shop could create unpleasant odors in the clothing store.

MANAGEMENT CONTRACTS

Employing the manager

The contract between the principal and the manager should clearly define the responsibilities, obligations, and duties of the manager and the owner (see figure 13.1). The contract should include the following basic items:

1. The length of the contract
2. The terms of the contract
3. The management fees
4. The authority vested in the agent
5. The budget for operating expenses
6. Some provision for monthly accounting by the manager to the owner

At the end of each month, the manager should give a detailed accounting of expenditures and disbursements to the owners. The manager's job is to try to control expenses and produce the greatest net return possible for the owners. He supervises the maintenance employees to ascertain that the work is skillfully accomplished with materials acquired at a reasonable rate. By insisting upon proper vouchers and receipts, he maintains efficient control of costs.

MANAGEMENT AGREEMENT

_____(hereinafter called Owner), and _____
(hereinafter called Agent), agree as follows:

A. The Owner hereby employs the Agent exclusively to rent and manage the property known as _____
upon the terms hereinafter set forth, for a period of ___years beginning on the ___day of _____, 19___, and ending on the ___day of _____, 19___, and thereafter for yearly periods from time to time, unless on or before _____ the expiration of any such renewal period, either party hereto shall notify the other in writing that it decides to terminate this Agreement, in which case this Agreement shall be thereby terminated on said last mentioned date.

B. The Agent Agrees:

1. To accept the management of the above mentioned property and agrees to furnish services for the rental operation and management of the Premises.

2. To render a monthly statement of receipts, disbursements and charges to the Owner and to remit each month the net proceeds (provided Agent is not required to make any mortgage, escrow or tax payment on the first day of the following month). Agent will remit the net proceeds or the balance thereof after making allowance for such payments to the Owner. In case the disbursements and charges shall be in excess of the receipts, the Owner agrees to pay such excess promptly, nothing herein contained shall obligate the Agent to advance its own funds on behalf of the Owner.

3. The Agent agrees to have all employees who handle any money to be bonded.

C. The Owner Agrees: To give the Agent the following authority and powers (all or any which may be exercised in the name of the Owner) and agrees to assume all expenses in connection therewith:

1. To advertise the property, to display signs, and to rent said property. Agent will investigate prospective tenants and to sign leases, renew and or cancel existing leases and prepare and execute the new lease. To terminate tenancies and to sign and serve such notices as are deemed needful by the Agent; to institute and prosecute actions to remove tenants and to recover possession of the property; to sue for and recover rent: and, when expedient, to settle, compromise and release such actions or suits, or reinstate such tenancies.

2. To collect rents due or to become due and issue receipts to deposit all funds collected hereunder in the Agent's custodial account.

3. To refund tenants' security deposits at the expiration of leases.

4. To hire, discharge and pay all caretakers and other employees; to make all ordinary repairs and replacements necessary to preserve the property in its present condition and for the operating efficiency thereof and all alterations and decorating required to comply with lease requirements and to enter into agreements for all necessary repairs and maintenance; to purchase supplies and pay all bills.

    a. To indemnify, defend and save the Agent harmless from all suits in connection with the Premises and from liability for damage to property and injuries to or death of any employee or other person whomsoever, and to carry at his (its) own expense public liability, and workmen's compensation insurance naming the Owner and the Agent and adequate to protect their interests.

5. To pay any expenses incurred by the Agent, including, without limitation, attorney's fees for counsel employed to represent the Agent or the Owner.

6. Owner agrees to pay to said agent ___per month or ___percent(___%) of the monthly gross receipts from the operation of the Premises during the period this Agreement remains in full force and effect, whichever is the greater amount.

7. This Agreement may be cancelled by Owner before the termination date specified in Paragraph 1 on not less than ___days prior written notice to the Agent, provided that such notice is accompanied by payment to the Agent of a cancellation fee in an amount equal to ___% of the management fee that would accrue over the remainder of the stated term of the Agreement. For this purpose the monthly management fee for the remainder of the stated term shall be presumed to be the same as that of the last month prior to service of the notice of cancellation.

IN WITNESS WHEREOF, the parties hereto have affixed or caused to be affixed their respective signatures this ___day of _____, 19___.

_____   _____
Witness   Owner

_____   _____
Witness   Agent

FIGURE 13.1 An example of a management contract.

RENTING THE SPACE

The primary goal of the manager is to market the client's space to yield the greatest net return. Whether the space is living accommodations, office space, or commercial space, the prospective tenant will be seeking the most advantageous location for his needs at the best price available.

The manager may need to adjust the rental rate if the supply of rentals is greater than the demand. However, he must be careful not to favor any one tenant by reducing rent on a particular unit.

The manager's duties

In leasing commercial areas it is wise to reserve space for a growing tenant to expand into by filling in with smaller tenants. Allowing the larger tenant an area for expansion may prevent the business from moving at a later date.

EMPLOYEES

The property manager will select personnel with care since she is accountable to her employer for their actions. By carefully interviewing applicants to evaluate their abilities, desires, and ambitions, and following up with a good training program and adequate supervision, the manager can build a staff of conscientious employees. As word of the manager's expertise spreads, her business will expand.

TYPICAL BUDGETS

A typical **management budget** for an apartment complex should contain the following items:

I. Expenses
   A. Operating expenses and maintenance service
      1. supplies
      2. painting and decorating
      3. salaries
      4. services
      5. repairs
   B. Utility expenses
      1. heating fuel
      2. electricity
      3. gas
      4. water
   C. Fixed charges
      1. real estate taxes
      2. insurance

The property manager should create a monthly written income and expense report for the owner. A typical report on an apartment complex would be similar to the example in figure 13.2.

Income & Expense Report

Property Address: 12534 Money Lane   June, 1987

Income:

18 units @ $375	$ 6,750	
8 units @ $350	$ 2,800	
6 units @ $325	$ 1,950	
Total	$11,500	

Less vacancy

1 unit @ $375 $ 375

Total rent $11,125

Other income:

Garages – 20 @ $15 $ 300   300
          TOTAL INCOME $11,425

Expenses:

Salaries:		
Resident manager	500	
Property manager	1,000	1,500
Fixed expenses		
Insurance	305	
Taxes	380	685
Variable expenses		
Maintenance	402	
Utilities	500	902
Capitol expenditures		
1 refrigerator	420	
Paint	30	450

TOTAL EXPENSES	$3,537	
NET INCOME		$7,888.00
DEBT SERVICE	$4,400	
CASH FLOW		$3,488.00

FIGURE 13.2 A typical income and expense report on an apartment complex.

THE NATIONAL INSTITUTE OF REAL ESTATE MANAGEMENT

The **National Institute of Real Estate Management** was organized by the National Association of Realtors in 1933. Their code of ethics requires the property manager to be loyal to clients and diligent in the maintenance and protection of their properties.

Offering educational courses to further prepare its members for the broad field of management, the association awards **CPM (Certified Property Manager)** designations to candidates who fulfill the program's requisites. This professional recognition goes to specialists in the field of property management.

The code of the NIREM follows.

CODE OF PROFESSIONAL ETHICS FOR THE INSTITUTE OF REAL ESTATE MANAGEMENT

Preamble

The objective of this professional code is the continuing enhancement of professional performance by Certified Property Managers through acceptance and conformance with those procedures that are the necessary elements of a mutually beneficial relationship between the Certified Property Manager, his or her fellow CPMs, fellow Realtors, clients, employers, and the public at large.

A CPM shall be bound by the following professional Pledge:

"I pledge myself to the advancement of professional property management through the mutual efforts of members of the Institute of Real Estate Management and by any other proper means available to me.

"I pledge myself to seek and maintain an equitable, honorable, and cooperative association with fellow members of the Institute and with all others who may become a part of my business and professional life.

"I pledge myself to place honesty, integrity, and industriousness above all else; to pursue my gainful efforts with diligent study and dedication to the end that service to my clients shall always be maintained at the highest possible level.

"I pledge myself to comply with the principles and declarations of the Institute of Real Estate Management as set forth in its bylaws and regulations and this code of professional ethics."

Article I

The Code of Ethics of the National Association of Real Estate Boards as in effect from time to time is incorporated into this code by reference.

Article II

A CPM shall not use or permit the use of the CPM designation in any manner that shall adversely affect the objectives or high purposes of the Institute of Real Estate Management.

Article III

A CPM shall not make or authorize or otherwise encourage any oral or written statements of a derogatory nature concerning another CPM or his or her business practices.

Article IV

SECTION 1 A CPM shall neither in his or her own behalf nor for others solicit the services of any employee known to be under the supervision of another CPM without prior knowledge by the other member.

SECTION 2 A CPM shall not offer his or her services to the client of another CPM whose services have heretofore been satisfactory by basing solicitation on the inducement of a reduced management fee.

Article V

A CPM shall not accept association with or employment by an individual, partnership, group, or other organization unless to the best of his or her knowledge and belief such organization complies with all applicable governmental laws, ordinances, rules, and regulations and with this code of professional ethics.

Article VI

A CPM shall at all times be loyal to his or her clients, and shall be diligent in the maintenance and protection of their reputations and properties.

Article VII

A CPM shall not represent divergent or conflicting interests, nor engage in any activity reasonably calculated to be contrary to the best interests of his or her clients or clients' property, unless the clients have been previously notified.

Article VIII

A CPM shall not receive directly or indirectly any rebate, fee, commission, discount, or other benefit, whether monetary or otherwise, without the full knowledge and prior consent of the client concerned.

Article IX

A CPM shall not disclose to a third party confidential information concerning the business or personal affairs of his or her clients without prior authorization, except upon legal demands by competent governmental authority.

Article X

A CPM shall keep his or her clients currently advised in all matters concerning their respective properties or welfare. A CPM shall cause to be furnished to each client at agreed intervals a complete, regular accounting in respect to the operation of that client's properties.

Article XI

A CPM shall exert due diligence for the protection of his or her client's funds against all foreseeable contingencies. The deposit of such funds in account with a reputable banking institute shall constitute due diligence.

Article XII

A CPM shall at all times keep and maintain accurate accounting records, properly marked for identification concerning the properties managed for each client, and such records shall be available for inspection at all reasonable times by each respective client.

Article XIII

The interpretation of compliance with this professional code is the responsibility of the Ethics and Discipline Committee of the Institute of Real Estate Management.

Disciplinary action for violation of any portion of this code shall be instituted by the Governing Council of IREM in accordance with rules and regulations established by that Governing Council and approved by the membership.

SUMMARY

The need for responsible management to supervise and administrate property investments is discussed in this chapter. Many investors pool their funds in joint ventures with others and employ management firms to supervise their investments. While some investors may purchase farmland, others buy shopping centers, office buildings, or residential complexes. Since investments vary so greatly, specialization in management is required. A great deal of expertise is mandatory since the property manager must try to protect the owner's investment and obtain the largest net return the property is capable of producing.

Property management firms are increasing in numbers as more and more people are investing in real estate. Some real estate firms have separate management departments to handle the properties they have sold to investors. The management fee varies in different areas of the country and also is dependent on the type of property managed and the quantity of units. For example, twenty-four single-family homes will create more work than a twenty-four-unit apartment building.

While investing in real estate provides a hedge against inflation, the time involved in renting and maintaining the property can be a troublesome chore for the investor. S/He often prefers to pay a fee to have a professional handle the management details.

The obligations and duties of the property manager are defined in the contract between the parties. The manager is the liaison between the owners and the tenants, handling the tenants' complaints and guarding the owner's interests. The manager sees to the physical care of the building and hires maintenance personnel and resident managers (when a residential complex is involved).

At the end of each month a detailed accounting of expenditures and disbursements must be given to the owners. A typical manager's budget for an apartment complex is included in the chapter.

KEY WORDS AND CONCEPTS

Certified Property Manager (CPM): A designation awarded to candidates who fulfill requisites as outlined by the National Institute of Real Estate Management.

Fiduciary: One who holds a relationship of faith, trust, and confidence as between a property manager and client.

Institute of Real Estate Management: A branch of the National Association of Realtors offering specified educational courses in property management.

Management budget: A monthly written income and expense report.

Neighborhood shopping center: Several buildings grouped together into retail bays easily accessible to the nearby neighborhood.

Property management: A specialized branch of the real estate business that involves overseeing the leasing, managing, and maintenance of another's property.

Regional center: A large complex housing several national retail stores with a broad mix of shops that draw customers from a great distance.

Strip center: A number of units (bays) in a single building.

REVIEW QUESTIONS

1. A property management contract should contain
   a. the duties of the manager.
   b. the terms of the contract.
   c. both of the above
   d. neither of the above

2. The manager's responsibilities include
   a. selecting tenants on the basis of the space they require.
   b. selecting and retaining tenants.
   c. keeping an accurate account of his or her own salary.
   d. advertising only when the building becomes 15 percent vacant.

3. Upon signing a management contract with an owner, a broker becomes a
   a. trustee
   b. receiver
   c. management director
   d. fiduciary

4. All of the following would be included in a typical manager's operating budget except
   a. roof repairs
   b. decorating and painting
   c. the manager's salary
   d. cleaning supplies

5. Management is needed by which of the following?
   a. an absentee owner
   b. an investment syndicate
   c. busy investors
   d. all of the above

6. The following considerations are important in selecting tenants:
   a. the compatibility of tenants
   b. the ethnic background of tenants, since this would be proof of stability
   c. the number of employees in the tenant's business and the number of customers they will serve
   d. obtaining percentage leases from tenants of office space

7. An apartment manager under contract will usually perform the following duties:
   a. efficient marketing of the space
   b. instituting legal proceedings for rent payments in arrears
   c. both of the above
   d. neither of the above

8. A property manager's responsibilities include all of the following except
   a. paying utilities
   b. investing profits
   c. renting units
   d. collecting security deposits

9. When calculating operating income, a property manager would include which of the following:
   a. income taxes
   b. allowance for vacancies and collections
   c. mortgage payments
   d. allowance for depreciation

10. In a period of climbing inflation, a property manager would be reluctant to negotiate which of the following?
    a. a graduated lease
    b. a fixed-rent lease
    c. a price-index lease
    d. a reappraisal clause in a lease

Investment and Tax Aspects of Ownership | 14

Since food, clothing, and shelter are essential to our very existence, most Americans decide it is more prudent to permanently own that shelter than to rent. Ownership of real estate creates the greatest portion of the estate the average person acquires. The inflation of recent years has contributed to the appreciation of real estate and most homeowners soon become cognizant of the equity building up in their homes. Depending on the sector of the country where the property is located and the local demands for housing, it was not unusual for a home to appreciate 5 to 20 percent annually in the 1970s. The high interest rates of the early 1980s slowed that appreciation to a standstill in many parts of the country. As interest rates began to drop in the latter part of 1982, real estate transfers again began to increase. In early 1986 interest rates dropped to 10 and 10.5 percent. A rash of refinancing kept financial institutions busy as homeowners sought the lower rates. Home sales were brisk with the backlog of consumers who felt they could now afford to purchase a home. In early 1987 interest rates had dropped to 8 and 8.5 percent, something not seen for many years, making home ownership even more within the realm of possibility for the average American.

This chapter will explain the advantages of home ownership as an investment, illustrating the true principal and interest payments when the interest and tax deductions are considered. The income benefits the investor in real property receives will also be covered.

HOME OWNERSHIP AS AN INVESTMENT

Home ownership provides more than shelter, it is one of the most substantial investments that can be made. Owning a home not only enhances pride and self-worth, but also provides a hedge against inflation.

The tax reform bill of 1986 brought some sweeping changes to the nation's tax laws, some of which affect the real estate investment market. However, the benefits of home ownership remain intact. Itemized deductions are retained on real estate taxes and mortgage interest will continue to be deductible for first and second homes. This means that the owner of a primary residence *and* a second vacation home can still deduct interest paid on the mortgages and the real estate taxes. Since interest is deductible from taxable income, it creates an added incentive to purchase real estate.

Interest & property tax deductible

Taxpayers will be allowed to borrow on their homes up to the original purchase price, plus any added improvements, and such interest will be deductible. The bill did include the stipulation that loans backed by the appreciated value of a home but used for purposes other than home improvements (consumer loans) would not be deductible unless the proceeds are used for tuition or other educational costs, or medical expenses. Generally, it is not permissible to deduct interest paid on loans above the market value of the property.

Figure 14.1 shows the 1987 and 1988 tax rate schedule for married couples filing jointly and for the single taxpayer. Looking at the chart, assume that the combined income of a couple for 1987 is $50,000. Their taxes would be computed as such:

11% of $3,000 earned	= $	330 taxes
15% of $25,000 earned	= $	3750 taxes
28% of $17,000 earned	= $	4760 taxes
35% of $5,000 earned	= $	1750 taxes
		$10,590 taxes paid

There are five rates in 1987, but in 1988 the taxation of individuals will be reduced to a three-step process.

In 1988, depending on your filing status, a certain portion of your taxable income will be subject to a 15 percent rate and any amount over that will be taxed at 28 percent. A third rate of 33 percent will be imposed on higher levels of taxable income (in effect, a 5% surcharge). This will result in a phasing out of the 15 percent rate and the personal exemption.

Personal exemptions have been increased from $1,900 in 1987 to $1,950 in 1988 to $2,000 in 1989. As the chart indicates, standard deductions are also increased.

1987

	Taxable Income	Rate	Standard Deduction
Married filing jointly	$0–$3,000	11 %	$3,800
	$3,000–$28,000	15 %	
	$28,000–$45,000	28 %	
	$45,000–$90,000	35 %	
	Over $90,000	38.5 %	
Single	$0–$1,800	11 %	$2,570
	$1,800–$16,800	15 %	
	$16,800–$27,000	28 %	
	$27,000–$54,000	35 %	
	Over $54,000	38.5 %	

1988

	Taxable Income	Rate	Standard Deduction
Married filing jointly	$0–$29,750	15 %	$5,000
	$29,750–$71,900	28 %	
	$71,900–$149,250	33 %	
	Over $149,250	28 %	
Single	$0–$17,850	15 %	$3,000
	$17,850–$43,150	28 %	
	$43,150–$89,560	33 %	
	Over $89,560	28 %	

FIGURE 14.1 Chart for 1987 and 1988 taxable income for single persons and married filing jointly.

To find the overall percent they were taxed, divide the $10,590 by the earnings of $50,000 which equals 21 percent.

They are paying on a $60,000 mortgage at 10 percent interest.

$60,000 *mortgage*
× .10 *interest rate*
$ 6,000 *annual interest*
× .21 *tax bracket*
$ 1,260 *tax deduction allowable*

Now assume the mortgage is for 15 years. Payments would be 10.75 per $1,000 (see amortization chart in Chapter 9), or $645 per month. With the tax deduction for interest paid the monthly payment is in actuality lowered by $105.00 ($1260 taxes ÷ 12 months) to $540.00.

In addition to this the homeowner may also deduct the property taxes paid. Assume the taxes are $1800 per year: 21% of $1800 = $378.00 tax deductible. $378 ÷ 12 months reduces the monthly payment another $31.50, leaving an actual monthly house payment of $508.50. Add to these tax advantages the fact that equity is building and that the investment is appreciating in value.

Appreciation and Home Ownership

Investing in a commodity that will appreciate in value produces a present income plus a gain in worth. Such investments may include buying silver, gold, coins, paintings, stamps, automobiles and other desirable collector items. However, an element of risk is involved in these investments since they are speculative, liquidating them may prove difficult, and the true value may not be obtained. On the other hand, the demand for housing helps insure at least some degree of appreciation in home ownership.

Depreciation

A home owner cannot depreciate the property where he resides. If, however, he uses a portion of that residence as an office, depreciation is allowable along with deductions for his expenses. In effect, the law refrains from considering the building a residence if a portion is used for business. For example, if one room in a six-room house is used as an office, then one-sixth of the expenses of that residence may be deductible.

When a residence is depreciable

Sale of a Residence

If an owner sells his home and purchases another within a twenty-four month period, and if the cost of the replacement is equal to or more than the home he sold, he is exempt from paying tax on any gains realized on the sale. The tax may be deferred.

Deferring Gains Tax

When a capital gains tax is deferred, any improvements made to the first home are added to the original purchase price. Costs incurred in the sale are deductible from the amount realized. These selling expenses are the actual costs involved in the sale, such as the broker's commission, legal fees, state transfer fees, and title insurance or abstract fees.

The **basis** is **adjusted**; that is, the gain on the old residence is subtracted from the costs of the new residence. For example:

1980 purchase price	$55,000
1982 added family room	8,500
Adjusted basis	$63,500
1987 sale price	78,000
Less selling expenses	5,680
	$72,140
Less adjusted basis	63,500
Gains from sale	8,640
New purchase	85,000
Less gain from sale	8,640
Adjusted basis	$76,360

Tax Free Sale

The $100,000 exclusion for home owners fifty-five years of age or older was introduced by the Revenue Act of 1978. It has since been increased to $125,000 and generally applies to residences sold or exchanged after July 20, 1981. To qualify for this exclusion, the taxpayer must file an election and meet these qualifications:

1. The taxpayer must have reached the age of 55 before the date of the sale or exchange; and
2. The taxpayer must have owned and used the property as a principal residence for at least three of the five years just before the sale.

REAL ESTATE AS AN INVESTMENT

Investing in real estate

The investment in real estate serves many functions. With the realization that real estate is a great hedge against inflation, the number of people investing in income-producing property has grown. Leading economists have found by tracking real estate values through the years that real property prices keep pace with inflation.

Purchasing Real Estate vs. Fixed Income Investment

The primary purpose of the investor is to generate income (cash flow). Income gained other than through one's labor can be realized by limiting present spending in favor of future benefits. If the investor is seeking a fixed return, this can be accomplished with treasury bills, certificates of deposit, municipal bonds, or savings accounts. These forms of savings are secure and produce a fixed income that is easily converted to cash. However, inflation erodes the future purchasing power of these investment dollars. In the case of real estate, appreciation has been a big factor in attracting investors; however, income is the compelling motive for most of them.

Cash Flow

Ideally, an investment property will yield a **positive cash flow**. The cash flow represents the net proceeds after all expenses are met. If an investor has a property that generates an annual income of $44,000 and expenses total $35,000, a net return (cash flow) of $9,000 has been earned.

Income from office building		$44,000
Expenses	22,000	
Debt service (mortgage payment)	18,000	
Cash flow		
		$ 4,000

If the tax deductible expenses involved in a property are greater than the income, there will be, for tax purposes, a **negative cash flow**. To some investors this negative cash flow is desirable because their main concern is to have a **tax shelter**. A tax shelter is best defined as a *book loss*, it is simply a phrase used to describe some of the advantages of real estate investments. Since investment property can be depreciated as an expense when figuring income tax, it provides a tax shelter for its owner. For example:

Income		$44,000
Expenses	22,000	
Interest deduction	16,000	
Depreciation deduction	8,000	
	$46,000	$44,000 = ($2,000 loss)

The owner has a book loss of $2,000. Prior to the passage of the Tax Reform Act of 1986, owning improved real estate proved to be one of the few, as well as one of the best, methods for sheltering income. The optimum situation results when the property shows a book loss but still has a positive cash flow.

With the new Tax Reform Act of 1986, such special tax treatment as has been accorded to taxpayers' investment activities will be phased out. Generally the bill considers these investments (including rental properties) as passive; that is, not containing the taxpayers' active involvement. Previously a taxpayer's income or loss from all sources were combined and the net amount taxed (with the exception of capital gains or losses) at the graduated rates. Today there are three classifications for income:

1. *Active income*: earned by salaries or a business in which the taxpayer materially participates.
2. *Portfolio income*: interest, annuities, dividends, royalties and profit from the sale of portfolio assets.
3. *Passive activity income*: invested funds.

Losses from passive investments may no longer be used to offset ordinary income. The taxpayer may only deduct these losses from passive investments against income from that investment; they may not be applied against active or portfolio income. The IRS has described passive investments as all rental income, interests in limited partnerships, and all other business involvements where the taxpayer is not involved in the operation on a regular and substantial basis. Exempt are working oil and gas properties.

Passive income

Losses up to $25,000 from real estate rental activities in which the taxpayer actively participates may be used to offset salaries and active business income. This $25,000 amount, however, is phased down to a 50 percent ratio for those taxpayers with income between $100,000 and $150,000. Any losses on real estate investments in excess of these amounts will be treated as passive investment losses and the $25,000 amount is eliminated entirely.

INCOME FROM REAL ESTATE INVESTMENTS

The return on the individual's cash investment can vary greatly, depending on the ratio of cash invested to the purchase price, and also on the cost of financing.

The investor now has additional taxable income; that is, he has spendable income plus the capital gains or equity income in the property. However, he can depreciate his real estate holdings, and the interest on the loan is deductible. The *taxable income* is the investment net, less interest and depreciation. The *spendable income* is the investment net, less principal, interest, and tax costs. The *equity income* is the investment net, less the income and interest, but adding the appreciation of the investment.

Rate of Return

To evaluate the feasibility of an investment, the investors decide what percentage of return they want on their investment, and examine the return on the actual investment. If they know they can receive a 10 percent return on certificates of deposit or treasury bonds, they will expect more from a real estate investment because of the risks involved. However, income tax must be paid on the interest earned from savings. With a real estate investment, the earnings can be sheltered since the improvements can be depreciated.

Determining return on investment

In the income approach technique for evaluating property investments, the property's income is divided by the desired rate of return. If an investor requires a 12 percent annual return and the property has a $15,000 net annual income, he should pay no more than $125,000.

$$\frac{15,000 \ (income)}{12\% \ (rate\ of\ return)} = \$125,000 \ (property\ value)$$

The rate of return relates net operating income to the investment.

In using this capitalization method of evaluating an income producing property, the future income is converted to present value. Since a property will depreciate and lessen in value as its economic life is depleted, this must be taken into consideration when analyzing the possibility of recapturing the investment. If the remaining life of the property is twenty-five years and it is depreciated on a straight-line basis, the property will depreciate at 4 percent a year. As the property depreciates, the income will likewise decline. Since the investor desires a 12 percent return on his investment, the 4 percent (*recapture rate*) must be added to supply the full return on his investment. Thus, in looking for a 16 percent return, the value of the property in the previous example is now reduced to $93,750.

Depreciation Methods

While we will evaluate the four types of depreciation methods, the 1986 Tax Reform Act requires that residential rental property investments placed in service *after* January 1, 1987 must be depreciated on a straight-line basis over 27½ years. Nonresidential real estate will be depreciated on a straight-line basis over 31½ years. Automobiles and light trucks may be written off over 5 years. Most manufacturing equipment will be written off over 7 years.

Depreciation is available only to an investor in real estate. Depreciation actually converts net operating income into capital gains. For accounting and tax purposes, it is based on estimates of a property's future decrease in value. Even as the investor depreciates his property, it continues to increase in value due to rising construction costs and land values. The realization of this depreciation allowance is further enhanced if the investor has used little of his resources to purchase the property. (For example, if a $60,000 property was acquired with $12,000 in cash and the balance from a loan, the investor was still able to depreciate on the *full* value of the structure.) After the value of its **useful life** (economic life) is over, the **salvage value** remains. This is generally 5 to 10 percent of the property's depreciable basis. Depreciation cannot be taken on the land, only on the improvements thereon. Land does not diminish in value since it literally does not wear out. Tax assessors separate the land and improvements when they appraise the property for tax purposes. A typical example follows:

Remaining value after depletion

Address: 7007 Mulberry Drive
Legal: Lot 3, Block 7, Fall Rapids Subdivision
Land Value $30,000
Improvements $90,000
Assessed Value $120,000

Prior to the Tax Recovery Law of 1981, an investor chose one of four available methods to depreciate real property: **component depreciation, straight-line composite depreciation, sum-of-the-years digits,** or **double-declining balance.** These depreciation methods apply to real estate purchased before January 1, 1981.

Component depreciation. In the aforementioned example, the ratio of land value ($30,000) to improvements $90,000) is one to three. A depreciation schedule of the improvements must now be set up. If we estimate the usable life of the building to be twenty-five years, components such as heating, air conditioning, plumbing, and roofing will need to be replaced prior to the end of that twenty-five years. The owner now has a choice of allowing a straight-line depreciation of 4 percent for the twenty-five-year period, which amounts to 100 percent over the twenty-five years, or of breaking down the component parts and depreciating each, thus realizing greater depreciation benefits over the first years.

Depreciating parts individually

For example, the duplex at 7007 Mulberry Drive has an appraised value of $30,000 for land and $90,000 for improvements. The following schedule illustrates the component-depreciation method.

	Value	Life of Component	Rate	Annual Depreciation
Heating	$ 2,000	10 years	10%	$ 200
Air Conditioning	1,800	10 years	10%	180
Plumbing	4,000	10 years	10%	400
Roof	5,000	10 years	10%	500
Fixtures	8,000	15 years	6.6%	533
Base Building	69,200	25 years	4%	2,768
	$90,000			$4,581

Straight-line composite depreciation. If the life of the duplex is set as twenty-five years and straight-line composite depreciation is used, 4 percent of the

$90,000 value of the improvements would give the owner an annual depreciation of $3,600, as opposed to the $4,581 depreciable under the component parts method.

Building Value	Life of Structure	Yearly Depreciation	Annual Depreciation
$90,000	25 years	4%	$3,600

Sum-of-the-years digits. The **sum-of-the-years digits** is a method of depreciation that provides for a greater depreciation in the early years of ownership and less in later years. The idea is to shift the taxable income towards the end of the structure's life. This is achieved by multiplying the economic life of the building times a proportion of the whole each year.

Totaling years for accelerated depreciation

If the economic life of the property is twenty-five years, each year is added—25 + 24 + 23 and so on through 1—for a total of 325. Taking the $90,000 building value times 25 years and dividing it by 325, the owner can depreciate $6,923.08 the first year. The following year he takes 24 years times $90,000 and divides it by 325, allowing $6,728.97 in depreciation. The process is continued each succeeding year. The first year's depreciation will be 25 times greater than the last year's. It's easy to see that the investor realizes the greatest tax advantage the first several years.

Depreciating by the 200 percent method

Double-declining balance. The **double-declining balance** method is an accelerated method of depreciation that provides the owner with the greatest depreciation in the first years of the building's life. This method allows 200 percent depreciation. Assuming the economic life of our structure is twenty-five years, 4 percent of 200 equals 8 percent. The $90,000 value multiplied by 8 percent allows $7,200 depreciation the first year.

The second year the $7,200 is subtracted from the $90,000 leaving $82,800. Multiplying $82,800 by 8 percent allows $6624 depreciation the following year. Each year the investor continues this process of depreciating the improvement. This depreciation schedule cannot be used on all income-producing properties.

The first owner of residential income-producing property may use the 200 percent double-declining balance. A second owner may use 125 percent declining balance if there is a remaining economic life of twenty years or more.

If a nonresidential property (as an office building) is being depreciated, the owner cannot use more than 150 percent declining balance. Owners of all other depreciable real estate are limited to using the straight-line method.

Leverage

The investor may borrow money to finance the greater share of an investment. By using other people's money, the investor's buying power is increased. This use of borrowed funds is called **leverage**. The investor will want to put the least possible amount down and obtain the lowest available interest rate over the longest period of time. This allows the investor to accumulate the maximum amount of real estate with the minimum amount of personal funds.

However for the investor expecting a cash flow, the expenses and mortgage costs may well exceed the returns if too much leverage is used. While tax shelters, appreciation, and cash flow are all great motivators for purchasing, the investment must not be leveraged to the point that a cash flow is impossible. The choice the investor selects must have reasonable likelihood of satisfying the objective of increasing the purchaser's net worth. Not only does the present value need to be considered, but its future income stream should be analyzed. Mentioned earlier in this text were the forces that influence value. If the investor buys with the intention of selling or conditions develop that necessitate a sale, economic conditions may not be conducive to a quick sale. The lack of liqudity is one of the biggest risk factors involved in owning real estate.

Let us take a property and analyze the difference on the rate of return when cash is paid vs. leveraging with a mortgage.

1. Cash investment:
   $125,000 investment $15,000 net income
   $15,000 ÷ $125,000 = 12 percent return

2. Investment financed:
   $125,000 investment
   $93,750 mortgage (75%) = $31,250 equity invested
   subtract 1 year's interest at 10% ($9375.00) from $15,000 net income = $5,625 net income.
   $5,625 (net income) ÷ $31,250 (initial investment) = 18% return annually.

Remember, the above figures on investment/financing are predicated on the rate of return on the investment. To many investors this is more meaningful since it considers only the amount of cash they have invested.

There are various types of real estate investments to choose from. The investor may purchase single family homes, duplexes, four-plexes, apartments, condominiums, office buildings, strip shopping centers, farms, acreage, or bare development land. There is literally something for everyone. If the investor needs immediate income, vacant land would be a poor choice. Holding power is needed since property taxes, interest, and insurance are constant costs. The speculator gambles on the premise that the land will increase in value, a risk that all investors are not ready to assume. *Investment opportunities*

Consider a typical American couple who own their own home. They have been able to accumulate $6000 in savings, $5000 of which they decide to use to purchase a rental house. After searching every weekend for the perfect unit, they make concessions and finally decide on an older two-story house in a modest neighborhood that has been converted into two apartments. Inspections reveal newer wiring and two modern furnaces. No measurable deferred maintenance is observed. They purchase the property for $45,000 at 10 percent interest for 20 years. Monthly payments are $386.40. Insurance coverage costs $240.00 a year. The units rent for $280 and $320 each.

Income
> $280 @ 12 mos. = $3360.00
> $320 @ 12 mos. = 3840.00
>   Gross income   = $7200.00

Expenses

Insurance policy	$140.00	
Supplies & materials	180.00	
Taxes	450.00	
Maintenance	320.00	
Mortgage payments	4636.80	
	$5726.80	$7200.00 (income)
Net Income		1473.20

This is not taking into consideration income tax deductions for interest and real estate taxes.

All physical labor such as yard care and minor repairs are done by the owners. Technically they should place a value on their time. Had the investors taken their $5,000 and invested it in a certificate of deposit at 7 percent, the annual yield would have been $350, before taxes.

They realize that their profit can be wiped out if a unit remains vacant for a period of time. They have discussed with one tenant carpet replacement for his unit, with the tenant agreeing to a raise in rent from $280 to $305 a month. To recover the cost of the carpet will take 2½ years, but they are assured of a happy tenant who will not vacate the unit. The couple are pleased with their investment and when their savings build up they plan to search for another property.

The principle of increasing and decreasing returns must be acnowledged. Continued improvement of a property will eventually reach a leveling off point beyond which rents cannot be raised. To place microwaves, fireplaces and jacuzzis in the units would not be a justifiable expense and would result in overimprovement.

The couple's upkeep and care of the property has enhanced its value and they can use the equity in that investment to leverage buying another. They could either draw some of the equity out or use it as collateral for a blanket mortgage that could cover both properties.

Now the pyramiding begins. If they were to continue the process, a portfolio of investments could be secured. The careful investor will not over-leverage or the pyramid will come tumbling down. It should be built with the stability of an Egyptian pyramid and withstand all foreseeable obstacles.

DEFERRING GAINS TAXES

Refinancing vs. Selling

Equity builds up in an investment property through increased value of the property and principal reduction on the amortized loan. The owner can then refinance the property with a new loan and use the tax-free money to purchase another property. Since this is borrowed money, it is not taxable. By refinancing, taxes on gains are avoided since taxes are payable only on the sale of the property. The owner is now able to purchase additional properties with the money obtained through refinancing and thus can pyramid his holdings. By carefully choosing properties that increase in value, the owner can refinance each after holding the property for a reasonable period of time, depending on current market conditions, and use the money to purchase other properties. If the investor so chooses, s/he can avoid taxes forever by leaving the properties to his or her heirs.

Tax-Deferred Exchanges

Trading investment property

To defer capital gains, an investor can make a **tax-free exchange** of his property for another like property. This simply means that real estate must be exchanged for real estate. A duplex could be exchanged for a six-plex, or an apartment could be traded for an office building. The quality of the property is not questioned, "like kind" refers to the nature, class, or character of the real property. If it is not an equal exchange and additional money or goods are included, then the extra money is called "boot" and is taxed at the time of transfer. The depreciated book value of the old property will be carried to the new and the adjustments for the additional compensation (boot) will be added to the property.

Had the investor of the duplex at 7007 Mulberry Lane exchanged his property for another, taxes could have been deferred as follows:

Duplex sale price	$120,000	New 4-plex	$180,000
Adjusted basis	41,000	Boot needed	60,000

The new basis for the four-plex is $101,000. This is the basis of the duplex, $41,000, carried over to the new purchase, plus the boot of $60,000.

Capital Gains

The 1986 Tax Reform Act repealed the long term capital gains deduction for gains realized. Capital gains income will be taxed as ordinary income, with a top bracket of 28 percent. Most affected by this ruling will be the recapture of depreciation since profit from a sale is now treated as ordinary income.

GROUP BUSINESS VENTURE

Many times business enterprises are formed by a group of individuals who have a common purpose in mind. Partnerships, corporations, syndications, and trusts hold real estate for business purposes. Investors join others in a joint venture or limited partnership since they can acquire larger properties by pooling their funds. *Joint venture*

Partnerships are formed by two or more people who join forces to carry out an idea together for profit-making reasons. The partnership may be operated in the name of the owners or a trade name selected by the partners. *Pooling funds with other investors*

Two types of legally recognized partnerships exist: the general partnership and the limited partnership.

In the *general partnership* the individuals involved manage and operate the business. The partners take total responsibility for both profits and loses. Some of the disadvantages are that *General partnership*

1. Each partner is personally liable for any debts incurred and their personal assets may be attached;
2. One partner can obligate the others;
3. Death will terminate the partnership;
4. Consent of all partners for decisions; and
5. Lack of liquidity, since it may be difficult to sell a partnership interest.

The advantages include the following:

1. The partnership is not taxed (as a corporation is); and
2. Partners can share their money and expertise to build a business.

A *limited partnership* involves a general partner and two or more limited partners. Although the limited partners are the investors, they do not take an active role in management but are passive investors, and a general manager is paid to handle the investment. The limited partners are held responsible for losses only in the amount of their investment; the general manager usually conceives and organizes the partnership. The agreement is so drawn that the death or withdrawal of one of the partners does not affect the partnership. *Limited partnership*

The investors' liability is limited and they have no management obligations; the general manager, however, must be capable and have a good track record. Furthermore, limited partnership shares are difficult to transfer since all partners must agree to the transfer. There are many combinations of limited partnerships. A typical joint venture is illustrated in figure 14.2.

The joint purchasers of the property outlined in figure 14.2 have an additional gross income added to the total cost:

$3,000,000 *cost to acquire property*
 1,000,000 *gross income*
$4,000,000 *sale price to limited partners*

The development and management expenses are deducted from the gross income:

$1,000,000 *gross income*
   475.000 *expenses*
$ 525,000 *net income*

The limited partners will receive the full amount of their invested funds plus a percentage—say 10 percent. The balance of the profits will be evenly divided between the limited partners and the general manager.

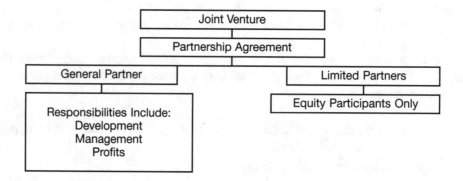

FIGURE 14.2
A typical joint venture in real estate.

Corporations are legal entities formed by two or more parties and are considered by law as individual "persons." The stockholders of a corporation may obtain money without becoming personally liable. Unlike a partner, a stockholder has only his or her own investment at stake. The corporation may hold title to property and enter into contracts under its articles of declaration. There is a cost to incorporate and corporations are subject to double taxation: the corporation pays taxes on its earnings, and when the stockholders receive dividends they are personally taxed on the income.

The *Subchapter S corporation* permits investors to avoid double taxation resulting from earnings of the shareholders and of the corporation. Income is not taxed at the corporate levels, but Subchapter S corporations are limited to 25 shareholders. The type of income allowed is limited and there are firm limitations on losses.

Syndication is a term used to denote multiple participation in a real estate investment. A syndication group is composed of a general partner and two or more limited partners. Although the limited partners are the investors, they do not take an active role in management. The general partner is paid to manage the investment.

A syndication must comply with federal and state regulations. If the syndication is formed with the intent of making money on the investment, it is considered a security and must be registered with the Security Exchange Commission (SEC).

Real Estate Investment Trusts (REIT) make available the investment in real estate to individuals by selling shares in large investment properties. By pooling the funds of many investors, the trust can purchase large properties. Income received from the properties goes to the beneficiaries (investors). The trustee (manager) manages the properties for the investors. Shares are easily transferrable. One of the advantages of REIT is that the revenue is not treated as corporate income; that is, it is not taxed twice.

REAL ESTATE OFFERINGS AS SECURITIES

If real estate is purchased for investment it will be considered a *security* and subject to jurisdiction under the Securities Act when it meets the four elements of an "investment contract" as defined by the Federal Securities Act of 1933. Four elements must be present for it to be considered a security:

1. it must be an investment of money;
2. it must be in a common enterprise;
3. it must be undertaken with the prospect of making a profit; and
4. it must be one in which profit will be derived solely or substantially from the management efforts of others (whose efforts affect the success or failure of the enterprise).

A typical example of a security would be a limited partnership where shares are sold.

The purpose of the Securities Act was to provide full and fair disclosure of securities sold in interstate commerce and through the mails and to prevent frauds in the sale of securites.

Anyone selling a security must register it with the Federal SEC before offering the security for sale. A disclosure statement giving basic preliminary information of the enterprise must be delivered prior to or with any solicitation of an offer for the sale of the securities. This statement is referred to as a **prospectus**. A detailed accounting must be included, revealing the number of investors the partnership is seeking, all pertinent data pertaining to the property offered, and the distribution of profits and losses.

There are exceptions, as when the offering is intrastate—that is, offered solely in the state where the issuer resides and does business. However, the offering will need to be registered in that particular state, unless it would be exempt as a private offering. A private offering is of a limited scope, and is directed to a selected type of sophisticated investor who doesn't need the protection offered by the SEC disclosure.

Exceptions to SEC filing

A securities license is required of anyone who offers securities for sale. The securities laws which regulate the registration and sale of securities were passed to prevent people from buying or selling a "piece of the blue sky," thus the reason for referring to the laws as Blue Sky Laws.

SUMMARY

The many aspects of real estate as an investment have been covered in this chapter. The advantages include

1. The continual rise of property values has been a great hedge against inflation;
2. The attractive high rate of return on the investment;
3. The leverage available since the investor borrows money to finance the purchase, his buying power is substantially increased; and
4. The investor's equity buildup, since a portion of the payments apply to reducing the principal.

The major disadvantages of a real estate investment are

1. The nonliquidity. While stocks and bonds can be sold quickly through a stockbroker, it usually takes a period of time to find a buyer for real estate.
2. The risk. An investor must be a knowledgeable buyer and understand the risks involved, which include
   a. the importance of property location,
   b. the ratio of rental returns to payments,
   c. the maintenance of the structures, and
   d. the management of the property (if the investors do not have the time, a professional management service will need to be hired).

Many investors are not overly concerned if the property does not create an immediate return on the capital invested since they use their real estate investments in part as tax shelters. However, the Tax Reform Act of 1986 will affect the passive investor involved only for purposes of sheltering income.

Depreciation schedules used in investment properties are discussed in this chapter along with a brief analysis of the need for reinvesting to avoid capital gains when the property is sold. The importance of tax-free exchanges to defer the resulting gains in the investment are also covered.

For the serious investor who wants to accumulate wealth through real estate ownership and have a steady flow of income, the new tax reform law will not detour investing. Proponents of the 1986 Tax Reform Bill felt such changes were necessary because of a glut of properties built with no concern for real use or occupation. Called *see-through buildings* because of the lack of tenants, they are an example of the abuse of the law by people seeking merely tax shelters.

KEY WORDS AND CONCEPTS

Adjusted basis: The basis, plus cost of any physical improvement to the property, minus depreciation.

Basis: The initial cost of the property, the financial interest of the owner.

Cash flow: The cash income or return on an investment.

Depreciation: An expense deduction taken when depreciating the value of an income producing property for income tax purposes.

Gain: Any profit received upon the sale of an asset, the difference between the adjusted basis and the net selling price.

Leverage: The use of other people's money (OPM) to finance the bulk of an investment.

Limited partnership: A group of passive investors with a sponsor or general partner who manages the investment portfolio.

Negative cash flow: Occurs when the expenses are greater than the income produced.

Prospectus: Preliminary information on an enterprise that is required by the SEC to be given to prospective investors.

Passive income: Income derived from the efforts of another, as an investment in a syndication or limited partnership.

REIT: Real Estate Investment Trust, they offer shares in large investment properties.

Salvage value: The value after the useful life is over (usually 5 to 10% of the property's depreciable basis).

SEC: Securities Exchange Commission, they monitor the sale of securities.

Syndication: A group of people who pool their funds and invest in a common enterprise.

Tax free exchange: Exchanging income producing property for a like property and thus enabling the investor to defer taxes on the gain.

Tax shelter: An investment that acts to reduce income tax.

Useful life: The number of years an investment will be useful to the investor. The shorter the useful life, the larger the depreciation deduction per year.

REVIEW QUESTIONS

1. When expenses are greater than the income produced, it is called
   a. taxable income
   b. cash flow
   c. negative cash flow
   d. adjusted basis

2. Depreciation of real property is available to
   a. home owners
   b. investors
   c. both of the above
   d. neither of the above

3. The function of a real estate investment is to give the investor
   a. equity gains
   b. appreciation
   c. income
   d. all of the above

4. All of the following are methods of depreciation, except
   a. straight-line
   b. sum-of-the-years digits
   c. cost reproduction
   d. double-declining balance

5. Capital gains occur when
   a. a home owner sells his home and reinvests in a like property.
   b. an investor sells property at a loss.
   c. an investor sells depreciated property and does not reinvest.
   d. none of the above

6. A disclosure statement that describes an investment opportunity is called a(n)
   a. contract
   b. shelter
   c. option to purchase
   d. prospectus

7. Leverage is best defined as
   a. borrow the least amount of money for the shortest period of time.
   b. put the least amount down, obtain the lowest interest for the longest period of time.
   c. a tax free exchange.
   d. postponing capital gains.

8. An owner is exempt from paying taxes on gains realized from a sale
   a. if he purchases another home within a twenty-four-month period.
   b. if the new purchase is at least equal in value to the property sold.
   c. both of the above
   d. neither of the above

9. The following factor(s) have influenced people to invest in real estate:
   a. the inflation of real estate values
   b. the need for shelter
   c. both of the above
   d. neither of the above

10. Investments that can be depreciated include
    a. a home, when a room is used solely as an office
    b. a private residence
    c. savings deposited in a federally insured bank
    d. none of the above

11. A home owner has recorded the following expenditures: $2,300 mortgage interest, $1,250 property tax, $1,800 depreciation, $700 addition of a garage and $1,500 sale of an easement. What would the allowable income tax deduction be?
    a. $3,550
    b. $5,350
    c. $6,050
    d. $7,550

12. After the economic life of an apartment complex has been exhausted, the owner has left
    a. an unearned value
    b. pure profit
    c. salvage value
    d. adjusted basis

13. A retired person on a pension buys a twenty-four-unit apartment complex. What would he most likely be looking for:
    a. depreciation
    b. gross income
    c. rent income
    d. net spendable money

14. Professor Smith purchases a home for $60,000. She installs a $12,000 tennis court and a $3,000 air conditioner. Five years later she sells the home for $96,000. Her taxable income is
    a. $78,000
    b. $36,000
    c. $21,000
    d. $18,000

15. Upon the sale of an investment property, any profits in excess of straight-line depreciation are considered
    a. ordinary income
    b. earned income
    c. 30 percent tax sheltered
    d. entirely tax sheltered

16. A person is in the 28 percent tax bracket. If he has a $126 monthly interest payment, how much less will his income tax be if he can deduct 100 percent of his interest?
    a. $800
    b. $600.51
    c. $1,512
    d. $423.36

17. An investment is considered a security when all of the following components are present, except
    a. It is an investment of money.
    b. It is a common enterprise.
    c. The investor hopes to make a profit.
    d. All the investors share in managerial duties.

18. The Federal Securities Act of 1933 was enacted to do all of the following, except
    a. Monitor intrastate sale of securities.
    b. Provide full disclosure of securities offered for sale.
    c. Prevent fraud in the sale of securities.
    d. Prevent consumers from buying "blue sky."

19. The 1986 Tax Reform Act brought forth some sweeping new changes to the tax laws. It had the greatest impact on
    a. Homeowners
    b. Investment property
    c. Vacation homes
    d. Motor homes

20. The term that best describes a group of people who pool their funds in a joint venture to acquire a real estate investment is
    a. Portfolio
    b. Risk takers
    c. Syndication
    d. Co-ownership

The Appraisal Process | 15

Appraising is far from an exact science, but a degree of relative uniformity may be achieved by applying proven appraisal techniques along with the use of factual information. Many professional appraisers concentrate all their time on the profession and are recognized for their knowledge, skill, and experience in the field. They interpret the facts in an unbiased manner from pertinent available information. An independent fee appraiser may be called upon to support his or her opinions in a court of law, so diligent care is taken with each parcel appraised. While real estate brokers and salespersons need not qualify as professional appraisers, they should be familiar with the three approaches to determining value by means of the appraisal process and be capable of arriving at the market value of the property they intend to list.

This chapter will explore the many different purposes for which the fee appraiser may be requested to determine valuation of a property, the steps in an appraisal, and how valuation is arrived at and shown in the written, documented appraisal report furnished to the client.

APPRAISALS

An **appraisal** means simply an *estimate of value*. It is an opinion as to the worth of a particular piece of property. An appraiser must measure the value of each parcel of real estate s/he appraises, and furnish a supportable opinion.

A definite sequence of steps is followed in the appraisal process.

1. Defining the problem: identifying the parcel of real estate by legal or street address and stating the purpose of the appraisal
2. Collecting the data
   a. economic data
   b. neighborhood data
   c. the property's data
3. Analyzing and applying the three approaches
   a. comparison approach
   b. cost approach
   c. income approach
4. Correlating the data and analyzing the results
5. Writing the appraisal report

THE PURPOSE OF AN APPRAISAL

Since value means different things to different people, the purpose of the appraisal is the first question asked by the appraiser. To the owner of the property, value would be considered as market value, investment value, and value in use. The insurance agent will think in terms of insured value while the lender is concerned with loan value. When the appraiser makes his report he will clearly state the nature of the assignment. Valuation may be sought to determine any of the following:

1. **Market value:** Market value is commonly referred to as the highest probable price at which a willing seller will sell and a willing buyer will buy, with neither being under abnormal pressure. It is the highest price a property is expected to bring if exposed for sale on the open market, allowing a reasonable amount of time to find a purchaser who is fully aware of the uses to which the property may be put. Keep in mind that value is created by the desire of people for a commodity or service. *Market price* is the actual sale price of the property. This may differ from the market value if the seller needs to sell quickly.

2. **Loan value:** Prior to committing to a loan, a lending institution has an appraiser give a report on the property's value since it is the collateral for the loan. Many large savings and loan companies have staff appraisers to determine loan value.

3. **Insurance value:** The lender requires the borrower to insure the property to protect the lender's interest. The insurance policy will need to cover the amount of the loan, with the lender named as cobeneficiary.

The property owner will also want to insure the investment, regardless of whether or not a loan is involved. In case of damage or destruction, the owner is assured of sufficient coverage to replace the structure.

4. **Estate tax value:** The value of a deceased person's real property will need to be determined for inheritance tax purposes.

5. **Lease interest:** If a commercial property carries a long-term lease, it may contain a reappraisal clause since the leasehold value may change over a period of time. Some properties are also built on leased land, such as vacation homes or commercial buildings, and the land value may vary over the length of the lease.

Methods of determining value for taxation

6. **Tax assessment:** Real property is assessed for taxation purposes according to its value. This is known as an **ad valorem tax.** The county assessor's office appraises the property for taxation purposes and the assessed value is provided by the law of the municipality. The city council or governing board then sets the mill levy according to the amount of money needed to meet the budget and expenses of the local government. This budget is submitted by the county auditor and approved by the council.

To determine the amount of taxes on a property, the assessed value is multiplied by the mill levy. (A mill equals one-tenth of a cent.)

For example:		
	$70,000	*appraised value*
	.30	*percentage taxed*
	$21,000	*assessed value*
	.070	*mill levy*
	$ 1,470	*annual taxes*

Taxes are sometimes expressed in dollars, as $2.00 per $100 of appraised value. Thus, the $70,000 appraised value times $2.00 would equal $1,400 annual taxes.

7. **Eminent domain:** As we learned in Chapter 2, under the right of eminent domain the police power of a governmental body may take the property of an individual for public use. The property is condemned and appraisers determine its *fair market value*.

Property condemned for public use

When a fraction of an individual's property is condemned and taken (as under the right of eminent domain), the appraiser determines what the value of the property was before that portion was taken and what the remainder is now worth. This before-and-after method awards just compensation to the condemnee for the loss of that portion of land.

FIGURE 15.1
The appraiser establishes how much the original value has been diminished.

8. **Financial statement:** If a person needs to borrow capital, the lender may require a current appraisal of the borrower's real property holdings to establish the net worth of the individual.

9. **Third-party companies:** An appraisal will serve as a basis for corporations or third-party companies that buy out (purchase) the homes of transferred employees.

10. **Liquidation:** In the situation of a forced sale or auction, a liquidation value will be necessary.

At this point the difference between a competitive market analysis (CMA) as discussed in Chapter 6 and a fee appraisal should be clarified. The CMA is different in both purpose and form. The broker and salesperson need to arrive at the probable market value each time they list a property. This is approached by comparing the selling price of similar properties that recently sold and the listed price of comparable properties currently offered for sale. They also check the listed price of expired listings. Through continuous evaluation of listings and sales, the broker and salesperson keep abreast of prices and the changing market conditions that affect them. However, they are not expected to give written and certified reports such as the fee appraiser prepares. The real estate salesperson's only concern is pricing the property at a realistic selling price in today's market.

COLLECTING THE DATA

The appraiser maintains a data bank of information as a ready resource. General data on the region, the city, and the neighborhood will be collected and maintained in the data bank.

Regional and city information includes knowledge of the economic conditions of the area. For example, an influx of new industry creates additional employment, which in turn brings new families, children, bank accounts, and retail sales into the area. Diversified employment provides a healthy economic outlook. The environmental or physical conditions that affect property values include parks, highways,

Regional factors that affect value

airports, public transportation, available utilities, and shopping centers in the region. The political conditions in regional and local governments are also considered. Understanding social factors includes evaluating the population trends of the area. The prevalent age groups determine the demand for various types of housing, such as single-family homes, condominiums, apartments, or retirement complexes.

The neighborhood data is information on the area within certain street boundaries in which the dwellings are of comparable price range and age. The average income and age of residents, convenience to shopping, public transportation, churches, and schools are other factors considered.

After assembling the regional, city, and neighborhood data the appraiser begins analyzing the property itself. The site is evaluated and the lot size determined. The square footage and street frontage are measured. Any special assessments against the property are recorded in the report. (A *special assessment* is a charge against real property to pay for the cost of a public improvement to the property. This assessment is made by a unit of government. Special tax assessments are levied against the property for the cost of street paving, curbing, sidewalks, and sewers.)

Primary Forces Affecting Value

The appraiser must consider the forces that continually affect value. Property values are influenced at national, regional, and the local community level. The four major forces that have the greatest influence on residential real estate values are

1. governmental (political)
2. economic (financial)
3. physical
4. sociological

These four forces can modify value, can create value, or can destroy value. The influence of federal control over policies that affect inflation have an impact on the cost of housing. Interest rates are directly responsive to government action that determines how many people will be buying real estate.

While housing values are affected at the regional level due to political stability, economic conditions, and employment statistics, the most important levels of influence are conditions at the local level. The physical location of a property in a community affects its value. Certain neighborhoods in a given area will be in greater demand and command higher sale prices. The topography may also be a factor, affecting construction costs.

Sociological factors reflect the attitude of the people in the community. Property taxes and services rendered to the residents are local forces that affect property values. How the residents feel towards the local government—their opinion of the community as a good place to live—also has an impact on value. Cultural amenities such as theatre, arts, parks, and recreational facilities are all amenities that enhance the lives of the area residents.

In the final analysis, value is created when there is

1. *desire:* The commodity must be wanted.
2. *utility:* This considers the degree to which it can be used.
3. *scarcity:* Supply is limited.
4. *effective purchasing power:* Money is available to buy it.

Other Factors Affecting Appraisal

Three approaches are used in the appraisal of real property: the **cost approach,** the **market data approach,** and the **income approach.** Before the appraiser begins to analyze each of these approaches to value he/she must apply certain basic principles that affect the worth in any method of appraising real property. These principles are discussed below.

When we speak of the **highest and best** use of property, we are referring to the most profitable use to which it can be put. Briefly, the highest and best use can be defined as the use that, at the time of the appraisal, is most likely to produce the greatest net return on the land and/or building over a given period of time. *Net return* is the key phrase in this definition. It means whatever is left from gross yield after all costs are met. Sometimes net return takes a form that may not bring the greatest monetary return: for example, land for a children's zoo or a forest preserve that will give enjoyment to thousands every year.

Highest and best use

If the property can be *substituted* for another, then its value is set to an extent by the cost of acquiring the like property. The knowledgable purchaser today will "shop" and compare properties before making his selection. This is the *principle of substitution,* used in the comparison approach to appraising.

The *utility value* of a property, how it can be used, is also important in deter- mining value. A lovely wooded lot may appear to be a perfect location for a home site, but investigation uncovers that it has a ravine running through it, leaving no feasible spot for a building site. Zoning laws and restrictive covenants can also affect the use of a property. A location that may seem ideal for a commercial building but which is zoned only for office buildings will be limited to the use designated by the zoning ordinance. Protective covenants in an area may prohibit the building of a two-story house since it would obscure the views of surrounding home owners. When appraisers put a valuation on a particular property, they must carefully weigh its utility value.

Use dictates value

Functional utility refers to the usability of a building. A contractor may build one house with a highly desirable, very livable floor plan and choose a plan for another house with a poorly arranged interior. The latter may lack good window placement, have a traffic pattern that necessitates walking through the middle of one room to reach another, or lack storage area.

The *principle of contribution* is the principle the appraiser applies to the return on improvements to the property. To improve a property may not necessarily mean that the total cost of the improvement can be added to the value of the building. While a recreation room will expand the living space of the home and make it more desirable to a buyer, the owner may not recapture the entire cost of the remodeling. Enclosing porches and updating kitchens and baths may add appeal to the property but may not return the seller's total costs.

Principles of change acknowledge that the life cycle of a building dictates change. As a neighborhood ages, new land uses may be introduced, for example, by a demand for multifamily units in a once affluent neighborhood. New uses also develop through rezoning. As new styles and plans are built in the suburbs, people on a higher economic scale gravitate outwards from the city's urban area. A great thrust in many cities has been to revitalize the older sectors in an effort to slow suburban sprawl and prevent the decay of the innercity areas.

Age changes value

Amenities are the extras attached to a property. A desirable view, a wooded lot, or the privacy or location of a particular property can all be considered amenities.

The amenities desired may vary with different buyers. The proximity to transportation, a shopping center, or schools may be prime considerations for one purchaser, while special energy-conserving features may be most important to another.

APPROACHES TO APPRAISAL

When using the three approaches to value, the appraiser makes the decision as to which approach best typifies the subject property. Little credence is given to the income approach when appraising single family residences since few are purchased for rental purposes. For these appraisals, greater reliance is placed on the cost and comparison approaches. Conversely, these approaches to value would not be given as much weight in appraising an income-producing property. When appraising a single-purpose building, such as a church, the cost approach would be most applicable since comparable properties would be difficult to locate and the church is not considered income producing.

Comparison Approach

Determining value by comparison

The *market-data* approach is often referred to as the **comparison approach** to value, because the subject property (property being appraised) is compared to properties recently sold in the same general area or in neighborhoods of similar value.

The appraiser will seek comparable properties that have recently sold. Properties currently on the market for sale are not considered since no agreed upon contract between buyer and seller exists. A minimum of three comparables provide the appraiser with the necessary data to form an opinion as to the value of the subject property. The more similar the properties are, the easier it is to conclude value. Allowances and adjustments are made for any differences in the properties. The comparable approach to value is the most commonly used in appraising residential property as it depends on what similar properties are actually selling for.

When locating comparables, the appraiser will first look for recently sold properties in the immediate location of the subject property. If no recent sales are available in the neighborhood, an area similar in value should be searched. It is important that the comparables have sold within the past six months; this is especially true if the market is volatile. Depending on local conditions, adjustments for time lapsed are made either upwards or down.

It is necessary to locate the same style of house; for instance, two-story houses are not compared with ranch style houses. Adjustments are made for any differences in square footage, time of sale, garages, landscaping, lot size, the general condition of the property, and the financing terms of the sale.

Figure 15.2 indicates the process used in comparing residential properties. Let us analyze each step. Our subject property is at 1040 Clear Street, which is the model used throughout this book.

A. This line lists the property addresses. All three comparables are in the same subdivision as the subject property.

B. This line states the sale price of the comparable properties.

C. Line C allows for the change in value that occurs since the time of sales. The appraiser must track carefully any economic changes that have occurred since the sale date of the properties. If property is selling for less it will be necessary to adjust the comparables down. In the example, the area is in demand and properties do not have a long market time even though prices have leveled off and inflation has slowed. In view of this information, comparable #1 needs no adjustment since

	Subject	Comparables					
	1040 Clear Street	**1155 Clear Street**		**2201 Main Street**		**3215 Lincoln Street**	
A. Address	1040 Clear Street	1155 Clear Street		2201 Main Street		3215 Lincoln Street	
B. Sale Price		$86,000		$84,000		$85,500	
C. Time Adjustment		1 mo.	0	6 mos. add 2%	+ 1,680	3 mos. add 1%	+ 850
D. No. of rooms	6	6	0	6	0	6	0
E. No. of Bedrooms, baths	3-2	3-2	0	3-2	0	3-2	0
F. Square Footage	1350	1300 50 less	+ 2,500	1400 50 more	− 2,500	1350	0
G. Style, Const.	Ranch, frame	Ranch, fr.	0	Ranch, fr.	0	Ranch, fr.	0
H. Garage	2 car attd.	2 car attd.	0	1 car attd.	+ 1,500	2 car attd.	0
I. Age, Condition	7 yrs., good	4 yrs. excellent	− 2,500	7 yrs. excellent	− 1,000	15 yrs. good	+ 1,800
K. Lot, size extras	85 x 120	80 x 120	0	85 x 110	0	90 x 110	0
L. Special Features	wood deck, fenced	wood deck, fenced	0	patio, view	0	new carpet, fenced	0
M. Method of Sale		loan assumption	− 1,000	conv.	0	VA	− 2,000
N. Net Adjustments			− 1,000		+ 320		+ 650
O. Adjusted Market Price			$85,000		$84,320		$86,150
P. Indicated Value	$85,000						

FIGURE 15.2 Comparing resdential properties.

it sold just one month ago. Comparable #2 sold six months ago and its value has increased 2% and comparable #3 sold three months ago and has a 1% increase.

Remember, adjustments must be made to the comparable properties and not the subject. This is sometimes difficult for the person first approaching the appraisal process to understand. Think of it in terms of the fact that since the value of the subject property is unknown we cannot make adjustments to it.

D,E. No adjustments are necessary here since there are no variations.

F. Property #1 is 50 square feet smaller, so considering that the cost per square foot is $50.00 x 50 square feet, + $2500 is given to the property. Comparable #2 has 50 square feet more so we give it a - $2500.

G. Style and construction of the properties are all the same.

H. Comparable #2 has a 1 car garage, so we added $1500. This takes into consideration that it would be worth an additional $1500 if it had an extra garage.

I. Allowance need to be made for the differences in the age and condition of properties. Comparable #1 is only four years old and in excellent condition. Since it is three years newer than the subject and in excellent condition, a minus $2500 is given. Comparable #2 is the same age as the subject property; however, its condition is excellent so a minus $1000 is credited to it. Comparable #3 is fifteen years old so it has developed eight years of additional depreciation and $1800 is added to it.

K. Lot sizes vary so slightly that no allowances are made.

L. Special features can have a great affect on the sale price of a property. Wood decks and fenced yards are very fashionable in this area. While comparable #2 has neither, it does have a spectacular view that the appraiser felt "equalled out" not having the former. Properties that are treed, that offer privacy, or that are unusually well landscaped have amenities that also enhance value. Houses with professionally decorated interiors, that sparkle with cleanliness, or that have extra features such as built-in appliances, skylights, and jacuzzis have enhanced market value.

M. The financing involved in the sale can influence the price paid for the property. If a seller carries financing or an existing loan is assumed the purchaser may pay more for favorable loan terms. The appropriate adjustments were made on comparables #1 and #3.

N. The net adjustments are totalled.

O. The adjusted market price reflects the adjustments.

P. When looking at the three comparables, no correlation is necessary since the three properties are all very similar to the subject property. We give equal value to each of the properties and the indicated market value is $85,000. After the correlation of the properties, the appraiser states the conclusion; the final step for the appraiser is to certify the report.

Cost Approach

The **cost approach** to appraising is sometimes referred to as the *replacement cost method* or the *summation approach*. In this approach, an estimate is made of the cost to replace the improvements at today's prices, less depreciation, and adding the value of the land as if it were vacant and used to its highest potential as governed by covenants and zoning laws. Keep in mind that to replace a dwelling is to construct a building similar in design and quality. To actually reproduce a structure would probably not be feasible, as it would mean recreating the structure exactly as it is.

In implementing the cost approach, the appraiser first estimates replacement costs by using the square foot method (see figure 15.3). Cost data from recent construction of a similar structure will be divided by the square footage of the building, thus establishing the cost per square foot. The base cost estimate of the actual property is found by multiplying the square footage times the cost per foot.

Remember that in the cost approach, *replacement cost* less *depreciation* plus *land value* gives us the *appraisal value*. Figure 15.4 indicates how the appraised value of the example property located at 1040 Clear Street was determined. The appraiser did not feel the seven year old residence suffered from functional or economic obsolescence. The annual physical depreciation of ½% was multiplied times the seven years, and the resulting 3.5 percent was then multiplied times the replacement cost (including the concrete). Figure 15.5 (page 215) is a more in-depth form appraisal report that includes taxes, neighborhood data, and construction details. Most lenders now require appraisers to use the form approved by Freddie Mac and Fanny Mae (see figure 15.6 on page 216).

In a new building, a contractor may use the **unit-in-place** cost approach. In this approach, the cost of all the component parts, including the kitchen cabinets ($8700), the built-in appliances ($2300), the fireplace ($2200), and so on, are computed.

If contractors want a very precise cost breakdown, they can use the **quantity survey** method. This is the most detailed approach to appraising. Forty-two kitchen cabinet hinges may cost $1.30 each, nineteen drawer pulls .93 cents each, and so on. The cost of the labor is then added and contractors can come very close to figuring the exact cost of constructing the house. They can then decide the percentage of profit they desire for time and labor and add this to the cost of the building.

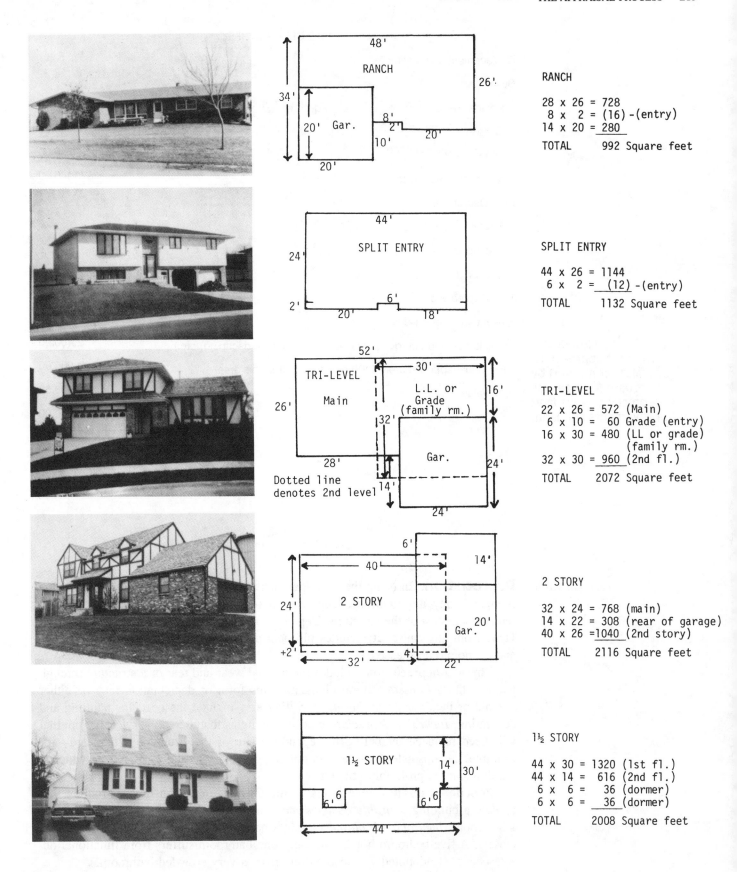

RANCH

28 x 26 = 728
 8 x 2 = (16) -(entry)
14 x 20 = 280
TOTAL   992 Square feet

SPLIT ENTRY

44 x 26 = 1144
 6 x 2 = (12) -(entry)
TOTAL   1132 Square feet

TRI-LEVEL

22 x 26 = 572 (Main)
 6 x 10 = 60 Grade (entry)
16 x 30 = 480 (LL or grade)
               (family rm.)
32 x 30 = 960 (2nd fl.)
TOTAL   2072 Square feet

2 STORY

32 x 24 = 768 (main)
14 x 22 = 308 (rear of garage)
40 x 26 =1040 (2nd story)
TOTAL   2116 Square feet

1½ STORY

44 x 30 = 1320 (1st fl.)
44 x 14 = 616 (2nd fl.)
 6 x 6 =   36 (dormer)
 6 x 6 =   36 (dormer)
TOTAL   2008 Square feet

FIGURE 15.3 A guide to measuring the square footage of various floor plans.

1040 CLEAR STREET

Replacement cost estimate:

Buildings:

Residence _____1350_____ sq. ft. at $50.00 _____ $67,500.00

Garage __2-car attd. 400__ sq. ft. at __12.00__ 4,800.00

Other __(concrete) 700__ sq. ft. at __1.20__ 840.00

Total Replacement Cost _____ $73,140.00

Less Depreciation:

Physical __(½%)__ $2,530.50

Functional __(0)__ -0-

Economic __(0)__ -0-

Total Depreciation $ 2,530.50

Present value of building $70,609.50

FIGURE 15.4 Net value of land improvements (walks, fences, landscaping, etc.) 2,400.00
The cost approach to
appraisal, computed by Land value (approximately $100 per front foot in this area) 11,900.00
square footage less
depreciation plus land Total Value $84,908.50
improvements and land.
Say: $85,000.00

Losses in value **Depreciation.** In using the cost approach method, the appraiser must determine if there is any **depreciation.** Depreciation of the property is subtracted from the replacement cost of the structure. Depreciation of real property is defined as loss of value from any cause. It includes physical deterioration, functional obsolescence, and economic obsolescence.

Physical depreciation includes the normal wear and tear of a structure through use and the actions of natural elements. This form of depreciation may be either curable or incurable. *Curable depreciation* may include the need for painting and decorating. *Incurable depreciation* occurs on items that are still serviceable but that will need replacement before the economic life of the structure is depleted—for example, an obsolete furnace. Economic life refers to the period over which a building can be profitably utilized.

Functional obsolescence refers to the changes in design or construction that outdate a building. *Curable obsolescence* might include the need for modernizing a bathroom. *Incurable obsolescence* might be a poor floor plan or a serious lack of closets. A five-bedroom home with only one bathroom suffers from functional obsolescence. (Undoubtedly, it also suffers from a very crowded bathroom!)

Economic obsolescence relates to conditions external to the property, such as the desirability of the neighborhood or changes in nearby land use. The value of a

RESIDENTIAL APPRAISAL

Owner's Name __Wender, Harvey & Della__   DATE OF APPRAISAL— __3-8-87__

LOCATION OF PROPERTY:

City, town or village __Big Red__   County __Kent__   State __Nebraska__

Street number __1040__ on __east__ side __Clear Street__
(AVENUE, STREET, ROAD, BOULEVARD

Legal Description - Lot No. __8__   Block No. __1__   Subdivision __Confusion Hill__

Lot size __85__ ft. (Frontage) x __110__ ft. (Depth)

TAXES AND ASSESSMENTS:

Assessed Valuation $ __land-9000, improvements 75,400__ Annual Taxes (Estimate) $ __1550.00__

(NOTE - The market value should include the value of all improvements and should not be reduced by unpaid liens for such improvements.)

NEIGHBORHOOD

Price Range of Typical Houses   Ages of Typical Houses   Income Range of Typical Families

$ __70,000__ to $ __95,000__   to __5 to 15__ yrs. $ _____ to $ _____

TYPE OF NEIGHBORHOOD	UTILITIES	STREET IMPROVEMENTS	AMENITIES
(Predominantly)	☒ City Water	☒ Paved	Shopping __1__ miles
☒ Single Family	☐ Community Water	☐ Unpaved	Churches __2__ miles
☐ Multiple Family	☐ Well ☐ Storm Sewer	☐ Curbs	Schools __8 blks.__ miles
☐ Commercial ☐ Industrial	☒ Sanitary Sewer	☐ Sidewalks	Public Transportation 1 miles
TREND OF NEIGHBORHOOD	☐ Septic System		
☐ Developing	☒ Electricity ☒ Gas	TRAFFIC CONDITIONS:	
☒ Static ☐ Declining	☐	☒ Light ☐ Heavy	

CONSTRUCTION DETAILS

YEAR BUILT __1980__

ARCHITECTURE	BASEMENT	EXTERIOR WALLS	CAR STORAGE
☒ Single Story	☒ Full ☐ Crawl Space ☐ Slab	☒ Wood Siding	☒ Garage ☐ Carport
☐ Two Story	☐	☐ Wood Shingles	☒ Attached ☐ Detached
☐ Tri-Level	FOUNDATION	☐ Stucco ☐ Brick Veneer	☐ In Basement ☒ 2 Car ☐ 1 Car
☐	☒ Block	☐ Brick on Block ☐ Stone Facing	☒ Auto. Door
	☐ Poured Concrete	☐ Asbestos Shingle	DRIVE:
FLOOR CONSTRUCTION	☐ Tile ☐ Brick	☐ Aluminum ☐ Masonite	☒ Paved ☐ Unpaved
☐ Concrete Slab	ROOF	INTERIOR FINISH	
☒ Wood	☒ Asphalt Shingles	☒ Plaster	OTHER FEATURES
☐	☐ Wood Shingles	☒ Drywall	☒ Fireplaces (1)
	☐	☒ Wood Trim ☐ Metal	☒ Cent. Air Conditioning
HEATING	PLUMBING	KITCHEN	☐ Lawn Sprinkler System
☒ Gas ☐ Base Board	☐ Galv. Iron	☒ Built-in Oven	☐ Family Room
☐ Oil ☐ Water	☒ Copper	☒ Built-in Range	☒ Rec. Room in Basement
☐ Electric ☐ Steam	☐	☒ Dishwasher	☒ Storms & Screens
☒ Forced Air ☐ Radiant	LANDSCAPING	☒ Garbage Disposal	☐ Swimming Pool
☐ Radiators ☐ Space-Heater	☐ Above Avg. ☐ Below Avg.	☒ Exhaust Fan	(_____ ft. x _____ ft.)
	☒ Average		☒ Fenced yard

GENERAL COMMENTS: (State any adverse soil and flood conditions, etc.)

REQUIRED REPAIRS: (If there are any repairs or deferred maintenance required to make the property salable, indicate below.)

Description (Identify Area)   Estimated Cost

__none__ $ _____

REPLACEMENT COST ESTIMATE:

Buildings:

Residence __1350__ sq. ft. x $ __50__ $ __67,500__

Garage __400__ sq. ft. x $ __12__ $ __4,800__

Other __rec room__ $ __2,000__

   Total Replacement Costs $ __74,300__

Less Depreciaton:

*Physical (__½__ %) x 7 yrs. $ __2530.50__

Functional (__0__ %) $ _____

Economic (__0__ %) $ _____

   Total Depreciation   ($ __2,530.50__)

   Present Value of Building $ __71,769.50__

Net Value of Land Improvements (Walks, Fences, Landscaping, etc.) $ __14,000.00__

Land Value $ __85,769.50__

   Total Value $ __85,800.00__

Explanation of Depreciation:

* This amount should reflect required repairs indicated above.

FIGURE 15.5 A more detailed cost-approach appraisal.

| Valuation Section | **UNIFORM RESIDENTIAL APPRAISAL REPORT** | File No. |

Purpose of Appraisal is to estimate Market Value as defined in the Certification & Statement of Limiting Conditions.

COST APPROACH

BUILDING SKETCH (SHOW GROSS LIVING AREA ABOVE GRADE)
If for Freddie Mac or Fannie Mae, show only square foot calculations and cost approach comments in this space

ESTIMATED REPRODUCTION COST–NEW–OF IMPROVEMENTS:

Dwelling _____ Sq. Ft. @ $ _____	= $ _____
_____ Sq. Ft. @ $ _____	= _____
Extras _____	= _____
	= _____
Special Energy Efficient Items _____	= _____
Porches, Patios, etc. _____	= _____
Garage/Carport _____ Sq. Ft. @ $ _____	= _____
Total Estimated Cost New	= $ _____

	Physical	Functional	External
Less			
Depreciation _____			= $ _____

Depreciated Value of Improvements	= $ _____
Site Imp. "as is" (driveway, landscaping, etc.)	= $ _____
ESTIMATED SITE VALUE	= $ _____
(If leasehold, show only leasehold value.)	
INDICATED VALUE BY COST APPROACH	= $ _____

(Not Required by Freddie Mac and Fannie Mae)

Does property conform to applicable HUD/VA property standards? ☐ Yes ☐ No

If No, explain: _____

Construction Warranty	☐ Yes ☐ No
Name of Warranty Program	_____
Warranty Coverage Expires	_____

SALES COMPARISON ANALYSIS

The undersigned has recited three recent sales of properties most similar and proximate to subject and has considered these in the market analysis. The description includes a dollar adjustment, reflecting market reaction to those items of significant variation between the subject and comparable properties. If a significant item in the comparable property is superior to, or more favorable than, the subject property, a minus (–) adjustment is made, thus reducing the indicated value of subject; if a significant item in the comparable is inferior to, or less favorable than, the subject property, a plus (+) adjustment is made, thus increasing the indicated value of the subject.

ITEM	SUBJECT	COMPARABLE NO. 1		COMPARABLE NO. 2		COMPARABLE NO. 3	
Address							
Proximity to Subject							
Sales Price	$		$		$		$
Price/Gross Liv. Area	$	☐ $		$	☐	$	☐
Data Source							
VALUE ADJUSTMENTS	DESCRIPTION	DESCRIPTION	+ (–) $ Adjustment	DESCRIPTION	+ (–) $ Adjustment	DESCRIPTION	+ (–) $ Adjustment
Sales or Financing Concessions							
Date of Sale/Time							
Location							
Site/View							
Design and Appeal							
Quality of Construction							
Age							
Condition							
Above Grade Room Count	Total Bdrms Baths	Total Bdrms Baths		Total Bdrms Baths		Total Bdrms Baths	
Gross Living Area	Sq. Ft.	Sq. Ft.		Sq. Ft.		Sq. Ft.	
Basement & Finished Rooms Below Grade							
Functional Utility							
Heating/Cooling							
Garage/Carport							
Porches, Patio, Pools, etc.							
Special Energy Efficient Items							
Fireplace(s)							
Other (e.g. kitchen equip., remodeling)							
Net Adj. (total)		☐ + ☐ – $		☐ + ☐ – $		☐ + ☐ – $	
Indicated Value of Subject		$		$		$	

Comments on Sales Comparison: _____

INDICATED VALUE BY SALES COMPARISON APPROACH .... $ _____

INDICATED VALUE BY INCOME APPROACH (If Applicable) Estimated Market Rent $ _____ /Mo. x Gross Rent Multiplier _____ = $ _____

This appraisal is made ☐ "as is" ☐ subject to the repairs, alterations, inspections or conditions listed below ☐ completion per plans and specifications.

Comments and Conditions of Appraisal: _____

Final Reconciliation: _____

RECONCILIATION

This appraisal is based upon the above requirements, the certification, contingent and limiting conditions, and Market Value definition that are stated in

☐ FmHA, HUD &/or VA instructions.

☐ Freddie Mac Form 439 (Rev. 7/86)/Fannie Mae Form 1004B (Rev. 7/86) filed with client _____ 19 ___ ☐ attached.

I (WE) ESTIMATE THE MARKET VALUE, AS DEFINED, OF THE SUBJECT PROPERTY AS OF _____ 19 ___ to be $ _____

I (We) certify: that to the best of my (our) knowledge and belief the facts and data used herein are true and correct; that I (we) personally inspected the subject property, both inside and out, and have made an exterior inspection of all comparable sales cited in this report; and that I (we) have no undisclosed interest, present or prospective therein.

Appraiser(s) SIGNATURE _____   Review Appraiser SIGNATURE _____   ☐ Did ☐ Did Not
NAME _____   (if applicable) NAME _____   Inspect Property

Freddie Mac Form 70 10/86 **12Ch.** **AB** Forms and Worms Inc.® 315 Whitney Ave., New Haven, CT 06511 1(800) 243-4545   Item #130960   Fannie Mae Form 1004 10/86

FIGURE 15.6 The appraisal form currently required by most lenders.

Property Description & Analysis **UNIFORM RESIDENTIAL APPRAISAL REPORT** File No.

SUBJECT				
Property Address		Census Tract		LENDER DISCRETIONARY USE
City	County	State	Zip Code	Sale Price $
Legal Description				Date
Owner/Occupant		Map Reference		Mortgage Amount $
Sale Price $	Date of Sale		PROPERTY RIGHTS APPRAISED	Mortgage Type
Loan charges/concessions to be paid by seller $			☐ Fee Simple	Discount Points and Other Concessions
R.E. Taxes $	Tax Year	HOA $/Mo.	☐ Leasehold	Paid by Seller $
Lender/Client			☐ Condominium (HUD/VA)	
			☐ De Minimis PUD	Source

NEIGHBORHOOD

LOCATION	☐ Urban	☐ Suburban	☐ Rural	NEIGHBORHOOD ANALYSIS	Good	Avg.	Fair	Poor
BUILT UP	☐ Over 75%	☐ 25-75%	☐ Under 25%	Employment Stability	☐	☐	☐	☐
GROWTH RATE	☐ Rapid	☐ Stable	☐ Slow	Convenience to Employment	☐	☐	☐	☐
PROPERTY VALUES	☐ Increasing	☐ Stable	☐ Declining	Convenience to Shopping	☐	☐	☐	☐
DEMAND/SUPPLY	☐ Shortage	☐ In Balance	☐ Over Supply	Convenience to Schools	☐	☐	☐	☐
MARKETING TIME	☐ Under 3 Mos.	☐ 3-6 Mos.	☐ Over 6 Mos.	Adequacy of Public Transportation	☐	☐	☐	☐

PRESENT LAND USE %	LAND USE CHANGE	PREDOMINANT	SINGLE FAMILY HOUSING		Recreation Facilities	☐	☐	☐	☐
			PRICE $ (000)	AGE (yrs)					
Single Family	Not Likely	OCCUPANCY			Adequacy of Utilities	☐	☐	☐	☐
2-4 Family	Likely	☐ Owner			Property Compatibility	☐	☐	☐	☐
Multi-family	In process	☐ Tenant	Low		Protection from Detrimental Cond.	☐	☐	☐	☐
Commercial	To:	☐ Vacant (0-5%)	High		Police & Fire Protection	☐	☐	☐	☐
Industrial		☐ Vacant (over 5%)	Predominant		General Appearance of Properties	☐	☐	☐	☐
Vacant			—		Appeal to Market	☐	☐	☐	☐

Note: Race or the racial composition of the neighborhood are not considered reliable appraisal factors.

COMMENTS:

SITE

Dimensions		Topography
Site Area		Size
Zoning Classification	Corner Lot	Shape
	Zoning Compliance	Drainage
HIGHEST & BEST USE: Present Use	Other Use	

UTILITIES	Public	Other	SITE IMPROVEMENTS	Type	Public	Private	View	
Electricity	☐		Street		☐	☐	Landscaping	
Gas	☐		Curb/Gutter		☐	☐	Driveway	
Water	☐		Sidewalk		☐	☐	Apparent Easements	
Sanitary Sewer	☐		Street Lights		☐	☐	FEMA Flood Hazard Yes* ___ No ___	
Storm Sewer	☐		Alley		☐	☐	FEMA* Map/Zone	

COMMENTS (Apparent adverse easements, encroachments, special assessments, slide areas, etc.):

IMPROVEMENTS

GENERAL DESCRIPTION	EXTERIOR DESCRIPTION	FOUNDATION	BASEMENT	INSULATION
Units	Foundation	Slab	Area Sq. Ft.	Roof ☐
Stories	Exterior Walls	Crawl Space	% Finished	Ceiling ☐
Type (Det./Att.)	Roof Surface	Basement	Ceiling	Walls ☐
Design (Style)	Gutters & Dwnspts.	Sump Pump	Walls	Floor ☐
Existing	Window Type	Dampness	Floor	None ☐
Proposed	Storm Sash	Settlement	Outside Entry	Adequacy
Under Construction	Screens	Infestation		Energy Efficient Items:
Age (Yrs.)	Manufactured House			
Effective Age (Yrs.)				

ROOM LIST

ROOMS	Foyer	Living	Dining	Kitchen	Den	Family Rm.	Rec. Rm.	Bedrooms	# Baths	Laundry	Other	Area Sq. Ft.
Basement												
Level 1												
Level 2												

Finished area **above** grade contains: ___ Rooms; ___ Bedroom(s); ___ Bath(s); ___ Square Feet of Gross Living Area

INTERIOR

SURFACES	Materials/Condition	HEATING	KITCHEN EQUIP.	ATTIC	IMPROVEMENT ANALYSIS	Good	Avg.	Fair	Poor
Floors		Type	Refrigerator	None	Quality of Construction	☐	☐	☐	☐
Walls		Fuel	Range/Oven	Stairs	Condition of Improvements	☐	☐	☐	☐
Trim/Finish		Condition	Disposal	Drop Stair	Room Sizes/Layout	☐	☐	☐	☐
Bath Floor		Adequacy	Dishwasher	Scuttle	Closets and Storage	☐	☐	☐	☐
Bath Wainscot		COOLING	Fan/Hood	Floor	Energy Efficiency	☐	☐	☐	☐
Doors		Central	Compactor	Heated	Plumbing-Adequacy & Condition	☐	☐	☐	☐
		Other	Washer/Dryer	Finished	Electrical-Adequacy & Condition	☐	☐	☐	☐
		Condition	Microwave		Kitchen Cabinets-Adequacy & Cond.	☐	☐	☐	☐
Fireplace(s) #		Adequacy	Intercom		Compatibility to Neighborhood	☐	☐	☐	☐
CAR STORAGE:	Garage	Attached	Adequate	House Entry	Appeal & Marketability	☐	☐	☐	☐
No. Cars	Carport	Detached	Inadequate	Outside Entry	Estimated Remaining Economic Life				Yrs.
Condition	None	Built-In	Electric Door	Basement Entry	Estimated Remaining Physical Life				Yrs.

Additional features:

COMMENTS

Depreciation (Physical, functional and external inadequacies, repairs needed, modernization, etc.):

General market conditions and prevalence and impact in subject/market area regarding loan discounts, interest buydowns and concessions:

Freddie Mac Form 70 10/86 **12Ch.** AB Forms and Worms Inc.,® 315 Whitney Ave., New Haven, CT 06511 1(800) 243-4545 Item #130960 Fannie Mae Form 1004 10/86

FIGURE 15.6, continued

property might be diminished if the surrounding structures were not compatible. Overimprovement of a home may also result in economic obsolescence, since a $50,000 home surrounded by $25,000 homes would be less likely to attract $50,000 purchasers.

Income Approach

Value determined by income production

The **income approach** is also referred to as the *capitalization* approach to value. It is based on the net income produced by the property. The net income is determined by subtracting the operating expenses from the gross income. The net income is then divided by the capitalization rate (as a percentage) to find the appraised value. This capitalization rate provides for the return of the investor's capital and the return on the capital invested (the recapture rate). See figure 15.7 for an example of the income approach to appraisal.

Gross rent multipliers. The indicator of value can be obtained from similar rental properties. This figure is known as the *gross rent multiplier,* and is calculated by dividing the price by the annual gross income.

Comparative items on the income property would include price, terms, location, time of sale, income produced, and expenses. A brief analysis follows:

Subject Number	Date	Price	Annual Gross Income	Income Multiplier
1	12-87	$430,000	$85,000	5.06
2	1-87	480,000	90,000	5.33
3	2-87	390,000	72,000	5.41
4	3-87	375,000	70,000	5.36

Working from this table, greatest consideration would be given to the examples that are most similar to the subject. The multiplier would be determined from this. If it were 5.30, we would then take the rent from the subject property, $85,500 x 5.30 for an indicated value of $453,150.

Application of the income approach is useful to the person desiring to purchase an investment property. Since risk is involved, the investor will want a greater return than the money market or a savings account would bring. The simplest method to determine what to pay for a property is to decide what return is desirable and divide the net income by the return. For example, if a building produces $15,000 net per year and the investor wants a 10 percent return, it is feasible to spend $150,000 for the property: $15,000 ÷ 10% (or .1) = $150,000. Other factors must be taken into consideration and these are covered in the investment chapter.

While the gross rent multiplier is used on commercial and industrial property, the gross monthly income is used for residential real estate. For example, a monthly rental income of $450.00 is received on a house that sells for $64,000. The GRM would be:

$$\frac{\$64,000 \text{ (sale price)}}{\$450.00 \text{ (monthly rent)}} = 104.2 \text{ GRM}$$

The income approach gains importance when the property being appraised is older and the cost approach is less convincing because of depreciation considerations.

Gross annual income		$85,500
10 units @ $300 per month × 12 ($36,000)		
15 units @ $275 per month × 12 ($49,500)		
Laundry facility income		500
Annual Gross Income		$86,000
Vacancy and rent loss—5%		4,275
Effective Gross Income		$81,725
Expenses		
Real Estate Taxes	$7,200	
Insurance	1,100	
Management (resident 6%)	4,900	
Utilities—water, gas, electricity	2,100	
Maintenance and repair	3,200	
Redecorating	1,800	
Replacement (appliances, equipment)	2,600	
Accounting services	700	
Advertising	500	
Total Expenses		$24,100
Net Income		$57,625

If the capitalization rate is 12 percent, the indicated value will be:

$$\frac{57,625}{.12} = \$480,209$$

FIGURE 15.7
The income approach to appraisal.

The appraiser needs to analyze the rental history, with past and present rentals serving as guides in estimating future rentals. Comparing what competitive properties are renting for in the area will be another important factor in determining value. Any change in rent anticipation will need to be documented and supported by the appraiser. Not only the quantity of rent, but its durability and quality are taken into consideration.

Correlation of Value

Any one of the three mentioned approaches to value may be used to determine the appraisal of the subject property, but they will not necessarily yield the same value. It may be that replacing a structure would cost less than the prevailing market value if the demand were especially great.

Application of different approaches to value

In income-producing property, the capitalization approach is usually given the most credence. If the subject is a single-family dwelling, the income approach is generally not used. The use of the cost approach is of value if the home is comparatively new. The market value would probably come closest to the real value of our example property. If the appraisal is to be made on a property for which recent comparison sales are not obtainable—for example, a pickle factory or a church—then the cost approach will probably carry the greatest weight.

The final step in the appraisal procedure is the written report. The purpose of the appraisal will determine the length and depth of the formal report.

THE APPRAISAL REPORT

The final step for the appraiser is delivery of the report. This may be done by one of four methods: an oral report, a letter, a form appraisal, or a narrative report. The reports may vary in length and type, depending on the request from the client. Regardless of the type of report submitted, the appraiser has gathered his information by the same process.

The minimum requirements of any report should include

1. Identification of the property
2. Purpose of the appraisal
3. Date valuation was made
4. Data used to support the conclusion
5. State any limiting conditions and appraiser assumptions, if any
6. Indication of value
7. Certification by appraiser
8. Signature of appraiser

Oral report

The *oral report* is given verbally by the appraiser, either in person or by telephone to the person who requested the appraisal. Since there is no documentation to substantiate the findings it does not carry the credence of a written document. The oral report is used when time is of the essence and a quick report is needed.

Letter report

The *letter report* is a formal written appraisal in letter form that identifies the property, states the purpose of the appraisal, and briefly summarizes the appraiser's findings. Usage of this simplified form is not encouraged among the professional appraisers since pertinent and crucial facts could be omitted.

Form report

The *form report* is used extensively by appraisers who need a standarized method for their clients or employers. Mortgage lenders and mortgage insurers generally request use of the approved FHMA (Fannie Mae) and FHLMC (Freddie Mac) form, since they often anticipate selling their loans on the secondary market. All FHA and VA loans must be accompanied by an approved appraisal form since all information FHA and VA require is on this form, eliminating any problem of missing facts (see figure 15.6).

The form report contains the appropriate boxes to check and blanks to complete. The appraiser has the responsibility to add any additional comments pertinent to the findings. Currently this form is the most popular means of submitting appraisals.

Narrative report

The *narrative report* permits the appraiser to present the appraisal in summary form. A narrative report can contain a very few pages or a hundred pages. The appraiser must use good judgment in not becoming too elaborate in his writing. Many will begin the report with a one or two page synopsis of the findings, enabling the reader to obtain a quick overview of the appraisal. The reader can then proceed through the report for verification and substantiation of the appraiser's opinion of the properties' value. The narrative will include the complete steps taken in the analysis used in reaching the conclusion. Included will be neighborhood data and exhibits of comparables.

Some of the professional appraisal societies require a demonstration narrative appraisal prior to acceptance in the organization and some universities and colleges require a narrative report to be completed by the student who is studying real estate appraisal.

THE APPRAISER

The independent fee appraiser is a disinterested third party who follows an orderly process in determining the value of a property. The appraiser certifies that s/he has no present or future contemplated interest in the real estate being appraised and that his or her employment or fee is not contingent upon the determined value. The appraiser will use substantial, logical comparables.

In the early 1980s appraisers came under the scrutiny of the Federal Home Loan Bank because lending institutions held large numbers of defaulted loans on properties that were overvalued. If the owner of a highly leveraged property needed to sell and found the market value to be less than the loan, defaults occurred. Additionally, with the vast number of homeowners refinancing their properties in 1986 when interest rates plunged to a long-time low, lenders were concerned that with the rush for refinancing and the resultant backlog of appraisals, carelessness could occur.

The National Association of Review Appraisers and Mortgage Underwriters has developed a form to be used in the review of narrative or residential appraisal reports. It is their intent that use of the form will substantially reduce loan loss of financial institutions by calling attention to the strengths and weaknesses of the appraisal report that they rely upon when making real estate loans. It is, however, the function of the autonomous reviewer to see that the valuation is based on sound judgment (see figure 15.8).

Review form

Some states require appraisers to be licensed, while in other states a real estate broker's license is sufficient. Continued education and minimum standards of performance are criteria sought by the appraisal institutes, and some states are now passing legislation to insure these requirements are met.

As professionalism has developed among appraisers, organizations and designations have followed. Rigid appraisal education requirements must be met by appraisers seeking membership and designations in these associations. With local chapters across the country, appraisal techniques are taught for appraising urban, rural, and industrial properties.

Among the societies and councils, the following are well known across the country.

- American Institute of Real Estate Appraisers. *Designations:* RM (Resident Member), MAI (Member, Appraisal Institute).
- American Society of Appraisers. *Designations:* ASA (Senior Member), FASA (Fellow).
- American Association of Certified Appraisers, Inc. *Designations:* Non-certified—Affiliate and R-1 (Residential first level); Certified—CA-R (Certified Appraiser—Residential), CA-S (Certified Appraiser—Senior), CA-C (Certified Appraiser—Consultant).
- Society of Real Estate Appraisers. *Designations:* SRA (Senior Residential Appraiser), SRPA (Senior Real Estate Appraiser), SREA (Senior Real Estate Analyst).
- American Society of Farm Managers & Rural Appraisers, Inc. *Designations:* AFM (Accredited Farm Manager), ARA (Accredited Rural Appraiser).
- National Association of Review Appraisers. *Designation:* CRA (Certified Review Appraiser).
- National Association of Independent Fee Appraisers, Inc. *Designations:* IFA (Member), IFAS (Senior Member), IFAC (Appraiser-Counselor).

RESIDENTIAL APPRAISAL REVIEW FORM

Lending Institution _____

Lender's Address _____

Name of Borrower _____

Property Address _____

Loan Number _____

Lender's Appraiser _____ Phone _____

Appraiser's Address _____

Appraised Value $ _____ Date _____

Review Appraiser _____ Phone _____

Reviewer's Address _____

Reviewer's Value Opinion $ _____ Varience % _____ $ _____

The reviewer will analyze the appraisal in light of the following questions. In addition, the Reviewer will sum up the results of his or her analysis by completing the "Reviewer's Comments" appearing at the end of each section. Questions that do not apply can be marked N/A.

FORMAT AND PRESENTATION

YES NO

1. Is the appraisal report in conformance with company ☐ ☐
appraisal requirements?
Reviewer's Comments _____
_____
_____
_____
_____

LENDER SECTION

YES NO

2. Is the lender section of the report complete and ☐ ☐
accurate?
Reviewer's Comments _____
_____
_____
_____
_____

NEIGHBORHOOD SECTION

YES NO

3. Is the neighborhood section of the report complete and accurate? ☐ ☐
4. Does the neighborhood section provide the reviewer an adequate understanding with respect to locational factors, growth rate and economic trends, property values, housing supply, marketing time, land use, price ranges, convenience to employment and amenities, adequacy of utilities and recreational facilities, property compatibility, appearance of properties, detrimental conditions and marketability? ☐ ☐
5. Does the appraisal report enable the reviewer to spot healthy growth patterns or trends that may indicate a deteriorating neighborhood with limited market appeal? ☐ ☐
6. Are comments in the neighborhood section relevant and do they give insight into those conditions which positively or negatively affect the appraised properties value and marketability? ☐ ☐

YES NO

7. Have all fair and poor ratings in the neighborhood section been explained? ☐ ☐
8. If marketing time is over six months, has the appraiser commented on the reasons for slow market conditions in the subject area? ☐ ☐
9. If the market is slow, has the appraiser indicated whether or not this has resulted in a decline in values? ☐ ☐
Reviewer's Comments _____
_____
_____
_____
_____
_____

SITE SECTION

YES NO

10. Is the site section of the appraisal report complete and accurate? ☐ ☐
11. Has the appraiser commented on unfavorable site factors? ☐ ☐
12. Does the appraiser indicate whether or not the subject property meets all the criteria for a desirable lot in the area? ☐ ☐
13. Has the appraiser addressed and commented on problems relating to poor drainage, flood conditions, adverse easements, encroachments or other detrimental factors? ☐ ☐
14. Does the appraiser indicate the subject's zoning and whether or not the subject conforms with present zoning requirements? ☐ ☐

YES NO

15. Has the appraiser accurately indicated the dimensions and size of the subject lot? ☐ ☐
16. Does the appraisal report reveal whether or not site improvements and services to the site are adequate and acceptable in the market place? ☐ ☐
Reviewer's Comments _____
_____
_____
_____

IMPROVEMENTS SECTION

YES NO

17. Is the improvement section of the report complete and accurate? ☐ ☐
18. If the subject property is a condominium, are the project improvements and project rating sections complete and accurate? ☐ ☐
19. Did the appraiser comment on physical and functional inadequacies and indicate whether or not repairs and modernization are needed? ☐ ☐
20. Has the appraiser explained fair or poor improvement ratings? ☐ ☐
21. Does the appraiser indicate whether or not factors receiving poor or fair ratings, adversely affect the property's marketability? ☐ ☐

YES NO

22. Have factors relating to age, condition, quality of construction, finish and equipment, as well as size and utility been properly handled? ☐ ☐
23. Has the appraiser given serious attention to structural problems? ☐ ☐
24. Did the appraiser comment on unusual layouts, peculiar floor plans, inadequate equipment and amenities? ☐ ☐
25. Has the appraiser indicated whether or not factors relating to unusual layouts, peculiar floor plans, inadequate equipment and amenities, limit the value and market appeal of the subject? ☐ ☐
26. If there is evidence of dampness, termites or settlement, did the appraiser comment on these factors? ☐ ☐

FIGURE 15.8

Review Form No. 2002

IMPROVEMENTS SECTION Continued

YES NO

27. Has the appraiser provided the reviewer with a clear and accurate understanding of the physical and functioning attributes of the subject property? ☐ ☐
28. Is the property rating section accurate as well as consistent with other data contained in the report? ☐ ☐
29. Has the appraiser presented information on construction features in a manner that gives an accurate and adequate view of the subject property? ☐ ☐
30. Has information relating to the improvements been well handled? ☐ ☐

YES NO

31. In the reviewer's opinion, is the descriptive section of the appraisal report (page one) acceptable? ☐ ☐
Reviewer's Comments_____

COST SECTION

YES NO

32. Is the cost section complete and accurate? ☐ ☐
33. Are the appraiser's measurements for gross living area correct? ☐ ☐
34. Has the appraiser commented on functional and economic obsolescence? ☐ ☐
35. In estimating reproduction costs, has the appraiser used cost figures that are appropriate for the local market? ☐ ☐
36. Do figures for physical, functional and economic depreciation appear reasonable in light of the subject's age, condition, state of modernization, size and utility, and location? ☐ ☐
37. Is the estimate of land value appropriate? ☐ ☐

YES NO

38. Has the appraiser used construction cost figures rather than market data to arrive at the subject's market value? ☐ ☐
39. Are the appraiser's mathematical calculations accurate? ☐ ☐
40. Is the budget analysis section accurate and complete (if condo)? ☐ ☐
Reviewer's Comments_____

MARKET ANALYSIS SECTION

YES NO

41. Is the market analysis section complete and accurate? ☐ ☐
42. Has the appraiser selected his or her comparables from the subject neighborhood? ☐ ☐
43. If not, has the appraiser explained why comparables were selected from a different neighborhood? ☐ ☐
44. In your opinion, are the comparables really similar with respect to location, site, design and style, quality and amenities, as well as size and utility? ☐ ☐
45. Are all of the comparables recent sales of similar properties from the subject neighborhood? ☐ ☐
46. If the comparables are over three months old, has the appraiser explained why he or she failed to use recent sales? ☐ ☐
47. Are room counts and square foot areas of the subject and comparables similar? ☐ ☐
48. Do the sales prices and prices per square foot of the comparables correlate and indicate comparability? ☐ ☐
49. Are there large differences in the price per unit and per square foot between the subject and comparable properties? ☐ ☐
50. Has the appraiser bracketed his or her sales data (before making adjustments)? ☐ ☐
51. Do time adjustments, for date of sale, appear reasonable in light of market trends and current market conditions? ☐ ☐
52. Has the appraiser made excessive adjustments (gross adjustment figures that are 25% or more of comparable sales prices and individual line adjustments that are 10% or more of comparable sales prices)? ☐ ☐
53. Has the appraiser made numerous large adjustments? ☐ ☐
54. Has the appraiser adjusted all three comparables in a reasonable and consistent manner? ☐ ☐
55. Does the appraiser make unsupportable or faulty adjustments? ☐ ☐
56. Is there missing or inaccurate information in the market analysis section? ☐ ☐
57. Are the appraiser's mathematical calculations accurate? ☐ ☐
58. Is there a convincing value range with respect to the three adjusted comparables? In brief, are the adjusted value conclusions reasonably similar? ☐ ☐
59. Does the appraiser's final value conclusion relate to the adjusted comparables? ☐ ☐
60. Has the appraiser selected good market data and handled it well? ☐ ☐
61. Has the appraiser commented on the subject's marketability? ☐ ☐
62. Does the appraisers marketability information appear to be accurate? ☐ ☐

YES NO

63. Does it appear that the appraiser is backing into any or all of the approaches to value? ☐ ☐
64. Is there a lack of clarity with respect to the appraiser's reasoning? ☐ ☐
65. Can you read the appraisal report, step by step, and arrive at the same conclusion of value as the appraiser? ☐ ☐
66. Does the appraiser appear to be an advocate rather than an individual offering an independent and impartial third party opinion of value? ☐ ☐
67. Are there missing photographs or photographs that do not adequately show the subject and surrounding properties? ☐ ☐
68. Is other illustrative material missing or poorly done? ☐ ☐
69. If the appraiser is using computer generated data, are the facts and comments in the report accurate and applicable to the subject and comparable properties? ☐ ☐
70. Does it appear that the appraiser is using the computer as a substitute for thinking? ☐ ☐
71. Are the appraiser's comments and final reconciliation of value adequate and does the appraisal give insight into the value and marketability of the subject property? ☐ ☐
72. Is the appraiser's value conclusion reasonable? ☐ ☐
73. Do you wind up with a different value conclusion than the appraiser, based upon data contained within the report? ☐ ☐
74. In your opinion, has the appraiser failed to prove his or her case? ☐ ☐
75. Does it appear that the subject property has been over appraised? ☐ ☐
76. Has the appraiser signed the report and typed his or her name under the signature? ☐ ☐
77. Is there a phone number on the report and/or cover letter which would enable the reviewer to contact the appraiser and clarify a questionable appraisal report? ☐ ☐
78. Is the valuation section of the report (page two) acceptable? ☐ ☐
Reviewer's Comments_____

REVIEWER'S SUMMARY

(To be completed by the lender's appraisal, quality control or underwriting department.)

Appraisal Report was: Acceptable ☐ Unacceptable ☐

Recommendations, comments and summary of action taken (if any).

Reviewer's Signature _____ Date of Review _____

Review Form No. 2002

FIGURE 15.8, continued

• National Association of Master Appraisers (NAMA). *Designations:* MRA (Master Residential Appraiser), MFIA (Master Farm & Land Appraiser), MSA (Master Senior Appraiser).

SUMMARY

There are three main appraisal techniques: the cost approach, the market-data approach, and the income approach. Each of these approaches to the value of real property is explained in this chapter. The appraiser should always begin by requesting the purpose for the appraisal. Keep in mind that an appraisal is an estimate of value. While this estimate of value can be arrived at by any one of the three different approaches, the choice of the method depends on the purpose of the appraisal.

The appraisal procedure is carried out in a sequence of steps, from defining the problem and collecting the data to analyzing the subject property and applying one of the three approaches.

Depreciation affects value. The highest and best use of the property and the various principles involved in creating value are discussed in the chapter.

While there are many more facets involved in the appraisal of real property, the techniques and definitions presented here should be adequate to introduce you to the field of appraisal. In-depth studies of land and building residual techniques and complete detailed appraisal reports can be found in textbooks written strictly on appraisal.

KEY WORDS AND CONCEPTS

Ad valorem: The assessed valuation of property; *ad valorem* taxes are based on this valuation.

Appraisal: An estimate of value; an opinion as to the worth of the property.

Assessment: A charge against real property made by a unit of government.

Comparison approach: Comparing market values of similar properties to the subject property.

Cost approach: Determining the cost of replacing the subject property with a new structure similar in design.

Depreciation: Loss in value from any cause.

Economic obsolescence: Loss in value due to a changing neighborhood; the introduction of other usage for property in the area.

Functional obsolescence: Depreciation caused by outmoded or poor design.

Highest and best use: The greatest net return over a given period of time.

Income approach: Gross income less costs; net income is used in appraising income-producing property.

Market value: The highest probable price at which a willing seller will sell and a willing buyer will buy.

Obsolescence: The quality of being outdated or outmoded; causes loss in value.

Physical depreciation: Loss in value due to normal wear and tear.

Quantity survey: A survey listing the cost and quantity of each item used in construction plus the labor required to install it.

Unit-in-place: Cost of component parts of the improvement.

REVIEW QUESTIONS

1. In analyzing a parcel of land to estimate its value, what is the first thing necessary to determine?
   a. the market value
   b. the cost appraisal
   c. the reason for the appraisal
   d. the availability of public transportation

2. Functional obsolescence is due to
   a. normal wear and tear
   b. poor design or floor plan
   c. poor location
   d. none of these

3. On what type of property would the cost approach be the most accurate?
   a. a six-month-old residence
   b. an apartment house
   c. an older property with economic obsolescence
   d. a fifteen-year-old residence

4. The market value of a property is commonly defined as
   a. the highest and best use of the property
   b. the highest price at which a willing seller will sell and a willing buyer will buy
   c. the income the property is annually producing
   d. amenities attached to the property

5. The definition of depreciation is
   a. loss in value
   b. mortgage foreclosures
   c. loss from scarcity of a product
   d. none of these

6. Physical depreciation is brought about by
   a. conditions outside the property
   b. functional obsolescence
   c. normal wear and tear
   d. none of the above

7. Economic obsolescence is related to
   a. lack of closet space
   b. poor drainage in the yard
   c. faulty heating systems
   d. conditions external to the property

8. A four-bedroom home with one bathroom suffers from
   a. economic obsolescence
   b. functional obsolescense
   c. physical depreciation
   d. all of the above

9. The value of a property can be lowered by
   a. a changing neighborhood
   b. economic obsolescence
   c. zoning laws
   d. all of the above

10. The formula of replacement-cost-less-depreciation-plus-value-of-land is called the
    a. income approach
    b. market-data approach
    c. comparison approach
    d. summation approach

11. The summation approach to value is best used on
    a. commercial property
    b. service-type buildings
    c. land
    d. older homes

12. The depreciation most difficult to remedy would be
    a. physical
    b. economic
    c. wear and tear
    d. functional

13. The replacement-cost method of appraising
    a. tends to set the upper limits of value.
    b. tends to set the lower limits of value.
    c. is best applied to income property.
    d. is best applied to older homes.

14. Utilizing a property to its greatest economic advantage is commonly referred to as
    a. mobilization
    b. economic utility
    c. market value
    d. highest and best use

15. When applying the cost approach to value, the appraiser allows for depreciation
    a. on land
    b. on improvements
    c. both a and b
    d. neither a nor b

16. When preparing a comparable analysis of real estate, all of the following should be considered, except
    a. the dates comparable properties were sold
    b. amenities attached to the property
    c. the racial makeup of the neighborhood
    d. the desirability of the location

17. The average home buyer is most concerned with
    a. floor plan
    b. architectural design
    c. location
    d. tax basis

18. In preparing an appraisal report, the appraiser's first step is to
    a. collect the data
    b. apply the cost approach
    c. write the appraisal report
    d. define the problem

19. The appraisal approach that is concerned with the present worth of future benefits of the property is called
    a. capitalization
    b. cost approach
    c. comparison approach
    d. summation approach

20. Functional obsolescence would least likely include
    a. rotting wood
    b. poor architecture
    c. an outdated kitchen
    d. bad design

21. A twenty-five-year-old home is sound and in good condition, but has an outdated bath. The bath is suffering from
    a. normal depreciation
    b. physical obsolescence
    c. functional obsolescence
    d. deterioration

22. When an appraiser measures the area of a house, s/he measures
    a. each individual room
    b. inside wall measurements, excluding partitions
    c. the exterior of home
    d. all of the above

23. What value may an appraiser be employed to determine?
    a. market value
    b. loan value
    c. condemnation value
    d. all of the above

24. When an appraiser determines the fair market value of a property, he/she should furnish the following information to the owner who requested the appraisal:
    a. a statement revealing how the value was determined
    b. data showing recent comparable sales
    c. both a and b
    d. neither a nor b

25. The best definition of an appraisal is
    a. a means of determining depreciation
    b. a method to keep values current with reproduction costs
    c. a statement of facts that may not necessarily be true
    d. an estimate of value

Land Use Controls | 16

It is important that our land is wisely utilized. At the beginning of this country's history, the authors of the constitution determined that the government would exercise control of the land. Title to land was granted by the federal government to individuals. Most titles can be traced back to the original land grant or patent. The grant provided for allodial ownership with fee simple title. To encourage settlement, especially of the western territories, land was sold at auction and offered as a bonus to soldiers who served in the Continental Army.

FEDERAL CONTROLS ON LAND USAGE

From the start, some land was set aside for park areas. In 1872, Congress created the first national park preserve in the world. Yellowstone National Park was followed by twenty-nine other preserves containing mountains, volcanoes, glaciers, and spacious virgin forests. Today all fifty states have established parks within their boundaries as recreational areas for picnicking and camping. Cities have also developed parks for the enjoyment of their residents.

Reserving land for parks

With the growth of our country many additional laws covering the disposition and use of real estate have been enacted. Controls by the federal government include the Real Estate Settlement Procedures Act (RESPA), which covers conditions that must be adhered to in the transfer of real estate (see chapter 8).

In 1968, the federal government enacted the Interstate Land Sales Disclosure Act, which regulates subdivided land. The U.S. Department of Housing and Urban Development (HUD) requires developers to register interstate land sales with the Office of Interstate Land Sales Registration (OILSR) if the development contains fifty or more units. A property report must be given to a prospective buyer a minimum of three days before a contract to purchase may be entered into. This "cooling-off" period allows the buyer to analyze the wisdom of his or her decision. This law was implemented to protect people from purchasing land presented as a great opportunity that may in truth be greatly misrepresented.

Laws covering interstate land sales

In July 1982, Congress passed a law stating that Savings and Loan Institutions do not have to allow mortgages to be assumed upon transfer of title. This superseded law that had been mandated in some states to the contrary. Finally, the Civil Rights Act of 1969 provides for fair housing throughout the United States (see Chapter 7).

While all fifty states have control over land within their boundaries, the federal interstate highways, parks, and schools are examples of land under the jurisdiction of the United States government.

STATE AND LOCAL CONTROLS ON LAND USAGE

Regulating land use in communities

States exercise control over their highways, parks, lakes and government buildings. The governmental powers within a local municipality impose controls and restrictions over the private use of land. This power of the government to regulate land use is referred to as **police power** and must be used in the interests of the public. These controls ensure that the growth of a city, whether a large metropolis or an incorporated village, proceeds in a coordinated and harmonious manner.

Since the desire for land is concentrated around employment areas, land is more in demand in and near large cities. City planning, with a broader outlook to the future, is under constant study by urban governmental agencies. Overcrowding and traffic congestion have been special objects of study, with master planning needed to meet the ever-changing social and economic needs of communities. With a *master plan,* growth will proceed in the manner that best promotes the general welfare of the citizens and protects their real estate investments. The properties in a given area will be **homogeneous** or compatible, thus stabilizing values.

In exercising its police power, the local government establishes the **zoning** ordinances that regulate and control land use. Zoning falls into three categories; residential, commercial, and industrial. Since it is wise to have homogeneous divisions, each of these three categories is further divided into more specific areas. The zoning laws of the municipality govern the type of structure one can erect and the use to which it can be adapted. Most cities require, through legislative enactment, that the use of land be regulated within a one-to-three mile radius of the city. Zoning limits the rights of property owners, specifying what is allowable and what specific uses will be prohibited.

SUBDIVISION DEVELOPMENT

Site Selection

Subdividing raw land

When a developer wishes to subdivide raw land into housing sites, the site selection should be made in a location that follows the growth of the area. The location can make the difference between the success or failure of the subdivision. It should be convenient to utilities and employment centers. The general plan should be competitive with and measure up to surrounding developments.

Once the site is selected, the subdivider usually hires an experienced subdivision planner to develop layout concepts in conformance with current styles and trends. Environmental concerns should be considered, along with lot views and street placement.

An engineer site grades the land and plans the paving design, the utilities design, and drainage.

The Plat

The subdivider must submit the proposed plans for development, or the *plat* to the city planning department. Subdivision regulations are laws enacted by a local governing body to control the conversion of bare land into building sites. This places legal control over the community's design, thus eliminating the misuse of property and protecting community values, health, and safety.

The plat is reviewed by various professionals and city officials, including the planning department, city engineer, health department, utility officials, and the parks and recreation department.

The preliminary plat usually has areas designated for schools and parks and the required number of streets laid out. In the covenants, the subdivider dedicates these streets to the city (or county, if the area is outside the city limits). In addition, areas must be reserved or dedicated for public use, public utilities must be installed, and lots and blocks must be clearly specified as to size and length. Once approval of the plat is obtained, the subdivider begins construction of the subdivision improvements. The final plat is certified by the engineer and the subdivider and is then recorded.

Covenants

Covenants concerning building lines, setbacks, and side yards must be stipulated in the subdivider's plan. **Covenants** are restrictions or agreements that regulate the land. Use restrictions are always for the public good and generally relate to how the land can be best utilized and the sort of construction permissible. These covenants and restrictions will protect the purchaser's investment. The square footage required in a dwelling, the architectural design, whether outbuildings may be constructed, or whether one- or two-car garages are required are examples of restrictions placed in covenants. (See the example of covenants and restrictions at the end of this chapter.) Restrictive covenants remain in effect for specific time periods—for example, for ten years, twenty years, or in perpetuity.

ZONING

Local zoning regulations and restrictive covenants filed with the plat plan for a particular subdivision regulate the distance from the perimeter of the property that a building may be erected. Referred to as a **setback,** this applies to front, side, and rear yards.

Zoning protects property rights

Building permits are required each time a contractor starts to construct a building, thus ensuring compliance with the zoning ordinances. Permits are also required to remodel an existing structure or even to erect a fence. The building must not violate a covenant or deed restriction of the area, or the contractor will be stopped in mid-construction. It is the responsibility of neighboring home owners to enforce their covenants.

Sometimes a developer will gather together two or more parcels of land to make the whole more valuable. This is known as **assemblage.**

A **nonconforming** use of property is a use in violation of present zoning laws but lawful at the time the use was begun. *Grandfather rights* exist in a situation like this, since zoning regulations cannot be retroactive. For example, consider a grocery store built in 1965 on the edge of an undeveloped area. In 1983, a developer plats out the remaining land into large single-family lots. The grocery store is not compatible, so it is now considered a nonconforming use. The grocer is not required to close down, but no one could open a new grocery in the area now.

Spot zoning is zoning of isolated properties for activities other than called for in existing regulations. The law generally does not favor spot zoning since it is inconsistent with the present zoning of the area. A vacant lot presently zoned residential but rezoned for commercial use would be an example of spot zoning. A change to allow construction of a multiunit building in a neighborhood of single-family residences is another example of spot zoning.

If an individual owner needs an exception to the zoning ordinance and if his or her use is not detrimental to the public, a **variance** can be requested. For instance, an owner may wish to build a garage, but is unable to adhere to the zoning laws because the structure will be five feet from the lot line and the regulations in her subdivision call for setbacks of seven feet from lot lines. In such a case, a variance would probably be granted. Usually variances are granted only when compliance with local zoning laws would cause undue hardship to the owner in need of the exception.

LOT VARIATIONS

New lot variations have become popular in some areas of the country. Greater density can be achieved by clustering homes. *Cluster house lots* are usually only half the size of conventional house lots; however, they can provide as much privacy and green space as the normal lots. Instead of breaking up the areas into front, side, and rear yards, the aggregate of all the yards is molded into one open space around the homes. With proper design and variance in roof and window placements, visual and noise barriers will exist between the homes. Because the structures are clustered, the developer can pass the savings of less sidewalks and utility connections on to the purchasers.

Zero lot line is another concept in lot use whereby single-family homes are built on the lot line, with the owner having an easement, usually five feet, on his neighbor's lot so he may paint or repair his house. This saves land since the owner has just one side yard, which is more usable than two small side yards (see figure 16.1).

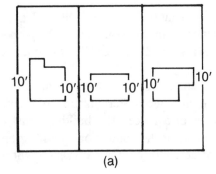 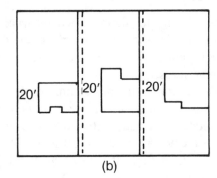

(a)   (b)

FIGURE 16.1
(a) Normal lot with ten-foot side yards.
(b) Zero lot line – dotted lines denote easements.

EASEMENTS

Right of way through another's land

If there are easements on a segment of land this will also be outlined in the covenants. Since an easement represents an interest in another's land, it must be in writing to conform with the statute of frauds. An **easement** is a right of way through the land of another, referred to as the right of *ingress* and *egress* (entering and leaving) over another's land.

Each easement is classified as either an **easement appurtenance** or an **easement in gross.** An easement appurtenance goes along with the land. Examples of an easement appurtenance include shared driveways and party walls. The two pieces of land must be adjacent to each other and owned by separate individuals for an appurtenant easement to exist. For example, in figure 16.2, A and B share a common driveway; thus, each has the right to use the adjoining land of the other. Most easement appurtenances are specially written in the deed or by express written contract.

An easement in gross is personal and is generally not assigned to another. Examples would be large billboards or signs erected on another's property, pipelines,

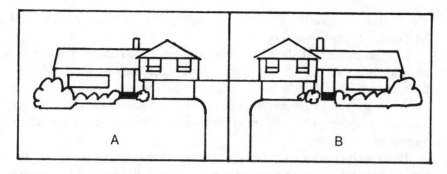

FIGURE 16.2
An easement appurtenance.

utility lines, sewer lines, and power lines (see figure 16.3). The easement in gross to an individual is not an appurtenance and does not automatically pass with the land. If a purchaser wants an existing easement in gross to pass with title it would be necessary to state this in the deed.

Since an easement in gross is for an individual's lifetime, a landowner should issue a **license** if he has any reservations about giving a permanent easement to the other person. A license is revocable at the grantor's option and is not transferable.

FIGURE 16.3
The billboard and telephone lines are easements in gross.

Easements of Necessity and Other Easements

An *easement of necessity* arises when there is a special need, as in the case of a landlocked owner. For example, in figure 16.4, X sold the back portion of her land to Y and an easement was necessary for Y to get to his land. The *dominant* tenant (Y) receives the easement and the *servient* tenant (X) gives the easement. Easements granted by one party to another cannot be rescinded by the owner of the land. The

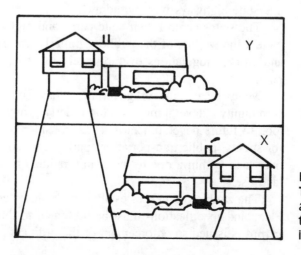

FIGURE 16.4
The easement to Y is an *appurtenance* (it goes with the land), the easement to X is an *encumbrance*.

land in this example has no other access; since a purchaser cannot be landlocked, the easement was mandatory.

If a servient tenant allows the dominant tenant to remove minerals or soils from his land, it is called *profit a 'pendre*. These rights may be extended to just the one dominant tenant or they may be assignable to a future owner of the land.

An *easement by prescription* is the right acquired through continuous use of another's property. This use must be in an adverse manner; that is, without the consent of the owner.

Party wall easements exist between two owners when a common wall separates two structures, as in row houses or condominiums. Each owner has the responsibility to maintain her side of the wall and each has an easement on the other owner's side. Party wall easements may also exist when a fence separates the boundaries of two properties.

ENCROACHMENT

An **encroachment** exists when one owner's property infinges onto another's land. Examples of common encroachments include fences carelessly erected on neighboring land or driveways and patios extending onto the adjoining property. Tree branches or shrubbery hanging over the property line can create an encroachment.

Since encroachments are generally not covered by title insurance, it is important for a purchaser to have a survey if there is any doubt concerning the accuracy of the boundaries. If the encroachment has existed long enough an easement by prescription may be in effect.

The following document in figure 16.5 provides an example of covenants and restrictions.

SUMMARY

While ownership of real estate legally gives one a bundle of rights that extends below the earth's surface and into the sky, the use of land is controlled by various units of government. The federal government maintains jurisdiction over its national parks and freeways. An example of freeway control was the fifty-five mile per hour speed limit. If states did not enforce the speed law, federal funds to maintain the interstate highways were withdrawn.

The states control their state parks and highways and may adopt regulations to protect the welfare of the public. Similarly, country and city governments establish and enforce regulations over privately owned property under their right of police power.

Many local units of government have planning commissions that study the community's development so that orderly growth will be established. A broad outlook to future development must be considered and a general master plan laid out for streets, public transportation, park areas, and utility services. Keeping controls over land within a one-to-three mile radius of the city further assists in regulating land use.

The zoning ordinances established by local governments also regulate land use. Plans and specifications must be presented to the planning board before a building permit is issued so enforcement of the ordinances is assured.

**Declaration of
Covenants, Conditions, and Restrictions
for Confusion Hill
Lots 1 through 123 Inclusive**

THIS DECLARATION, made on the date hereinafter set forth by Buford Builders, Inc., a Nebraska Corporation, hereinafter referred to as the "Declarant,"

WITNESSETH:

WHEREAS, the Declarant is the Owner of the following described real property:

Lots 1 through 123, inclusive, in Confusion Hill, a Subdivision, as surveyed, platted and recorded in Kent County, Nebraska, and

WHEREAS, the Declarant will convey said lots, subject to certain protective covenants, conditions, restrictions, reservations, liens, and charges as hereinafter set forth,

NOW, THEREFORE, the Declarant hereby declares that all of the lots described above shall be held, sold, and conveyed subject to the following easements, restrictions, covenants, and conditions, all of which are for the purpose of enhancing and protecting the value, desirability and attractiveness of said lots. These easements, covenants, restrictions, and conditions, shall run with said real property, and shall be binding upon all parties having or acquiring any right, title or interest in the above described lots, or any part thereof, and they shall inure to the benefit of each owner thereof.

PART A. RESTRICTIONS FOR THE SINGLE-FAMILY RESIDENTIAL AREA

A-1. No building shall be created, altered, placed, or permitted to remain on any lot other than one detached single-family dwelling, not to exceed two stories in height, nor containing finished living areas, exclusive of porches, breezeways, carports, and garages of less than the following: A one-story dwelling house constructed on any of said residential lots shall have a ground floor area of not less than 1,200 square feet. A one and one-half story dwelling house or two story dwelling house shall have a ground floor area of not less than 1,000 square feet. Dwelling houses constructed on a split-entry ranch plan or split-level plan shall have not less than 1,200 square feet on the main living floor level. That said areas are exclusive of porches or attached garages. Each house shall have a garage for not less than two automobiles.

A-2. No lot shall be used except for residential purposes.

A-3. No structure of a temporary character, trailer, basement, tent, shack, barn or other outbuilding shall be erected upon, or used, on any lot at any time as a residence, either temporarily or permanently.

A-4. No unused building material, junk or rubbish shall be left exposed on any lot. No repair of automobiles will be permitted outside of garages or on any lot at any time.

A-5. No boat, camper trailer, auto-drawn trailer of any kind, mobile home, truck, jeep, motorcycle, grading or excavating equipment or other heavy machinery or equipment, vehicle undergoing repair, van or aircrft shall be stored outside the garage or in any manner left exposed on any lot at any time.

FIGURE 16.5
An example of covenant and conditions.

A-6. No animals, livestock, fowl or poultry of any kind shall be raised, bred or kept on any lot, except that dogs, cats, or other household pets maintained within the dwelling may be kept, provided they are not kept, bred, or maintained for commercial purpose. This is intended specifically to prohibit horses, ponies, or other animals sheltered outside the main dwelling except for a single dog house.

A-7. Exposed portions of the foundation on the front of each dwelling are to be covered with either siding or brick and exposed portions of the foundation on the sides and rear of each dwelling shall be either covered with brick or siding or shall be painted.

A-8. A dwelling on which construction has begun must be completed within one (1) year from the date the foundation was dug for said dwelling.

A-9. Public sidewalks shall be constructed of concrete four feet wide by four inches thick in front of each built-upon lot and along the street side of each built-upon corner lot. The sidewalks shall be placed five feet back of the street curb line and shall be constructed by the then owner of the lot prior to time of completion of the main structure and before occupancy or use thereof; however, this provision shall be varied to the extent required to comply with any subsequent requirements of the City of Big Red.

A-10. No building, fence, wall, driveway, patio, patio enclosure, rock garden, swimming pool, dog house, tree house, television antenna, flag pole, radio antenna, or other external improvement above or below the surface of the ground shall be erected, replaced, altered, or permitted to remain on any building plot, nor shall any grading, excavation or tree removal be commenced, until the construction plans and specifications, a site-grading plan and a plot plan showing the location of the structure or improvement have been approved in writing by Declarant, or any person, firm, corporation, partnership or entity designated in writing by the Declarant, which shall consider such plans and specifications with regard to type, quality and use of exterior materials, exterior design, location of improvements upon the building plot, and proposed finished grades; provided that Declarant and its designee specifically reserve the right to deny permission to construct any type of structure or improvement which it determines will not conform to the master plan for development of the subdivision.

A-11. No incinerator or trash burner shall be permitted on any lot unless the same is incorporated into the dwelling and not exposed to view from the outside of the dwelling. No garbage or trash can or container or fuel tank shall be permitted to remain outside of any dwelling unless completely screened from view from every street and from all other lots in the subdivision. No garden, lawn or maintenance equipment of any kind whatsoever shall be stored or permitted to remain outside of any dwelling except when in actual use unless completely screened from view from the street and from all other lots in the subdivision. No clotheslines shall be permitted outside of any dwelling at any time except one umbrella-type clothesline per lot. Any exterior air-conditioning condenser unit shall be placed in the rear or side yard. No garage door shall be permitted to remain open except when entry to and exit from the garage are required.

PART B. EASEMENTS AND LICENSES

B-1. A perpetual license and easement is hereby reserved in favor of and granted to Great Red Telephone Company and to Big Red Public Power District, their successors, and assigns, to erect and operate, maintain, repair, and renew cables, conduits, and other instrumentalities and to extend wires for the carrying and transmission of electric current for light, heat and power and for all telephone and telegraph message service under a

FIGURE 16.5, continued

five-foot strip of land adjoining the rear and side boundary lines of said lots, and license being granted for the use and benefit of all present and future owners of said lots; provided, however, that said side lot line easement is granted upon the specific conditions that if both said utility companies fail to construct wires or conduits along any of the said lot lines within 36 months of the date hereof, or if any wires or conduits are constructed but hereafter removed without replacement within 60 days after their removal, then this side lot line easement shall automatically terminate and become void as to such unused or abandoned easementways, but the same may be used for gardens, shrubs, landscaping and other purposes that do not then or later interfere with the aforesaid uses or rights herein granted.

B-2. All telephone and electric power service lines from property line to dwelling shall be underground.

PART C. GENERAL PROVISIONS

C-1. For the purpose of these restrictions, two-story height as hereinbefore mentioned in Part A-1 shall, when the basement wall is exposed, be measured from the basement ceiling on the exposed side(s) to the eave of the structure on the same side(s).

C-2. The Declarant or any owner of a lot named herein shall have the right to enforce by a proceeding at law or in equity, all restrictions, conditions, covenants, and reservations, now or hereinafter imposed by the provisions of this Declaration, either to prevent or restrain any violation of same, or to recover damages or other dues for such violation. Failure by the Declarant or by any owner to enforce any covenant or restriction herein contained shall in no event be deemed a waiver of the right to do so thereafter.

C-3. The covenants and restrictions of this Declaration shall run with and bind the land for a term of twenty-five (25) years from the date this Declaration is recorded. This Declaration may be amended by the Declarant, or any person, firm, corporation, partnership, or entity designated in writing by the Declarant, in any manner it shall determine in its full and absolute discretion for a period of five (5) years from the date hereof. Thereafter this Declaration may be amended by an instrument signed by the owners of not less than ninety percent (90%) of the lots covered by this Declaration.

C-4. Invalidation of any one of these covenants by judgment or court order shall in no way affect any of the other provisions hereof which shall remain in full force and effect.

IN WITNESS WHEREOF, the Declarant has caused these presents to be executed this _____ day _____, 19____

BUFORD BUILDERS, INC.
A Nebraska Corporation

_____, President **FIGURE 16.5, continued**

Private control over land is exercised by subdividers, who establish the covenants and restrictions for their developments. The surrounding owners may enforce these restrictions if a violation occurs.

An easement is a right of way or interest in the land of another. Common easements include shared driveways and party walls. Any protrusion over a property line is an encroachment. Encroachments are not covered by title insurance and should thus be carefully checked by a prospective buyer.

KEY WORDS AND CONCEPTS

Appurtenance: Something that goes with the land, as a right of way.

Assemblage: Gathering two or more parcels of land to make the whole more valuable.

Building code: A group of ordinances that legislate building construction within a community.

Covenant: An agreement or restriction that regulates the use of land.

Easement: Right of way through another's land.

Easement in gross: A personal easement that is not automatically assignable.

Encroachment: Anything protruding onto another's property.

Homogeneous: Compatible; land use is regulated by zoning to create homogeneity and stabilize values.

License: A right to use, revocable at the will of the giver.

Party wall: A common wall between two adjoining properties.

Police power: Power of government to regulate the use of land.

Setback: The distance between a structure and the perimeter of the property.

Variance: Use granted to an individual in exception of zoning regulations.

Zoning: Regulating and controlling the use and character of a parcel of land.

REVIEW QUESTIONS

1. To the owner of the land it runs across, an easement is
   a. an appurtenance
   b. an encumbrance
   c. a common interest
   d. an attachment

2. Zoning laws are the utilization of a governing body's
   a. police power
   b. power of eminent domain
   c. escheat
   d. all of the above

3. A use not in compliance with present zoning, but legal when it was enacted is called a(n)
   a. variance
   b. spot zoning use
   c. nonconforming use
   d. encroachment

4. The gathering together of two or more parcels to make the whole more valuable is a(n)
   a. easement
   b. appurtenance
   c. subdividing
   d. assemblage

5. If there is a party wall between two lots, which of the following is true?
   a. Each person must be responsible for its maintenance.
   b. Each person owns a common interest in the wall.
   c. Both of the above are true.
   d. Neither of the above are true.

6. Ingress and egress refer to
   a. appurtenance
   b. an easement
   c. subservience
   d. police power

7. Which of the following restrict the use of land?
   a. townships
   b. monuments
   c. surveys
   d. covenants

8. Communities regulate the use of land by means of
   a. controlling the population
   b. exercising governmental power
   c. buying and selling land themselves
   d. annexing nearby towns

9. Mr. Jones's good friend, Charlie Smith, lives next door and uses a portion of Jones's land as a driveway. As much as Jones likes his friend, he does not want to grant him the use of the land in perpetuity. Since he wants to retain the privilege of reviewing the situation on a regular basis, Jones should grant his friend
   a. a license
   b. an easement
   c. an easement appurtenance
   d. a permit

10. All of the following are established by the private sector, except
   a. building styles
   b. restrictive covenants
   c. subdivision plats
   d. building codes

11. The governmental regulations that most affect the value of real property are
   a. zoning ordinances
   b. covenants of deed restrictions
   c. laws of escheat
   d. Federal Housing Authority regulations

12. The police power of a city is used to enforce all of the following except
   a. building codes
   b. zoning restrictions
   c. deed restrictions
   d. subdivision regulations

13. The government of a municipality holds control over real property through all of the following except
   a. taxation
   b. assessments
   c. encumbrance
   d. eminent domain

14. The following is an example of an easement appurtenance
   a. a shared driveway
   b. a power line
   c. both a and b
   d. neither a nor b

15. A gas station was built in 1960 in an area that was rezoned to residential in 1980. The gas station constitutes
   a. a variance
   b. a nonconforming use
   c. spot zoning
   d. a violation

16. In a condominium, the center wall was built nine inches into the next person's unit. The builder will need to
   a. have the building inspector issue a variance.
   b. consult an attorney to have an easement established.
   c. tear down the building and start over.
   d. ask the engineers to change the lot line.

17. A building complied with the zoning laws except for the setback. The owners need to request
   a. spot zoning
   b. a variance
   c. a nonconforming use
   d. a compliance

18. To increase open space and conserve land, a developer will group lots together by
   a. deed restrictions
   b. placing cul de sacs in the plat
   c. clustering
   d. building apartments

Federal Fair Housing and License Laws

Fair Housing Laws 17

THE LAW

Every person engaged in the business of real estate should be familiar with the **fair housing laws** as they relate to the sale and rental of all residential property. Federal, state, and local laws provide for equal opportunity in housing. This is the law of the land and the right of every person in this country without regard to race, color, religion, sex, or national origin.

Real estate salespersons, brokers, and owners must be cognizant of and must put into practice the law that prohibits **discrimination.** Every person has a right to purchase or rent housing in any area they desire to live in, as long as they can assume the financial responsibility.

The Civil Rights Act of 1866

It is the policy of the United States to provide within its constitutional limitations for fair housing throughout the country. Fair housing law dates back to the Civil Rights Act of 1866, which prohibited discrimination based on race only. This act provided that "all citizens of the United States shall have the same right, in every state and territory, as is enjoyed by white citizens thereof to inherit, purchase, lease, sell, hold, and convey real and personal property."

Equal housing opportunities for all

The Civil Rights Act of 1964

Title VI, the Civil Rights Act of 1964, was passed by Congress to prohibit discrimination when a program receives federal financial assistance. The intent of Congress was to insure that no program utilizing federal financial aid should be tainted by discriminatory acts. **HUD** (Department of Housing and Urban Development) has set aside funds under sections 235 and 236 respectively to give assistance to low-income citizens in home ownership and low-rent public housing.

The Fair Housing Act of 1968

In June of 1968, the United States Supreme Court upheld the 1866 civil rights act in the case of Jones vs. Mayer. The original act proclaimed that all *racial* discrimination was illegal when selling or renting property; the Court extended it to include color, religion, national origin, and sex. In the case of Jones vs. Mayer, a black person sued for an injunction and other relief with an allegation that the defendant had refused to sell him a home solely on racial grounds.

Provisions of fair housing law

The Fair Housing Act of 1968, under Title VIII of the Civil Rights Act of 1968, prohibits the following acts:

1. Refusing to sell, rent, negotiate, or deal with any person.
2. Quoting different terms or conditions for renting or buying housing to persons of different races, colors, religions, or national origins.
3. Advertising that property is available only to certain races, colors, religions, or national origins.
4. Not being truthful about the availability of homes for rent or sale.
5. **Block busting,** or inducing owners, for profit, to sell or rent their homes by threatening the movements of minority groups into neighborhoods.
6. Lenders varying terms or conditions for home loans in an effort to discriminate.
7. Discriminating in real estate services, multiple listing services, or broker organizations by denying membership or limiting participation.

These laws apply to single-family housing under the following conditions:

1. When single-family housing is privately owned and the owner employs a real estate firm (or any other person who sells or rents).
2. When single-family homes are not privately owned.
3. When discriminatory advertising is used for single-family homes.
4. When single-family homes are owned by private individuals who own more than three such houses and who, in any two-year period, sell more than one in which the individual was not the most recent resident.

These laws apply to multi-family housing under the following conditions:

1. When multi-family dwellings contain five or more rooms or units are rented.
2. When multi-family dwellings of four or less units or rooms are rented, if none of the units is occupied by the owner of the property.

Who must comply with fair housing law?

These laws do not affect the sale or rental of single-family houses owned by a private individual if the person owns three or fewer such single-family houses and if

1. A real estate broker is not used.
2. Discriminatory advertising is not used.
3. No more than one house in which the owner was not the most recent resident is sold during any two-year period.
4. Rooms or units in owner-occupied multi-dwellings for two to four families are rented, and discriminatory advertising is not used.
5. The sale, rental, or occupancy of dwellings that a religious organization owns or operates for other than a commercial purpose is limited to persons of the same religion, if membership in that religion is not restricted on account of race, color, or national origin.
6. The rental or occupancy of lodging that a private club owns or operates for other than a commercial purpose is limited to the club's members.

There are three means provided for obtaining compliance with the Fair Housing   *Filing complaints*
Law:

1. Complaints can be sent to HUD at

> Fair Housing
> Department of Housing and Urban Development
> Washington, D.C. 20410

or to Fair Housing, in care of the nearest HUD regional office.

The complaint will be notarized, if possible, and must be sent to HUD within 180 days of the alleged discriminatory act or the same shall be waived.

HUD will investigate the complaint. If it is covered by law and the secretary decides to resolve the complaint, HUD may attempt informal, confidential conciliation to end the discriminatory housing practice, or inform the **complainant** of the right to force immediate court action. In appropriate cases, HUD may refer the complaint to the attorney general.

The complaint may be referred by HUD to a state or local agency that administers the law with rights and remedies substantially equivalent to those of the federal law. If the state or local agency does not commence proceedings within 30 days and carry them forward with reasonable promptness, HUD may require the case to be returned. In any case, the complainant will be notified of the type of action to be taken.

Upon receipt of a complaint, HUD will furnish a copy to the person charged with the discriminatory act. The person charged may then file an answer in writing, which should also be notarized.

2. A person may take a complaint directly to the U.S. District Court or state or local court within 180 days of the alleged discriminatory act, whether or not a complaint has been filed with HUD. In appropriate cases, an attorney may be appointed for the complainant and the payment of fees, costs, or security can be waived.

If HUD or the state or local agency is unable to obtain voluntary compliance, the complainant may file suit in the appropriate district court. This must be done within 31 to 60 days after filing with HUD or after the complaint is returned to HUD from a state or local agency. In states with equivalent judicial rights and remedies, such a suit would have to be brought in state court.

The court can grant permanent or temporary injunctions, temporary restraining orders, or other appropriate relief. It may award actual damages and not more than $1,000 in punitive damages. The courts are also directed to expedite cases and assign them for hearing at the earliest practical date.

3. Information about possible discrimination in housing may also be brought to the attention of the Attorney General. If the resulting investigation indicates that there is a pattern or practice of resistance to full enjoyment of rights granted under Title Eight or that a group of persons has been denied such rights and the denial raises an issue of general public importance, the Attorney General may bring action to insure full enjoyment of the rights granted by Title Eight.

It is illegal to coerce, intimidate, threaten, or interfere with a person buying, renting, or selling housing, making a complaint of discrimination, or exercising any such rights in connection with this law.

The 1968 Civil Rights Law provides a quick, direct method of obtaining a remedy against racial discrimination in housing. The complainant may take the case directly to a federal court.

The court could stop the sale or rental of the desired housing to someone else. It could make it possible for the complainant to buy or rent the desired housing. It could award damages and court costs or take other appropriate action to benefit the complainant.

Denial of loan. Lenders who make residential real estate loans must not discriminate in fixing the amount, interest, rate duration, or terms or conditions of a loan because of race, color, religion, or national origin. This is not to say that the lender cannot refuse a loan if the borrower is financially unable to meet the commitment.

Lenders must comply with law

Redlining. The lender must not refuse to make loans in certain neighborhoods; to do so is called **redlining.** Refusal to offer financing in a particular section of the city can lead to the decay of the area. To assure compliance with the law, the federal government passed the Home Mortgage Disclosure Act in 1975. Large lenders with one or more offices in a particular area are required to issue annual reports on all loans, so that if redlining does exist it is easily detectable.

Real estate agents must not discriminate

Salesperson and broker obligations. Not only is the salesperson or broker bound by the Civil Rights Act, but as a member of the National Association of Realtors®, he or she must also abide by Article 10 of the Code of Ethics. Article 10 requires that "the Realtor® shall not deny equal professional service to any person for reasons of race, creed, sex, or country of national origin. The Realtor® shall not be a party to any plan or agreement to discriminate against a person or persons on the basis of race, creed, sex, or country of national origin."

Inducing owners to sell for profit

Block busting and panic peddling. The salesperson or broker must not induce nonminority home owners to sell their properties for profit because of the introduction of minorities in or near the neighborhood. This is referred to as **block busting** and is prohibited by law. Great care must be taken not to solicit listings on the premise that minority groups are moving into the area, insinuating that property may lessen in value. The salesperson's conduct must be above reproach and not give the impression that he is **panic peddling.** Intensive door-to-door canvassing in a changing neighborhood or adjacent to a changing or minority neighborhood would create suspicion.

The agent must affirmatively demonstrate full compliance with the fair housing laws and work in a like manner with all clients so s/he is not accused of giving less favorable treatment to a minority. This involves servicing customers equally and not ignoring a minority client, and submitting offers promptly and not offering the property on less favorable terms to a minority person.

Steering. The agent must not try to avoid showing property to minority customers in certain nonintegrated areas. To take them only to minority or changing neighborhoods is referred to as **steering.** Offering a wide range of properties in all areas will alleviate any such complaint. Conversely, the salesperson must show the nonminority customer homes in all neighborhoods to avoid being accused of discouraging a buyer from seeking housing in a minority or changing neighborhood.

Equal housing opportunity. In 1972, the Fair Housing Law was amended to include the requirement of equal opportunity posters. All real estate firms, model homes, and mortgage lenders must display the Equal Housing Opportunity poster, which states that housing is available equally to all people (see figure 17.1).

Equal Housing Opportunity

U.S. DEPARTMENT OF HOUSING AND URBAN DEVELOPMENT

NATIONAL ASSOCIATION OF REALTORS®

REALTOR®

Federal Fair Housing Law

(Title VIII of the Civil Rights Act of 1968)

It Is Illegal To Discriminate Against Any Person Because Of Race, Color, Religion, Sex, Or National Origin

- In the sale or rental of housing or residential lots

- In advertising the sale or rental of housing

- In the financing of housing

- In the provision of real estate brokerage services

  Blockbusting is also illegal

Those who feel they have been discriminated against should send complaint to

U.S. Department of Housing and Urban Development, Assistant Secretary for Equal Opportunity Washington, D.C. 20410

Code for Equal Opportunity

Omaha Board of REALTORS®

subscribes to the policy that equal opportunity in the acquisition of housing can best be accomplished through leadership, example, education, and the mutual cooperation of the real estate industry and the public. In the spirit of this endeavor, this board proclaims the following provisions of its Code for Equal Opportunity to which each member is obligated to adhere:

1. In the sale, purchase, exchange, rental, or lease of real property, REALTORS® and their REALTOR®-ASSOCIATES have the responsibility to offer equal service to all clients and prospects without regard to race, color, religion, sex, or national origin. This encompasses:

   A. Standing ready to enter broker-client relationships or to show property equally to members of all racial, creedal, or ethnic groups.

   B. Receiving all formal written offers and communicating them to the owner.

   C. Exerting their best efforts to conclude all transactions.

   D. Maintaining equal opportunity employment practices.

2. Members, individually and collectively, in performing their agency functions have no right or responsibility to volunteer information regarding the racial, creedal, or ethnic composition of any neighborhood or any part thereof.

3. Members shall not engage in any activity which has the purpose of inducing panic selling.

4. Members shall not print, display, or circulate any statement or advertisement with respect to the sale or rental of a dwelling that indicates any preference, limitations, or discrimination based on race, color, religion, sex, or ethnic background.

5. Members who violate the spirit or any provision of this Code of Equal Opportunity shall be subject to disciplinary action.

Those who feel they have been discriminated against may contact the management of this office or the Board of REALTORS®

FIGURE 17.1 The Equal Housing Opportunity poster.

Restrictive covenants. It is further unlawful to place any restrictive covenants in any transfer, sale, or rental of housing. Many states have enacted legislation that is consistent with the federal fair housing law. Complaints are then directed to the state and are handled by the appropriate agency within said state. If an incorporated city has enacted or adopted a resolution equivalent to the state's fair housing law, then complaints will be directed to the local agency. If the complaint is not handled with reasonable promptness, the state will regain jurisdiction of the complaint.

The purpose of the federal and state fair housing laws are to

1. Seek to eliminate and prevent discrimination in places of public accommodation because of race, color, sex, religion, national origin, or ancestry.

2. Effectuate the purpose of this act by conference conciliation, and persuasion so that persons may be guaranteed their civil rights and so that good will be fostered.

3. Formulate policies to enforce the purpose of this act and make recommendations to agencies and officers of the state or local subdivisions of government in aid of such policies and purposes.

4. Adopt rules and regulations to carry out the powers granted by this act.

5. Designate one or more members of the commission or the commission staff to conduct investigations of discrimination in race, color, sex, religion, national origin or ancestry and to attempt to resolve such complaints by conference, conciliation, and persuasion, and conduct such conciliation meetings and conferences as deemed necessary to resolve a particular complaint. Such meetings shall be held in the county in which the claim arose.

6. Determine that probable cause exists for crediting the allegations of a complaint.

7. Determine that a complaint cannot be resolved by conference, conciliation, or persuasion. Such a determination is to be made only at a meeting where a quorum is present.

8. Dismiss complaints where it is determined there is not probable cause to credit the allegations of a complaint.

9. Hold hearings, subpoena witnesses and compel their attendance, administer oaths, take the testimony of any person under oath, and in connection therewith require for examination any papers relating to any matter under investigation or in question before the commission.

10. Issue publications and the results of studies and research that tend to promote good will and to minimize or eliminate discrimination because of race, color, sex, religion, national origin, or ancestry.

SUMMARY

The original Civil Rights Act of 1866 was based on race only; however, the Federal Fair Housing Act of 1968 declared that discrimination based on race, color, religion, national origin, or sex is illegal in the rental or sale of housing. This includes vacant land that is offered for sale and zoned for residential use.

Many states have fair housing laws compatible with the federal law. Local organizations such as the Equal Opportunity Commission **(EOC)** and the Human Relations Board are formed in many cities to enforce the laws.

Any person seeking restitution because of discrimination should file a complaint with HUD within 180 days after the alleged violation occurred. If it appears to be covered by the law, HUD will attempt informal confidential conciliation in an effort to end the discriminatory practice. A person may take a complaint directly to court, but again, the violation must be acted upon within 180 days.

The licensed salesperson and broker must take diligent care to offer all properties to any person seeking housing. He must not attempt to induce a home owner to list her house for sale by representing to her that minorities are moving into the neighborhood, *even when the statement is accurate*. Membership in the multiple listing service or in real estate organizations must not be denied to any person because of race, color, religion, national origin, or sex.

The affirmative marketing agreement is a commitment made by many Realtors to demonstrate their compliance with fair housing laws. Real estate firms are required to display the Equal Opportunity poster in their offices. Anyone engaged in the real estate business must offer to all prospective purchasers equal opportunity to buy the real property of their choice.

KEY WORDS AND CONCEPTS

Block busting: Inducing an owner, for profit, to sell or rent his or her home by threatening the movement of minority groups into the neighborhood.

Complainant: A person who brings a complaint against another.

Discrimination: The act of making a distinction in favor or against a person on the basis of a group he belongs to.

EOC: Equal Opportunity Commission, a local agency that enforces fair housing laws.

Fair housing: Laws that prohibit discrimination in the rental or sale of housing because of race, color, religion, national origin, or sex.

HUD: Department of Housing and Urban Development, a federal agency that promotes fair housing and is involved in national housing programs.

Panic peddling: Creating unrest in a neighborhood by placing fear in the minds of property owners that the introduction of minorities in or near the area will lessen property values.

Redlining: Refusing to make mortgage loans in specific neighborhoods.

Respondent: A person against whom a complaint is made.

Steering: Limiting choice by channeling a buyer into specific neighborhoods.

REVIEW QUESTIONS

1. After receiving a complaint pursuant to the Federal Housing Act, the local agency to whom the complaint was referred must investigate within
   a. thirty days after receiving the complaint
   b. ninety days after receiving the complaint
   c. both of the above
   d. neither of the above

2. A complaint filed with the Federal Fair Housing Commission
   a. should be sworn to under oath.
   b. may be reasonably amended at any time.
   c. both of the above
   d. neither of the above

3. Under the federal Fair Housing Law, HUD may
   a. investigate when it appears discrimination may have occurred.
   b. investigate incidents reported to them.
   c. both of the above
   d. neither of the above

4. A complaint to the federal Fair Housing Commission must be
   a. filed within 180 days after the alleged discrimination.
   b. sworn to under oath by the complainant.
   c. both of the above
   d. neither of the above

5. Under the federal Fair Housing Act, the following people can be charged with discrimination for refusing to sell because of race:
   a. an individual who sells his home by himself and not through a real estate agent.
   b. an individual who refuses to rent a unit of a fourplex in which he resides.
   c. both of the above
   d. neither of the above

6. In regard to the federal Fair Housing Act, which of the following are true?
   a. In any complaint, the burden of proof is on the complainant.
   b. It is legal to quote different terms or conditions for rentals below $100 per month.
   c. both of the above
   d. neither of the above

7. The Fair Housing Act prohibits
   a. discrimination in housing because of race
   b. discrimination in housing because of religion
   c. both of the above
   d. neither of the above

8. The following are exempt from the Fair Housing Act:
   a. a real estate broker
   b. a religious group that limits rentals of property it owns to its own members
   c. both of the above
   d. neither of the above

9. Under the federal Fair Housing Act, the following are discriminatory practices:
   a. refusing to sell a house to a person of a minority race because she is unable to qualify for a loan
   b. advertising a preference in whom you will sell to
   c. both of the above
   d. neither of the above

10. The federal Fair Housing Act applies to
    a. denying a person the right to buy a home because of his national origin
    b. a discriminatory restrictive provision in a deed
    c. both of the above
    d. neither of the above

11. Under the housing discrimination laws, it is illegal to refuse to show real property to all of the following except
    a. a single person
    b. a minority group member
    c. a foreigner
    d. a person of another religion

12. Ms. Loring asked A-1 Realty to lease her home for four months while she was in Europe on vacation. She specified she preferred only white tenants. Under the Fair Housing Act, following her preference is
    a. illegal
    b. legal, since Ms. Loring is the owner-occupant
    c. legal upon acceptance of the lease agreement
    d. legal if the broker obtains the request in writing

13. Ms. Gomez and her three children went to Ace Realty to find a residence for rent. The firm assigned her to Mr. Alvarez in accordance with their policy of matching their client's race, interest, and so on as closely as possible. During the course of viewing property, Ms. Gomez asked to see an apartment in a white middle-class neighborhood that she had seen advertised in a newspaper. Mr. Alverez said the apartment was rented, when in fact it was not. Under the Fair Housing Act
    a. Mr. Alvarez committed illegal steering.
    b. Mr. Alvarez acted in his customer's best interest.
    c. it was legal, since it is approved office practice.
    d. it was illegal, because Ms. Gomez is a single parent.

14. Black families are beginning to move into a neighborhood that was previously all white. XYZ Realty wanted the whites to move out and wanted blacks to buy homes in the area. They ran an ad that said, "Sell now, don't wait, we can arrange special financing." The ad
    a. constitutes block busting.
    b. is not illegal.
    c. constitutes redlining.
    d. is intimidating.

15. This symbol represents
    a. HUD
    b. fair housing
    c. equal housing authority
    d. FHA

16. A nonprofit religious sect bought property and developed condominiums that they sold back to their church members exclusively. According to the Fair Housing Act, this was
    a. illegal, because a religious sect cannot build condominiums.
    b. illegal, because it is discriminatory.
    c. legal, because a religious sect is not subject to law.
    d. legal, because a religious sect is allowed to sell property exclusively to its members.

17. Ms. Andrews lives in an apartment complex on Garden Boulevard. Her single friend, Ms. Bloss, has two children and wants to live in the same complex. The owner refused to give her a lease because of her single-parent status, so Ms. Andrews filed a complaint with HUD alleging discrimination. Upon learning of the complaint, the owner evicted Ms. Andrews. The eviction was
    a. legal according to federal Fair Housing Law.
    b. illegal, because the owner can't retaliate for filing a complaint with federal Fair Housing.
    c. illegal because a landlord cannot break a lease without going to court.
    d. legal, because only Ms. Bloss can make the discrimination report.

18. The 1968 federal Fair Housing Act provides that
    a. white persons have a right to bring suits when acts of discrimination deny them the opportunity to have neighbors who are members of minority groups.
    b. undeveloped property zoned for residential use is not covered by the 1968 Fair Housing Act.
    c. both of the above
    d. neither of the above

License Law | 18

All fifty states have enacted legislation requiring the licensing of real estate salespersons and brokers. At this time there is no uniform **license law** covering the states, but basically their content is quite similar. The license law and the rules and regulations adopted by each individual state are for the express purpose of protecting the public. To further protect citizens from unscrupulous or incompetent practitioners, the law prescribes the standards and qualifications for licensing. This has elevated the standards of the real estate profession and protects licensees from unfair competition.

Mandatory education continues to be of primary concern to licensing officals in the belief that specified knowledge will better qualify the licensee to serve the public. Many states are now requiring completion of certified real estate courses prior to application to take the licensing examination. Other states require continuous education after becoming licensed so the licensee keeps abreast of new laws and practices.

WHO NEEDS A LICENSE?

While the laws vary from state to state, the majority of states require that anyone who negotiates or attempts to negotiate the business of selling, listing, purchasing, exchanging, renting, leasing, managing, optioning, or auctioning real property for a fee, commisssion, or other valuable compensation must be licensed.

Exceptions

Those persons who are generally exempt from needing a license include

1. An owner or lessor of real estate.
2. An attorney-in-fact (someone given power of attorney by the property owner).
3. An attorney-at-law in the performance of his or her duty as such attorney-at-law.
4. A receiver or trustee in bankruptcy.
5. The administrator or executor of a deceased estate.
6. A court-appointed guardian.
7. An officer or employee of a federal or state agency.
8. In many states, resident managers of apartment complexes.

Keep in mind that these exceptions do not permit a person to act in the capacity of a real estate firm without a license.

TYPES OF LICENSES

Broker's and salesperson's licenses

There are generally two types of licenses issued: that of a real estate **salesperson** and that of a real estate **broker.** A broker's license permits him to set up his own real estate office and to hire other brokers and salespersons to work for him. An associate broker is an individual who holds a broker's license and who has elected to work for another broker. A salesperson is always required to be in the employ of a broker.

The broker may set up her business using her own name, for example, Jane A. Smith, or may transact business under a trade name such as A-1 Real Estate Company. If the broker purchases a franchise, she will need to disclose her business name (whether she uses Jane A. Smith or A-1 Real Estate Company) along with the franchise name. The broker may further elect to form a partnership or corporation with another broker or brokers. All active members of the partnership or corporation must be licensed to conduct the business of a real estate agent.

If branch offices are opened, a broker or broker-associate must be in charge of each branch office. Again, this is to provide adequate supervision over the sales associates. Since the broker is responsible for the actions of the salesperson, she will supervise and guide the salesperson's performance so that the firm is properly and lawfully represented. The salesperson will list and sell property in the name of the broker and all advertising will be under the broker's business name.

LICENSING EXAMS

Competency tests for licensure

To obtain the license of salesperson or broker, the person must pass a written examination. This exam is designed to test real estate knowledge and competency to transact the duties of a real estate salesperson or broker. The examination is given by the state Real Estate Commission or regulatory agency at stated times throughout the year. Failure to pass the written examination is grounds for denial of a license without further hearing.

In the past, individual states prepared their own exams for evaluating the applicants' ability to conduct the business of real estate salesperson or broker. This placed the burden of writing, preparing, and grading the exam upon the state's real-estate governing body.

While approximately one-third of the states still adhere to this form of testing, many states now subscribe to exams prepared by the Educational Testing Service (ETS) of Princeton, New Jersey. This service prepares a uniform test consisting of eighty questions applicable to all the states and a minimum of thirty questions relating to the individual state's licensing laws. In addition to the license law questions, the uniform test covers the basic fundamentals of the principles and practices of real estate. The American College Testing (ACT) and Assessment Systems, Inc. (ASI) are other testing services used by state licensing officials.

The California multistate examination is presently utilized by several other states. The significant factor in this testing procedure is that the states adhering to the exam require that the licensee need only take the license law portion in a subscribing state if he desires to obtain a license in that state.

Exams differ for the salesperson and broker; a more comprehensive understanding is required from the broker. Since the broker can go into business for him- or herself, it is necessary that s/he understand closing procedures and the fundamentals of operating a real estate business.

REQUIREMENTS OF APPLICANTS

The minimum age requirement for license applicants is generally between eighteen and twenty-one years with a high school diploma or its equivalent. Most states require one to three years practical experience as a salesperson prior to applying for a broker's license. Nebraska accepts 18 credit hours or 180 classroom hours in accredited real estate courses in lieu of practical experience, while Arizona requires the equivalent of 12 class hours of continued education annually. Throughout the country, education requirements are constantly increasing to better ensure the public of being represented by qualified sales representatives.

Minimum age and education requirement

COMMISSIONS

Since the salesperson generally works as an independent contractor, s/he is considered self-employed and as such is responsible for his or her own social security. This means the salesperson should file a quarterly estimate of income. The broker does not offer fringe benefits such as accident and health insurance or retirement plans for self-employed persons.

Compensation for services

The salesperson generally earns a percentage of the commission paid to the real estate firm. Assuming the earned commission is 7 percent on a $50,000 property, the real estate firm pays the listing salesperson 30 percent of the commission and the selling salesperson another 30 percent. If the salesperson is both the listing and selling agent s/he would have received 60 percent or $2,100 of the $3,500 commission.

Percentages paid to sales associates on listing and sales are not uniform. The broker in this situation retained 40 percent, or $1,400, to cover the expenses of maintaining an office, paying salaries to the office staff (such as secretaries, receptionists, and bookkeepers) advertising, signs, materials, rents, management fees, and other fixed and miscellaneous expenses.

Many contract variations exist between employing brokers and sales associates. In some instances, the agent may receive 100 percent of the commission but will share in the office expenses, paying a percentage of the rent, utilities, secretarial costs, and so on. Under the 100 percent plan, the cost of advertising his listings and purchasing signs would be the salesperson's expense. While 100 percent commission may sound alluring, the agent must make payments on his share of the expenses even during months when he doesn't make any sales.

Commissions charged by brokerage firms vary; there is no set fee. Since the listing agreement constitutes a contract between the real estate firm and the property owner, they both determine the fee. Should a salesperson leave a company, any listings she may have remain with the firm under whom the listings were taken.

LICENSE FEES

The licensee pays a fee for the issuance of his or her license plus an annual renewal fee. In some states the renewal fee is paid for a two- or three-year period. This license remains in force unless revoked or suspended for just cause. Since a license is a privilege, committing an infraction of the license law is cause for **revocation** or **suspension.**

NONRESIDENT LICENSES

The right of reciprocity is in effect among many states. A nonresident may apply for a **reciprocal license** upon showing proof of being presently licensed and engaged in business in the state of residence. A nonresident salesperson must be employed by a broker holding a nonresident license. This salesperson must further sign a designation in writing that appoints the director of the real estate commission or regulatory agency to act as his or her licensee agent in the event that judicial or legal process is served upon him or her. This has the same effect as if it were served upon the licensee.

Fees for reciprocal licenses vary, but are generally higher than for resident licenses. This license permits the recipient to go to the other state and conduct business. However, should s/he move to that state permanently, s/he would need to meet the requirements of that state to work as a salesperson or broker.

GOVERNING BODIES

Regulatory agencies

The **Real Estate Commission** or regulatory body enforces the license laws, which are statutes that have been passed by the state legislature. Rules and regulations consistent with the law are promulgated by the state Real Estate Commission or governing body. The licensee is further bound by the local, state, and national Association of Realtors rules if s/he is a member of that organization. The governing body generally consists of licensees actively engaged in the real estate industry and persons-at-large to represent the public. They employ a director and staff to perform the administrative duties of the office. This position involves keeping records of all official acts of the governing body, conducting licensing exams, issuing and renewing licenses, holding educational seminars for licensees, and transacting any other duties the agency may require. The governing body has the full power to regulate the issuance of licenses and to revoke or suspend licenses for just cause.

TRUST ACCOUNTS

Placing funds in trust accounts

Brokers must set up a trust account in a bank located in the state where they are doing business. All money coming into their possession that belongs to others must be put in the designated noninterest-bearing trust account. This would include earnest money deposits, money advanced by a buyer or seller for payment of expenses in connection with a closing, the balance received from the buyer at the time of closing, and other trust funds. This account is subject to inspection by the real estate governing body and if found to be in an "unsound" condition would be cause for revoking or suspending the broker's license.

Earnest Deposits

Upon receipt of an accepted contract, the broker puts the earnest deposit in his or her trust account, where it remains until the transaction is consummated or terminated. If the sale was a cooperating broker's listing, the broker issues a check to the cooperating broker's trust account since the listing company closes the sale. In states where closing of the sale is done exclusively by escrow companies, the broker transfers the earnest deposit and purchase agreement into the possession of the escrow agent.

ADVERTISING

All advertising must be in the name of the firm and clearly indicate that it is indeed a Real Estate Company. No advertisements may simply give a box number or telephone number implying it may be a private party.

Newspaper ads

While the broker may "puff" the goods, he must not intentionally misrepresent the property or the terms under which it may be purchased. "Puffing" the goods refers to using terms to attractively describe the property, such as "treed lot with lovely view." While it must have a reasonable number of trees to qualify as "treed," it would be easy for the purchaser to ascertain for himself whether the property has a lovely view.

UNFAIR TRADE PRACTICES

Licenses are granted only to persons who bear a good reputation for honesty and integrity. If a broker, associate broker, or salesperson commits an infraction of the license law, the Real Estate Commission will investigate the actions of the licensee and has the power to **suspend** or **revoke** his license or **censure** him. The following are some of the unfair trade practices that result in such action.

Professionalism required of licensees

1. Discrimination regarding the offering for sale or rent of real property because of race, color, national origin, or ethnic group.
2. The use of misleading advertising.
3. All money coming into the possession of the licensee must be accounted for and placed in the broker's trust account unless the parties having an interest in the funds (seller and purchaser, in the case of a purchase contract) agree otherwise *in writing*. Placing the money directly into the broker's business or personal account is prohibited since it would constitute the commingling of funds.
4. Accepting, giving, or charging any undisclosed commission, rebate, or direct profit on expenditures made for a principal.
5. The salesperson or associate broker places his or her license with one broker and must never attempt to represent another broker or accept a commission from another broker unless her employing broker has given consent.
6. The licensee must disclose whether s/he has any interest in a property. S/He cannot act in a dual capacity as agent and principal without revealing this to all parties concerned.
7. Guaranteeing to the purchaser future profits from the resale of the real property.
8. In many states, *written* consent from the owners is needed before placing a "For Sale" sign on the property.
9. Offering property for sale on terms other than those authorized by the owner or his representative.
10. Inducing a party to break a contract for the purpose of substituting a new contract with another principal.
11. If an owner has an exclusive right to sell listing contract with another agent, all offers to purchase must be presented to the owner through his or her listing agent.

12. Paying a fee or compensation to an unlicensed person.

13. Most states require a fixed expiration date in a listing contract and require that a copy be left with the seller.

14. A copy of the accepted purchase agreement must be given to the seller and the purchaser.

15. When closing a transaction, a completed copy of the settlement statement showing all the receipts and disbursements must be given to both sellers and purchasers.

16. Failure to reduce an offer to writing when a prospective purchaser requests the same.

Violations of License Law

Penalties for disregarding license law

While the preceding license law violations vary from state to state, the basic necessity for ethical conduct appears in all the state license laws. When it appears to the Real Estate Commission that a licensee is in violation of a license law or upon receiving a sworn complaint in writing against a real estate broker or salesperson, the commission will investigate the actions of the licensee. If the investigation reveals no violation, the complaint will be dismissed. Should they determine justification for the complaint, a date will be set for a hearing. If the licensee is found guilty of an unfair trade practice his license will be revoked or suspended or he will be censured.

OUT-OF-STATE SUBDIVISIONS

Interstate land sales

To further protect purchasers, many states have strict regulations regarding the selling of lands within their state when such land is located in another state or is of a promotional nature. Under the Interstate Land Sales Full Disclosure Act, the Real Estate Commission requires from the applicant a full disclosure of the area of real estate being offered for sale. A recorded plat of the area, an audited financial statement, and copies of the instrument used to obtain title to the land must be submitted. If there is a mortgage on the property, the mortgagee must subordinate his or her interest to that of the purchaser. The Real Estate Commission may request a personal inspection of the property at the applicant's expense. If the purchaser has not seen the land prior to said purchase, the contract will allow him or her an unconditional right of refund on all payments made if s/he inspects the real estate within a period of not more than four months. The contract may be rescinded within fourteen days if s/he has not seen the land.

The **subdivider** will need to show proof in the form of performance bonds or other security that he can provide any promised public improvements to the property.

UNLICENSED PERSONS

When an unlicensed person acts in the capacity of a licensee and does not fall under the exceptions in his or her state, the real estate regulatory agency will bring this fact to the attention of the attorney general. Prosecution will be commenced against the violator in the district court in the county where such violation occurred.

SUMMARY

Considering that the purchase of real estate is the largest investment that the average person ever makes, it is understandable that all states have laws that govern the actions of the licensed salesperson and broker.

Educational requirements are mandatory in many states prior to licensing, and other states require continuing education. Since the financing of real estate has changed dramatically in the past four years, it is imperative that the salesperson keep abreast of these changes. Compulsory education is a means of giving added assurance of the licensee's competence to transact business.

The salesperson or broker who belongs to the National Association of Realtors is further bound by code of ethics to uphold fair practices and use diligence in preparing to conduct business as a licensee.

Anyone who conducts the business of listing, selling, exchanging, purchasing, renting, leasing, optioning, or managing real property for a fee, commission, or other valuable compensation must be licensed. This license is a privilege that can be rescinded if the licensee commits an infraction of the license law. Although there are differences in the laws among various states, license law is intended to protect the consumer from unfair real estate practices.

KEY WORDS AND CONCEPTS

Broker: A person licensed to negotiate between the parties to a real estate transaction. The broker may employ others to work for him or her.

Censure: To reprimand or express disapproval of the actions of a licensee.

License law: Authority given through the laws enacted by the state to regulate the actions of salesperson and broker.

Real Estate Commission: The regulatory body governing the actions of a licensee.

Reciprocal license: A license that enables the holder to practice the duties of a licensed salesperson in another state.

Revocation: To be taken away; a license is revoked when the licensee commits an infraction of the license law.

Salesperson: A person licensed to sell real estate while under the employ of a broker.

Statute: A law passed by the legislative body of government.

Subdivision: A parcel of land subdivided into individual lots.

Suspension: To be held in abeyance for a stipulated period of time.

REVIEW QUESTIONS

1. Which of the following are violations of real estate license laws?
   a. placing a "For Sale" sign on property without the written permission of the owner
   b. purchasing property as an undisclosed principal
   c. both a and b
   d. neither a nor b

2. Which of the following are true concerning a listing contract?
   a. a copy must be left with the sellers
   b. it must contain an expiration date
   c. both a and b
   d. neither a nor b

3. When a real estate broker advertises in the local newspaper, he must
   a. always state the price of the house.
   b. give the address of the house.
   c. both a and b
   d. neither a nor b

4. If a salesperson mishandles funds
   a. the person's license may be revoked.
   b. the broker who employs him or her may be subject to suspension.
   c. both a and b
   d. neither a nor b

5. When a nonresident broker requests a reciprocal license, she must
   a. provide a copy of the license she now holds in the state where she conducts business.
   b. give written consent that appoints the director of the regulatory agency to be her licensee agent.
   c. both a and b
   d. neither a nor b

6. A broker may place an earnest deposit
   a. in his personal account.
   b. in his business account.
   c. both a and b
   d. neither a nor b

7. The broker may lose his license if he fails to
   a. give a completed copy of the closing and purchase statements to both the buyer and the seller.
   b. retain a copy of the closing statement in his files.
   c. both a and b
   d. neither a nor b

8. A salaried employee selling tracts of land for a land developer
   a. must be licensed.
   b. must receive a commission on the sales he makes.
   c. both a and b
   d. neither a nor b

9. Which of the following are exempt from needing a license?
   a. the resident manager of an apartment complex
   b. the executor of a will
   c. both a and b
   d. neither a nor b

10. Real estate law is intended to
    a. protect the public.
    b. insure the salesperson he or she will be paid a commission.
    c. both a and b
    d. neither a nor b

11. The following people must be licensed to transact the business of real estate:
    a. resident apartment managers
    b. real estate secretaries
    c. both a and b
    d. neither a nor b

12. A real estate licensee may
    a. work on a part-time basis.
    b. lease property listed with the firm.
    c. both a and b
    d. neither a nor b

13. A license may be revoked upon proof of
    a. charging more than the usual rate of commission.
    b. refusal to accept a listing.
    c. both a and b
    d. neither a nor b

14. A broker could lose his or her license for
    a. withholding earnest money when the purchaser is rightfully entitled to return of same.
    b. dividing or splitting commissions with another broker.
    c. both a and b
    d. neither a nor b

15. A real estate salesperson can
    a. work independently.
    b. auction land.
    c. both a and b
    d. neither a nor b

16. Which of the following could result in revocation of a salesperson's license?
    a. failure to submit to an owner, before his acceptance, all formal written offers received on the property
    b. quoting a price other than that stipulated by the owner
    c. both a and b
    d. neither a nor b

17. A salesperson in a real estate transaction may accept compensation from
    a. the seller
    b. the buyer
    c. both a and b
    d. neither a nor b

18. A broker may
    a. buy property through a corporation without disclosing the fact that she is a broker.
    b. offer property for sale without disclosing the fact that she has an interest in the real estate.
    c. both a and b
    d. neither a nor b

19. A broker would be censured for commingling funds if he deposited earnest money in anything other than
    a. his general real estate account
    b. his personal account, because the portion of money was due him
    c. a separate checking account designated as a trust account
    d. a separate savings account designated as a trust account

20. Which of the following are in violation of license law?
    a. failure to offer property to a minority
    b. accepting an undisclosed rebate on an expenditure made for a principal
    c. both a and b
    d. neither a nor b

Basic Tools

Real Estate Math | 19

Salespersons and brokers must have an understanding of the basic mathematical principles involved in the real estate transaction. While we covered the ad valorem tax structure on real property in chapter 15, the amortization of a loan in chapter 8 and the proration of costs in the settlement procedure in chapter 10, it is necessary to further elaborate on the arithmetic involved in real estate transactions.

It is necessary to correctly measure the area (square footage) of a house or a parcel of land when the sales representative lists the property. Commercial land is generally priced per square foot so the exact amount of square footage must be determined by the agent. A contractor may price a plan by square footage. An appraiser determines value by the square footage when using the cost approach to value. Cubic footage may be important to the purchaser of a commercial building or to the contractor pouring a driveway or patio.

A general review of the approach used in percentage problems is important when fractions or percentages of a tract of land are being divided. Many of the areas of arithmetic covered in this chapter involve percentages. For example, our inflationary market results in rapidly increasing property values, so the techniques used to evaluate percentages of appreciation must be understood. If the property depreciates, the resulting loss in value must also be calculated. To an investor, the past history of the value increase on a particular piece of property is very important.

Another area of mathematics important to real estate involves taxation. Since all real property is subject to taxation, understanding the tax structure as expressed in dollars or mill levy is further explained in this chapter.

When analyzing the worth of a subdivided property, it is of value to both buyer and seller to determine the proportionate amount being sold. If a segment of a property is being taken under the right of eminent domain, the owner will want to know the proportion taken to determine the value of the land s/he is losing. Ratio problems concerning scales are also analyzed in this chapter since house plans are drawn to scale.

Determining the capitalization of an income-producing property is a prime concern of the investor, since he will want to know the rate of return on his investment.

Amortization is the liquidation of a loan by making monthly payments. This chapter explains how to determine the loan payment or to find the rate from the interest and principal payment. Discount problems when interest points are charged on a new loan are also included in this chapter.

When a property is sold, the financial responsibility of taxes, insurance, interest, and rents is divided (prorated) between the purchaser and seller. This is a bookkeeping procedure that the real estate agent should understand.

And lastly, the sales agent will be interested in computing commission problems. The split commission between real estate firms, broker-agent arrangements concerning commissions, and sliding-scale commission problems are presented in this chapter.

MEASUREMENT PROBLEMS

Let's review the following basic elements of arithmetic. The measurement of land and areas—square footage, cubic feet, acreages—are all of importance to the real estate salesperson. The following lists show the equivalents of various types of measures.

Linear measure
12 inches = 1 foot
36 inches = 3 feet or 1 yard

Square measure
144 inches = 1 square foot
9 square feet = 1 square yard

Cubic measure
1 cubic foot = 1,728 cubic inches
27 cubic feet = 1 cubic yard

Surveyor's measure
link = 7.92 inches
chain = 66 feet or 4 rods
rod = 16½ feet or 1 perch
mile = 5,280 feet
acre = 43,560 square feet, 4,840 square yards, or 160 square rods
section = 640 acres

Circular measure
60 seconds (″) = 1 minute (′)
60 minutes (′) = 1 degree (°)
90 minutes (′) = 1 quadrant
360 degrees (°) = a circle

Square Footage and Yardage

Area problems To find the *square footage* of a square or rectangular area, multiply the lengths of the two sides together.

AREA = LENGTH × WIDTH

By drawing the basic formula in a circle, the math procedure is simple to determine: just blot out the element you are looking for. Thus, if you have the total square footage and are looking for the width, divide the area by the length to obtain the width.

Example: A room measures 18 feet long and 12 feet wide. Find the area.

$\quad$ A = 18′ (L) × 12′ (W)
$\quad$ A = 216 square feet

Example: Compute the square footage of the house shown in the diagram.

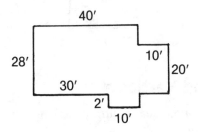

$\quad$ Square off the diagram as shown:
$\quad$ A = 40′ × 28′ $\quad$ = $\quad$ 1,120 square feet
$\quad$ B = 2′ × 10′ $\quad\quad$ = $\quad\quad$ 20 square feet
$\quad$ C = 20′ × 10′ $\quad$ = $\quad\quad$ 200 square feet
$\quad$ Total area $\quad\quad\quad$ = $\quad$ 1,340 square feet

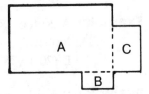

To find the *square yards*, divide the square feet by nine (there are nine square feet in a square yard).

Example: 216 square feet divided by 9 equals 24 square yards.

Example: Find the square yards of carpet needed to cover a 15-foot × 18-foot room.

$\quad$ 15′ × 18′ = 270 square feet
$\quad$ 270 square feet ÷ 9 = 30 square yards

To find the *area of a triangle*, multiply the base by the height and divide by two.

Area = half the base × the altitude.

The altitude is the distance from the base of the triangle to its peak, as shown here by the dotted line. Line CD is the base and line AB the altitude.

Example: A triangular lot has a base of 200 feet and an altitude of 150 feet. Find the area.

$\quad$ A = Half the base × the altitude
$\quad$ A = $\dfrac{200}{2}$ × 150
$\quad$ A = 100 × 150
$\quad$ A = 15,000 square feet

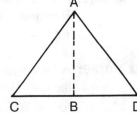

Example: To compute the square feet in the diagram, add the two widths, 40' + 50' = 90'. Then divide by two: 90' ÷ 2 = 45'. Now multiply by the length: 45' × 80' = 3,600 square feet

Note: When an angle is marked by an arc and "90°," it merely indicates it is a right angle.

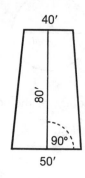

Cubic Footage and Yardage

To find the *cubic footage* of an area, multiply the length by the width by the height: L × W × H = cubic feet.

Example: A 20-foot × 12-foot room has a height of 8 feet. Compute the cubic footage.

L (20') x W (12') × H (18') = 1,920 cubic feet

Example: If a driveway measures 60 feet long by 8 feet wide and is 3 inches deep, what is the cubic footage?

60' × 8' × ¼' = 120 cubic feet

To find the *cubic yards*, divide the cubic feet by 27 (there are 27 cubic feet in a cubic yard).

Example: A driveway 54 feet long by 15 feet and 4 inches deep will be poured at a cost of $30 per cubic yard of concrete. Find the cost.

54' × 15' × ⅓' = 270 cubic feet
270 cubic feet ÷ 27 = 10 cubic yards
10 × $30 = $300

Linear Footage

Linear feet, sometimes referred to as running feet, are the measure of the distance from one point to another.

Example: A lot 100 feet wide by 150 feet deep is to be fenced on all four sides. How much fencing is needed?

100' + 100' + 150' + 150' = 500 feet

Example: A lot 65 feet wide by 80 feet deep will be fenced on both sides and the rear. How many linear feet of fencing is needed?

65' + 80' + 80' = 225 feet

PERCENTAGES

Decimals and percentages

It is necessary for salespeople and brokers to understand the conversion to percentages. Remember that the whole of anything is 100 percent. Anything less than the whole is a part or percentage of the whole. For example, think of $1.00 as being the whole and 50¢ as a part—in decimal form, .50. When converting a number to percentage, move the decimal point two places to the right and add the percentage symbol (%). Thus, you would write .50. as 50%. Another way to think of this is $\frac{50}{100}$.

Remember, to change a percent to a decimal, move the decimal point two places to the left: 50% = .50. To change a decimal to a percent, move the decimal point two places to the right: .05 = 5%, .108 = 10.8%, 1.00 = 100%.

To change the percent to a common fraction, express it as hundredths and reduce:

$$50\% = \frac{50}{100} = \frac{1}{2} \qquad 75\% = \frac{75}{100} = \frac{3}{4}$$

To change a fraction to a percentage, express it in hundredths and then as a percentage:

$$\frac{1}{2} = \frac{50}{100} = .50, \text{ or } 50\% \qquad \frac{3}{4} = \frac{75}{100} = .75, \text{ or } 75\%$$

Fractions must have common denominators before you can add or subtract them:

$$\frac{1}{3} = \frac{4}{12}$$
$$\frac{2}{4} = \frac{6}{12}$$
$$\overline{\frac{10}{12}, \text{ or } \frac{5}{6}}$$

As the example shows, 1/3 and 2/4 have a common denominator of 12. When they are added together, the answer, 10/12, is reduced to 5/6.

In multiplying fractions, the numerators are multiplied and the denominators are multiplied:

$$3\frac{1}{3} \times \frac{1}{2} =$$

Change 3 1/3 to an improper fraction and multiply numerators and denominators:

$$\frac{10}{3} \times \frac{1}{2} = \frac{10}{6} \text{ or } \frac{5}{3} = 1\frac{2}{3}$$

To divide a fraction, the divisor is inverted and then multiplied:

$$\frac{2}{3} \div \frac{4}{5} =$$
$$\frac{2}{3} \times \frac{5}{4} = \frac{10}{12} = \frac{5}{6}$$

Profit and Loss

Appreciation and depreciation problems

As we learned in the chapter on appraisal, depreciation is loss from any cause, whether it is physical deterioration, functional obsolescence, or economic obsolescence. If a property *depreciates* in value, it has simply lost value. If it *appreciates* in value, it has gained in value and is now worth more.

We begin with the original value of a building as 100 percent. If the useful life of a building is fifty years, it will depreciate 1/50 or 2 percent a year. Thus, if a property depreciates 2 percent a year for eight years, it has a 16 percent loss in value.

We subtract this loss from 100 percent:

$$100\% - 16\% = 84\%$$

If the property is now worth, say, $16,800, this represents 84% of its original value. To determine its original value, we divide:

$$\$16,800 \div 84\% = \$20,000 \text{ (original value)}$$

When appreciation occurs, it represents a gain in value. Assuming a property presently valued at $23,000 had appreciated 3 percent a year for the last five years, it would have gained 15 percent in value. Its present value would thus be 115 percent of the original value.

$$\$23,000 \div 115\% = \$20,000 \text{ (original value)}$$

Example: If a property sold for $12,100, gaining a 10 percent profit for the owner, what was the original cost of the property?

100% (cost) + 10% (profit) = 110% (selling price)

$$\frac{\$12,100}{110} = \$11,000 \text{ (original cost of property)}$$

Here we divided the selling price by its percentage to determine the original cost.

Example: A $40,000 house appreciates in value at the rate of 2.5 percent each succeeding year. What is the value of the house at the end of the second year?

$40,000 × 2.5% = $1,000 (appreciation the first year)
$40,000 + $1,000 = $41,000
$41,000 × 2.5% = $1,025 (appreciation the second year)
$41,000 + $1,025 = $42,025 (value after the second year)

The wording "each succeeding year" indicates compound interest; that is, the interest is added to the new balance at the end of *each* year.

Example: A $30,000 house appreciates 5 percent each year for five years. What is its present value? (In this problem we need only multiply the five years by 5 percent, for a total of 25 percent appreciation.)

25% × $30,000 = $7,500
$30,000 + $7,500 = $37,500 (present value)

If we know the value of a house was $20,000 ten years ago and that it depreciated 2 percent a year, we can find the present value by multiplying:

10 years × 2% = 20% (total depreciation)
The present value of the house is 80% (100% − 20% = 80%)
$20,000 × 80% = $16,000 (present value)

Example: A-1 Construction Company built a home in a new subdivision. It was sold six months after completion for $48,500, which represented a depreciation (loss) of 3 percent. What was the original asking price?

$48,500 ÷ 97% = $50,000 (asking price)

Example: A duplex depreciates 3 percent for five years. If the building originally cost $20,000, compute the present value of the duplex.

3% × 5 years = 15% (total depreciation)
$20,000 × 15% = $3,000
$20,000 − $3,000 = $17,000 (present value)

Example: Mr. Loser sells his house for $27,000, which represents a 10 percent loss over the price he originally paid for it. What did he pay for the house?

100% − 10% = 90%
$27,000 ÷ 90% = $30,000

TAXATION PROBLEMS

The property tax structure is an ad valorem (*according to value*) tax. This value is determined by a tax assessor, who appraises the value of each piece of property. An assessment roll is prepared that gives a description of the property, its assessed valuation, and the owner's name.

The tax rate is referred to either as *mill levy* or *in dollars*. In determining the taxation of a property, the assessed value is acquired by taking the percentage of the real value the taxes are based on; then the mill levy is multiplied by the assessed value. A mill represents 1/10 of one cent and is written as .001. Thus, 83 mills would be written as .083, and 6.5 mills would be written as .0065.

Taxation by mill levy

Example: A property valued at $35,000 is assessed at 40 percent of its value. The mill levy is 83. Compute the annual tax.

$35,000 (value of property) × 40% (percentage taxed) = $14,000 (assessed value)
$14,000 × .083 (mill levy) = $1,162 (annual taxes)

Example: If the assessed valuation is $20,000 and the tax rate is $4.00 per $100 of value, compute the annual tax.

Taxation by dollars

The $4.00 per hundred indicates that the $20,000 assessed valuation must be divided by 100.

$20,000 ÷ 100 = $200
$200 × $4 = $800 (tax)

RATIO AND PROPORTION

Comparing ratios   Ratio problems involve comparisons of two related numbers. A house plan or map is "scaled" so that one inch or a fraction of an inch equals a number of feet. The ratios must always be equal or in proportion.

Example: What is the scale of a house plan if a room 16 feet $\times$ 28 feet is shown on the scale as 4 inches $\times$ 7 inches?

$$\frac{4}{16} = \frac{1}{4} \qquad \frac{7}{28} = \frac{1}{4} \qquad \text{Scale is } \frac{1''}{4} = 1'$$

Example: What is the actual measurement of a property 6 inches in length by 8 inches wide if the scale is 1/8 inch = 1 foot?

If the scale is 1/8″ to 1′, 1″ = 8′.

$6 \times 8 = 48$

$8 \times 8 = 64$ The meaurement is 48′ $\times$ 64′

Example: In nine months a salesperson sells property to one out of every five prospective purchasers. How many sales would she make in three months if she showed property to 150 people? (Since the months involved are of no significance, we disregard the time element.)

$$\frac{5}{1} = \frac{150}{X}$$

$$\frac{150}{X} \times \frac{1}{5} = \frac{150}{5X}$$

$$\frac{150}{5} = X$$

$$X = 30 \text{ sales}$$

Proportion problems   **Example:** How many acres are there in plot A if plot B contains 25 acres?

$$\frac{900}{X} = \frac{1,350}{25}$$

$$\frac{900}{X} \times \frac{25}{1,350} = \frac{22,500}{1,350} = 16\frac{2}{3} \text{ acres}$$

```
        900'           1,350'
     ┌─────────┬─────────────────┐
     │         │                 │
     │    A    │        B        │
     │         │                 │
     └─────────┴─────────────────┘
```

Example: If the ratio of a salesperson's commission to that of his broker is 4:6, what amount does the salesperson earn from a $3,000 commission?

$4 + 6 = 10$ parts

$100\% \div 10 = 10\%$

$4 \times 10\% = 40\%$ and $6 \times 10\% = 60\%$

40% of $3,000 = $1,200

CAPITALIZATION AND OTHER FINANCE PROBLEMS

To solve income problems, use the formula P = R × B (principal equals rate × base). This is similar to using A = L × W in finding the square footage of an area.

P = principle (sum due)
R = rate (interest)
B = base (amount of value)

Use a circle and blot out the one unknown.

Example: $140 is 3½% of what amount?

principal ÷ interest rate = amount or base

$\dfrac{140 \ (P)}{.035 \ (R)} = B$

$140 ÷ .035 = $4,000

Always *divide* to find the base or rate.

Example: If the quarterly interest payments are $150 on a $12,000 loan, what is the annual interest rate?

$150 × 4 (4 quarters in a year) = $600

$\dfrac{\$600 \ (P)}{\$12,000 \ (B)} = R$

$600 ÷ $12,000 = 5%

To determine the percentage, divide the *income* by the *investment*. (This is usually the larger number into the smaller.)

Example: Compute the value of a property that has a net income of $5,480 and that returns 8 percent annually on the investment.

$\dfrac{\$5,480 \ (P)}{8\% \ (R)} = B$

$5,480 ÷ .08 = $68,500

Interest into return equals investment.

Determining value of income property

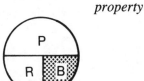

In this example, we divided the percentage rate into the net return to determine the value of the property.

Example: If the interest rate is 4½% and the monthly interest payments are $21.25, what is the sum due?

$21.25 × 12 months = $255 annual interest

$\dfrac{\$255 \ (P)}{.045 \ (R)} = B$

$255 ÷ .045 = $5,666.67

Example: A man obtains a 75% loan on a house with a value of $28,000. What is the interest percentage if his interest payments are $140 monthly?

75% × $28,000 = $21,000 loan

$140 × 12 months = $1,680 annual interest

$$\frac{\$1,680\,(P)}{\$21,000\,(B)} = R$$

$1,680 ÷ $21,000 = 8% interest

Example: If an investment valued at $350,000 returns 12 percent annually, what is the amount of income produced?

$350,000 (B) × 12% (R) = $42,000

Example: If the capitalization rate on a building that produces $20,000 annual income is 10 percent, find the estimated value of the structure.

$$\frac{\$20,000\,(P)}{10\%\,(R)} = B$$

$20,000 ÷ 10% = $200,000

Example: Compute the value if the same building had a capitalization rate of 5 percent.

$$\frac{\$20,000\,(P)}{.05\,(R)} = B$$

$20,000 ÷ .05 = $400,000

In using the capitalization approach, remember that the *higher* the cap rate, the *lower* the appraised value.

Loan Payments

The buyer's foremost concern when purchasing a home is what her monthly loan commitment will be. The amount borrowed will be *amortized* over a period of years in equal payments, a portion of which will be interest, with the remainder applied towards the principal payment to gradually reduce the loan.

Amortization problems

Example: Ms. Morley purchases a home with a $45,000 mortgage at 9¾% interest. If the monthly payments are $387.70, what amount is applied against the principal after the first payment?

$45,000 × .0975 = $4,387.50 annual interest

$4,387.50 ÷ 12 months = $365.63 first month's interest

$387.70 − $365.63 = $22.07 against principal

The $22.07 is deducted from the principal amount of $45,000, so that the second month begins with the remaining balance of $44,977.93.

To determine the total monthly payment if the interest is in addition to the stated principal payment, we compute the interest and add it to the principal payment.

Example: Mr. Winslow negotiates for a $30,000 loan with $200 monthly payments plus 9 percent interest.

$30,000 × .09 = $2,700 ÷ 12 months = $225 interest per month
$200 principal payment + $225 interest payment = $425 principal and interest.

If the loan amount is unknown, but the interest payment and rate of interest is given, we compute the amount as follows:

Example: The semiannual interest payments are $400 with interest of 5 percent annually.

$400 × 2 = $800 annual interest ÷ .05 = $16,000 loan amount

Further Examples of Interest Problems

Example: Mr. Jones wanted to remodel his business. He obtained a loan for $4,300 at 6 percent interest. He paid it off in eight months. What amount of interest did he pay?

$4,300 × .06 = $258 interest for year
$258 ÷ 12 months = $21.50 per month
$21.50 × 8 months = $172 interest paid

Example: A buyer purchases a home for $50,000. She takes out a 25-year loan for 75 percent of the purchase price. Assuming that her mortgage payments are equal and the interest payment is ¾ percent of the principal each month, what would be the amount of her first monthly payment?

$50,000 × .75 = $37,500 loan
25 years × 12 months = 300 months
$37,500 ÷ 300 months = $125 principal per month
¾% × 12 months = 9% interest per year
$37,500 × .09 = $3,375 ÷ 12 months = $281.25 interest
$125 + $281.25 = $406.25 principal and interest

Example: Jane Jones obtains an FHA loan on a $55,000 home. The down payment scale is 3 percent of the first $25,000 and 5 percent of the balance. There is a loan fee of two points that the buyer is to pay. What amount should Ms. Jones bring to the closing?

3% of $25,000 = $ 750 $56,000
5% of $31,000 = $1,550   − $2,300 down payment
                 $2,300 $53,700 loan

Two points would be .02 of the loan balance ($53,700) = $1,074
$2,300 + $1,074 = $3,374

Example: How much less are the monthly payments on a $36,000 home than on a $40,000 home if a 75 percent loan is obtained at $8.70 a month per $1,000 of value?

$40,000 − $36,000 = $4,000 × 75% = $3,000

$3 (thousands) × $8.70 = $26.10

Example: Ms. Randall purchases a home for $58,000 and puts 10 percent down. The 20-year loan is to be repaid with a constant principal payment, and interest will be charged at the rate of ¾ percent per month. Compute the amount of the first month's payment.

$58,000 − $5,800 (10% down) = $52,200 loan

20 years × 12 months = 240 months

52,200 ÷ 240 = $217.50 principal per month

¾% × 12 months = 9% × $52,200 = 4,698 ÷ 12 = $391.50 interest per month

$217.50 + $391.50 = $609 principal and interest

Discount Problems

A discount is an amount charged by the lender in excess of the closing costs. In addition to the interest rate, a percentage is charged on the *amount loaned* to the borrower. The effective yield to the loan company becomes greater when these discount points are charged. A "point" is really one percent of the amount of the loan. If one point is charged on a $20,000 loan, the lender collects 1 percent of $20,000, or $200. If 2½ points are charged, the fee would be $500.

Example: Mr. Corkle purchases a $55,000 home using FHA financing. He is required to put 3 percent down on the first $25,000 loaned with 5 percent on the balance of the purchase price. The lender is charging 3½ discount points. Compute the points the seller will have to pay.

$25,000 × .97 = $24,250

$30,000 × .95 = $28,500

$52,750 loan amount

$52,750 × .035 = $1,846.25 discount points

Prorations

Dividing expenses by prorating

Prorating means *dividing expenses* between buyer and seller. The person who uses must pay his share for the time he is using. In prorating, one must analyze the period of time involved and multiply it by the rate. Real estate prorating at the time of closing a sale may commonly include taxes, rents, insurance, or interest charges.

Example: Mr. Happy sells his home July 1, with closing and possession set for July 15. Since Ms. Stucky is assuming the loan, she has also decided to assume the insurance policy, which was paid March 1 for one year in the amount of $156. What amount will appear as a credit on Mr. Happy's closing statement?

March 1 to July 15 = 4½ months. (This represents the amount of insurance *used* by Mr. Happy, leaving 7½ months *unused*.)

$156 divided by 12 months = $13 monthly

$13 × 7½ months = $97.50 (amount due to Mr. Happy)

Example: The mortgage being assumed by Ms. Stucky is in the amount of $15,000 at 8 percent interest. The interest has been paid to June 1st. Mr. Happy is liable for the interest to the date of closing. Compute the amount he owes.

$15,000 × .08 = $1,200 ÷ 12 months = $100 for June, plus $50 for half of July

Total = $150

Example: I. M. Leach sold her home November 15 with possession set for December 5. Mr. Winner will assume the three-year insurance policy, which became effective July 15 of last year in the amount of $396. The annual taxes of $982.80 were paid by the owner for the first half of the year; the second half year's taxes are due and payable. What amounts are payable and by whom?

1. Insurance

   July 15 (last year) to December 5 = 1 year, 4 months, 20 days used
   (16 months and 20 days *used* or 19 months and 10 days *not used*)

$396 ÷ 36 months = $11 per month × 19 months = $209

$11 ÷ 30 days = $.366 per day × 10 days = $3.67

$209 + $3.67 = $212.67 (insurance paid for and not used will be refunded to Ms. Leach.)

2. Taxes

$982.80 ÷ 12 months = $81.90 per month

July 1 to December 5 = 5 months, 5 days taxes due

$81.90 × 5 = $409.50

$81.90 ÷ 30 days = $2.73 per day

$2.73 × 5 days = $13.65 + $409.50 = $423.15 (taxes due from seller)

$2.73 × 25 days = $68.25 (taxes due from buyer to complete year)

$212.68 insurance prorate due to I. M. Leach

$423.15 taxes due from Ms. Leach

$68.25 taxes due from Mr. Winner

Commissions

In the real estate business a salesperson normally is paid on a commission basis. *The sales commission* Instead of receiving a fixed salary, the salesperson is paid a percentage or proportion of the real property he or she sells or lists. This straight commission earning is received only if the salesperson produces. The real estate firm, of course, must retain a portion for its fixed expenses.

Example: If a property sells for $20,000 and a broker's commission is 6 percent, the broker's commission would be:

$20,000 × 6% = $1,200 commission

Example: If a salesperson receives 35 percent of a total commission from his broker, what is the broker's share if the property sold for $23,000 and the commission was on a 6 percent basis?

$23,000 × .06 = $1,380 (total commission)

100% − 35% = 65% (broker's share)

$1,380 × 65% = $897 (broker's portion)

Example: Tom Luck earns 6 percent on the first $50,000 of a $160,000 sale. If the total commission is $7,400, what percentage was paid on the remainder?

$50,000 × .06 = $3,000
$7,400 − $3,000 = $4,400
$160,000 − $50,000 = $110,000
So: $4,400 = what % of $110,000?
$4,400 (P) ÷ $110,000 (B) = .04 = 4% (R)

Example: Mr. Jones, a real estate broker, leases a property to Ms. Whitney for five years. Mr. Jones will receive a 5 percent commission. The rent will be $300 per month for the first year, with a $50-a-year increase each succeeding year. What is Mr. Jones's commission?

$300 @ 12 months = $3,600
$350 @ 12 months = $4,200
$400 @ 12 months = $4,800
$450 @ 12 months = $5,400
$500 @ 12 months = $6,000
$24,000 × .05 = $1,200 commission

REVIEW QUESTIONS

1. Find the square footage of the diagram, excluding the small area indicated in the lower right hand corner.
   a. 34,000 sq. ft.
   b. 33,800 sq. ft.
   c. 30,000 sq. ft.
   d. 33,600 sq. ft.

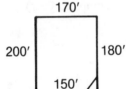

2. If a house depreciates at the rate of 2.5 percent per year for 10 years and has a present value of $12,500, what was the original value of the house?
   a. $14,000
   b. $16,666
   c. $18,000
   d. $17,000

3. An $11,000 house is assessed at 30 percent of its original cost. The school tax on the property is 12 mills. What was the approximate yearly tax (rounded off to the nearest dollar)?
   a. $396
   b. $400
   c. $600
   d. $40

4. A house is appraised for $25,000 and shows an assessed value of $20,000. If taxes on it are $300 yearly, what would the tax be on a house appraising at $45,000 with an assessed value of $40,000?
   a. $150
   b. $500
   c. $600
   d. $700

5. Mr. Lewis is working for Ms. Morris on a 50/50 basis. Mr. Lewis sells 360 acres at $150 an acre; another firm, ABC Realty, has the listing and splits on a 50/50 basis with Ms. Morris's firm. The commission rate is 5 percent on the first $25,000, 2½ percent on the next $20,000 and 1 percent on the balance. How much does Mr. Lewis earn?
   a. $920
   b. $1,840
   c. $460
   d. $230

6. What portion of the whole piece of land is lot A?
   a. 2/15
   b. 1/30
   c. 3/60
   d. 2/9

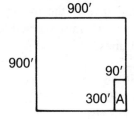

7. Find the actual measurement of a property shown as 5¾ inches long and 4½ inches wide if the scale is ⅛ inch = 1 foot.
   a. 12′ × 9′
   b. 24′ × 18′
   c. 36′ × 32′
   d. 46′ × 36′

8. A house sale is closed on July 15th. The taxes of $546 for the calendar year have been paid. The fire insurance premium of $102 for the calendar year has also been paid. What is the total prepaid portion that the buyer will owe back to the seller?
   a. $54
   b. $297
   c. $351
   d. $425

9. Shelly Ford pays her taxes of $660 for the calendar year. She sells her property and closes on June 15th. What is the remaining prepaid portion due back to her?
   a. $412.50
   b. $357.50
   c. $302.50
   d. $330

10. An apartment house has 10 units renting at $275 a month and 12 units at $250 a month. Expenses are $6,789 annually. The vacancy factor is 15 percent annually. If you desire to make 10 percent return on your investment, approximately what should you pay for the property?
    a. $518,610
    b. $585,000
    c. $612,000
    d. $62,100

11. Carol Reed purchases a $62,000 property on which she obtains an 80 percent loan. She pays 4 discount points, and the attorney's fees and miscellaneous costs amount to $2,500. How much money should she bring to the closing?
    a. $16,884
    b. $14,900
    c. $12,400
    d. $1,984

12. What was the selling price of a property if Jerry Brown paid $350 for taxes due, has a $12,500 mortgage, paid a 6 percent broker commission and net $7,000 on the sale?
    a. $21,041.00
    b. $21,117.02
    c. $13,621.00
    d. $15,500.00

13. A building that cost $300,000 to construct 10 years ago has depreciated 25 percent. The land cost $51,000. Find the current appraised value.
    a. $276,000
    b. $351,000
    c. $263,250
    d. $265,000

14. Mr. Landlover owns a lot measuring 80 feet × 120 feet. The city puts in a new street in front and to the side of his house and assesses him 6¢ a square foot based on the area of this lot. His costs are
    a. $480.00
    b. $48.00
    c. $57.60
    d. $576.00

15. If the documentary stamps are payable at the rate of 55¢ per $500 or part thereof, compute the grantor's cost on a $49,750 sale.
    a. $53.90
    b. $27.36
    c. $55.00
    d. $54.55

16. Ms. Dale buys a $20,000 property. She puts $1,000 down with the balance to be repaid over 20 years at 12 percent interest. Her monthly payments are $275. What is the amount of interest paid in the second month's payment?
    a. $85.00
    b. $190.00
    c. $189.15
    d. $75.00

17. What is the approximate amount of interest paid on the loan in problem 16 at its maturity?
    a. $19,000
    b. $66,000
    c. $45,000
    d. $47,000

18. The gross annual income for each of five apartments is $145 per month. The building is 90 percent occupied. The caretaker is paid 5 percent of the gross, and the total yearly maintenance is $1,400. Find the monthly net income of the apartments.
    a. $620.00
    b. $503.21
    c. $391.20
    d. $6038.51

19. James Stole manages an office building with leases of $60,000 per year. His management agreement is for seven years, with fees as follows: 7 percent the first year, 5 percent the second and third years, and 3 percent the remaining years. Find the total management fee the broker would receive.
    a. $9,000
    b. $12,000
    c. $14,400
    d. $17,400

20. Find the annual percentage rate of net return of an $88,000 investment if the weekly gross income is $225 and the monthly expenses are $370.
    a. 12½%
    b. 10%
    c. 8¼%
    d. 7%

21. Ms. Carlson owns a 110-acre orchard that yields an average net profit of $13,000. If she sells the land and invests the money at 5 percent, what price per acre must she sell for to match her present earnings?
    a. $2,250
    b. $236.36
    c. $21,500
    d. $2,363.64

22. A building worth $430,000 rents for $1,500 a month. What is the rate of capitalization?
    a. 23¾%
    b. 4%
    c. 8%
    d. 9%

23. An office building earns $850,000 a year; expenses run 35 percent of that amount. If the property is capitalized at 12 percent, what is its approximate value?
    a. $552,500
    b. $297,500
    c. $6,630,000
    d. $4,604,000

24. Mr. Jay buys a home and obtains a $20,000 loan on which monthly payments will be $7.50 per $1,000. Annual taxes are $360; a three-year fire insurance policy cost $54. What was the first payment, including taxes and insurance?
    a. $280.00
    b. $216.50
    c. $193.50
    d. $181.50

25. A map is drawn to scale and marked 13½ inches × 16½ inches. In reality that area equals 108 feet × 132 feet. What is the scale?
    a. 8″ = 1′
    b. ¼″ = 1′
    c. ⅛″ = 1′
    d. ⅜″ = 1′

26. A salesperson receives 8 percent of the first $90,000 he sells each month and 2 percent of the excess above that amount. In August, he made sales of $42,000, $48,000, $36,500, and $55,600. If he had been paid a flat 6 percent commission, how much more or less would he have made?
   a. less than $600 more
   b. less than $500 more
   c. more than $5,000
   d. less than $5,000 more

27. Ms. Randall's $85,000 condominium is assessed at 35 percent of value. The tax rate is $2.70 per $100 of value. If the tax increases $.35 per $100, her new tax will be
   a. $699.13
   b. $750.00
   c. $9073.80
   d. $907.38

28. A house is currently worth 50 percent of its original value. The land, however, has appreciated in five years from $60,000 to its present value of $96,000. Find the average annual rate of appreciation of the land over the five-year period.
   a. 16%
   b. 12%
   c. 63%
   d. 6¼%

29. Now that you are entering the real estate profession, you purchase a new four-door automobile costing $9,200. Your accountant advises that you deduct $2,300 as depreciation this year. What percentage are you deducting?
   a. 4%
   b. 12%
   c. 12½%
   d. 25%

30. The diagram contains:
   a. 5,600 square feet
   b. 6,800 square feet
   c. 8,000 square feet
   d. 8,500 square feet

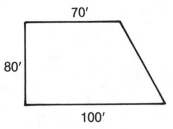

Answers to Chapter-End Review Questions

CHAPTER 2	CHAPTER 3	CHAPTER 4	CHAPTER 5	CHAPTER 6
1. a	1. d	1. b	1. d	1. b
2. d	2. c	2. b	2. c	2. a
3. b	3. d	3. d	3. a	3. b
4. b	4. a	4. c	4. a	4. c
5. c	5. d	5. d	5. c	5. a
6. d	6. c	6. c	6. b	6. b
7. d	7. c	7. b	7. a	7. b
8. d	8. a	8. a	8. c	8. c
9. d	9. c	9. b	9. c	9. d
10. a	10. a T10N,R2W	10. c	10. b	10. c
11. b	b T10N,R1E	11. c	11. d	11. a
12. d	c T8N,R2W	12. b	12. a	12. a
13. c	d T8N,R1E	13. b	13. b	13. a
14. a	11. b	14. a	14. d	14. b
15. b	12. d	15. d	15. c	15. b
16. b	13. a 40 acres	16. d		16. a
17. d	b 10 acres	17. d		17. c
18. c	c 20 acres	18. b		18. c
19. c	d 80 acres	19. a		19. e
20. d	14. b	20. a		20. a
	15. c	21. c		21. d
	16. b	22. c		22. b
	17. a			23. b
	18. b			24. b
				25. b

CHAPTER 7	CHAPTER 8	CHAPTER 9	CHAPTER 10	CHAPTER 11
1. c	1. c	1. c	1. b	1. b
2. b	2. d	2. a	2. a	2. a
3. d	3. b	3. a	3. c	3. a
4. c	4. d	4. b	4. c	4. b
5. c	5. c	5. d	5. b	5. e
6. a	6. c	6. b	6. a	6. c
7. b	7. a	7. b	7. a	7. d
8. b	8. a	8. a	8. c	8. d
9. d	9. a	9. a	9. b	9. b
10. a	10. b	10. a	10. d	10. b
11. a	11. b	11. b	11. c	11. c
12. a	12. a	12. b	12. a	12. d
13. d	13. b	13. b	13. a	13. d
14. b	14. c	14. b	14. a	14. c
15. a	15. a	15. c	15. d	15. a
16. d	16. d	16. d	16. a	16. b
17. b	17. c	17. c	17. c	17. c
18. a	18. c	18. d	18. b	
		19. c	19. c	
		20. b	20. d	
		21. b	21. b	
		22. b		
		23. a		
		24. a		
		25. b		

CHAPTER 12	CHAPTER 13	CHAPTER 14	CHAPTER 15
1. a	1. c	1. c	1. c
2. b	2. b	2. b	2. b
3. d	3. d	3. d	3. a
4. b	4. a	4. c	4. b
5. a	5. d	5. c	5. a
6. c	6. c	6. d	6. c
7. b	7. c	7. b	7. d
8. d	8. b	8. c	8. b
9. b	9. b	9. c	9. d
10. c	10. b	10. a	10. d
11. c		11. a	11. b
12. a		12. c	12. b
13. c		13. d	13. a
14. d		14. c	14. d
15. d		15. a	15. b
16. c		16. d	16. c
17. c		17. d	17. c
18. a		18. a	18. d
19. c		19. b	19. a
20. c		20. c	20. a
21. c			21. c
22. a			22. c
			23. d
			24. c
			25. d

CHAPTER 16	CHAPTER 17	CHAPTER 18
1. b	1. a	1. c
2. a	2. c	2. c
3. c	3. c	3. d
4. d	4. c	4. c
5. c	5. d	5. c
6. b	6. a	6. d
7. d	7. c	7. c
8. b	8. b	8. a
9. a	9. b	9. c
10. d	10. c	10. a
11. a	11. a	11. d
12. c	12. a	12. c
13. c	13. a	13. d
14. a	14. b	14. a
15. b	15. c	15. b
16. b	16. d	16. c
17. b	17. b	17. d
18. c	18. a	18. d
		19. c
		20. c

CHAPTER 19

1. b $200' \times 170' = 34,000$ sq. ft.
$20 \times 20 = 40$ sq. ft. $\div 2 = 200$ sq. ft.
$34,000$ sq. ft. $- 200$ sq. ft. $= 33,800$ sq. ft.

2. b $2.5 \times 10 = 25\%$ depreciation
$100\% - 25 = 75\%$
$12,500 \div .75 = \$16,666$

3. d $\$11,000 \times .30 = \$3,300$
$\$3,300 \times .012$ mills $= \$39.60$
(*approximate* tax is $40.00)

4. c $\$300 \div 20,000 = .015$ mill levy
$\$40,000 \times .015 = \$600$

5. c 360 acres $\times \$150 = \$54,000$
$\$25,000 \times .05 = \$1,250$
$\$20,000 \times .025 = \$500$
$9,000 \times .01 = \$90$
Total commission $= \$1,840$
Half to Morris's firm $= \$920$
Half of $920 to Mr. Lewis $= \$460$

6. b $900' \times 900' = 810,000$ sq. ft.
$300 \times 90 = 27,000$ sq. ft.
$810,000 \div 27,000 = 1/30$

7. d 1 foot $= 1/8$, or 8 ft. $= 1$ inch
$8 \times 5\frac{3}{4} = 46$
$8 \times 4\frac{1}{2} = 36$
area $= 46 \times 36$

8. b July 15 through December $31 = 5\frac{1}{2}$ months unused
$\$546 + \$102 = \$648 \div 12$ months $= \$54$ per month
$\$54 \times 5\frac{1}{2}$ months $= \$297$

9. b June 15 through December $31 = 6\frac{1}{2}$ months unused
$660 \div 12 = \$55$ month $\times 6\frac{1}{2}$ months $= \$357.50$

10. a $\$275 \times 10 = \$2,750$ per month $\times 12$ months $= \$33,000$ annual rent
$\$250 \times 12 = \$3,000$ per month $\times 12$ months $= \$36,000$ annual rent
$\$33,000 + \$36,000 = \$69,000 \times 15\%$ vacancy $= \$10,350$
$\$69,000 - \$10,350 = \$58,650 - \$6,789$ (expenses) $= \$51,861$
$\$51,861 \div 10\% = \$518,610$

11. a $\$62,000 \times .80 = \$49,600$ loan $\times .04 = \$1,984.00$ (discount points)
$\$1,984.00 + \$2,500 = \$4,484$
$\$62,000 - \$49,600 = \$12,400$ down payment plus $\$4,484 = \$16,884$ total

12. b $\$350 + \$12,500 + \$7,000 = \$19,850 \div .94 = \$21,117.02$

13. a 25% depreciation $\times \$300,000 = \$75,000$
$\$300,000 - \$75,000 = \$225,000 + \$51,000 = \$276,000$

14. d $120' \times 80' = 9,600$ sq. ft. $\times .06 = \$576.00$

15. c $\$50,000 \times 1.10 = \$55.00$

16. c $19,000 \times .12 = 2,280 \div 12 = \$190.00$ interest per month
$\$275 - \$190 = \$85.00$ towards principal
$19,000 - 85 = 18,915 \times 12 = 2,269.80 \div 12$ months $= \$189.15$

17. d 20 years $\times 12 = 240$ months
$\times \$275 = 66,000 - 19,000 = 47,000$

18. b $\$145 \times 5$ apartments $= \$725$ monthly
$\$725 \times 12$ months $= \$8,700 \times 90\% = \$7,830 \times .05 = \$391.50$
$\$1,400$ (expenses) $+ \$391.50 = \$1,791.50$ total expenses
$\$7,830$ (gross income) $- \$1791.50 = \$6038.50$ (yearly income)
$\$6,038.50 \div 12$ months $= \$503.21$

19. d 7% of $60,000 = 4,200$
5% of $60,000 = 3,000 \times 2$ years $= 6,000$
3% of $60,000 = 1,800 \times 4$ years $= 7,200$
$4,200 + 6,000 + 7,200 = \$17,400$

20. c $\$225 \times 52$ weeks $= \$11,700$
$\$370 \times 12$ months $= \$4,440$
$\$11,700 - \$4,400 = \$7,260$ net income
$\$7,260 \div 88,000 = .0825 = 8\frac{1}{4}\%$

21. d $\$13,000 = 5\%$ of what?
$\$13,000 \div 5\% = \$260,000 \div 110$ acres $= \$2,363.64$

22. b $\$1,500 \times 12 = 18,000 \div 430,000 = 4\%$

23. d $\$850,000 \times .35 = \$297,500$
$\$850,000 - \$297,500 = \$552,500$
$\$552,500 \div 12\% = \$4,604,166$

24. d $\$7.50 \times 20 = \$150$ payment
$\$360 \div 12$ months $= \$30$ taxes
$\$54 \div 36$ months $= \$1.50$ insurance
$\$150 + \$30 + \$1.50 = \$181.50$

25. c $108 \div 13.50 = 8$
$132 \div 16.50 = 8$
$1 \div 8 = \frac{1}{8}$; therefore $\frac{1}{8}'' = 1'$

26. d $\$42,000 + \$48,000 + \$36,500 + \$55,600 = \$182,100$
$\$90,000 \times 8\% = \$7,200$
$\$182,100 - \$90,000 = \$92,100 \times 2\% = \$1,842$
$\$1,842 + \$7,200 = \$9,042$ commission
$\$182,100 \times 6\% = \$10,926 - \$9,042 = \$1,884$ difference

27. d $\$85,000 \times .35 = \$29,750$ assessed value
$\$29,750 \div 100 = \$297.50$
$\$297.50 \times 3.05$ $(2.70 + .35) = \$907.38$

28. b $\$96,000 - \$60,000 = \$36,000 \div 5$ years $= \$7,200$ per year
$\$7,200 \div \$60,000 = 12\%$

29. d $\$2300 \div \$9200 = 25\%$

30. b $70' \times 80' = 5,600$ sq. ft.
$30' \times 80' = 2,400 \div 2 = 1,200$ sq. ft.
$5,600 + 1,200 = 6,800$ sq. ft.

Appendix: Real Estate Forms

This appendix of real estate forms includes various instruments and documents not previously introduced in the text. To facilitate ease of location they are listed according to subject matter.

Auction:
>buyer registration
>contract
>sale settlement

Buyer Forms:
>customer information
>estimated buyer's figures
>preliminary loan information
>what to bring to loan application

Deeds:
>corporate warranty
>general warranty
>joint tenancy warranty
>quitclaim
>warranty deed

Leases:
>farm lease
>house lease
>management contract
>quit notice

Listings:
>apartment listing
>commercial listing
>condominium listing
>house listing
>lot listing

Mortgages:
>deed of trust
>land contract
>mortgage

Purchase Agreement:
>addendum to purchase agreement
>indemnity agreement
>option to purchase
>purchase agreement

Seller Forms:
>comparable market analysis
>estimate of reasonable value
>estimated seller's figures
>listing worksheet

Date_____, 19___ **BUYER REGISTRATION** Page No._____

Sale_____ Location _____

BUYER NO.	NAME	ADDRESS	CITY & STATE	PHONE

TURN TO NEXT SHEET WHEN FULL - CONTINUE NUMBERS IN ORDER.

FIGURE A.1 Buyer registration for an auction.

Contract for Services for Conducting Auction

THIS CONTRACT entered into this .... day of .... ,19 ....

by and between ....

....

....

....

....

Parties of the first part and   Realty, of   , ...

.... parties of the second part, WITNESSETH:

Parties of the first part do by this contract employ and authorize   Realty ....

.... to arrange for, and conduct a public auction of the following described real estate, to-wit:

....

....

....

....

on the .... day of ...., 19 ......, and party of the first part agrees to pay party of the second part for services in arranging for and conducting said Auction of the above described real estate as follows, to-wit:

....

....

....

of the last bid made or received, said commission due and payable on day of Auction.

First parties agree that the property described herein will be sold to the highest bidder and will not be withdrawn from the sale either prior to sale or at time of sale, and that second party may advertise the fact that said described property will be sold to the highest bidder. Said first parties agree to furnish merchantable abstract of title and deliver premises by warranty deed.

Parties of the first part hereby appoint parties of the second part as their true and lawful attorneys-in-fact for the sole purpose of completing and filling in the consideration, down payment and purchaser at the close of the public auction of the above described property in the blank Agreement for Sale of Real Estate executed by parties of the second part, and to collect from said purchaser for first parties the down payment and to receipt for the same to the purchaser and hold such down payment in the trust account of second parties for first parties until final settlement is made for said property, and parties of the first part hereby ratify and confirm the acts of the parties of the second part in accordance with this Power of Attorney.

This contract made in duplicate, each signed copy of which is considered an original by all parties.

Witnesses   Party of the First Part

....

....

                                            ....

REALTY   **Parties of Second Part**
                                                REALTY

By ....

FIGURE A.2 Auction contract.

AUCTION SALE SETTLEMENT

Date _____ , 19_____

Owner _____

Address _____

Date of Sale _____

Location of Sale _____

Auctioneer _____ Clerk _____

Auctioneer's Commission $ _____

Clerk's Commission $ _____

Advertising Charges $ _____

Other Charges _____ $ _____

_____   _____

_____   _____

TOTAL CHARGES AND COMMISSIONS $ _____

Gross Proceeds of Sale $ _____

Less Charges and Commissions $ _____

TOTAL NET PROCEEDS OF SALE $ _____

I, _____ seller of merchandise, goods and/or property sold at public auction on (date) _____ at (location) _____ acknowledge and accept this settlement of proceeds of sale. I agree to accept all responsibility for providing merchantable title to all merchandise, goods and/or property sold, and for deliver of title to the purchasers.

_____   _____
(Date)   (Signed)

FIGURE A.3 Auction sale settlement.

CUSTOMER INFORMATION

NAME_____PHONE_____

ADDRESS_____CITY_____STATE_____ZIP_____

Please answer the following questions to aid us in finding the type of home you desire.

How many are there in your family?_____Adults___Children_____Children's Ages_____

How many bedrooms do you desire?_____How many baths?_____

What type of schools does your family require?　Elementary_____Junior High_____
Senior High_____College_____Parochial_____Other_____

In what area do you prefer to live?_____

Are you interested in city bus service?　Yes_____No_____

Do you want to be near a shopping center?　Yes_____No_____

What special features do you desire in a home? Family Room___Dining Room___Patio_____
Family Kitchen___Built-ins____Fireplace____Double Garage____Fence____Basement_____
Deck_____Hardwood Floors____Forced Air Heat_____Landscape_____Lot Size_____
Total Square Feet of Living Space_____

How soon must you move?_____Must you sell first?_____Do you want to trade?_____
Urgency_____Reason for buying_____

What is the most you feel you want to invest in a home?
 Price?_____Down Payment_____Monthly Payments_____

What type of financing do you prefer?
 Cash_____G.I._____FHA_____Conventional_____Loan Assumption_____

If new financing is required, we will need to know your approximate monthly or
annual earnings.　Monthly_____Annual_____

Where are you employed?_____Type of work_____

How long have you worked for your present employer?_____

Does your wife work?_____If so, where?_____

COMMENTS:_____

_____

APPOINTMENT RECORD: HOMES SHOWN:

FIGURE A.4 Customer information form.

ESTIMATED BUYER'S FIGURES

Property_____   Price_____

Tentative Closing Date_____

Total Initial Investment Needed   _____
Mortgage Balance   _____

Closing Costs

Credit Report   _____

Appraisal-FHA,VA,PMI,CONVENTIONAL   _____

Termite Inspection   _____

Attorney's Opinion/Title Insurance   _____

_____Percent Origination Fee   _____

Miscellaneous Savings and Loan Fees   _____

Interests   _____

Survey   _____

Recording   _____

_____   _____

_____   _____

TOTAL-------------------------------   _____   _____

ESCROW

(1) Year Hazard Insurance   _____

(1-2) Month Hazard Insurance   _____

(6-7) Month Taxes   _____

(1-2) Month FHA or PMI Insurance   _____

TOTAL-------------------------------   _____   _____

                            Estimate of Total Costs: _____

                            Less Amount Deposited: _____

                            Approximate Balance
                            Needed to Close
                            Transaction-------------   _____

Estimated Monthly Payment

Principal and Interest @_____% =   _____

Hazard Insurance (1/12)   =   _____

Taxes (1/12)   =   _____

Total Monthly Investment   =   _____

We understand that above figures are approximate and the approximate amount needed.

_____ _____   _____   _____
Purchaser   Date   Purchaser   Date

BY_____
   Salesman
                                      Reviewed by Sales Manager

FIGURE A.5 Estimated buyer's figures.

PRELIMINARY LOAN INFORMATION

NAME_____ ADDRESS _____

BORROWER'S EMPLOYMENT:

Monthly Salary (Base)_____ $_____

Overtime (if any)_____ $_____

Bonus and/or commission (per year)_____ $_____

Other Income (explain)_____

_____

Type of work_____

Employer_____ Number of years _____

CO-BORROWER'S EMPLOYMENT:

Monthly Salary_____ $_____

Occupation_____ Number of years employed_____

ESTIMATED LIQUID ASSETS:

Cash on hand or in the bank (including deposit) $_____
Approximate cash value of stocks and bonds $_____

Equity from sale of property (approximate) $_____

OBLIGATIONS:	Amount owed	Monthly Payment	Number of Months
Car Payment	$_____	$_____	_____
Other Monthly Payments	$_____	$_____	_____
_____	$_____	$_____	_____
_____	$_____	$_____	_____

Children: Number and ages_____

Does purchaser have any existing mortgage loans in his name?_____

Any suits or collections? _____Bankruptcies_____

Divorces?_____ If so, any alimony or child support obligations?_____

_____

_____   _____
Applicant   Date

FIGURE A.6 Preliminary loan information.

WHAT TO BRING TO LOAN APPLICATION

All Sources of Incomes
    Addresses of Companies
    Amount per month

All Accounts and Numbers
    Savings
    Checking
    Credit Union, Social Security Numbers

Stocks, Bonds, Certificates
    Their value
    Serial Numbers

Life Insurance
    Face Value
    Cash Value
    Who with

Estimate of Personal Property
    1. Cars & Boats
        Approximate value of each one
    2. All other Personal Property
        Estimate of value of everything you own (clothes, furniture
        dishes, all personal belongs-what replacement cost
        would be)

Debts
    Who you owe and how much
    Even if they have been paid off (this is excellent credit)

Marital Status
    If divorced and alimony or child support is required, a copy of
    Divorce Decree or substantiation of consistent payments for
    2 years are required

Checkbook
    You will need check for approximately $125-$150 for appraisal
    and credit check

FIGURE A.7 What to bring to loan application.

STATE OF..⎤
⎱ss.
County of..⎰

.... day of.................................... , 19........, at........................o'clock and....................minutes................M.,

and recorded in Book..........................of..at page..............................

....Reg. of Deeds

By..Deputy

Entered on numerical index and filed for record in the Register of Deeds Office of said County the

CORPORATION WARRANTY DEED

The grantor

a corporation organized and existing under and by virtue of the laws of the State of

in consideration of

received from grantee, does grant, bargain, sell convey and confirm unto

herein called the grantee whether one or more, the following described real property in

.... County, Nebraska:

To have and to hold the above described premises together with all tenements, hereditaments and appurtenances thereto belonging unto the grantee and to grantee's heirs and assigns forever.

And the grantor for itself and its successors does hereby covenant with the grantee and with grantee's heirs and assigns that grantor is lawfully seised of said premises; that they are free from encumbrance

that grantor has good right and lawful authority to convey the same: and that grantor warrants and will defend the title to said premises against the lawful claims of all persons whosoever.

In witness whereof, grantor has hereunto caused its corporate seal to be affixed and these presents signed by its   President.

Dated   19

....

By .... President

STATE OF NEBRASKA, County of ....:

Before me, a notary public qualified in said county, personally came

President of

, a corporation,

known to me to be the President and identical person who signed the foregoing instrument, and acknowledged the execution thereof to be his voluntary act and deed as such officer and the voluntary act and deed of said corporation and that its corporate seal was thereto affixed by its authority.

Witness my hand and notarial seal on ...., 19............

.... Notary Public.

My commission expires ...., 19......

FIGURE A.8
Corporate warranty deed.

GENERAL WARRANTY DEED

_____

_____ , Grantor,

whether one or more, in consideration of _____

_____Dollars ($ _____), receipt of

which is acknowledged, conveys to _____

_____ , Grantee,

whether one or more, the following described real estate (as defined in Neb. Rev. Stat. § 76-201) in

_____County

Grantor covenants (jointly and severally, if more than one) with the Grantee that Grantor:

(1) is lawfully seised of such real estate and that it is free from encumbrances _____

_____

_____

(2) has legal power and lawful authority to convey the same;
(3) warrants and will defend the title to the real estate against the lawful claims of all persons.

Executed: _____ , 19 _____ .

Grantor:

_____

_____

_____

STATE OF   COUNTY OF _____ :

The foregoing instrument was acknowledged before me on _____ ,

19 _____ , by _____ .

(Grantor)

_____

Notary Public

. . . .

STATE OF   COUNTY OF _____ :
Filed for record and entered in Numerical
Index on _____
at _____o'clock ___ .M., and recorded in Deed
Record _____
Page _____ .
By: _____
County or Deputy County Clerk
Register of Deeds or Deputy
Register of Deeds

FIGURE A.9 General warranty deed.

JOINT TENANCY WARRANTY DEED

_____

_____ , Grantor,

whether one or more, in consideration of _____

_____Dollars ($ _____), receipt of

which is acknowledged, conveys to _____

_____ , Grantees,

as joint tenants and not as tenants in common, the following described real estate (as defined in Neb. Rev. Stat.

§76-201) in _____County

Grantor covenants (jointly and severally, if more than one) with the Grantees that Grantor:

(1) is lawfully seised of such real estate and that it is free from encumbrances _____

_____

_____

(2) has legal power and lawful authority to convey the same;
(3) warrants and will defend the title to the real estate against the lawful claims of all persons.

It is the intention of all parties, that in the event of the death of either Grantee, the entire fee simple title to the real estate shall vest in the surviving Grantee.

Executed: _____ , 19 _____ .

Grantor:

_____

_____

_____

STATE OF   COUNTY OF _____ :

The foregoing instrument was acknowledged before me on _____ ,

19 _____ , by _____ .
                        (Grantor)

_____
                        Notary Public

. . . .

STATE OF   COUNTY OF _____ :
    Filed for record and entered in Numerical
Index on _____
at _____ o'clock ____ .M., and recorded in Deed
Record _____
Page _____ .
By: _____
    County or Deputy County Clerk
    Register of Deeds or Deputy
    Register of Deeds

FIGURE A.10 Joint tenancy warranty deed.

QUITCLAIM DEED

_____

_____ , Grantor,

whether one or more, in consideration of _____ ____

_____ Dollars ($ _____), receipt of

which is acknowledged, quitclaims and conveys to _____ ___

_____ , Grantee,

whether one or more, the following described real estate (as defined in Neb. Rev. Stat. §76-201) in

_____County

Executed: _____ , 19 _____ .

                Grantor:

                            _____

                            _____

                            _____

STATE OF   COUNTY OF _____ :

      The foregoing instrument was acknowledged before me on _____ ,

19 _____ , by _____ .

                                        (Grantor)

                        _____

                          Notary Public

. . . .

STATE OF   COUNTY OF _____ :

    Filed for record and entered in Numerical

Index on _____

at _____ o'clock ____.M., and recorded in Deed

Record _____

Page _____ .

By: _____

    County or Deputy County Clerk

    Register of Deeds or Deputy

    Register of Deeds

FIGURE A.11 Quitclaim deed.

-WARRANTY DEED

KNOW ALL MEN BY THESE PRESENTS:

THAT

of the County of   *and State of*   *for and in consideration of the sum of*

DOLLARS

in hand paid do   *hereby grant, bargain, sell, convey and confirm unto*

of the County of   *and State of*   *the following described real estate*
situated in   *in*   *County, and State of*   *to-wit:*

TO HAVE AND TO HOLD the premises above described, together with all the Tenements, Hereditaments and Appurtenances thereunto belonging, unto the said

     and to   *heirs and assigns forever.*
And   *do hereby covenant with the said Grantee*   *and with*   *heirs and assigns, that*
lawfully seized of said premises; that they are free from encumbrance

that   *have good right and lawful authority to sell the same; and*   *do*   *hereby covenant to warrant and*
defend the title to said premises against the lawful claims of all persons whomsoever.
     And the said   *hereby relinquishes all*

in and to the above described premises.

Signed this   *day of*   *, A. D. 19*

     In Presence of

_____

_____

_____

_____

STATE OF _____ } *ss.*   *On this* _____ *day of* _____ *, A. D. 19* ____ *, before*
_____ *County*   *me the undersigned* _____
a Notary Public, duly commissioned and qualified for and residing in said county,
personally came _____

_____

to me known to be the identical person _____ *whose name* _____
affixed to the foregoing instrument as grantor ____ *and acknowledged the same to*
be _____ *voluntary act and deed.*
Witness my hand and Notarial Seal the day and year last above written.

_____ *Notary Public.*

My Commission expires the _____ *day of* _____ *, 19* ____

FIGURE A.12 Warranty deed.

THIS AGREEMENT, Made and entered into this   day of

by and between

party of the first part, and

party of the second part, WITNESSETH, That the said party of the first part has this day leased unto the party of the second part the following described property, situated in the County of   and State of   to wit:

The   quarter of section   , in Township   , Range   of the P.M., together with the   buildings and improvements thereon from the   day of   , 19   to the   day of   , 19   and the said second party, in consideration of the leasing of the above premises, hereby covenants and agrees with the said party of the first party to pay the said party of the first part as rent for the same as follows, to-wit:

AND IT IS FURTHER EXPRESSLY AGREED between the parties hereto that the said party of the first part should   deem it necessary may, at the cost and expense of the party of the second part, employ men and equipment to go upon said premises and cultivate the crops and harvest them or to do anything that is necessary to promote their growth or save them at any time before they are in the granaries, the whole expense of the same to be a lien upon said second party's share of said crops.

AND IT IS FURTHER EXPRESSLY AGREED by the party of the second party that   will carefully protect all buildings, fences and improvements of every kind that are now on said premises or that may be erected thereon during the continuance of this lease; that   will promptly at the expiration of the term herein granted yield up possession of said premises, without notice, unto the party of the first part, in good repair.

AND IT IS FURTHER AGREED that the party of the first part and   agents may go upon said premises at any time to inspect the same or to make improvements thereon and to plow for future crops and to sow small grain in corn and stubble ground in the fall before the expiration of this lease.

AND IT IS FURTHER AGREED by the party of the second part that   will not sub-let nor in any manner release any part of the described premises without the consent of party of the first part.

The covenants herein shall extend to and be binding upon the heirs executors and administrators of the parties to this lease.

Signed this   day of   , 19

Witness

-------------------------------- -------------------------------------(SEAL)

-------------------------------- -------------------------------------(SEAL

-------------------------------- -------------------------------------(SEAL)

-------------------------------- -------------------------------------(SEAL)

FIGURE A.13 Farm lease.

THIS AGREEMENT Witnesseth: That I or we, _____

_____

_____

have this day rented to_____

_____

_____

in the present condition thereof, the premises known as;_____

_____

_____

_____

for the period of _____

from the _____day of _____, 19____, on the following terms and

conditions, to-wit: for the use and rent thereof the said lessee, hereby promises

to pay the lessor, or to his, her or their order _____

_____Dollars

per _____for the whole time above stated, and to pay the same _____

_____on the _____of each _____; that lessee
will not sub-let or allow any other tenant to come in with or under him, her or
them without the written consent of said lessor; that lessee will repair all injuries or damages done the premises during his, her or their occupancy, or pay for the
same; that all of his, her or their property, whether subject to legal exemption,
or not, shall be bound and subject to the payment of rents and damages thereof; that
lessee will comply with all city ordinances, will take good care of the buildings
and premises, and keep them free from filth, from danger or fire, and will keep the
side-walks free from ice and snow and the house and premises shall be kept clean.
If in default of the payment of rent for a period of _____days after the same
is due, lessee will at the request of said lessor quit and render to lessor the
peaceable possession thereof; but, for this cause, the obligation to pay shall not
cease; and finally at the end of lessees term, lessee will surrender to the said
lessor, his, her or their heirs and assigns, the peaceable possession of said demised premises with all the keys, bolts, latches and repairs, if any, in as good
condition as the same was received, the usual wear and tear.

   The said lessor reserves the privilege of entering and showing above property
to prospective renters during the last thirty-day period of this lease or for any
other reasonable purpose at any time._____

_____

_____

_____

_____

_____

   IN WITNESS WHEREOF the parties hereto have subscribed to two copies hereof, one
to be retained by each party.

   Dated this _____ day of _____, 19____.

Lessor_____   Lessee_____

Lessor_____   Lessee_____

FIGURE A.14 House lease.

MANAGEMENT AGREEMENT

_____(hereinafter called Owner), and _____
(hereinafter called Agent), agree as follows:

A. The Owner hereby employs the Agent exclusively to rent and manage the property known as _____
upon the terms hereinafter set forth, for a period of ___years beginning on the ___day of _____, 19___, and ending on the ___day of _____, 19___, and thereafter for yearly periods from time to time, unless on or before _____ the expiration of any such renewal period, either party hereto shall notify the other in writing that it decides to terminate this Agreement, in which case this Agreement shall be thereby terminated on said last mentioned date.

B. The Agent Agrees:

1. To accept the management of the above mentioned property and agrees to furnish services for the rental operation and management of the Premises.

2. To render a monthly statement of receipts, disbursements and charges to the Owner and to remit each month the net proceeds (provided Agent is not required to make any mortgage, escrow or tax payment on the first day of the following month). Agent will remit the net proceeds or the balance thereof after making allowance for such payments to the Owner. In case the disbursements and charges shall be in excess of the receipts, the Owner agrees to pay such excess promptly, nothing herein contained shall obligate the Agent to advance its own funds on behalf of the Owner.

3. The Agent agrees to have all employees who handle any money to be bonded.

C. The Owner Agrees: To give the Agent the following authority and powers (all or any which may be exercised in the name of the Owner) and agrees to assume all expenses in connection therewith:

1. To advertise the property, to display signs, and to rent said property. Agent will investigate prospective tenants and to sign leases, renew and or cancel existing leases and prepare and execute the new lease. To terminate tenancies and to sign and serve such notices as are deemed needful by the Agent; to institute and prosecute actions to remove tenants and to recover possession of the property; to sue for and recover rent: and, when expedient, to settle, compromise and release such actions or suits, or reinstate such tenancies.

2. To collect rents due or to become due and issue receipts to deposit all funds collected hereunder in the Agent's custodial account.

3. To refund tenants' security deposits at the expiration of leases.

4. To hire, discharge and pay all caretakers and other employees; to make all ordinary repairs and replacements necessary to preserve the property in its present condition and for the operating efficiency thereof and all alterations and decorating required to comply with lease requirements and to enter into agreements for all necessary repairs and maintenance; to purchase supplies and pay all bills.

a. To indemnify, defend and save the Agent harmless from all suits in connection with the Premises and from liability for damage to property and injuries to or death of any employee or other person whomsoever, and to carry at his (its) own expense public liability, and workmen's compensation insurance naming the Owner and the Agent and adequate to protect their interests.

5. To pay any expenses incurred by the Agent, including, without limitation, attorney's fees for counsel employed to represent the Agent or the Owner.

6. Owner agrees to pay to said agent ___per month or ___percent(___%) of the monthly gross receipts from the operation of the Premises during the period this Agreement remains in full force and effect, whichever is the greater amount.

7. This Agreement may be cancelled by Owner before the termination date specified in Paragraph 1 on not less than ___days prior written notice to the Agent, provided that such notice is accompanied by payment to the Agent of a cancellation fee in an amount equal to ___% of the management fee that would accrue over the remainder of the stated term of the Agreement. For this purpose the monthly management fee for the remainder of the stated term shall be presumed to be the same as that of the last month prior to service of the notice of cancellation.

IN WITNESS WHEREOF, the parties hereto have affixed or caused to be affixed their respective signatures this ___day of _____, 19___.

_____   _____
Witness   Owner

_____   _____
Witness   Agent

FIGURE A.15 Management contract.

THREE-DAY NOTICE TO QUIT

DATE: _____ _____

TO: _____
    _____
    _____

    Please be advised that this constitutes a Three-Day (3)-Day Notice to Quit as per the Nebraska Residential Landlord Tenant Act.

    You are hereby notified of the landlord's intent to terminate the lease three days subsequent to your receipt of this notice. If you fail to comply with the terms of your rental agreement within such period or to vacate the premises within said period, we shall be forced to commence legal action against you for possession of the premises and rent due and owing.

    This notice is premised upon the fact that you have failed to comply with the terms of your rental agreement by your non-payment of rent past due and owing for the month(s) of _____ , 19___ , in the amount of $_____.

    To avoid the applicable legal action for restitution and damages, you must deliver full payment to the undersigned within three (3) days of the receipt of this notice. Failure to so deliver the rent or possession will cause legal action to be commenced immediately.

FIGURE A.16 Quit notice.

APARTMENT LISTING

Name of Complex _____

Address _____

Owner _____ Phone_____

Number of Buildings _____ Number of Units _____

Number Furnished _____ Unfurnished _____

Elevator _____ Parking Stalls _____

Central Air _____ Garages _____

Heat _____

Lot Size _____ x _____

A. INCOME:

Studio _____ X $_____ = $_____
1 BR/1 Bath _____ X $_____ = $_____
2 BR/1 Bath _____ X $_____ = $_____
2 BR/2 Bath _____ X $_____ = $_____
__BR/__Bath _____ X $_____ = $_____

TOTAL MONTHLY INCOME. . . . . . . $_____ X 12 mos = $_____

Laundry room, vending machines $_____ X 12 mos = $_____

GROSS ANNUAL INCOME . . . .$_____

Less: _____% Vacancy Factor . . . . $_____

NET ANNUAL INCOME . . . .$_____

B. MORTGAGE DEBT SERVICE:

1st Mortgage
   Interest _____% Monthly Payment $_____ Annual $_____ Current Balance $_____
2nd Mortgage
   Interest _____% Monthly Payment $_____ Annual $_____ Current Balance $_____
3rd Mortgage
   Interest _____% Monthly Payment $_____ Annual $_____ Current Balance $_____

PER ANNUM MORTGAGE DEBT SERVICE $_____ Total $_____

C. FIXED EXPENSES:
   Taxes $_____
   Insurance $_____
   Licenses $_____
   Other $_____
TOTAL FIXED EXPENSES: $_____

SUMMARY:

   Net Annual Income $_____ $_____
   Mortgage debt service $_____
   Fixed Expenses $_____

   TOTAL EXPENSES $_____ $_____

CASH FLOW BEFORE DEPRECIATION
         AND TAXES $_____

D. OPERATING EXPENSES:
   Admin, Legal, Acctg. $_____
   Gas $_____
   Electricity $_____
   Water & Sewer $_____
   Telephone $_____
   Office Supplies $_____
   Janitor $_____
   Pool Supplies $_____
   Pool maintenance $_____
   Waste Disposal $_____
   Repairs & Maintenance $_____
   Management $_____
   Extermination $_____
   Other _____ $_____
   TOTAL OPERATING EXPENSE $_____

FIGURE A.17 Apartment listing.

(Execute in triplicate and file signed copy and typed data sheet with M.L.S. within 48 hours)

UNIFORM LISTING CONTRACT

....19.......

In consideration of your agreement to list and offer for sale the property hereafter described, and to use your efforts to find a purchaser therefore, I hereby give you the sole and exclusive right to and including ....to sell ....

....legal ....

....

together with electric and other attached fixtures, including shades, rods, venetian blinds, storm sash and screens, and TV antenna for the sum of $ ....,upon the following terms: ....

I agree to pay you a cash commission of ....% of the gross sales price, with minimum commission of $ ...., (whichever is greater) said commission to be payable on the happening of any one or more of the following events, to-wit:

If a sale is made, or a purchaser found, who is ready, willing and able to purchase the property before the expiration of this listing, by you, myself, or any other person, at the above price and terms or for any other price and terms I may agree to accept, or if this agreement is revoked or violated by me, or if you are prevented in closing the sale of this property by existing liens, judgments, or suits pending against this property, or the owners thereof, or if you are unfairly hindered by me in the showing of or attempting to sell said premises, within said period, or if within ....days after the expiration of this listing I make a sale of said premises to any one due to your efforts or advertising, done under this listing. This property is offered without respect to race, color, national origin or religion.

I hereby represent that to the best of my knowledge, information and belief the following describes the true condition of the hereinbefore described real estate and premises, to wit: a) there are no termites in the buildings; and b) the lower level or basement level under such residence is free from leakage or seepage of water. However, if termites or leakage or seepage are found in said building and it is known or discovered that any such condition existed prior to closing, I shall indemnify you for any loss or expense incurred by you as a result.

I agree to pay any assessments for paving, curb, sidewalk or utilities previously constructed or now under construction, but not yet assessed.

In case of the forfeiture, by a prospective purchaser, of any earnest money payment, upon the within described property, said earnest money, after expense incurred by you has been deducted, shall be divided one-half to the owners and one-half to the agent.

I agree to furnish a complete abstract certified to date of sale showing marketable title, or a Title Insurance Policy if necessary, to complete said sale

and to pay any expense incurred in perfecting the title in case the same is found defective, and convey within ....days

from date of sale, the property by warranty deed, or ....executed by all

persons having any interest therein, and clear of all encumbrances except ....

Possession to be given..

I agree to maintain until delivery of possession, the heating, air conditioning, water heater, sewer, plumbing and electrical systems and any built-in appliances in good and reasonable working condition. I further agree to hold you harmless from any and all causes of action, loss, damage or expense you may be subjected to arising in connection therewith.

For Sale sign and Lock Box permitted. Permission is given you to process, advertise and distribute this listing through the Multiple Listing Service to its participants.

Further, I authorize my mortgage lender to release all pertinent information relative to the status of my mortgage loan # .... on subject property, to the agent.

I hereby accept the above listing and agree to the terms thereon this day and date above written. Receipt of a copy of this agreement is hereby acknowledged.

Owners' Name (typed) ....   Owner..

....REALTOR® Owner..

....   Address..
Address   Phone

By ....   Telephone Residence .... Business ....

NOTES

The following will be used for computer search and is REQUIRED TO BE FILLED IN:

Lot Size *(Check One)*

☐ A — Less than ¼ acre	☐ D —1 to 3 acres
☐ B — ¼ to ½ acre	☐ E — 4 to 10 acres
☐ C — ½ to 1 acre	☐ F — More than 10 acres

Square Feet *(Check One)*

☐ A — 700 or Less	☐ F — 1800-2100
☐ B — 700-1000	☐ G —2100-2500
☐ C — 1000-1250	☐ H —2500-3000
☐ D — 1250-1500	☐ I — 3000-3500
☐ E — 1500-1800	☐ J — 3500-4000
	☐ K —4000 & more

See reverse side for data instructions
Rev. 9/79

COMMERCIAL				
Add			L #	
Bus Incl		Zoning	Area	
Bldg. Incl		Bldg Sz	Blk	
Inv. Incl		Sq Ft	CC	
Fix/Eq Incl		Stories	SCH OP INC	$
Heat		Age	VAC/LOSS	$
A/C		Ext	OP EXP	$
Swr.		Roof	NET OP INC.	$
Int Dec	Sn/La	Bsmt	1 Mtg	
Trash		Gar	Mtg. Bal	
Lease		Prk #	$	Int %
Renew	Tx Clse	Ceil Ht	Tax 19 $	
Lot Sz		Track	Elev	Terms
		Docks #	SpSys	
Legal				
Remarks:				
B #	P	A		R

This information, although believed to be accurate, is not guaranteed.

FIGURE A.18 Commercial listing.

(Execute in triplicate and file signed copy and typed data sheet with M.L.S. within 48 hours)
UNIFORM LISTING CONTRACT

....19 ....

In consideration of your agreement to list and offer for sale the property hereafter described, and to use your efforts to find a purchaser therefore, I hereby give you the sole and exclusive right to and including ....to sell ....

....legal ....

....

together with electric and other attached fixtures, including shades, rods, venetian blinds, storm sash and screens, and TV antenna for the sum of $ ....,upon the following terms:

I agree to pay you a cash commission of ....% of the gross sales price, with minimum commission of $ .... , (whichever is greater) said commission to be payable on the happening of any one or more of the following events, to-wit:

If a sale is made, or a purchaser found, who is ready, willing and able to purchase the property before the expiration of this listing, by you, myself, or any other person, at the above price and terms or for any other price and terms I may agree to accept, or if this agreement is revoked or violated by me, or if you are prevented in closing the sale of this property by existing liens, judgments, or suits pending against this property, or the owners thereof, or if you are unfairly hindered by me in the showing of or attempting to sell said premises, within said period, or if within ....days after the expiration of this listing I make a sale of said premises to any one due to your efforts or advertising, done under this listing. This property is offered without respect to race, color, national origin or religion.

I hereby represent that to the best of my knowledge, information and belief the following describes the true condition of the hereinbefore described real estate and premises, to wit: a) there are no termites in the buildings; and b) the lower level or basement level under such residence is free from leakage or seepage of water. However, if termites or leakage or seepage are found in said building and it is known or discovered that any such condition existed prior to closing, I shall indemnify you for any loss or expense incurred by you as a result.

I agree to pay any assessments for paving, curb, sidewalk or utilities previously constructed or now under construction, but not yet assessed.

In case of the forfeiture, by a prospective purchaser, of any earnest money payment, upon the within described property, said earnest money, after expense incurred by you has been deducted, shall be divided one-half to the owners and one-half to the agent.

I agree to furnish a complete abstract certified to date of sale showing marketable title, or a Title Insurance Policy if necessary, to complete said sale and to pay any expense incurred in perfecting the title in case the same is found defective, and convey within ....days from date of sale, the property by warranty deed, or...executed by all persons having any interest therein, and clear of all encumbrances except ....

Possession to be given...

I agree to maintain until delivery of possession, the heating, air conditioning, water heater, sewer, plumbing and electrical systems and any built-in appliances in good and reasonable working condition. I further agree to hold you harmless from any and all causes of action, loss, damage or expense you may be subjected to arising in connection therewith.

For Sale sign and Lock Box permitted. Permission is given you to process, advertise and distribute this listing through the Multiple Listing Service to its participants.

Further, I authorize my mortgage lender to release all pertinent information relative to the status of my mortgage loan # .... on subject property, to the agent.

I hereby accept the above listing and agree to the terms thereon this day and date above written. Receipt of a copy of this agreement is hereby acknowledged.

Owners' Name (typed) .... Owner ....

....REALTOR® Owner ....

.... Address ....
        Address   Phone

By .... Telephone Residence .... Business ....

NOTES

The following will be used for computer search and is REQUIRED TO BE FILLED IN:

Square Feet *(Check One)*

☐ A — 700 or Less	☐ F — 1800-2100
☐ B — 700-1000	☐ G — 2100-2500
☐ C — 1000-1250	☐ H — 2500-3000
☐ D — 1250-1500	☐ I — 3000-3500
☐ E — 1500-1800	☐ J — 3500-4000
	☐ K — 4000 & more

See reverse side for data instructions
Rev. 9/79

CONDOMINIUM

Add							L #	
Style		Poss		Oc	Age	Area		Bk
C	D	L	Room Size	Car	Gar	SID		LB
		LR		B%	WO	CC		
		DB		Ext	FP	1 MTG		
		Kit		RF	HT	MTG Bal.		
		FR		Fen	CA	Type		Int.
		RR		Pav	P/H	$		T	I
		BR		Swr	R/O	Tax 19		$
		BR		Wtr	Dsh	Conv		Eml
		BR		Gas	Disp	PMI		2 Fl
		BR		BA		LA		LL
Grd		J Hi				FHA		FinB
Par.		Hi				VA		FSF
Legal						Lot sz.		
						Mo. Asmt $		
Remarks					Inc.			
					Amen			
B #		P		A			R	

This information, although believed to be accurate, is not guaranteed.

FIGURE A.19 Condominium listing.

(Execute in triplicate and file signed copy and typed data sheet with M.L.S. within 48 hours)

UNIFORM LISTING CONTRACT

....19.......

In consideration of your agreement to list and offer for sale the property hereafter described, and to use your efforts to find a purchaser therefore, I hereby give you the sole and exclusive right to and including ....to sell ....

................................legal ....

....

together with electric and other attached fixtures, including shades, rods, venetian blinds, storm sash and screens, and TV antenna for the sum of $ ....,upon the following terms: ....

I agree to pay you a cash commission of ....% of the gross sales price, with minimum commission of $ .... , (whichever is greater) said commission to be payable on the happening of any one or more of the following events, to-wit:

If a sale is made, or a purchaser found, who is ready, willing and able to purchase the property before the expiration of this listing, by you, myself, or any other person, at the above price and terms or for any other price and terms I may agree to accept, or if this agreement is revoked or violated by me, or if you are prevented in closing the sale of this property by existing liens, judgments, or suits pending against this property, or the owners thereof, or if you are unfairly hindered by me in the showing of or attempting to sell said premises, within said period, or if within ....days after the expiration of this listing I make a sale of said premises to any one due to your efforts or advertising, done under this listing. This property is offered without respect to race, color, national origin or religion.

I hereby represent that to the best of my knowledge, information and belief the following describes the true condition of the hereinbefore described real estate and premises, to wit: a) there are no termites in the buildings; and b) the lower level or basement level under such residence is free from leakage or seepage of water. However, if termites or leakage or seepage are found in said building and it is known or discovered that any such condition existed prior to closing, I shall indemnify you for any loss or expense incurred by you as a result.

I agree to pay any assessments for paving, curb, sidewalk or utilities previously constructed or now under construction, but not yet assessed.

In case of the forfeiture, by a prospective purchaser, of any earnest money payment, upon the within described property, said earnest money, after expense incurred by you has been deducted, shall be divided one-half to the owners and one-half to the agent.

I agree to furnish a complete abstract certified to date of sale showing marketable title, or a Title Insurance Policy if necessary, to complete said sale and to pay any expense incurred in perfecting the title in case the same is found defective, and convey within ....days from date of sale, the property by warranty deed, or ....executed by all persons having any interest therein, and clear of all encumbrances except ....

Possession to be given................................

I agree to maintain until delivery of possession, the heating, air conditioning, water heater, sewer, plumbing and electrical systems and any built-in appliances in good and reasonable working condition. I further agree to hold you harmless from any and all causes of action, loss, damage or expense you may be subjected to arising in connection therewith.

For Sale sign and Lock Box permitted. Permission is given you to process, advertise and distribute this listing through the Multiple Listing Service to its participants.

Further, I authorize my mortgage lender to release all pertinent information relative to the status of my mortgage loan # .... on subject property, to the agent.

I hereby accept the above listing and agree to the terms thereon this day and date above written. Receipt of a copy of this agreement is hereby acknowledged.

Owners' Name (typed) .... Owner................................

................................REALTOR® Owner................................

.... Address................................
    Address   Phone

By .... Telephone Residence .... Business ....

NOTES

The following will be used for computer search and is REQUIRED TO BE FILLED IN.

Lot Size (Check One)

☐ A — Less than ¼ acre   ☐ D — 1 to 3 acres
☐ B — ¼ to ½ acre   ☐ E — 4 to 10 acres
☐ C — ½ to 1 acre   ☐ F — More than 10 acres

Square Feet *(Check One)*

☐ A — 700 or Less   ☐ F — 1800-2100
☐ B — 700-1000   ☐ G — 2100-2500
☐ C — 1000-1250   ☐ H — 2500-3000
☐ D — 1250-1500   ☐ I — 3000-3500
☐ E — 1500-1800   ☐ J — 3500-4000
                ☐ K — 4000 & more

See reverse side for data instructions
Rev. 9/79

RESIDENTIAL

Add					L #		
Style		Poss	Oc	Age	Area		Bk
C	D	L	Room Size	Car Gar	SID	LB	
		LR		B%	WO	CC	
		DR		Ext	FP	1 Mtg	
		Kit		RF	HT	Mtg. Bal	
		FR		Fen	CA	Type	Int	%
		RR		Pav	P/H	$	T	I
		BR		Swr	R/O	Tax 19	$
		BR		Wtr	Dsh	CONV	Eml
		BR		Gas	Disp	PMI	2 Fl
		BR		BA		LA	LL
Grd			J Hi		FHA	Fin B
Par			Hi		VA	FSF
Legal					Lot sz.	

Remarks

B #	P	A	R

This information, although believed to be accurate, is not guaranteed.

FIGURE A.20 House listing.

(Execute in triplicate and file signed copy and typed data sheet with M.L.S. within 48 hours)

UNIFORM LISTING CONTRACT

.... .19 ......

In consideration of your agreement to list and offer for sale the property hereafter described, and to use your efforts to find a purchaser therefore, I hereby give you the sole and exclusive right to and including .... to sell ....

.... legal ....

....

together with electric and other attached fixtures, including shades, rods, venetian blinds, storm sash and screens, and TV antenna for the sum of

$ .... upon the following terms: ....

I agree to pay you a cash commission of .... % of the gross sales price, with minimum commission of $ .... , (whichever is greater) said commission to be payable on the happening of any one or more of the following events, to-wit:

If a sale is made, or a purchaser found, who is ready, willing and able to purchase the property before the expiration of this listing, by you, myself, or any other person, at the above price and terms or for any other price and terms I may agree to accept, or if this agreement is revoked or violated by me, or if you are prevented in closing the sale of this property by existing liens, judgments, or suits pending against this property, or the owners thereof, or if you are unfairly hindered by me in the showing of or attempting to sell said premises, within said period, or if within .... days after the expiration of this listing I make a sale of said premises to any one due to your efforts or advertising, done under this listing. This property is offered without respect to race, color, national origin or religion.

I hereby represent that to the best of my knowledge, information and belief the following describes the true condition of the hereinbefore described real estate and premises, to wit: a) there are no termites in the buildings; and b) the lower level or basement level under such residence is free from leakage or seepage of water. However, if termites or leakage or seepage are found in said building and it is known or discovered that any such condition existed prior to closing, I shall indemnify you for any loss or expense incurred by you as a result.

I agree to pay any assessments for paving, curb, sidewalk or utilities previously constructed or now under construction, but not yet assessed.

In case of the forfeiture, by a prospective purchaser, of any earnest money payment, upon the within described property, said earnest money, after expense incurred by you has been deducted, shall be divided one-half to the owners and one-half to the agent.

I agree to furnish a complete abstract certified to date of sale showing marketable title, or a Title Insurance Policy if necessary, to complete said sale and to pay any expense incurred in perfecting the title in case the same is found defective, and convey within .... days

from date of sale, the property by warranty deed, or .... executed by all

persons having any interest therein, and clear of all encumbrances except ....

Possession to be given ....

I agree to maintain until delivery of possession, the heating, air conditioning, water heater, sewer, plumbing and electrical systems and any built-in appliances in good and reasonable working condition. I further agree to hold you harmless from any and all causes of action, loss, damage or expense you may be subjected to arising in connection therewith.

For Sale sign and Lock Box permitted. Permission is given you to process, advertise and distribute this listing through the Multiple Listing Service to its participants.

Further, I authorize my mortgage lender to release all pertinent information relative to the status of my mortgage loan # .... on subject property, to the agent.

I hereby accept the above listing and agree to the terms thereon this day and date above written. Receipt of a copy of this agreement is hereby acknowledged.

Owners' Name (typed) .... Owner ....

.... REALTOR® Owner ....

.... Address ....
         Address   Phone

By .... Telephone Residence .... Business ....

NOTES

GROUND OR LOT		
Add		L #
Zoning	Rstr.	Area
In City	Cov.	Blk
Corner	Sp. Asmt $	CC
Swr	SID #	Faces
Wtr	Paved	Lndscp
Gas	Curb	
Elec	Sdwk	Grade
Tax$	Alley	
Terms		
Lot Sz		
Legal		
Remarks:		

B #	P	A	R

This information, although believed to be accurate, is not guaranteed.

The following will be used for computer search and is REQUIRED TO BE FILLED IN:

Lot Size (Check One)

☐ A — Less than ¼ acre   ☐ D — 1 to 3 acres
☐ B — ¼ to ½ acre   ☐ E — 4 to 10 acres
☐ C — ½ to 1 acre   ☐ F — More than 10 acres

See reverse side for data instructions
Rev. 9/79

FIGURE A.21 Lot listing.

DEED OF TRUST

THIS DEED OF TRUST is made this.........................day of ....
19...., among the Trustor,...
....(herein "Borrower"),....   ....
....(herein "Trustee"), and the Beneficiary,
..   .., a corporation organized and
existing under the laws of................   ...., whose address is...............
...   .(herein "Lender").

BORROWER, in consideration of the indebtedness herein recited and the trust herein created, irrevocably grants and conveys to Trustee, in trust, with power of sale, the following described property located in the County of
...   ., State of

which has the address of...
[Street]   [City]
........................(herein "Property Address");
[State and Zip Code]

TOGETHER with all the improvements now or hereafter erected on the property, and all easements, rights, appurtenances, rents (subject however to the rights and authorities given herein to Lender to collect and apply such rents), royalties, mineral, oil and gas rights and profits, water, water rights, and water stock, and all fixtures now or hereafter attached to the property, all of which, including replacements and additions thereto, shall be deemed to be and remain a part of the property covered by this Deed of Trust; and all of the foregoing, together with said property (or the leasehold estate if this Deed of Trust is on a leasehold) are herein referred to as the "Property";

To SECURE to Lender (a) the repayment of the indebtedness evidenced by Borrower's note dated............
............(herein "Note"), in the principal sum of...
....Dollars, with interest thereon, providing for monthly installments of principal and interest, with the balance of the indebtedness, if not sooner paid, due and payable on............
....................................; the payment of all other sums, with interest thereon, advanced in accordance herewith to protect the security of this Deed of Trust; and the performance of the covenants and agreements of Borrower herein contained; and (b) the repayment of any future advances, with interest thereon, made to Borrower by Lender pursuant to paragraph 21 hereof (herein "Future Advances").

Borrower covenants that Borrower is lawfully seised of the estate hereby conveyed and has the right to grant and convey the Property, that the Property is unencumbered, and that Borrower will warrant and defend generally the title to the Property against all claims and demands, subject to any declarations, easements or restrictions listed in a schedule of exceptions to coverage in any title insurance policy insuring Lender's interest in the Property.

–1 to 4 Family—1/76—**FNMA/FHLMC UNIFORM INSTRUMENT**   (2653-4)
SAF (American Savings & Accounting Supply, Inc.)

FIGURE A.22(a) Deed of trust.

UNIFORM COVENANTS. Borrower and Lender covenant and agree as follows:

1. Payment of Principal and Interest. Borrower shall promptly pay when due the principal of and interest on the indebtedness evidenced by the Note, prepayment and late charges as provided in the Note, and the principal of and interest on any Future Advances secured by this Deed of Trust.

2. Funds for Taxes and Insurance. Subject to applicable law or to a written waiver by Lender, Borrower shall pay to Lender on the day monthly installments of principal and interest are payable under the Note, until the Note is paid in full, a sum (herein "Funds") equal to one-twelfth of the yearly taxes and assessments which may attain priority over this Deed of Trust, and ground rents on the Property, if any, plus one-twelfth of yearly premium installments for hazard insurance, plus one-twelfth of yearly premium installments for mortgage insurance, if any, all as reasonably estimated initially and from time to time by Lender on the basis of assessments and bills and reasonable estimates thereof.

The Funds shall be held in an institution the deposits or accounts of which are insured or guaranteed by a Federal or state agency (including Lender if Lender is such an institution). Lender shall apply the Funds to pay said taxes, assessments, insurance premiums and ground rents. Lender may not charge for so holding and applying the Funds, analyzing said account or verifying and compiling said assessments and bills, unless Lender pays Borrower interest on the Funds and applicable law permits Lender to make such a charge. Borrower and Lender may agree in writing at the time of execution of this Deed of Trust that interest on the Funds shall be paid to Borrower, and unless such agreement is made or applicable law requires such interest to be paid, Lender shall not be required to pay Borrower any interest or earnings on the Funds. Lender shall give to Borrower, without charge, an annual accounting of the Funds showing credits and debits to the Funds and the purpose for which each debit to the Funds was made. The Funds are pledged as additional security for the sums secured by this Deed of Trust.

If the amount of the Funds held by Lender, together with the future monthly installments of Funds payable prior to the due dates of taxes, assessments, insurance premiums and ground rents, shall exceed the amount required to pay said taxes, assessments, insurance premiums and ground rents as they fall due, such excess shall be, at Borrower's option, either promptly repaid to Borrower or credited to Borrower on monthly installments of Funds. If the amount of the Funds held by Lender shall not be sufficient to pay taxes, assessments, insurance premiums and ground rents as they fall due, Borrower shall pay to Lender any amount necessary to make up the deficiency within 30 days from the date notice is mailed by Lender to Borrower requesting payment thereof.

Upon payment in full of all sums secured by this Deed of Trust, Lender shall promptly refund to Borrower any Funds held by Lender. If under paragraph 18 hereof the Property is sold or the Property is otherwise acquired by Lender, Lender shall apply, no later than immediately prior to the sale of the Property or its acquisition by Lender, any Funds held by Lender at the time of application as a credit against the sums secured by this Deed of Trust.

3. Application of Payments. Unless applicable law provides otherwise, all payments received by Lender under the Note and paragraphs 1 and 2 hereof shall be applied by Lender first in payment of amounts payable to Lender by Borrower under paragraph 2 hereof, then to interest payable on the Note, then to the principal of the Note, and then to interest and principal on any Future Advances.

4. Charges; Liens. Borrower shall pay all taxes, assessments and other charges, fines and impositions attributable to the Property which may attain a priority over this Deed of Trust, and leasehold payments or ground rents, if any, in the manner provided under paragraph 2 hereof or, if not paid in such manner, by Borrower making payment, when due, directly to the payee thereof. Borrower shall promptly furnish to Lender all notices of amounts due under this paragraph, and in the event Borrower shall make payment directly, Borrower shall promptly furnish to Lender receipts evidencing such payments. Borrower shall promptly discharge any lien which has priority over this Deed of Trust; provided, that Borrower shall not be required to discharge any such lien so long as Borrower shall agree in writing to the payment of the obligation secured by such lien in a manner acceptable to Lender, or shall in good faith contest such lien by, or defend enforcement of such lien in, legal proceedings which operate to prevent the enforcement of the lien or forfeiture of the Property or any part thereof.

5. Hazard Insurance. Borrower shall keep the improvements now existing or hereafter erected on the Property insured against loss by fire, hazards included within the term "extended coverage", and such other hazards as Lender may require and in such amounts and for such periods as Lender may require; provided, that Lender shall not require that the amount of such coverage exceed that amount of coverage required to pay the sums secured by this Deed of Trust.

The insurance carrier providing the insurance shall be chosen by Borrower subject to approval by Lender; provided, that such approval shall not be unreasonably withheld. All premiums on insurance policies shall be paid in the manner provided under paragraph 2 hereof or, if not paid in such manner, by Borrower making payment, when due, directly to the insurance carrier.

All insurance policies and renewals thereof shall be in form acceptable to Lender and shall include a standard mortgage clause in favor of and in form acceptable to Lender. Lender shall have the right to hold the policies and renewals thereof, and Borrower shall promptly furnish to Lender all renewal notices and all receipts of paid premiums. In the event of loss, Borrower shall give prompt notice to the insurance carrier and Lender. Lender may make proof of loss if not made promptly by Borrower.

Unless Lender and Borrower otherwise agree in writing, insurance proceeds shall be applied to restoration or repair of the Property damaged, provided such restoration or repair is economically feasible and the security of this Deed of Trust is not thereby impaired. If such restoration or repair is not economically feasible or if the security of this Deed of Trust would be impaired, the insurance proceeds shall be applied to the sums secured by this Deed of Trust, with the excess, if any, paid to Borrower. If the Property is abandoned by Borrower, or if Borrower fails to respond to Lender within 30 days from the date notice is mailed by Lender to Borrower that the insurance carrier offers to settle a claim for insurance benefits, Lender is authorized to collect and apply the insurance proceeds at Lender's option either to restoration or repair of the Property or to the sums secured by this Deed of Trust.

Unless Lender and Borrower otherwise agree in writing, any such application of proceeds to principal shall not extend or postpone the due date of the monthly installments referred to in paragraphs 1 and 2 hereof or change the amount of such installments. If under paragraph 18 hereof the Property is acquired by Lender, all right, title and interest of Borrower in and to any insurance policies and in and to the proceeds thereof resulting from damage to the Property prior to the sale or acquisition shall pass to Lender to the extent of the sums secured by this Deed of Trust immediately prior to such sale or acquisition.

6. Preservation and Maintenance of Property; Leaseholds; Condominiums; Planned Unit Developments. Borrower shall keep the Property in good repair and shall not commit waste or permit impairment or deterioration of the Property and shall comply with the provisions of any lease if this Deed of Trust is on a leasehold. If this Deed of Trust is on a unit in a condominium or a planned unit development, Borrower shall perform all of Borrower's obligations under the declaration or covenants creating or governing the condominium or planned unit development, the by-laws and regulations of the condominium or planned unit development, and constituent documents. If a condominium or planned unit development rider is executed by Borrower and recorded together with this Deed of Trust, the covenants and agreements of such rider shall be incorporated into and shall amend and supplement the covenants and agreements of this Deed of Trust as if the rider were a part hereof.

7. Protection of Lender's Security. If Borrower fails to perform the covenants and agreements contained in this Deed of Trust, or if any action or proceeding is commenced which materially affects Lender's interest in the Property, including, but not limited to, eminent domain, insolvency, code enforcement, or arrangements or proceedings involving a bankrupt or decedent, then Lender at Lender's option, upon notice to Borrower, may make such appearances, disburse such sums and take such action as is necessary to protect Lender's interest, including, but not limited to, disbursement of reasonable attorney's fees and entry upon the Property to make repairs. If Lender required mortgage insurance as a condition of making the loan secured by this Deed of Trust, Borrower shall pay the premiums required to maintain such insurance in effect until such time as the requirement for such insurance terminates in accordance with Borrower's and Lender's written agreement or applicable law. Borrower shall pay the amount of all mortgage insurance premiums in the manner provided under paragraph 2 hereof.

Any amounts disbursed by Lender pursuant to this paragraph 7, with interest thereon, shall become additional indebtedness of Borrower secured by this Deed of Trust. Unless Borrower and Lender agree to other terms of payment, such amounts shall be payable upon notice from Lender to Borrower requesting payment thereof, and shall bear interest from the date of disbursement at the rate payable from time to time on outstanding principal under the Note unless payment of interest at such rate would be contrary to applicable law, in which event such amounts shall bear interest at the highest rate permissible under applicable law. Nothing contained in this paragraph 7 shall require Lender to incur any expense or take any action hereunder.

8. Inspection. Lender may make or cause to be made reasonable entries upon and inspections of the Property, provided that Lender shall give Borrower notice prior to any such inspection specifying reasonable cause therefor related to Lender's interest in the Property.

FIGURE A.22(b) Deed of trust (continued).

9. Condemnation. The proceeds of any award or claim for damages, direct or consequential, in connection with any condemnation or other taking of the Property, or part thereof, or for conveyance in lieu of condemnation, are hereby assigned and shall be paid to Lender.

In the event of a total taking of the Property, the proceeds shall be applied to the sums secured by this Deed of Trust, with the excess, if any, paid to Borrower. In the event of a partial taking of the Property, unless Borrower and Lender otherwise agree in writing, there shall be applied to the sums secured by this Deed of Trust such proportion of the proceeds as is equal to that proportion which the amount of the sums secured by this Deed of Trust immediately prior to the date of taking bears to the fair market value of the Property immediately prior to the date of taking, with the balance of the proceeds paid to Borrower.

If the Property is abandoned by Borrower, or if, after notice by Lender to Borrower that the condemnor offers to make an award or settle a claim for damages, Borrower fails to respond to Lender within 30 days after the date such notice is mailed, Lender is authorized to collect and apply the proceeds, at Lender's option, either to restoration or repair of the Property or to the sums secured by this Deed of Trust.

Unless Lender and Borrower otherwise agree in writing, any such application of proceeds to principal shall not extend or postpone the due date of the monthly installments referred to in paragraphs 1 and 2 hereof or change the amount of such installments.

10. Borrower Not Released. Extension of the time for payment or modification of amortization of the sums secured by this Deed of Trust granted by Lender to any successor in interest of Borrower shall not operate to release, in any manner, the liability of the original Borrower and Borrower's successors in interest. Lender shall not be required to commence proceedings against such successor or refuse to extend time for payment or otherwise modify amortization of the sums secured by this Deed of Trust by reason of any demand made by the original Borrower and Borrower's successors in interest.

11. Forbearance by Lender Not a Waiver. Any forbearance by Lender in exercising any right or remedy hereunder, or otherwise afforded by applicable law, shall not be a waiver of or preclude the exercise of any such right or remedy. The procurement of insurance or the payment of taxes or other liens or charges by Lender shall not be a waiver of Lender's right to accelerate the maturity of the indebtedness secured by this Deed of Trust.

12. Remedies Cumulative. All remedies provided in this Deed of Trust are distinct and cumulative to any other right or remedy under this Deed of Trust or afforded by law or equity, and may be exercised concurrently, independently or successively.

13. Successors and Assigns Bound; Joint and Several Liability; Captions. The covenants and agreements herein contained shall bind, and the rights hereunder shall inure to, the respective successors and assigns of Lender and Borrower, subject to the provisions of paragraph 17 hereof. All covenants and agreements of Borrower shall be joint and several. The captions and headings of the paragraphs of this Deed of Trust are for convenience only and are not to be used to interpret or define the provisions hereof.

14. Notice. Except for any notice required under applicable law to be given in another manner, (a) any notice to Borrower provided for in this Deed of Trust shall be given by mailing such notice by certified mail addressed to Borrower at the Property Address or at such other address as Borrower may designate by notice to Lender as provided herein, and (b) any notice to Lender shall be given by certified mail, return receipt requested, to Lender's address stated herein or to such other address as Lender may designate by notice to Borrower as provided herein. Any notice provided for in this Deed of Trust shall be deemed to have been given to Borrower or Lender when given in the manner designated herein.

15. Uniform Deed of Trust; Governing Law; Severability. This form of deed of trust combines uniform covenants for national use and non-uniform covenants with limited variations by jurisdiction to constitute a uniform security instrument covering real property. This Deed of Trust shall be governed by the law of the jurisdiction in which the Property is located. In the event that any provision or clause of this Deed of Trust or the Note conflicts with applicable law, such conflict shall not affect other provisions of this Deed of Trust or the Note which can be given effect without the conflicting provision, and to this end the provisions of the Deed of Trust and the Note are declared to be severable.

16. Borrower's Copy. Borrower shall be furnished a conformed copy of the Note and of this Deed of Trust at the time of execution or after recordation hereof.

17. Transfer of the Property; Assumption. If all or any part of the Property or an interest therein is sold or transferred by Borrower without Lender's prior written consent, excluding (a) the creation of a lien or encumbrance subordinate to this Deed of Trust, (b) the creation of a purchase money security interest for household appliances, (c) a transfer by devise, descent or by operation of law upon the death of a joint tenant or (d) the grant of any leasehold interest of three years or less not containing an option to purchase, Lender may, at Lender's option, declare all the sums secured by this Deed of Trust to be immediately due and payable. Lender shall have waived such option to accelerate if, prior to the sale or transfer, Lender and the person to whom the Property is to be sold or transferred reach agreement in writing that the credit of such person is satisfactory to Lender and that the interest payable on the sums secured by this Deed of Trust shall be at such rate as Lender shall request. If Lender has waived the option to accelerate provided in this paragraph 17, and if Borrower's successor in interest has executed a written assumption agreement accepted in writing by Lender, Lender shall release Borrower from all obligations under this Deed of Trust and the Note.

If Lender exercises such option to accelerate, Lender shall mail Borrower notice of acceleration in accordance with paragraph 14 hereof. Such notice shall provide a period of not less than 30 days from the date the notice is mailed within which Borrower may pay the sums declared due. If Borrower fails to pay such sums prior to the expiration of such period, Lender may, without further notice or demand on Borrower, invoke any remedies permitted by paragraph 18 hereof.

Non-Uniform Covenants. Borrower and Lender further covenant and agree as follows:

18. Acceleration; Remedies. Except as provided in paragraph 17 hereof, upon Borrower's breach of any covenant or agreement of Borrower in this Deed of Trust, including the covenants to pay when due any sums secured by this Deed of Trust, Lender prior to acceleration shall mail notice to Borrower as provided in paragraph 14 hereof specifying: (1) the breach; (2) the action required to cure such breach; (3) a date, not less than 30 days from the date the notice is mailed to Borrower, by which such breach must be cured; and (4) that failure to cure such breach on or before the date specified in the notice may result in acceleration of the sums secured by this Deed of Trust and sale of the Property. The notice shall further inform Borrower of the right to reinstate after acceleration and the right to bring a court action to assert the non-existence of a default or any other defense of Borrower to acceleration and sale. If the breach is not cured on or before the date specified in the notice, Lender at Lender's option may declare all of the sums secured by this Deed of Trust to be immediately due and payable without further demand and may invoke the power of sale and any other remedies permitted by applicable law. Lender shall be entitled to collect all reasonable costs and expenses incurred in pursuing the remedies provided in this paragraph 18, including, but not limited to, reasonable attorney's fees.

If the power of sale is invoked, Trustee shall record a notice of default in each county in which the Property or some part thereof is located and shall mail copies of such notice in the manner prescribed by applicable law to Borrower and to the other persons prescribed by applicable law. After the lapse of such time as may be required by applicable law, Trustee shall give public notice of sale to the persons and in the manner prescribed by applicable law. Trustee, without demand on Borrower, shall sell the Property at public auction to the highest bidder at the time and place and under the terms designated in the notice of sale in one or more parcels and in such order as Trustee may determine. Trustee may postpone sale of all or any parcel of the Property by public announcement at the time and place of any previously scheduled sale. Lender or Lender's designee may purchase the Property at any sale.

Upon receipt of payment of the price bid, Trustee shall deliver to the purchaser Trustee's deed conveying the Property sold. The recitals in the Trustee's deed shall be prima facie evidence of the truth of the statements made therein. Trustee shall apply the proceeds of the sale in the following order: (a) to all reasonable costs and expenses of the sale, including, but not limited to, Trustee's fees of not more than ½ of 1 % of the gross sale price, reasonable attorney's fees and costs of title evidence; (b) to all sums secured by this Deed of Trust; and (c) the excess, if any, to the person or persons legally entitled thereto.

19. Borrower's Right to Reinstate. Notwithstanding Lender's acceleration of the sums secured by this Deed of Trust, Borrower shall have the right to have any proceedings begun by Lender to enforce this Deed of Trust discontinued at any time prior to the earlier to occur of (i) the fifth day before the sale of the Property pursuant to the power of sale contained in this Deed of Trust or (ii) entry of a judgment enforcing this Deed of Trust if: (a) Borrower pays Lender all sums which would be then due under this Deed of Trust, the Note and notes securing Future Advances, if any, had no acceleration occurred; (b) Borrower cures all breaches of any other covenants or agreements of Borrower contained in this Deed of Trust; (c) Borrower pays all reasonable expenses incurred by Lender and Trustee in enforcing the covenants and agreements of Borrower contained in this Deed of Trust and in enforcing Lender's and Trustee's remedies as provided in paragraph 18 hereof, including, but not limited to, reasonable attorney's fees; and (d) Borrower takes such action as Lender may reasonably require to assure that the lien of this Deed of Trust, Lender's interest in the Property and Borrower's obligation to pay

FIGURE A.22(c) Deed of trust (continued).

the sums secured by this Deed of Trust shall continue unimpaired. Upon such payment and cure by Borrower, this Deed of Trust and the obligations secured hereby shall remain in full force and effect as if no acceleration had occurred.

20. Assignment of Rents; Appointment of Receiver; Lender in Possession. As additional security hereunder, Borrower hereby assigns to Lender the rents of the Property, provided that Borrower shall, prior to acceleration under paragraph 18 hereof or abandonment of the Property, have the right to collect and retain such rents as they become due and payable.

Upon acceleration under paragraph 18 hereof or abandonment of the Property, Lender, in person, by agent or by judicially appointed receiver, shall be entitled to enter upon, take possession of and manage the Property and to collect the rents of the Property including those past due. All rents collected by Lender or the receiver shall be applied first to payment of the costs of management of the Property and collection of rents, including, but not limited to, receiver's fees, premiums on receiver's bonds and reasonable attorney's fees, and then to the sums secured by this Deed of Trust. Lender and the receiver shall be liable to account only for those rents actually received.

21. Future Advances. Upon request of Borrower, Lender, at Lender's option, prior to full reconveyance of the Property by Trustee to Borrower, may make Future Advances to Borrower. Such Future Advances, with interest thereon, shall be secured by this Deed of Trust when evidenced by promissory notes stating that said notes are secured hereby. At no time shall the principal amount of the indebtedness secured by this Deed of Trust, not including sums advanced in accordance herewith to protect the security of this Deed of Trust, exceed the original amount of the Note plus US $ . . . .

22. Reconveyance. Upon payment of all sums secured by this Deed of Trust, Lender shall request Trustee to reconvey the Property and shall surrender this Deed of Trust and all notes evidencing indebtedness secured by this Deed of Trust to Trustee. Trustee shall reconvey the Property without warranty and without charge to the person or persons legally entitled thereto. Such person or persons shall pay all costs of recordation, if any.

23. Substitute Trustee. Lender, at Lender's option, may from time to time remove Trustee and appoint a successor trustee to any Trustee appointed hereunder by an instrument recorded in the county in which this Deed of Trust is recorded. Without conveyance of the Property, the successor trustee shall succeed to all the title, power and duties conferred upon the Trustee herein and by applicable law.

24. Request for Notices. Borrower requests that copies of the notice of default and notice of sale be sent to Borrower's address which is the Property Address.

IN WITNESS WHEREOF, Borrower has executed this Deed of Trust.

. . . . —Borrower

. . . . —Borrower

STATE OF . . . . .County ss:

On this . . . . .day of. . . . ., 19. . . ., before me, the undersigned, a Notary Public duly commissioned and qualified for said county, personally came. . . . .
. . . ., to me known to be the identical person(s) whose name(s) are subscribed to the foregoing instrument and acknowledged the execution thereof to be. . . . . .voluntary act and deed.

Witness my hand and notarial seal at. . . . . .in said county, the date aforesaid.

My Commission expires:

. . . .
Notary Public

REQUEST FOR RECONVEYANCE

TO TRUSTEE:

The undersigned is the holder of the note or notes secured by this Deed of Trust. Said note or notes, together with all other indebtedness secured by this Deed of Trust, have been paid in full. You are hereby directed to cancel said note or notes and this Deed of Trust, which are delivered hereby, and to reconvey, without warranty, all the estate now held by you under this Deed of Trust to the person or persons legally entitled thereto.

Date:. . . . .

——————————— (Space Below This Line Reserved For Lender and Recorder) ———————————

FIGURE A.22(d)   Deed of trust (continued).

LAND CONTRACT

THIS AGREEMENT, made the _____ day of _____ A.D. 19_____

between_____

part_____ of the first part, and _____

_____ part_____ of the second part.

WITNESSETH, that said part_____ of the first part agree _____ to sell and

convey to said part_____ of the second part, for the price and upon the terms

hereinafter mentioned, the following described real estate, situate in the County

of _____ and State of _____, to wit:_____

_____

_____

_____

Said part_____ of the second part agree _____ to purchase said real

estate from said part _____ of the first part, and to pay to _____

_____, as the purchase price for the same, the sum of _____

_____DOLLARS, in payment as follows:

_____

_____

_____

Payments to bear interest at the rate of _____ per cent per annum, payable
_____ annually, until paid.

If money is not paid when the same is due, then in that case, the whole of
said sum and interest shall immediately become due and payable; or if the taxes
and assessments of every nature, which are assessed or levied against said
premises, are not paid at the time when the same are by law made due and payable,
then the whole sum shall immediately become due and payable.

As soon as said purchase money and interest thereon shall be fully paid,
said part_____ of the first part agree_____ to make, execute and
deliver to said part _____ of the second part, a Warranty Deed conveying said
real estate to party of the first part in fee simple, free of all incumbrances.
If said part_____ of the second part shall refuse or fail to pay said purchase
money and interest as above stated and agreed, _____ shall forfeit
any and all rights in and to said real estate acquired under and by virtue of
this agreement, and shall forfeit any money paid for the purchase of the same,
unless said part_____ of the first part shall elect otherwise.

Said part _____ of the second part shall be entitled to the possession
of said land so long as the conditions of this agreement shall remain unbroken by
_____; but upon failure to comply with the same, said right of possession
shall terminate and said part _____ of the first part shall be entitled to the
possession of said land and the improvements thereon.

Any assignment of this contract shall be made only with approval of the
grantor _____ endorsed hereon.

Said parties respectively bind their heirs, assigns and legal representatives
IN WITNESS WHEREOF, the said parties have hereunto set their hands this day
and year as stated above.

SIGNED IN PRESENCE OF

_____   _____

_____   _____

                                    _____

FIGURE A.23 Land contract.

PREPAYMENT PENALTY

M O R T G A G E   N O T E

PRINCIPAL NOTE

...., Nebraska

Date ....

FOR VALUE RECEIVED, the undersigned ("Borrower") promise(s) to pay to the order of

.("Lender"), the principal sum

of ....Dollars (US $..................................)

.with interest on the unpaid balance from the date of this Note, until paid, at the rate of ....

.... (................%) percent per annum. Principal and interest shall be payable at

or such other

place as the Note holder may designate, in consecutive monthly installments of ....

...................................Dollars (US $...............................), on the first day of each month beginning ...., 19........

Such monthly installments shall continue until the entire indebtedness evidenced by this Note is fully paid, except that any remaining indebtedness, if not sooner paid, shall be due and payable on .... In the event the first installment due date is sixty (60) days after date of this note, interest on the unpaid balance shall be paid as accrued on the first of each month.

In addition to the payment of principal and interest, the Borrower also agrees to pay monthly installments sufficient to anticipate the payment of taxes, insurance premiums and similar items which shall accrue against or in connection with the mortgaged real estate, and agree to pay such items to said Lender and agree that such payment may be held by the Lender and commingled with other funds and the Lender's own funds and the Lender may pay such items from its own funds, and the Lender shall not be liable for interest or dividends on such funds.

The Borrower shall pay to the Note holder hereof a late charge of 5 percent of any monthly installment of principal and interest not received within 15 days after the installment is due.

If any monthly installment under this Note is not paid when due and remains unpaid after a date specified by a notice to Borrower, the entire principal amount outstanding and accrued interest thereon is then in default and shall at once become due and payable at the option of the Note holder. The date specified shall not be less than thirty days from the date such notice is mailed. The Note holder may exercise this option to accelerate during any default by Borrower regardless of any prior forbearance.

This Note shall bear interest after default at the rate of eleven (11) percent per annum until paid, whether the same becomes due by the exercise of the option provided for herein, or by the lapse of time according to its terms. Should suit be commenced to collect this Note, or to foreclose the mortgage securing the same, a reasonable attorney's fee shall be allowed and shall become a part of the judgment or decree rendered.

A prepayment penalty of US $..................................., equal to .... percent of the original principal amount of the loan will be assessed if this loan is paid in full during the first .... years from date of first monthly installment. Borrower may prepay the principal amount outstanding in part and Note holder can require that any partial prepayments (i) be made on the date monthly installments are due and (ii) be in the amount of that part of one or more monthly installments which would be applicable to principal. Any partial prepayment shall be applied against the principal amount outstanding and shall not postpone the due date of any subsequent monthly installments or change the amount of such installments, unless the Note holder shall otherwise agree in writing.

Presentment, notice of dishonor, and protest are hereby waived by all makers, sureties, guarantors and endorsers hereof. The Note shall be the joint and several obligation of all makers, sureties, guarantors and endorsers, and shall be binding upon them and their successors and assigns.

Any notice to Borrower provided for in this Note shall be given by mailing such notice certified mail addressed to Borrower at the Property Address stated below, or to such other address as Borrower may designate by notice to the Note holder. Any notice to the Note holder shall be given by mailing such notice by certified mail to the Note holder at the address stated in the first paragraph of this Note, or at such other address as may have been designated by notice to Borrower.

This Note is given for actual loan on the above amount, and is secured by a mortgage of even date herewith, which is a first lien on certain Real Estate described therein, in .... County,

Property Address: ....

....

Borrower

....

Borrower

FIGURE A.24 Mortgage note.

ADDENDUM TO PURCHASE AGREEMENT

FIRST RIGHT OF REFUSAL

THIS ADDENDUM shall become a part of the Purchase Agreement dated _____
19_____, between _____
as Sellers and _____
_____ as Purchasers with respect to the following described property:

Seller grants to Purchaser a "First Right of Refusal" for a period of _____
days ending at midnight on _____, 19_____. During said time period,
the property described above shall remain for sale on the open market. In the
event another written offer to purchase is obtained, satisfactory to the Sellers,
within the above stated period of time, the Purchaser shall have twenty-four
hours after receiving notice thereof to execute a Purchase Agreement at the
price and on the terms of the newly submitted written offer to purchase. In
the event that the Purchaser fails or refuses to exercise his first right of
refusal, he shall waive any and all rights to purchase the property described
above, shall nullify this privilege, and the Sellers shall then be at liberty to
sell the premises as stated in the written offer.

DATED: _____, 19_____.

_____   _____
Purchaser   Seller

_____   _____
Purchaser   Seller

_____   _____
Witness   Witness

FIGURE A.25 Addendum to purchase agreement.

This Warranty Agreement from the Sellers to the Buyers identifies the obligations of said Seller.

AGREEMENT

To:_____ Date:_____

The undersigned Seller being duly sworn, upon oath, represents and warrants as follows:

1. There are no unpaid bills, fees, costs, or other charges for labor or material furnished for the construction, erection, repair or improvement to the building and property located at _____ and legally described as:_____
_____
_____
_____

and in addition there is no agreement or order for any such work which could be the basis for any claims of a mechanic's lien against said property, whether or not of record.

2. There have been no public improvements affecting the property prior to date of closing that would give rise to the special property tax assessment against the property after the date of closing. All taxes and assessments for public improvements (paving, sidewalk, water, sewer, gas, etc.) which have been levied or assessed against the property have been fully paid. There are no public improvements in the vicinity under construction, or completed but not levied or assessed, which could be a basis for any special assessment liens against said property.

3. If any lien described above, or any other lien, actually now exists or comes into existence from Seller's ownership or occupancy, Seller at Seller's sole expense, upon receipt of written demand from Buyer, shall promptly and fully pay or satisfy each and all such liens and procure and record the full release or discharge on said property. In addition, Seller shall fully indemnify the Buyer against any and all payments and expenses of legal action in regard to any mechanic's liens that may be filed upon the above described premises as a result of any improvements made or caused to be made by me prior to my surrendering possession to you.

4. Expressly agree that all personal or real property items, attached or detached, mentioned in either the listing agreement or purchase agreement as being included in the sale shall remain on the premises, including specifically:
_____
_____
_____

5. Agrees to maintain the heating, air conditioning, if any, water heater, sewer, plumbing and electrical systems and any built-in appliances in working condition, to the date of possession.

6. Indemnifies and holds harmless my agent, _____ REAL ESTATE COMPANY, from any claim or court action that may arise from my failure to consummate any terms of the listing agreement and purchase agreement of sale.

7. The terms "Seller" and "Buyer" shall be construed singular or plural as the case may be. If there is more than one Seller, the obligations shall be joint and several, and any references shall be deemed to refer to one separately as well as to all.

This agreement is executed and delivered to Buyer to form a part of the sale of the above described property.

_____   _____
Seller   Seller

STATE OF _____, County of _____) ss.

Subscribed in my presence and sworn to before me this _____ day of _____, 19_____.

_____
Notary Public

FIGURE A.26 Warranty agreement containing indemnity clause (number 6).

OPTION

Know hereby that: _____
of the City of _____ County of _____, and State of _____
for the consideration of the sum of _____($_____) DOLLARS
in hand paid,

of the _____ of _____ County of _____, and
State of _____ have agreed and do hereby agree to hold until the _____
day of _____, A.D. 19_____, at 12 o'clock ____.M., time being
the essence and important part of this option, subject to the order of the said
_____, or assigns, the following described
property, to-wit:

or to transfer the said property at any time within the time above prescribed, to
the said _____ or such person or
persons as he or they may direct at and for the price of _____
_____($_____) DOLLARS payable on the following terms:

In the event that the holder(s) of this option shall decide to purchase the
said property at the above price and terms within the said time, then and in that
case, the said amount paid for this option shall be credited upon the said purchase
price, but in the event the holder(s) hereof do not conclude the purchase above
named within the time prescribed, then and in that case the said amount paid for
this option shall be retained by the undersigned in full satisfaction for holding
the property subject to the said order for the said time.

In case there should be any delay on the part of the undersigned in perfecting
the title to the above property for more than _____ days after notice of the
election of the holder(s) hereof to purchase the said property, then and in that
case the holder(s) hereof reserves the right to cancel this option and receive
back the consideration herefor or to extend the time until said title is perfected.

Dated at _____   _____(Seal)

this _____ day of _____, A.D. 19___   _____(Seal)

FIGURE A.27   Option to purchase.

(This is a legally binding contract. If not understood, seek legal advice.)

UNIFORM PURCHASE AGREEMENT

_____ , REALTORS _____ 19 _____

I, the undersigned Purchaser, hereby agree to purchase the property described as follows:

Address _____

Legal Description _____

including all fixtures and equipment permanently attached to said premises. The only personal property included is as follows: _____

Subject, however, and on condition that the owner thereof has good, valid and marketable title, in fee simple, and said owner agrees to convey title to said property to me or my nominees by warranty deed or _____ free and clear of all liens, encumbrances or special taxes levied or assessed, except _____

Subject, however, to all building and use restrictions, utility easements not exceeding 10 feet in width abutting the boundary of said property, and covenants now of record. Seller agrees to pay any assessments for paving, curb, sidewalk or utilities previously constructed or now under construction but not yet assessed.

I agree to pay for same _____ ($ _____) DOLLARS, on the following terms: $ _____ deposited herewith as evidence by your receipt attached below. Balance to be paid only as shown in following paragraphs _____ :

#1 All Cash

Balance of $ _____ to be paid in cash or by certified check at time of delivery of deed, no financing being required.

#2 Conditional Upon Loan

Balance of $ _____ to be paid in cash or by certified check at time of delivery of deed, conditional however, upon my ability to obtain a loan, to be secured by first mortgage, or deed of trust, on above described property in the amount of $ _____ . Said loan to be VA _____ , FHA _____ , CONVENTIONAL _____ , P.M.I. _____ , or VA/FHA _____ , with terms providing for stated interest not exceeding _____ % per annum, and monthly payments of approximately $ _____ plus taxes and insurance. Loan origination fee/service fee to be paid by purchaser. I agree to make application for said loan within 5 days of acceptance of this offer. I hereby authorize you to negotiate for a loan on the above basis and I agree to sign all papers and pay all costs in connection therewith, and to establish escrow reserves as required. If said loan is not approved within _____ days from date of acceptance hereof, this offer to be null and void, and the money paid herewith to be returned to me. However, if processing of the application has not been completed by the lending agency within the above time, such time limit shall be automatically extended until the lending agency has in the normal course of its business advised either approval or rejection.

#3 Assume Existing Mortgage

I agree to assume and pay existing mortgage balance in favor of _____ in the approximate amount of $ _____ and pay the balance in cash or by certified check at the time of delivery of deed; it being understood that present mortgage terms call for stated interest rate of _____ % per annum and payments of $ _____ per _____ . Said payment includes _____ . Stated interest on existing loan to be prorated to date of closing. I also agree to reimburse the Seller for the amount in the escrow reserve account which is to be assigned to me.

#4 Land Contract

Balance to be evidenced by land contract with present owner, providing for additional cash payment or certified check of $ _____ at time of execution of the contract, and remainder $ _____ to be paid in monthly payments of $ _____ , or more, which monthly payments shall include stated interest at the rate of _____ % per annum computed monthly on the unpaid portion of the principal. All other terms and conditions of the land contract to be as mutually agreed.

#5

_____
_____
_____

#6 Urban Taxes

ALL consolidated real estate taxes which will become delinquent in the year 19 ____ will be treated as though all are current taxes, and those taxes and rents, if now rented, shall be pro-rated as of date of possession _____ .

#7 Rural Taxes

ALL consolidated real estate taxes for the year 19 ____ (based on current assessment and mill levy) and rents, if now rented, shall be pro-rated as of date of possession _____ .

Possession of said premises shall be delivered to me on or before _____ at _____ o'clock _____ .M.

Within _____ days from the date of acceptance of this offer, or loan approval, Seller shall furnish to Purchaser either a complete abstract of title (certified to date by a bonded abstracter) or a title insurance commitment (binder), as determined by Seller. Within ten (10) days thereafter, Purchaser shall deliver to Seller a copy of attorney's opinion, or notice, showing defects, if any, in the title. If title defects are found, Seller, after written notice thereof, shall endeavor to correct the same to Purchaser's satisfaction within a reasonable period of time. If the defects are not cured within a reasonable time, then either Purchaser or Seller may rescind this agreement and Seller shall refund to Purchaser the deposit made hereunder. Purchaser agrees to close said purchase within _____ days after delivery of said abstract of title, or title commitment (binder), or in the event defects are found in said title, within ten (10) days after such defects are cured. **The cost of title insurance policy issued in connection with this sale shall be equally divided between Purchaser and Seller.** It is understood that the documentary revenue on the conveyance is to paid for by Seller.

This offer is based upon my personal inspection or investigation of the premises and not upon any representation or warranties of condition by the Seller or his agent. Seller agrees to maintain, until delivery of possession, the heating, air condition, water heater, sewer, plumbing and electrical systems and any built-in appliances in working conditions.

Any risk of loss to the property shall be borne by the Seller until title has been conveyed to the Purchaser. In the event, prior to closing, the structures on said property are materially damaged by fire, explosion or any other cause, Purchaser shall have the right to rescind this agreement, whereupon Seller shall then refund to Purchaser the deposit made hereunder. Seller, except for V.A. loan, agrees to pay the cost of a termite inspection of the house and attached structures, and Seller agress to pay for any treatment or repair work found necessary. If repairs are found to be needed for issuance of termite warranty, upon completion of repairs, Purchaser agrees to accept said treated real estate.

WITNESS: _____ , Purchaser

                                                           _____ , Purchaser

_____   Address _____ Phone _____

NAMES FOR DEED:
RECEIVED FROM _____

the sum of _____ ($ _____) DOLLARS (by _____) to apply on the purchase price of the above described property on terms and conditions as stated herein, it being hereby agreed and understood that in the event of the above offer is not accepted by the owner of said property within the time hereinafter specified, or that in the event there are any defects in the title which cannot be cured as specified above, the money hereby paid is to be refunded. In the event of refusal or failure of the purchaser to consummate the purchase, the owner may, at his option, retain the said money hereby paid as liquidated damages for such failure to carry out said agreement of sale, subject to the terms of the listing agreement.

This receipt is not an acceptance of the above offer, it being understood that the above proposition is taken subject to the written approval and acceptance by the owner on or before _____ .

                                                           _____ REALTORS®

                                  BY _____

OFFICE ADDRESS   PHONE #

Rev. 3/79   ACCEPTANCE ON REVERSE SIDE

FIGURE A.28(a) Purchase agreement.

#5 Continued _____
_____
_____
_____
_____
_____

ACCEPTANCE

_____ ,

_____ , 19 _____

The undersigned accept the foregoing proposition on the terms stated and agree to convey title to said property, deliver possession, and perform all the

terms and conditions set forth. _____

_____
_____
_____
_____

The undersigned further agree to pay to the named REALTORS $ _____ cash for professional services and understand that this

offer is conditioned upon the purchasers' ability to obtain a _____ loan and that _____ may be obligated to pay

a discount fee of _____ per cent of the amount of purchasers' loan.

Receipt of executed copy of this agreement is acknowledged this _____ day of _____ , 19 _____ .

Witness _____   _____

                                                 _____
                                                            SELLER

                                 State of   ) ss.
                                 County of   )
                                 The foregoing Purchase Agreement was acknowledged before the

                                 undersigned on _____ , 19 _____ ,

                                 by _____

                                 _____

                                 (Seal)   _____
                                                        Notary Public

Receipt of executed copy of this instrument is acknowledged this _____ day of _____ , 19 _____ .

                                                 _____
                                                 _____
                                                          Buyers Names

VA ESCAPE CLAUSE
AMENDATORY TO SALES CONTRACT OR PURCHASE AGREEMENT

Dated _____ , 19 _____ , on

property located at _____

"It is expressly agreed that, notwithstanding any other provisions of this contract, the purchaser shall not incur any penalty by forfeiture of earnest money or otherwise or be obligated to complete the purchase of the property described herein, if the contract purchase price or cost exceeds the reasonable value of the property established by the Veterans Administration. The purchaser shall, however, have the privilege and option of proceeding with the consummation of this contract without regard to the amount of reasonable value established by the VA".

Seller _____   Purchaser _____

Seller _____   Purchaser _____

Date _____   Date _____

FHA ESCAPE CLAUSE

"It is expressly agreed that, notwithstanding any other provisions of this contract, the purchaser shall not be obligated to complete the purchase of the property described herein or to incur any penalty by forfeiture of earnest money deposits or otherwise unless the seller has delivered to the purchaser a written statement issued by the Federal Housing Commissioner setting forth the appraised value of the property (excluding closing costs) of not less than $ _____ which statement the seller hereby agrees to deliver to the purchaser promptly after such appraised value statement is made available to the seller. The purchaser shall, however, have the privilege and option of proceeding with the consummation of the contract without regard to the amount of the appraised valuation made by the Federal Housing Commissioner. The appraised valuation is arrived at to determine the maximum mortgage the Department of Housing and Urban Development will insure. HUD does not warrant the value or the condition of the property. The purchaser should satisfy himself/herself that the price and the condition of the property are acceptable."

Seller _____   Purchaser _____

Seller _____   Purchaser _____

Date _____   Date _____

PURCHASER PLEASE NOTE

In closing your purchase, we, as agents, are required to have cash, or its equivalent, upon conveyance of title. Please bring cash, certified check or cashier's check for the balance of your payments. This will permit us to deliver papers promptly. If property is to be used as your principal residence, check with County Assessor's Office for a Homestead Exemption Application.

SELLER PLEASE NOTE

Upon termination of Seller's insurance at closing. Seller should insure all personal property remaining on the premises prior to delivering possession.

FIGURE A.28(b) Purchase agreement (continued).

FIGURE A.29 Comparable market analysis.

SUBJECT PROPERTY _____ DATE _____

COMPARABLE "SOLD"	STYLE	ROOMS	BDRS.	BATHS	GAR.	SQ.FT. ABOVE GRADE	SQ.FT. BELOW GRADE	AGE	SPECIAL FEATURES	SALE DATE	PIC#	LIST PRICE	SALE PRICE	D.O.M.	TERMS

COMPETITION	STYLE	ROOMS	BDRS.	BATHS	GAR.	SQ.FT. ABOVE GRADE	SQ.FT. BELOW GRADE	AGE	SPECIAL FEATURES	AVERAGES BOOK# PIC#	CONDITION	LIST PRICE	TERMS

COMPARISONS	STYLE	ROOMS	BDRS.	BATHS	GAR	SQ.FT ABOVE GRADE	SQ.FT. BELOW GRADE	AGE	SPECIAL FEATURES	AVERAGE PRICE AREA	LIST PRICE	SALE PRICE	D.O.M.	TERMS
COMPARABLE AVERAGE														
SUBJECT PROPERTY														
COMPETITION AVGE.														

MLS SALES STATISTICS FOR DISTRICT # _____ FROM ABOVE _____

AVERAGE SALE PRICE $ _____ DAYS FROM ABOVE _____

PERCENT OF PRICE OBTAINED _____

AVERAGE MARKET TIME _____

BEDROOMS _____   AREA FINANCING

VA - FHA _____% LAND CONTRACT _____% CASH _____%

CONVENTIONAL _____% ASSUMPTION _____%

ESTIMATE OF REASONABLE VALUE

NAME _____ DATE _____ STYLE _____

ADDRESS_____ HOME PHONE_____

Sq. Ft. First Level, L.L. _____ X _____ _____
Sq. Ft. Second/Third Level _____ X _____ _____
Sq. Ft. Finished Basement _____ X _____ _____

FEATURES:
Single Garage, Attached $ 2,000.00 _____ _____
Double Garage, Attached   3,000.00 _____ _____
Single Garage, Built-in   700.00 _____ _____
Double Garage, Built-in   1,200.00 _____ _____
Fireplace   1,000.00-2,500.00 _____ _____
Log Lighter   125.00 _____ _____
Central Air   250.00 per ton _____ _____
Wood Shingles   1,500.00-2,000.00 _____ _____
Power Humidifier   150.00 _____ _____
Electronic Air Filter   350.00 _____ _____
Intercom System   250.00 _____ _____
Dishwasher   275.00 _____ _____
Oven & Stove   350.00 _____ __ _____
Oven & Range/self-cleaning   400.00 _____ _____
Disposal   50.00-75.00 _____ _____
Patio or Porch   1.00 sq. ft. _____ _____
Fenced Yard   2.00-6.00 ft. _____ _____
Redwood deck   3.00-5.00 sq. ft. _____ _____
Additional full bath   1,000.00 _____ _____
Additional 3/4 bath   750.00 _____ _____
Additional 1/2 bath   450.00 _____ _____
Trash Compactor   200.00 _____ _____
Garage Door Opener   200.00 each _____ _____
Storage Shed   250.00 _____ _____
Wet Bar   500.00 _____ _____
Gas Grill   155.00 _____ _____
Swimming Pool   10.00 sq. ft. _____ _____
TOTAL FROM ABOVE--
Lot   75.00-110.00 fr. ft. ___ _____

LESS DEPRECIATION_____

Rule of thumb depreciation   Note #1:

_____% per year   Price/sq. ft. first floor

TOTAL ESTIMATE _____   25.00-35.00 _____

SELLING RANGE _____   Price/sq ft. second floor

                                            18.00-25.00 _____

                                        Price/sq. ft. finished basement

                                            6.00-10.00 _____

THIS IS NOT A CERTIFIED APPRAISAL. ABOVE PRICE RANGES ARE A GUIDE.

                                     _____

                                     SALES REPRESENTATIVE

FIGURE A.30 Estimate of reasonable value.

ESTIMATED SELLERS FIGURES

DATE: _____ PROPERTY: _____

TENTATIVE CLOSING DATE: _____

SALES PRICE   _____

EXPENSES:

Discount_____%   _____

Tax @ _____Month

From_____ To_____   _____   _____

Abstracting/Title Insurance   _____

State Revenue Stamps   _____

Termite Inspection   _____

Loan Payoff   _____

Inspections   _____

Professional Services Fee   _____

One month interest in arrears   _____

To show/record release MTG   _____

Prepayment privilege   _____

Allowance to buyer   _____

Escrow account   _____   _____

Total debit and credit   _____   _____

Estimated net to Seller   _____

LESS ANY LIENS OR SPECIALS   _____

While the above is an estimate
and we anticipate figures to be
close, some items may change.
Receipts will be furnished for
all expenses.
_____REAL ESTATE CO.   We acknowledge receipt of copy

BY_____   _____
                                                 Date

                               _____
                                                 Date

                               Reviewed by (Sales Manager)

                               _____
                                                 Date

Figure A.31 Estimate of seller's figures.

LISTING WORKSHEET

OWNERS_____ ADDRESS_____

LEGAL DESCRIPTION_____

LOAN COMPANY_____ LOAN NUMBER_____

LOAN BALANCE_____ TYPE OF LOAN_____

LOAN ASSUMABLE_____ COMMENTS_____

INTEREST RATE_____ MONTHLY PAYMENTS_____

INCLUDE TAX _____ INCLUDE INSURANCE_____ 19___ TAX_____

ESCROW BALANCE_____

URGENCY_____

STYLE_____ CENTRAL AIR_____ LOT SIZE_____

NUMBER OF ROOMS_____ HEAT_____ PATIO SIZE_____

NUMBER OF BEDROOMS_____ POWER HUMIDIFIER_____ DECK SIZE_____

_____CAR GARAGE_____ ELECTRIC AIR FILTER_____ TRASH COMPACTOR_____

BASEMENT %_____ FIREPLACE_____ STORAGE SHED_____

WALK-OUT_____ LOG LIGHTER_____ WET BAR_____

STORY_____ RANGE/OVEN_____ GAS GRILL_____

EXTERIOR SIDING_____ DISPOSAL_____ GARAGE OPENER_____

SEWER_____ DISHWASHER_____ GRADE SCHOOL_____

WATER_____ FENCE_____ JR. HIGH_____

GAS_____ ROOF_____ SR. HIGH_____

PAVING_____ AGE_____ PARISH_____

Rooms	Level	Carpet	Drapes	Room Size
Living Room				x
Dining Room				x
Kitchen				x
Family Room				x
Rec. Room				x
Bedroom				x
Bedroom				x
Bedroom				x
Bedroom				x
Bedroom				x
Baths: Full				
3/4				
1/2				

Figure A.32 Listing worksheet.

Glossary

abandonment   Terminating rights and title to property.

abstract   A publicly available summary of the title changes on a specific property, beginning with the original land grant.

acceleration clause   The clause that allows the lender to advance the time when the entire sum owed is due and payable.

accretion   Addition to the land through natural causes, usually by a change in water flow.

acknowledgment   The act of going before an authorized officer or notary public and declaring a legal document to be one's voluntary act and deed.

acre   A parcel of land that measures 43,560 square feet, or 208.71 feet square.

actual eviction   The lessee is evicted by the lessor for failure to live up to the terms of the lease.

actual notice   Notice given, knowledge of a condition.

adjustable rate mortgage   The rate will be renegotiated at set times to adjust to current interest rates.

adjusted basis   The reduction or increase of the original basis of a property caused by expenses or improvement to the property.

administrator   A person appointed by the court to settle the estate of one who died without leaving a will.

ad valorem tax   An assessment of property according to value.

adverse possession   Rightful owner loses land to occupant who has taken possession in a hostile, distinct, continuous, visible, and actual way for the statutory period.

affidavit   A written statement sworn to under oath.

agency   The legal relationship between owner and agent that arises out of the contract.

agreement of sale   A written agreement between buyer and seller for the purchase and sale of real estate. The owner retains title until the sale is consummated.

air lot   A unit of space in a high-rise condominium.

air rights   The right to use or occupy air space above a designated property.

alienation   The transfer of real property from one person to another.

allodial   The system of land ownership that permits individuals to own land in fee simple title.

alluvion   Gain of land along the shore of a waterway due to accretion.

alta   American Land Title Association, a national association of title insurance companies, abstractors, and attorneys specializing in real estate law.

amenities   Attractive features of a property that add to the pleasure of home ownership.

amortization   The liquidation of a financial debt on the installment basis.

annuity   A series of periodic payments; for example, money received in a long-term lease.

appraisal   An estimate of value made after analysis of the facts and data.

appreciation   The increased value of property due to economic or related causes, whether temporary or permanent.

appurtenance   Rights that pass with the title to real property, such as an easement over an adjoining land.

assemblage   Gathering together two or more parcels of land to make the whole more valuable.

assessed valuation   Value placed upon real estate for taxation purposes.

assessment   A charge against real property by a unit of government, as a tax levy or a special assessment.

assessor   A public official who evaluates property for the purpose of taxation.

assessor's map book   Prepared for county records from plats the developer of the land files with the county.

assignee   The person to whom an interest has been assigned, as in the sale of a mortgage.

assignment   The transfer of interests, rights, and title, as in the assignment of a mortgage, deed, lease or option.

assignment of rents   The clause in a mortgage that permits the lender to collect rents directly from a tenant upon default of mortgage payments by mortgagor.

assignor   The person who makes an assignment to the assignee.

assumption of mortgage   The obligation of a purchaser to be personally liable for payment of an existing note secured by the mortgage he assumes.

attachment   Legal seizure of property to force payment of a debt.

attorney in fact   A person who has power of attorney for another, allowing him to execute legal documents.

avulsion   Loss of land due to sudden change in the flow of water.

balloon payment   A final payment on a note that is larger than previous payments and that repays the full debt.

bargain-and-sale deed   A deed that conveys property and in which warranties are implied by the grantor.

base and meridian   Imaginary lines used by surveyors in locating and establishing the boundaries of lands.

basis   The original cost of a property.

before-and-after method   An appraisal technique used when a part of the property has been condemned, as under the right of eminent domain.

bench mark   Identification symbols on a permanent marker used in measuring land elevations.

beneficiary   A person designated to receive a benefit, as in a trust deed.

bequeath   To transfer personal property by will.

bequest   A gift of personal property by will.

biannual   Semiannual; twice a year.

biennial   Taking place once every two years.

bilateral contract   A promise on the part of each party to a contract, as in a purchase agreement.

bill of sale   Transfers title to personal property.

binder   A commitment; the temporary means to insure one's interest; or an agreement that covers a down payment on the purchase of real estate.

blanket mortgage   A single mortgage that covers two or more properties.

blend mortgage   The merging of a new mortgage with an existing loan, blending the interest rate of both loans.

block busting   To induce any person to sell or rent real property by insinuating that a person of a particular race, color, religion or national origin will soon move into the neighborhood.

bond   A written obligation given as security on a mortgage.

broker   A person licensed to transact real estate negotiations for another.

building line   The distance from the perimeter of a property within which no structure may be built; a set back.

building restrictions   Limit property use and outline size of structures as set forth in the deed covenants.

bundle or rights   The legal rights an owner of real estate has in his property.

buyer's agency   The buyer hires a real estate agent to represent his or her interests.

bylaws   The rules and regulations of a condominium association that relate the duties and obligations of the members.

capitalization   The process of converting future income into present capital value.

capitalization rate   The rate of interest considered a reasonable return on an investment.

caveat emptor   "Let the buyer beware"; the buyer examines the property and buys at his own risk.

certificate of no defense   An instrument executed by the mortgagor to the assignee upon the sale of the mortgage, revealing the amount owed. Also known as "declaration of no set off" and "estoppel certificate."

certificate of title   A written opinion by an attorney or title company that certifies the condition of the title.

cession deed   Given by a subdivider when he dedicates the streets in the subdivision to a governing body.

chain   A unit of measurement used in land surveying—sixty-six feet.

chain of title   A record of the past owners of a property, beginning with the original land grant.

chattel   Personal property, movable in nature.

check   A measurement of land; twenty-four square miles containing sixteen townships.

cite   To quote as authority; refer to; to summon; to notify a person of legal proceedings against her and require her appearance in court.

client   Hires another to represent him/her.

closing   Finalization of a sale, signing and transferring the title and distributing the money.

closing statement   A final settlement statement that enumerates the debits and credits of purchaser and seller.

cloud on title   A claim or interest revealed by a title search that may affect the title.

codicil   An addition to a will that may alter the provisions of the will.

collateral   Security given on a debt.

color of title   A title that appears to be good but upon the title search is found to be defective.

commingling   Unauthorized mixing of personal funds with the funds of a client.

commission   The fee earned by a real estate agent for services rendered.

common area   Land that is jointly used by all residents of the area, as in a condominium regime. Includes such items as pools, walkways, elevators, and clubhouses.

common law   Law derived from general usage.

community property   Property acquired by either the husband or wife during their marriage.

comparable market analysis   The evaluating of recent sales that are comparable to the subject property in an attempt to place a market value on the subject property.

comparison approach   An appraisal method that compares the subject property to similar properties recently sold.

compound interest   Interest computed on the original sum plus accrued interest.

concurrent ownership   Property held by two or more parties, as in joint tenancy or tenancy in common.

condemnation   Taking private property for public use with just compensation to the owner.

condemnee   The person whose property has been condemned (as by right of eminent domain).

condominium   Individual ownership of a single unit in a multiunit structure, with joint ownership of common elements.

consideration   The price or substance that induces a contract.

constant-payment mortgage   A mortgage with the reduction of the loan in fixed monthly payments, a portion applying to repayment of principal and a portion to interest.

construction loan   Interim financing used during construction of the building.

constructive eviction   The breach of a covenant in a lease whereby the landlord failed to live up to terms of the lease.

constructive notice   Legal notice given.

consummate   Conclude; bring to completion.

contract   An agreement between competent parties to perform a legal act.

conveyance   A written instrument used to transfer real estate.

cooperative   Ownership of shares or stock in a corporation for which the owner obtains a proprietary lease.

corporeal   Tangible real or personal property, as buildings and fences.

correction deed   Corrects an error that has occurred in a deed, such as the misspelling of a name.

correction lines   Placed by surveyors at 24 mile intervals to compensate for the earth's curvature.

correlation of value   The appraiser's final step in reconciling the value by analyzing the three approaches to arrive at an estimate of value.

cost approach   A method of appraisal based on replacement cost minus depreciation plus land value.

covenant   Agreements or restrictions that stipulate the use of property.

credit report   Relates the credit history of a borrower, a necessary step for the lender to assure the credit worthiness of the borrower.

cul de sac   A road with one outlet, usually ending in a circle.

curtesy   The right of a husband to his wife's estate upon her death.

customer   Purchaser of a commodity, is not represented by an agent.

datum   The spot where the surveyor begins measurement of a specific parcel.

debenture   An unsecured note given as evidence of a debt, secured only by the reputation of the maker.

dedication   Real property given by an individual to the public, as land for a park.

deed   A written instrument transferring ownership of real property.

deed of trust   A deed that secures repayment of a debt, held by a trustee until the note is paid.

default   Failure to meet an obligation, as defaulting on a mortgage.

defeasance clause   The clause in a mortgage that allows the mortgagor the right to redeem his property upon payment of his obligation.

deficiency judgment   Judgment against a debtor for the amount due the lender minus the funds derived from foreclosure.

demise   The conveyance of an estate under lease.

deposit   Earnest money tendered in conjunction with an offer to purchase real property.

depreciation   Loss of value from any cause.

devise   A gift of real estate by will.

devisee   The person to whom a gift of real estate is given by will.

direct reduction mortgage   A set amount of the principal is paid at stated periods. Payments will vary since the interest will be less with each payment.

director's deed   Issued when a public agency sells surplus land.

discount points   A percentage charged by the lender to increase the yield of the loan. Each point represents 1 percent of the loan amount.

disintermediation   Funds that leave the savings and loans to go to the higher-paying money markets.

distraint   Legal seizure of goods when rent is in arrears.

doctrine of prior appropriation   The first owner or user has the right to divert water for his/her use.

dominant estate   An estate that enjoys the rights of an easement through an adjoining estate known as the servient.

donee   A person who receives a gift.

donor   A person who makes a gift.

dower   The right of a wife in her husband's estate at the time of his death.

dual contract   Two contracts written with different terms and financing in an attempt to obtain a larger loan; a fraudulent practice.

duress   Unlawful constraint; insisting someone perform against his or her will.

earnest money   A deposit made by the purchaser at the time the purchase is written.

easement   Interest in another's land, as a right of way.

easement appurtenance   An easement that runs with the land, as a shared driveway.

easement in gross   An easement that does not run with the land, but is personal in nature.

easement by prescription   Rights to the land of another gained through continuous use.

easement of necessity   Created by law when a landlocked party needs access to his or her property.

economic life   The period over which a property may be profitably utilized.

economic obsolescence   A loss in value caused by conditions external to the property and over which the owner has little or no control, such as a deteriorating neighborhood.

economic rent   The base rent justifiably payable in the open market.

egress   Exit; the right to leave a tract of land.

eminent domain   Right of the government to take private property for public use upon just payment to the owner.

encroachment   The act of trespassing upon the domain of another.

encumbrance   An interest in real property that diminishes value, such as a lien or mortgage.

equitable title   The right to obtain absolute title to a property as in a land contract or an accepted purchase agreement.

equity   The value of real property above indebtedness.

equity of redemption   The right of an owner to reclaim property before it is sold in a mortgage foreclosure.

erosion   The gradual wearing away of land from natural causes.

errors and omission insurance   Insures for errors, mistakes, or liabilities in the practice of real estate.

escalator clause   The clause in a lease or mortgage allowing the holder to vary the interest rate.

escheat   Right of the sovereign state to succeed to the property of an intestate without heirs.

escrow   An agreement held by a disinterested third party until terms and conditions of the instrument are met.

escrow closing   The closing of a sale by means of a third party not involved in the sale, such as a title company or an attorney.

estate   Rights in property and possessions; quantity of ownership.

estate of inheritance   Permits owner of real property to distribute his or her estate by will.

estate for years   A leasehold interest extending for a definite period of time.

estoppel certificate   See *certificate of no defense*.

et al.   A term meaning "and others."

et ux   Term meaning "and wife."

eviction   Legal proceedings to recover possession of leased premises.

examination of title   Title opinion based on the abstract or title search.

exclusive agency   A listing that gives one brokerage firm the exclusive right to sell while the owner retains permission to sell without paying a commission.

exclusive right to sell   A listing that gives the brokerage firm the sole right to sell the property during the term of the agreement.

execution   Dispossession of property.

executor   The person named in a will to carry out the terms of the will.

executor's deed   Issued by the executor of an estate; carries no warranties.

executory contract   A contract not completed, as a purchase agreement.

expressed contract   Either oral or written, especially states obligations of parties.

ex rel   "Examination relating to."

Fannie Mae (FNMA)   Federal National Mortgage Association; purchases loans from qualified lenders.

Federal Fair Housing Act of 1968   This law prohibits discrimination in housing based on race, color, religion, national origin, or sex.

Federal Housing Administration (FHA)   A government agency that insures approved loans.

fee   See *fee simple*.

fee conditional   A fee simple estate subject to the happening or nonhappening of a stated condition.

fee determinable   An estate in fee simple for a certain period of time, after which it reverts to the grantor or his estate.

fee simple   The greatest and most complete interest in land, with absolute ownership in real property.

fee tail   Specially named heirs are to inherit the estate; if such heirs are not available, the estate reverts to the grantor or her heirs.

feudal system   System whereby the governing body of the land retains ownership of real property.

FHLMC   Federal Home Loan Mortgage Corporation; purchases loans from savings and loans that belong to the Federal Home Loan Bank System.

fiduciary   Involving confidence and trust, as in the relationship between agent and principal.

finder's fee   A fee paid to an individual for bringing together the parties to a transaction.

fixtures   Personal property permanently affixed to real property, such as a light fixture, oven and range, or bookcase.

foreclosure   The legal process by which the mortgagee cuts out the equity of the defaulting mortgagor.

forfeiture   Giving up something of value due to failure to perform (delinquent taxes or failure to make mortgage payments both constitute forfeiture).

fraud   The outright intention to deceive.

Freddie Mac (FHLMC)   Federal Home Loan Mortgage Corporation; acts as a secondary market for loans of member banks.

freehold estate   An estate that lasts an indefinite time, such as fee simple or life estate.

front foot   Measurement applied to the width of a lot at the street frontage. Residential lots are often priced by the front foot.

functional obsolescence   A loss in value due to poor design or age that outmodes an improvement, such as a poor floor plan, outdated electrical wiring, or poor closet space.

general warranty deed A deed giving fee simple title; the grantor guarantees title through himself, his heirs, and his predecessors.

Ginny Mae (GNMA) Government National Mortgage Association; provides reduced interest rates for low-income purchasers.

GNP (Gross National Product) The value of all goods and services produced and used in this country.

graduated lease A lease providing for a stipulated rent for an initial period, with increases or decreases at stated intervals.

graduated payment plan (GPM) Monthly payments begin at a lower than normal rate with increases periodically as the borrower's income increases.

grandfather rights A clause permitting continued use of a property that does not conform to present zoning; referred to as a nonconforming right.

grant The transfer of title to real property.

grant deed The grantor warrants the validity of the deed and guarantees that s/he has not conveyed any interest in the property to someone else.

grantee The purchase of real estate.

grantor The seller who conveys his or her interest in real property.

G.R.I. Graduate Realtors Institute; a professional designation earned upon completion of prescribed courses of study.

gross lease A straight lease; the lessee pays only rent to the owner, as in an apartment lease.

gross rent multiplier Using comparable sales that are divided by the monthly rent and multiplying this factor by the actual rent of the subject property to arrive at a rough estimate of the property's market value.

ground lease Rent on unimproved land.

ground rent Earnings from unimproved land.

ground water The water beneath the earth's surface.

growing equity mortgage (GEM) The monthly payment increases annually, with the increase applying to the principal.

guarantor The person giving a guarantee.

guardian The person appointed by the court to administer the affairs of a minor or other legally incapable person.

guardian's deed Conveys title to the estate of a minor or other person under guardianship.

habendum clause The "to have and hold" clause, which defines or limits the quantity of the estate the grantor is deeding.

heir The person who may succeed or inherit real property if there is no will.

heirs and assigns The term used in deeds and wills to provide that the recipient receives a fee simple estate in lands.

hereditaments Inheritable property, real or personal.

highest and best use As determined at the time of appraisal, the use that will produce the greatest net return over a given period of time.

holdover tenant A lessee who remains in possession of the premises after termination of the lease.

homeowner's insurance Insurance to cover major perils to the property; required by lenders as protection for the loan placed on the property and desired by the home-owner as protection on the investment.

homestead An estate in land occupied as a residence; some states exempt an amount from a forced sale to satisfy the debts of the home owner.

home warranty insurance Offers the buyer coverage on the component parts of a house. Usually insures major appliances, electrical, plumbing, heating, and air conditioning.

homogeneous Compatible, stabilizing the area.

HUD Federal Department of Housing and Urban Development; involved in housing activities, such as rehabilitation loans, urban renewal, subsidy programs, and public housing. HUD has jurisdiction over FHA and GNMA.

hypothecate To give as security, as when pledging a mortgage.

inchoate Incomplete, not finished, as a wife's right to her husband' estate under dower rights.

income approach An appraisal method whereby the net income of an income-producing property is divided by the capitlization rate to determine the property's value.

incorporeal rights Intangible interest in real property, such as an easement.

indemnification Reimbursement of loss.

indenture A binding agreement in writing, such as a deed.

independent contractor Individual employed but paid only upon production; no salary or normal fringe benefits are paid by the employer.

index lease Provides for rent adjustments that conform to changes in a price index.

ingress The right to enter land.

in lieu of Instead of; in place of.

instrument A written document capable of being recorded.

intangible property Property that is not visible, as the "good will" of a business.

interest A percentage charged for the use of a principal sum.

interim financing Temporary financing, as a construction loan.

intestate Person who dies without leaving a will.

irrevocable Unalterable; not changeable.

joint tenancy Ownership by two or more persons with rights of survivorship.

judgment A court decree to determine a settlement.

judgment lien A charge upon the lands of a debtor resulting from a court decree.

junior mortgage A mortgage subordinate to an existing or subsequent lien.

key lot   A lot that has one side adjoining the rear of another lot; usually on a corner. Key lots are valued for their locations.

laches   A delay in asserting one's legal rights, causing forfeiture of these rights.

land contract   Seller finances purchaser and retains title; purchaser obtains equitable title.

landmark   A monument or marker that establishes a certain spot, such as the boundary of a property.

latent defect   A defect that is hidden from view, such as defective plumbing.

lease   A contract giving the lessee (tenant) the right to use property owned by the lessor (landlord) for a stated period of time and for a specific purpose.

leasehold   The interest a lessee has in a lease.

lease option   A clause in a lease that affords the lessee first right to purchase the property.

legal description   The description of property boundaries recognized by law.

lessee   The tenant or person renting property under a lease contract.

lessor   The owner of property leased to a lessee.

less than freehold estate   Holder has leasehold rights in real property.

leverage   The investor takes the largest loan possible for the longest period of time with the smallest down payment.

license   A personal privilege or right that is nontransferable.

lien   A charge or claim against a debtor's property.

lien theory   Mortgage is a security for the debt, with the mortgagor the title holder.

lien waiver   An affidavit signed by the sellers attesting to the fact that there are no unpaid bills against the property.

life estate   The right to the ownership and use of property by a designated person during his or her lifetime.

life tenant   The holder of a life estate; ceases to exist upon death of the holder.

limited common areas   Common elements that are for the exclusive use of certain residents; as parking stalls and storage units.

link   In land measurements, a link equals 7.92 inches.

livery of seizen   Transfer of possession.

lis pendens   Notice of a suit pending that could affect ownership of land.

listing contract   The contract between the broker and the principal to negotiate the sale of the principal's property.

littoral rights   Rights along a shoreline, as in riparian rights.

loan commitment   A loan approval by the lender of the loan.

loan-to-value ratio   The ratio of a mortgage to the appraised value of a property.

lot   A plot of land with fixed boundaries.

lot and block number   The final plotting of a housing subdivision.

majority   The age at which a perosn is legally entitled to handle his or her own affairs.

marginal land   Land that barely repays the cost of production.

marketable title   A title without defect.

market price   The price paid for a property.

market value   The highest price for which the willing seller will sell and the willing buyer will buy.

master deed   The deed that is recorded and is the principal document that conveys ownership of the overall condominium regime.

MBS   Mortgage Backed Securities; act as security for mortgages that are pooled together and sold to investors.

mechanic's lien   The right of a contractor to place a lien against property for work completed but not paid for.

meeting of minds   An agreement on specified subject matter, such as a seller accepting the offer of a buyer.

meridian   Used in the government rectangular survey system; lines that run north and south across the country.

metes and bounds   Measurements and boundaries that describe a property.

MGIC   Mortgage Guarantee Insurance Corporation; an independent insurance corporation that insures loans made by approved lenders.

mile   A measurement of distance; 5,280 feet.

mill   One-tenth of one cent, used to compute property taxes.

minor   A person not of legal age.

misrepresentation   An erroneous statement made with the intention of deceiving.

monument   A stone or fixed object used to establish a land boundary.

monument survey   Description of a property in terms of natural and artificial boundaries.

moratorium   The legal period of delay for meeting a financial obligation.

mortgage   The pledge that secures the lender's investment and that accompanies the note.

mortgage broker   Person or firm acting as an intermediary between borrower and lender.

mortgage correspondent   Agent for a lender who places a loan for a borrower.

mortgage lender   A lending institution that makes and services mortgage loans.

mortgagee   The lender or holder of the mortgage.

mortgagee in possession   The mortgagee becomes in possession of a property when the mortgagor defaults on the note, permitting the lender to collect rents from tenant.

mortgagor   The debtor or borrower; the owner of property put up as security for a mortgage.

multiple listing service   A group of brokers that pools listings and cooperates to sell any listing of a member firm.

National Association of Realtors®   A national organization that promotes fair and ethical practices among its members. All members are entitled to use the trademark realtor.®

negative amortization   The monthly payment is less than needed to reduce the mortgage debt and thus results in an increase in the original indebtedness.

negative cash flow   An investment yields less than the expenses, causing a loss to the investor.

negotiable instrument   A promissory note that, upon meeting certain legal requirements, may be circulated freely in commerce.

negotiate   To arrange for, to transact business, as negotiating the sale of a property.

net lease   A lease whereby the lessee assumes some or all of the expenses normally paid by the owner.

net listing   Property listing at an agreed-upon net price the seller wishes to receive with any excess going to the agent as commission.

nonconforming use   Use in violation of present zoning laws but permitted because the usage was in effect before the law. The user is said to have "grandfather rights."

nonfungible   Cannot substitute one parcel of real property for another; no two are alike.

nonhomogeneous   A characteristic of real property; no two parcels are alike.

notary public   A lawfully authorized official who attests to and certifies documents by his hand and official seal.

note   A written promise to pay a certain sum of money within a specified time.

notice to quit   A notice to a tenant to vacate the premises.

novation   The substitution of a new contract for an existing contract.

obsolescence   Lessening in value due to functional, economic, or physical conditions.

offer   A promise by the purchaser to complete the terms of the contract upon acceptance by the seller.

offeree   Owner of property.

offeror   Buyer who "offers" to purchaser.

open-end mortgage   A mortgage that allows the mortgagor to borrow additional funds and extend the amount of the loan without changing the terms of the mortgage.

open listing   A nonexclusive listing, generally oral, available to any number of brokers with a commission paid to the selling firm.

open mortgage   A mortgage overdue and up for payment.

opinion of title   A legal opinion to determine if title is clear and marketable.

option   The right to buy within a specified time.

ordinance   A city or county legislative enactment, such as a zoning law.

origination fee   A finance charge to the borrower for making a loan that covers costs of preparing the loan.

ownership   The right to possess and use property to the exclusion of all others.

package mortgage   A mortgage that especially designates all personal property included in the sale.

parol evidence   Oral evidence; not in writing.

partition   Legal division of real estate by owners in order to sever their ownership.

partnership   Two or more parties join together in an enterprise.

party wall   A common partition between adjoining properties for the use of both parties.

passive income   Income derived solely from an investment of money in an enterprise that is managed by another, such as a limited partnership.

patent   A land grant by the U.S. government to an individual.

patent defect   A material defect that can be seen upon inspection.

percentage lease   A lease whereby the lessee pays a flat sum plus a percentage of the volume of business transacted on the premises.

percolating water   Underground water that is sufficient enough to be tapped for a well.

periodic tenancy   A lease that continues from period to period with no set termination date.

personal property   Movable items not affixed to real property, such as chattels.

personality   Chattel; personal property not permanently affixed to the real property.

planned-unit development (PUD)   A community planned to allow better use of land.

plat   A map of a certain area of land.

plat book   A public record of information concerning land.

pledge   Security held by the lender until a debt is paid off.

plottage   The assembling of several parcels of land into one ownership.

points   See *discount points*.

police power   Right of the government to pass legislation protecting the safety and welfare of the public.

positive cash flow   An investment produces a net return over and above expenses.

power of attorney   An instrument in writing authorizing one person to act for another.

prepayment clause   A mortgage clause stating the penalty for payment of the mortgage before the actual due date.

prescription   Rights in property acquired through continuous use.

principal   The property owner who employs an agent to sell her property.

principal meridian   A survey line running due north and south, as established by the Rectangular System of Survey.

promissory note   The note signed by the mortgagor that promises repayment of the debt.

property   Owner's interest and rights in her property to the exclusion of all others.

proprietary lease   The right to occupy a cooperative unit by the shareholder.

prorations   The dividing of expenses and credits between buyer and seller.

prospectus   A preliminary statement about an enterprise, to give advance information.

public records   Publicly available notice of matters concerning land.

public trustee   A disinterested third party who serves as an escrow agent under the terms of an agreement.

purchase-money mortgage   A mortgage carried by the seller to secure an unpaid balance of the purchase price.

qualified fee   A fee simple estate with limitations set by the grantor.

quiet enjoyment   The right to use property without disruption by the grantor or the landlord.

quiet title action   Action in court to either establish title or to remove a cloud on a title.

quitclaim deed   A deed containing no warranties, in which the grantor relinquishes any claims or rights he may have.

quit notice   Notice given to a tenant to vacate the premises.

quorum   The minimum number of members needed at any official meeting in order to conduct business (usually more than half).

real property   The land and anything permanently attached, such as buildings, fences, and fixtures.

Realtist   A member of a group of real estate brokers whose organization is made up of minority brokers.

realtor®   A coined trade name that refers to members of the National Association of Realtors.

reappraisal lease   A clause in a long-term lease that requires periodic appraisals to determine the economic rent.

receiver   Recipient; a person appointed under a statute to wind up a business.

recission   To revert back to the original conditions.

recordation   The act of giving public notice by recording a legal document.

redemption   The act of repurchasing real property after the mortgage is in default.

reduction certificate   A document showing the balance due on a mortgage at the time the transaction is closed.

reformation   Action taken to correct a mistake in a deed or other instrument.

regulation Z   Implements the truth-in-lending law through the Federal Reserve Board.

reliction   The gradual increase of land due to receding waters.

remainder estate   What is left from a life estate.

reproduction cost   The cost of duplicating or replacing a property.

remainderman   The person who receives an estate after the termination of a life estate.

rescind   Revoke, annul, or cancel (as a contract).

residual   Remainder, as the residual value of land after the economic life of the building is over.

RESPA (Real Estate Settlement Procedures Act)   A law requiring full disclosure of closing costs to buyer and seller.

restrictive covenant   A condition limiting the use of land, as stated in a deed.

reverse annuity mortgage   The retired homeowner receives income from the equity in the home.

reversion   The interest that reverts to a grantor or his heirs.

right of first refusal   Gives a person first opportunity to buy or lease.

right of redemption   The period within which a debtor may redeem his/her property after default.

right of way   An easement through the land of another.

riparian rights   The rights a land owner has in the use of water adjoining his property.

rollover mortgage   A renegotiable mortgage that calls for changes in interest rate at set intervals.

sale and leaseback   The owner sells her property with the stipulation that she may lease it back from the new owner.

salvage value   The value that remains after the useful life is exhausted.

sandwich lease   A leasehold interest involving a lessor, lessee, and sublessee.

satisfaction piece   An instrument that is recorded to announce payment of the debt; a mortgage release.

sea level   Zero feet, base from which measurements begin.

secondary mortgage market   The sale of existing mortages by the primary lender to the secondary mortgage market lenders, thus affording greater liquidity of mortgages.

second mortgage   A mortgage second in priority to a first mortgage; pledges the owner's equity in the property.

section   A division of land; 640 acres or one square mile.

security deposit   Lessor requires a deposit that is refundable at expiration of the lease if the property has not been damaged.

servient estate   An estate that includes an easement existing in favor of the dominant estate.

setback   The distance that zoning regulations require a structure to be located from the front, rear, and side property lines.

settlement closing   The broker prorates and adjusts the credits and costs for the buyer and seller upon closing the transaction.

severable   Capable of being divided.

severalty   Sole ownership by one person.

shared appreciation mortgage (SAM)   The mortgagee participates in any appreciation of the property in exchange for a fixed, below-market interest rate.

sheriff's deed   Transfers property sold at a public sale; usually the result of a foreclosure.

simple interest   Interest paid on the declining balance of a loan; thus the interest payments lower as the principal amount is paid off.

site   The location of a particular parcel of land.

situs   The location or site of a real property; value is partially based on a properties situs.

sky lease   A lease with the right to occupy the space of another above the leased real estate.

special assessment   A tax levied against property for the cost of a public improvement.

special warranty deed   A deed wherein the grantor guarantees title through himself and his heirs but not his predecessors.

specific performance   A remedy in a court of equity to carry out the terms of a contract.

spot zoning   Land use in violation of a zoning ordinance, differing from current usage of surrounding property.

steering   Limiting the choice of a buyer or renter of housing by channeling them to certain neighborhoods.

strawman   Person who purchases for another unidentified buyer; used when confidentiality is important.

sublet   Lessee retains lease but rents a portion of the premises to a sublessee.

subordination clause   A clause found in a mortgage or lease that states the rights of the holder are secondary to any existing or subsequent encumbrance.

subpoena   A legal summons requiring court appearance to give testimony.

subrogation   Substituting one person for another regarding a claim—as in a loan assumption.

summons   Notification to appear.

surety   Legal liability for another's debt.

surrender and acceptance   Mutual consent by lessee and lessor to cancel the lease.

tax deed   Real property sold at a public sale due to delinquent taxes.

tax sale   The sale of property for nonpayment of taxes.

tax shelter   A phrase used to describe advantages of real estate investments—such as deductions for taxes, interest, and depreciation—resulting in the postponement, reduction, or elimination of income tax.

temporary buydown   A mortgage differential allowance program that allows the seller to place funds with the lender to reduce the borrower's payments for the first two to three years.

tenancy at sufferance   The tenant remains in possession of the leased premises after expiration of the lease.

tenancy at will   Use of the property at the will of the landlord. Either party can terminate the lease at any time since there is no set termination date.

tenancy by the entireties   Ownership by husband and wife with both spouses sharing an equal, undivided interest in the whole property.

tenancy for years   A leasehold estate that grants the lessee use for a specified period of time.

tenancy in common   An interest in real estate held by two or more persons without right of survivorship.

tenant   Lessee; a person given the right to use real estate owned by another.

tender   To fulfill; to offer to perform as the terms of a contract state.

term mortgage   Short duration loans that are not amortized and are used for brief periods of time, such as construction loans.

testate   A person who dies leaving a will that designates the distribution of his or her estate.

testator   A person who leaves a will or who has died testate.

time share   Joint ownership of a single unit by several purchasers that gives use for a specified time.

title   Evidence of ownership in real estate.

title insurance   Insures the holder of the policy against defects in the title.

title search   An examination of public records to establish ownership of real estate.

title theory   Mortgagee has legal title to the property; as with a trust deed, the mortgagor acquires equitable title.

Torrens System   The system of land registration whereby a certificate of title is issued.

tort   An actionable wrong, a violation of a legal right.

townhouse   A type of structure generally in a clustered group which is usually two stories with common walls between the units.

township   A parcel of land that contains thirty-six sections and that is six miles square.

trade fixture   Personal property that has been affixed to leased property by a tenant who uses it in his or her business.

trust account   A non-interest-bearing account in which the real estate broker places all money entrusted to him/her by or on behalf of the principal and the customer.

trust deed   A deed held in trust by a third party until the obligation is paid; it is used to mortgage land.

trustee   A third party to a trust deed: the one who holds the trust deed.

trustor   The owner of the property under a trust deed.

truth-in-lending   A federal law requiring disclosure of costs involved in obtaining a loan.

Uniform Commercial Code   Requires the recording of personal property that is sold for in excess of $500.00 so that the creditor may file a financial statement and reclaim the property if the debtor defaults.

uniform landlord/tenant act   Regulates the landlord-tenant relationship on residential leases.

unilateral contract   A promise on the part of one party to perform a specific act.

U.S. government land survey   Rectangular land survey; a method of land description.

useful life   The economic life of an improvement; period of time over which it can be profitably utilized.

usury   The act of charging in excess of the legal interest rate.

vacation license   A right to occupy a unit in a condominium regime for a specified period of time without fee title; pre-paid lodging.

valid contract   A contract that complies with the law and is legally sufficient and enforceable.

valuation   The estimated worth of a property.

variable rate mortgage   Allows the lender to increase or decrease the interest rate within the perimeters set down in the mortgage rate.

variance   Permission given to an individual to use land in a way that varies from current zoning laws when compliance with zoning ordinance would create an undue hardship.

vendee   The purchaser of real property, who receives equity title under the terms of a land contract.

vendor   The seller of real property, who retains title in his name under terms of a land contract.

verify   To substantiate under oath.

vested   With an interest in; owned by a right in real property.

voidable contract   A contract that can be terminated even though it appears valid, as a contract with a minor can be rescinded by the minor.

void contract   A contract entered into for illegal purposes.

waiver   The voluntary surrender of rights or claims.

words of conveyance   Words in a deed that expressly grant the title to the grantee.

wraparound mortgage   Lenders refinance a property by lending an amount more than the existing mortgage, leaving the first mortgage in place. The complete package is considered as one loan, with the mortgagee of the wrap paying the obligation to the first mortgage.

zero lot line   The placing of a structure on the lot line without being required to have a setback from the perimeter of the property.

zoning   The regulation over the use of land within a specific municipality.

Bibliography

American Institute of Real Estate Appraisers. *The Appraisal of Real Estate*. Chicago: American Institute of Real Estate Appraisers, 1978.

Beaton, William R. *Real Estate Finance*. Englewood Cliffs, NJ: Prentice-Hall, 1975.

Beaton, William R., and Robertson, Terry. *Real Estate Investment*. Englewood Cliffs, NJ: Prentice-Hall, 1977.

Cyr, John E., and Sobeck, Joan M. *Real Estate Brokerage: A Success Guide*. Chicago: Real Estate Education Company, 1982.

Dennis, Marshall W. *Fundamentals of Mortgage Lending*. Reston, VA: Reston Publishing, 1978.

Irvin, Carol K., and Irvin, James D. *Ohio Real Estate Law,* 3rd Ed. Scottsdale, AZ: Gorsuch Scarisbrick, 1986.

Jacobus, Charles J., and Levi, Donald R. *Real Estate Law*. Reston, VA: Reston Publishing, 1980.

Kratovil, Robert and Werner, Raymond J. *Real Estate Law*. Englewood Cliffs, NJ: Prentice-Hall, 1979.

Kyle, Robert C., and Kennehan, Ann M. *Property Management*. Chicago: Real Estate Education Company, 1979.

Lindeman, Bruce. *Real Estate Brokerage and Management*. Reston, VA: Reston Publishing, 1981.

Miller, George H., and Gilbeau, Kenneth W. *Residential Real Estate Appraisal*. Englewood Cliffs, NJ: Prentice-Hall, 1980.

Palmer, Ralph A. *Real Estate Principles: The Real Estate Examination Guide,* 2nd Ed. Scottsdale, AZ: Gorsuch Scarisbrick, 1987.

Pyhrr, Stephen A., and Cooper, James R. *Real Estate Investment: Strategy, Analysis, Decisions*. Boston: Warren, Gorham and Lamont, 1982.

Reilly, John W. *The Language of Real Estate*. Chicago: Real Estate Education Company, 1977.

Ring, Alfred A., and Dasso, Jerome. *Real Estate Principles and Practices*. Englewood Cliffs, NJ: Prentice-Hall, 1981.

Shenkel, William M. *Marketing Real Estate*. Englewood Cliffs, NJ: Prentice-Hall, 1980.

Sirota, David. *Essentials of Real Estate*. Reston, VA: Reston Publishing, 1981.

Sirota, David, *Essentials of Real Estate Finance*. Chicago: Real Estate Education Company, 1983.

Smith, Halbert C., Tschappat, Carl J., and Racster, Ronald L. *Real Estate and Urban Development*. Homewood, IL: Richard D. Irwin, 1977.

Unger, Maurice A. *Elements of Real Estate Appraisal*. New York: John Wiley and Sons, 1982.

Unger, Maurice A., and Karvel, George R. *Real Estate Principles and Practices*. West Chicago: South-Western Publishing Company, 1979.

Ventolo, William L. Jr., and Williams, Martha R. *Fundamentals of Real Estate Appraisal*. Chicago: Real Estate Education Company, 1977.

Walters, William Jr. *The Practice of Real Estate Management*. Chicago: Institute of Real Estate Management, 1979.

INDEX